Class Matters

EARLY AMERICAN STUDIES

Daniel K. Richter and Kathleen M. Brown, Series Editors

Exploring neglected aspects of our colonial, revolutionary, and early national history and culture, Early American Studies reinterprets familiar themes and events in fresh ways. Interdisciplinary in character, and with a special emphasis on the period from about 1600 to 1850, the series is published in partnership with the McNeil Center for Early American Studies.

A complete list of books in the series is available from the publisher.

Class Matters

Early North America and the
Atlantic World

Edited by Simon Middleton
and Billy G. Smith

PENN

University of Pennsylvania Press
Philadelphia

Published by
University of Pennsylvania Press
Philadelphia, Pennsylvania 19104-4112

Printed in the United States of America on acid-free paper

10 9 8 7 6 5 4 3 2 1

A Cataloging-in-Publication record is available from the Library of Congress
ISBN 978-0-8122-4063-4

To Sage for her sixteenth and Michelle for her sixtieth

To Carolyn, and for Gerald Sider, who got me started on class

Contents

Of all the hokum with which this country [the United States] is riddled, the most odd is the common notion that it is free of class distinctions.
—W. Somerset Maugham

Though the conditions of mankind are various, they may with propriety be included under three denominations—the rich, the middling class, and the poor.
—"An American" (Pennsylvania Gazette, *December 24, 1794*)

The fears of one class of men are not the measure of the rights of another.
—George Bancroft

Introduction

Simon Middleton and Billy G. Smith

As a mode of historical analysis of early North America and the Atlantic World, class is dead—or so it has been reported for the last two decades. A combination of scholarly critiques and global structural changes has enervated a once vigorous historiography relating to class formation and struggles in the eighteenth and early nineteenth centuries. The academic focus on the importance of cultural rather than economic factors of historical causality and on the influence of language in constructing collective identities undermined class analysis as a mode of inquiry. At the same time, the dissolution of the Soviet Union and most socialist nations, the lurch of Western political parties to the right, the growing strength of global capitalism (and concomitant weakening of labor organizations), and the deindustrialization of wealthy nations all discouraged examination of the past (or present) from a class perspective.[1]

This volume confronts the devaluation of class and seeks to reinvigorate its study. Although differing in their interpretative approaches and priorities, the contributors to this collection all agree that class analysis is indispensable to understanding early North America and the Atlantic World and to explaining the historical processes that marked the transition from the early modern to the modern eras. To appreciate why this collection is necessary and valuable, the introduction reviews how class emerged and flourished as a category of analysis in the twentieth century then lost its purchase in Anglo-American historiography in the 1980s and 1990s. Thereafter, the introduction evaluates the global structural changes during the past quarter century that have affected the theoretical approaches to class and that inform the departure point for the chapters included in this collection.

Compared to other categories of difference—including race, gender, sexual orientation, religion, and culture—class has become the least fashionable among historians. Yet, we believe that class matters vitally. Fortunately, during the past four or five years, class analysis of early North America and the Atlantic World is recovering from its wilted stage and enjoying a state of renewed growth.[2] Indeed, the chapters in this collection point the way toward a variety of new methods and of new subjects for study that recognize the vital importance of class issues. Such a renaissance will benefit not only the writing of history, but also our understanding of our own world. Our goal, ultimately, is not to prescribe strict, dogmatic guidelines about one correct approach to class analysis, but rather, by considering various possibilities in this book, to water with interpretations, fertilize with ideas, and otherwise quicken the flowering of class studies that once again are beginning to take root.

"Class" initially entered English usage in the seventeenth century as a description of the "order or distribution of people according to their several degrees."[3] During the next two centuries, class gradually eclipsed notions of estate and degree as the preferred term of social classification for different "sorts" of people who were distinguished by increasingly fluid considerations of status, manners, and wealth.[4] For some scholars, the emerging preference for class in social description reflected a critical shift in economic relations, as interactions centered on subsistence agriculture and local markets mediated by long-established private and public obligations gave way to relations based on commercial agriculture, manufacturing, large-scale markets, and exchanges arbitrated by individual ambition and the cash nexus. Witnessing this transformation, and drawing upon a century or more of social and economic commentary, Karl Marx formulated his view of class as derived from the productive relations into which men and women have to enter in order to survive. He also posited an important distinction between class as an objective condition and class as a generative historical force with the potential to transform society. The first attribute reflected an individual's relationship to the means of production. The second developed only as members of a given class realized the political and historical implications of their structurally determined position as subjects. Marx thus deployed class not only as a term of social description but also as an analytic category that explained the history of virtually all societies and even provided a guide for the future.[5]

In the first half of the twentieth century, class enjoyed a prominent position in historical debate; some scholars argued for the salience of class identities and class struggles, although others offered interpretations based on a liberal, consensual view of early modern Anglo-American history.[6] At mid-century, one particular conceptualization came to dominate the historiography about class. It began with a gifted generation of English Marxist literary critics and historians who questioned the academic focus on "high culture" and valorized local intellectual idioms and popular traditions of social criticism and resistance.[7] They celebrated the aesthetic qualities and historical significance of common men and women and, in time, this encouraged others to adopt a perspective of history "from the bottom up." In this intellectual milieu, Edward P. Thompson developed his influential critique of the economic determinism of contemporary Marxist theory and its concentration on the behavior of "systems" and "laws" that supposedly operated within the social relations of production. Thompson instead reconsidered the mode of production itself as "a kernel of human relationship from which all else grows."[8] In 1963, *The Making of the English Working Class* set out Thompson's agenda, identifying class formation and struggle with the sense of shared difficulties and objectives that emanated from the lived experience of ordinary human beings.[9]

Thompson's emphasis on the *experience* of social conditions and the manner in which it gave rise to a collective social consciousness heavily shaped the chronological focus of his study and the many others that were inspired by his approach. These accounts of class formation and struggle centered on the process of proletarianization: the economic and political transformations in which artisans and small farmers lost control of their skills and lands and were increasingly forced to sell their labor for wages. The processes that enabled these changes—the enclosure of common land, the development of new technologies, the movement of population from country to city, and the emergence of free labor—had long and complex histories extending over many generations. Many class historians identified the late eighteenth century and the early nineteenth as the critical period during which the shared experiences of workers nurtured a common consciousness and political response to their collective predicament.[10]

Ironically, this chronological emphasis encouraged a noteworthy concurrence between some class historians and their neoclassical liberal contemporaries regarding the supposed "classless" condition of what became, by default, the "preindustrial" or "traditional" early modern era. Yet, the question nagged: how best to explain the obvious economic exploitation and social conflict that so clearly characterized the sixteenth, seventeenth, and eighteenth centuries in Britain and North America? Many historians argued that moral considerations rather than apolitical, spasmodic reactions to the "belly factors" of desperate hunger and want informed these struggles. But scholars also generally agreed that the limits set by a localized and deferential political culture differentiated these early modern contests from later, "mature" class struggles wherein leading protagonists were distinguished by their "horizontal" political consciousness and their articulation of an alternative social vision.[11] In this way, the identification of class with the particular consciousness and struggles of late eighteenth- and early nineteenth-century workers curtailed the analytic possibilities of applying a class analysis in earlier eras.

In the United States, the historiography of class developed in a somewhat different fashion, even as the ultimate interpretive trajectory shared many similarities with scholarship in Britain. "The myth of America as a 'classless society,'" as Greg Nobles has observed, "often diverted academic analysis away from class relations," thereby placing blinders on many historians in the United States.[12] Directly challenging the dominant consensus school of interpretation, and drawing inspiration instead from earlier Progressive historians, Jesse Lemisch forcefully argued that early Anglo-America was commonly depicted as being "classless" primarily because "historians have chosen to see it that way." The counterpart in the United States to Edward P. Thompson, Lemisch inspired many scholars, notably Staughton Lynd, Gary B. Nash, and Alfred F. Young, to explore class issues. Moreover, as people from working-class backgrounds began to enter the historical profession for the first time, they often responded enthusiastically to viewing "history from the bottom up" as a way to transform our understanding of colonial and Revolutionary America.[13]

The enormous power of Thompson's conceptualization of class reflected not only the originality of his insights but also the status of his major work, *The Making of the English Working Class*, which became an archetype of social history inquiry into the everyday lives and concerns of laboring men and women. By the early 1970s, this long and difficult book had become as well known for establishing the experience and political consciousness of ordinary subjects as a vital historical field as for its particular analysis of social relations of production in early nineteenth-century England. Thompson's oft noted determination to rescue his subjects from the "enormous condescension of posterity" echoed the cry of "new social historians" in the United States against previous approaches that obscured or ignored the significance of ordinary lives considered in the aggregate, as parents, workers, women, and slaves. Social historians focused on how objective conditions provided a foundation on the basis of which they could decipher the *mentalité* of past people.[14] In so doing, some advocated a dichotomous view of society composed of objective (economic and demographic) and subjective (ideas and interests) realms, wherein the former exerted causal primacy.[15] To mitigate the materialism implicit in this approach, scholars emphasized the interplay between objective and subjective realms, deploying the concept of hegemony and describing the dialectical interplay of culture and ideology to demonstrate the potential for autonomous mental worlds wherein even the most vulnerable of subjects participated in the creation of meaning. Using obscure and previously undervalued sources, new social historians also emphasized the force of "experience" in the production of consciousness and agency among previously marginalized groups such as women, African Americans, Native Americans, and working-class people.

For all that they shared conceptually, however, feminist and subalternist scholars were also critical of class historians for failing to take account of women, slaves, and Native Americans in histories focused on white, usually skilled, working men.[16] For conservative scholars, who lamented the baleful influence of what they considered the dogmatic triptych of "race, class, and gender," these disputes between new social historians fueled fears about the rise of "political correctness" and the supposed decline of historical objectivity. Conservative reaction fed the culture wars of the 1980s and 1990s, culminating with a bitter conflict over the National History Standards and an effort by some to establish an alternative professional association.[17] Yet, the most telling critiques of the burgeoning historiography relating to class issued not from detractors on the political left or right but from scholars schooled in linguistic and literary theory who questioned the epistemic foundations of historical study. Historians embroiled in the culture wars disagreed regarding the methodological problems and ethical issues posed by tracing sequences of cause and effect from social and economic conditions to political and cultural expressions. Yet, most of them accepted that knowledge of these causes and effects and of the relationship between the objective realities and subjective experience was recoverable, albeit in partial and fragmented form, through an intensive study of primary sources. Beginning in the 1960s, however, a series of critiques, loosely if clumsily classified as postmodern, challenged these foundational assumptions as outmoded and, in the view of the harshest critics, indicative of historians' willful methodological naïveté.[18]

For pre-postmodern historians, the most damning charge concerned the interpretive weight that scholars placed on the language found in the records, in particular, the reliance on this language as evidence of subjects' intentions based, for example, on their experiences of material causes that predated the creation of the documentary source. Critics argued that rather than simply reflecting anterior causes and motives, the language of the document had to be considered as a system of meaning with its own history and, as such, as a context that actively mediated and construed meaning for both contemporaries and later historians. If this were the case, then the language that social historians had relied upon in even the most mundane of historical sources provided less of a window on the past and the objective world "beyond the text" and more of a glimpse of linguistic patterning, rhetorical strategizing, and word games carried on within endlessly shifting but ultimately finite and ergo, at least in some sense, determinative linguistic structures. Thus scholarly assessments of the determinative connections between earlier material conditions (knowledge of which was also only recoverable through the study of equally problematic textual sources) and subsequent political and cultural expressions could only ever rest on inference at best and hubris at worst. To understand the records, critics argued, historians had to appreciate the formal and vernacular structures within which the language was produced and, within these structures, the subjective and discursive processes that differentiated between normative and deviant claims and positions that provided for the coherence and clarity of meaning that made intersubjective communication possible and effective.[19]

The ramifications of this "linguistic turn," as the concentration on the mediating function of language in history became known, was a categorical challenge to social historians' ontological conception of their subjects as meaning-giving agents who reliably spoke their own history. Rather than arising out of their shared "experience" of external conditions and exploitative social practices, the claims of workers, women, and slaves concerning their identities and shared political consciousness could be more accurately understood as relational, composed within systems of difference, and reflective of power imbalances and conflicting cultural forces. In this case, postmodernists argued, the social historians' acceptance of representations of individual and group consciousness at face value left uninvestigated and even risked obscuring the fact that whatever coherence was evident in the documents depended largely on the suppression of claims and interests that threatened the façade of common identities.

These critiques severely undermined the claims of the previous influential explanation about how a shared experience of proto-industrial immiseration had given rise to the horizontal political consciousness that served as the defining characteristic of an Anglo-American working class, whose "making" and maturing heralded the endpoint of early modernity and the advent of the modern world. By the 1990s, this class identity was taken by many to be indicative of nothing more (or less) than a historically contingent configuration of linguistic exchanges between a subsection of white, male, skilled workers and their employers: a set of discursive encounters that re-volved around workers' attempts to justify claims for political and economic equality in the languages of republicanism and liberalism, the form and function of which owed as much to the influence of constitutional traditions, gendered preconceptions, and the shifting meaning of liberty and virtue, as they did to the material hardships associated with the movement of popula-tion, the rise of factory production, and the shift to waged labor.[20]

This linguistic challenge to social historians' view of their subjects' sense of both themselves and their political consciousness and, by implication, to the facticity of historical identities met with a variety of responses. Embrac-ing the linguistic turn, many feminist and subalternist scholars and theoreti-cians traced the discursive forces and power relations operative in the creation of essentialized subjects, such as women, slaves, and Indians. In a ground-breaking article, Joan Scott reoriented the earlier investigation of "women's history" toward the broader and more fruitful study of the con-struction of femininity and masculinity in different times and places.[21] Demonstrating that gendered thinking figured as a constitutive element in all social interaction and served as a primary mode for the signification of rela-tionships of power, Scott also questioned the interpretive weight placed on the evidence of "experience." The growing interest in "whiteness" and the reconceptualization of encounters among Europeans and indigenous peo-ples that occurred on the "middle ground" suggested parallel developments in erstwhile similarly essentialist fields of African American and Native American history.[22]

The response of class historians to postmodern critiques ranged from thoughtful engagement to disinterested and, in some cases, ill-tempered dis-missal. Leading European scholars joined the theoretical debate, questioning the Thompsonian conceptualization of class and seeking a post-materialist rhetoric within which to consider the social and political contests of the late eighteenth and early nineteenth centuries.[23] In North America, however, the majority of social and labor historians demonstrated little interest in such projects; those who entered the theoretical debate frequently did so to take on what they considered voguish and, in their view, implicitly conservative linguistic and literary approaches.[24] These scholars acknowledged the need for a less exclusively white and masculine conception of who comprised the working class. Nevertheless, they mostly remained committed to a view that the shared experience of structural inequalities generated the collective po-litical consciousness that served as the key indicator of "mature" class iden-tity. It was this disinclination to pursue the "linguistic turn" which, at least in part, ensured the stalling of debate in the late 1990s and the diminishing purchase of class as an analytic category in the historiographical mainstream.[25]

Besides intellectual developments and shifting academic fashions, including postmodern skepticism of the quintessentially modern narrative of Marxism, worldwide political and economic transformations in the 1990s diverted the attention of many scholars away from class issues and toward other topics and methods that appeared to hold more significance for contemporary times. The dissolution of socialist nations that had been ostensibly committed to creating classless societies, and the subsequent revelations about the malfunctioning of communist societies such as the Soviet Union diluted the idealism about the potential of moderating class inequality. However, the disappointment of socialism to date does not necessarily mean that scholars should abandon class analysis as lacking explanatory power in the past or present. Discarding class solely in reaction to shattered socialist dreams is akin to accepting the age-old warnings about throwing out the baby with the bath water or cutting off one's nose to spite one's face. It makes for neither happy babies, nor pleased parents, nor handsome features, nor effective historical analysis.[26]

In the 1990s, the intensifying process of globalization likewise discouraged many scholars of early British America from employing class analysis. The growing power of capitalism on an international scale produced conditions with similarities to those of the Gilded Age in the late nineteenth-century United States, when robber barons enjoyed considerable power and wealth in a national arena. Strengthened by strong state support for "open markets" at the end of the twentieth century, capital flowed around the world much more quickly and easily than did the ability of workers to organize to protect their interests. Outsourcing of industrial jobs ended many of the relatively well-paid, manufacturing occupations in wealthy nations, reducing much of the work force to employment in the service sector, and it created sweatshop conditions in many poorer nations. The ability of employers to shift production offshore limited the bargaining power of laboring people in rich nations. Working-class communities and sources of identification and labor unions declined precipitously in Britain and especially in the United States, carving into a foundation that previously encouraged scholars in those nations to pursue class studies.

Capitalists in rich nations have rarely had it so good, as they reaped the benefit of huge profits resulting from globalization and favorable government policies, both of which helped redistribute resources up the economic ladder. Wealth inequality, as is now widely acknowledged even by conservative scholars and commentators, grew rapidly in the late twentieth century; it increased more quickly during the past several decades than at any time in human history. Meanwhile, incomes for the middle classes in rich nations stagnated. To the extent that their standard of living grows, it is based on acquiring cheaper goods produced by workers in foreign countries who earn a pittance. All of these phenomena are depressing to many scholars. However, rather than interpret these as discouraging trends that point historians away from class analysis, we believe they should be a summons to research how these kinds of processes operated in the past, particularly in early North America and the Atlantic World in the early modern era.

What can we learn from these contentious theoretical debates concerning class and from the structural transformations in our world during the past two decades? How does what we learn inform us about the direction of class studies in general and about this collection in particular? Given the manifest divisions left over from these scholarly deliberations, it is doubtful that anyone will devise a concept of class that will command the kind of dominance once enjoyed by the version advanced by E. P. Thompson and his counterparts in the United States. The contributors to this collection reflect a new and exciting range of interpretations and approaches in contemporary historiography. Several authors attempt to define the nature of class identities, even as they sometimes candidly admit uncertainty in their case studies. Others invoke social and economic conditions and behavioral traits as the most likely indicators of collective social *mentalité*. Some authors maintain the focus on experience as the mediation between productive relations and class consciousness. Others conceive of class more broadly—as interwoven with questions of inequality, hierarchy, and stratification—and as articulated in radically different ways from the form it assumed in the era of industrialization in the late eighteenth and early nineteenth centuries. Laudably, these authors embrace rather than react against the shattering of earlier ideological and conceptual uniformity. In agreement with the authors in this volume, we strongly encourage a host of new modes as well as new subjects of inquiry as the best way to advance class studies.

Devising a single conception of class analysis with universal appeal is not only unlikely but also even undesirable at this point in the historiography, when a newly invigorated study of class has the potential of producing dozens of different blooms. We learn this lesson from previous mistakes committed by well-meaning but overly dogmatic scholars, many of them Marxists, who endorsed a "purity" of class analysis that delegitimized approaches that did not adhere to a single party line. However, the buds on the tree of class (or any other) scholarship are discouraged from flowering in an environment in which the gardeners are too concerned about the rectitude of approaches.[27] Instead, as do the chapters in this book, we need to recognize the significance of class in various early modern (and preindustrial) contexts rather than try to construct a single master template that describes class in a supposedly unadulterated form that applies uniformly across time and in all societies. We asked the authors, where appropriate, to address the larger issues of class as part of their case studies.

Responding to the intellectual debates described above, we can suggest a broad framework that permits a redeploying of class away from its customary identification with the experiences of an essentialized worker subject and toward an analysis that combines class with the insights provided by scholars who focus on race and gender in transnational settings. Clearly, this framework needs to take account of the residual skepticism left over from postmodern critiques of the viability of class as a historical category as well as more recent concerns. Engaging the former challenge requires class historians to devise the kind of conceptual compromises formulated by other scholars who have benefited from but ultimately moved beyond linguistic and literary challenges to the epistemic assumptions of historical scholarship.[28]

Pierre Bourdieu's response to the question of what makes a social class provides a starting point. He begins by distinguishing between the objective and subjective conceptions of class that frame much of the debate. The former treats class as an aspect of reality with empirically verifiable properties and boundaries. The latter treats class as a theoretical construct fashioned by both historical actors and subsequent commentators in an effort to impose meaning on the undifferentiated continuum of the social world. The core of the subjective challenge to the objective view, which Bourdieu accepts, is that it is always possible to challenge claims made on behalf of classes conceived as homogenous groups of economically and socially differentiated individuals by pointing to those excluded by criteria of inclusion that are imposed upon, rather than derived from, material life. His most useful insight, however, is to identify the social space and subject positions that exist between the objective and subjective realms. In these terms, what makes social class are the relationships between individuals and groups that derive from differential access to various forms of capital—economic, cultural, symbolic—and social power. These relationships confer advantages and disadvantages in the competition for valued resources, which are signified in the discursive processes that this competition engenders and reflects. The historical specificities of these processes are difficult to grasp because the conditions, dispo- sitions, and interests that signify class relationships become construed as "real" and, in so doing, nurture common practices, representations, and identification among historical subjects. This naturalizing of conditions and representations that began as constructs produces what Bourdieu calls "a sense of one's place" and, equally importantly, a sense of the place of others. In this fashion, objective and empirically recoverable processes of social dif- ferentiation are reproduced and elucidated in subjective cultural and politi- cal expression. It is this slippage between the objective and subjective realms that makes a knowledge of class so elusive, "because the object of this knowl- edge is made *both of and by* knowing subjects."[29]

In recent years, others working at the intersection of class, race, and gen- der have taken similar steps beyond the enduring but ultimately irresolvable debate between objective and subjective conceptions of class and considered the realities constituted by the relationships between different social spaces and subject positions.[30] In these studies, class becomes neither simply a re- flection of the productive relations of the objective world nor a subjectively constructed identity fashioned from available linguistic and cultural re- sources. Instead, it comprises a constitutive element of social relationships emerging from inequalities in material conditions and social and cultural capital that serves as a primary way of signifying relationships of power. This understanding holds considerable promise for historians of class.[31]

In addition, scholars can employ class analysis to write histories valu- able for our own times, ones that address the types of issues associated with globalization discussed above. This effort involves enlarging the time frames, the subjects, and the geographic space considered by class studies. First, var- ious versions of the traditional account of the artisan-to-worker transition during the late eighteenth and early nineteenth centuries remain important parts of the story, both for the history of industrialized nations and because they speak to the experiences of so many workers in countries with emerging economies today. However, to understand more fully the development of the industrial classes, scholars clearly also need to explore the era before the exis- tence of factories from a class perspective. As Greg Nobles persuasively argues (and executes), historians need to trace the "origins of more explicit class re- lations back into the colonial era."[32] Second, the *subjects* of our histories also need to be broadened if we are better to comprehend the nature of class his- torically and in the present. Class relations both in the early modern era and in our own times are often defined outside of rather than by the manufactur- ing system. The "proletariat," broadly identified, comprises many more

subjects and groups than factory workers, and these groups demand our attention. Third, class scholars need to adopt a more far-reaching geographic
vision, continuing the work begun by scholars such as Peter Linebaugh and
Marcus Rediker in their *Many-Headed Hydra*. Admirably, the chapters in this
book greatly expand the times, subjects, and physical space on which most
previous class scholars have focused.[33]

Considered collectively, then, the chapters in this book explore the subject positions and relationships that exist in between objective class conditions and the signification of these conditions in cultural and discursive
practice: the impact of class formation and class struggle and the processes of
social differentiation—some long established, some novel, and some radical
and disjunctive—that marked the emergence of an early modern commercial
system. Although formally separated, autonomous, and supervised by their
respective European backers, the colonies, enclaves, and regions that comprised European empires in the Americas were bound together by ideological and commercial ties and by common possibilities, challenges, and
experiences. The initial half dozen chapters consider specific locales and their
interconnection within the wider Atlantic World. In eighteenth-century
Glasgow, as Simon Newman argues, the financial and political influence accrued by the city's "tobacco lords" affected the changing working conditions
and configuration of class relations on the River Clyde. Newman also sets the
foundation for other chapters by considering how class operated throughout
the Atlantic World. Breaking with the reluctance of many historians of Native Americans to employ class analysis, Daniel Richter and Daniel Mandell
demonstrate how indigenous communities felt similar shock waves, which
were, in turn, reshaped by local conditions and systems of native stratification that rested on the redistribution rather than accumulation of highly valued symbolic trade goods. A world away, on the Cape Coast described by Ty
Reese, the Europeans' need for labor motivated the enslavement and exploitation of some West African peoples, even as other Africans, determined
to participate in the market on their own terms, forced the interlopers to accommodate local practices and expectations.

In the West Indies and other slave societies, questions of profitability
were complicated by additional threats to security posed by real and imagined slave conspiracies and slave resistance. In St. Kitts, according to Natalie
Zacek, the struggle between yeomen and "Grandy Men" over the distribution
of plantation land raised questions concerning geopolitical and social stability. While the wealthy and powerful secured their ends, the presence and allegiance of poor white planters could never be taken for granted; in the

compromise of class interests among freeborn Europeans lay the discursive dynamic for social differentiation of African workers in terms of race. Wherever conflicts butted up against inequalities in the distribution of social power exercised in the competition for the means of survival and valued goods, however, class concerns were evident in their character and negotiated resolution. Thus, in New Amsterdam and early New York City, as Simon Middleton argues, community survival and the harmonious pursuit of profit by the city's elite and their subaltern charges were mediated by negotiations conducted in a civic language of rights and privileges that held all to publicly acknowledged standards of behavior and governance.

Significantly, the developments identified by these chapters occurred across the early modern era and over the course of many decades rather than at one particular time and place. Wherever and whenever the Atlantic economy proffered opportunities and exacted costs, it stimulated processes of social differentiation and class formation. In these terms, the development of class formation and struggle in the early modern Atlantic World is best considered not as a linear progression from traditional to modern. Instead, it operated more as a sedimentary process in which successive layers of change formed the contours of an increasingly exploitative and profitable Atlantic World commercial system—a process that continues on an even wider scale to this day.[34]

Derived from unequal access to forms of capital, these processes of social differentiation ensured the discriminatory distribution of power that stressed and strained communities in Europe and the Americas. For all its informal coherence, the Atlantic World was divided by competing and colliding interests. Varying conceptions of authority and contests between immigrants and indigenous peoples, within individual colonies, and between colonies and their presumptive imperial governors added to the complex competitions.[35] Social tension drew upon the contingencies of colonial conditions and the continuing force of Old World commitments to local practices and customs as well as religious, ethnic, and familial networks.

In the late seventeenth and early eighteenth centuries, the disjunctive experience of imperial settlement, religious change, and the commercial revolution created conditions enabling the articulation of new identities according to mutable and interlocked categories of class, race, and gender.[36] This was especially evident in the appearance and development of the middle classes—the topic of Chapters 7 to 11 in this volume. Konstantin Dierks analyzes the broader issues associated with the nascent development of a new class as he examines epistolary culture. Conduct books addressed the concerns and ambitions of men (and some women) seeking status and fortune in the commercializing economy. Aspirational people devoured the advice that prescribed self-mastery and the support and security of genteel associations and friendships to deal with the hectic and uncertain world of merchant commerce. These books provided one explanation for the emergence of an in-between social space created by the Atlantic economy that urged readers to occupy their economic and cultural niche within rather than against the existing social structure. Pursuing genteel lives in the burgeoning consumer empire, this new middling sort eventually articulated a clearer sense of their social distinctiveness, economic interests, and political objectives. The appropriate use and display of consumer goods, for example, offered status and symbols of social superiority for some affluent people as it excluded others. Even as middling colonists sought common cause with one other and the fashionable metropolitans they considered their peers, they sharpened distinctions in colonial communities and nurtured resentment among those who lacked the wherewithal to acquire the trappings of respectability.[37]

During and after the American Revolution, the emerging middle class assumed new forms. Jennifer Goloboy details the shift among Charleston merchants from relying on personal relationships to impersonal connections in carrying out their business. Andrew Schocket traces the materialization of corporate identities that stretched across the Atlantic World, and Lawrence Peskin analyzes the new rhetorical celebration of industrialization. Of course, new definitions of class had a gender component as well, and Susan Branson notes the struggle of Ann Carson to define herself according to middle-class values. All of these episodes reflected the reconfiguration of class relations and the newer ways of conceptualizing the differences between men and women, and between black and white people along increasingly restrictive lines.

Thomas Humphrey and the final chapters shift the focus to poorer people in Anglo-America. Humphrey situates his study of tenants within a broader perspective of class and class conflict in early North America and assesses how elite Americans exercised the political and social power they acquired by virtue of their property to structure the lives and deaths of poorer people in their communities. Simultaneously, "lower-class Americans struggled to make the best of societal conditions that were working against them." Gabriele Gottlieb reveals the class nature of capital punishment in the late eighteenth century, with poorer Americans enduring execution much more often than did richer citizens. Sharon Sundue discloses how elites used pauper apprenticeships as a system of cheap labor and a way to maintain class distinctions.

Class, Raymond Williams once observed, is a "difficult word, both in its range of meanings and in its complexity in that particular meaning where it describes a social division."[38] The chapters presented here only begin to address the range and complexity of meanings of class and class struggles in the context of early North America and the Atlantic World. Another group of scholars would have doubtless produced different chapters and somewhat different perspectives. One alternative perspective is outlined by Christopher Tomlins's Afterword, which calls for a more forthright engagement with the legacies of historical materialism. Tomlins insists that class historians reflect on their relationship to what he considers the epistemic restraint of a professionalized historical discourse content with the endless historicization of new subjects and self-gratifying debates about complexity and significance. Invoking Walter Benjamin's *Theses on the Philosophy of History* as an inspirational example of the still untapped imaginative promise of historical materialism, Tomlins calls for history that seduces, unnerves, angers, and threatens its readers. Failure to take up this challenge, he concludes, leaves class historians as "prospectors in a dusty landscape" engaged in the interminable pursuit of an ever greater knowledge of class in the service of arid historiographical debate. In his meditative essay, Tomlins critiques some of the approaches taken in this book, pushing the debate in new directions and demonstrating that this is a propitious moment to revivify the study of class in our examination of the past and its relation to the present. Speaking in one voice with the authors, we hope this book energizes that study.

1

Theorizing Class in Glasgow and the Atlantic World

Simon P. Newman

By 1850 Glasgow was rapidly emerging as one of Britain's greatest industrial cities, the Second City of the empire. It was the year that the Factory Act restricted women and children to workdays of no more than ten and a half hours, but in the pages of the *Glasgow Herald* seventy-seven-year-old Robert Reid evoked images of Glasgow's bucolic past. During his childhood Reid's "grandmother, who was born in the year 1715," had recalled a time when such city-center streets as Candleriggs, King Street, and Princes Street were "open fields, which were occasionally sown with corn." Reid contextualized these distant memories, recalling that "it was during this year (1715) that the first newspaper was published in Glasgow, price one penny. Three years later (1718) the first Glasgow ship crossed the Atlantic."[1]

In reminiscing that Glasgow's Merchant City neighborhood had recently been farmland on the edge of a royal burgh no larger than a medieval market town, Reid ended his recollection with an observation about the first Glaswegian ship to cross the Atlantic, which was fitting since Atlantic trade and commerce fueled the city's meteoric rise. Following the Act of Union, Glaswegians took full advantage of their integration into Britain's infant empire, as vast quantities of American tobacco and sugar arrived in Glasgow and its outlying ports of Port Glasgow and Greenock. The Atlantic trade helped trigger significant expansion of local manufacturing, as Glaswegians produced items from coal to linen to shoes for export to Britain's mainland and Caribbean colonies.[2] The enormous profits generated by the tobacco trade, together with Glasgow's increasing economic diversification, were what saved the city during the American Revolution. Merchants who held on to their extensive stocks of tobacco saw prices rise so high during the War for Independence that they were able to realize huge profits. Moreover, the loss of much of the tobacco trade was "amply compensated by the great increase in manufactures; the merchants having, of late, turned their attention more to improve the manufactures, which had been begun among them, and to establish new ones, which promise to be a much more permanent source of wealth."[3] Thereafter the city focused more than ever before on the production of commodities, especially fabric, for an expanding British Empire and beyond.

The people and the city of early modern Glasgow demonstrate the utility of the Atlantic World in providing both a narrative framework and an analytical focus for the study of those whose lives were transformed by the dramatic expansion in the movement of people and goods within and between the communities surrounding the ocean. Change came in different ways and with very different effects to these communities, and changes in ownership and modes of production transformed class relationships and political and economic power among people as distant and diverse as the indigenous peoples of mainland North America, the communities on the western coast of Africa, and the urban populations of the British Isles. Local circumstances conditioned the effects of this new Atlantic World, but the working lives and the developing class experiences and identities of all were touched by it.

The working population of Glasgow, which was destined to become the Second City of Britain's developing empire, was among those who in the eighteenth and early nineteenth centuries experienced the greatest transformation of their class status and identity. Beginning with the great "tobacco lords" of the eighteenth century, Glasgow's mercantile and financial leaders accrued such extensive financial, political, and legal power that they were able to mold the nature and the conditions of employment—and thus the conditions of life—for the fast-growing working class. The consolidation of elite power came at a time when the rights and liberties of the lower sort were at their lowest ebb, as more and more rural folk were cleared from the land, a process that was politicized and expanded in the wake of the failed Jacobite Rebellion of 1745–46 and the beginning of the Highland Clearances in earnest. The displaced Highlanders who flooded into Glasgow or who traveled across the Atlantic as indentured servants had been "greatly oppressed and reduced to Indigent and necessitous Circumstances," and they regarded their debased condition as "but one degree removed from slavery."[4] With no money or power, those who sought work in Glasgow were at the mercy of powerful mercantile and manufacturing leaders, yet some workers—especially the weavers—could and did begin to embrace and defend a class identity, often employing the language and forms of protest that were shared around the British Atlantic World. It would not be until the late nineteenth and early twentieth centuries, however, that the working-class politics of "Red Clyde" would demonstrate that Glasgow's workers had become sufficiently powerful and self-assured to assert their claim to power over the terms and forms of their employment.

Eighteenth- and early nineteenth-century Glaswegian workers thus enjoyed relatively little control over the nature and terms of their employment, although there is ample evidence of their willingness to articulate and protest in defense of what they understood to be their rights. In comparison, the class relations within many of the coastal West African communities changed relatively little during the eighteenth and early nineteenth centuries. Local African leaders continued to monopolize gold production and to profit from the small-scale production of various foodstuffs and commodities by local populations; in many cases, European trade enabled such leaders to consolidate their wealth and power. Europeans, however, exercised little power beyond the confines of their fortified trading posts and castles, and local African workers—from canoemen to farmers to fishermen—continued to function much as they had for centuries. For those Africans transported in chains across the Atlantic it was a very different story, and in the British West Indies and the Chesapeake colonies these men, women, and children were molded into the most servile of classes. Slave-owning planters enjoyed almost unlimited power over their workforces, and as these societies developed the existence of an enslaved working class conditioned class relations for all people, free and unfree alike. Native Americans in the mainland British colonies provide a third example of people whose working lives were transformed by the advent of the Atlantic World. As the flow of Europeans and their goods across the Atlantic increased, Native Americans lost more and more land, and their ability to survive in traditional ways on the land was so compromised as to threaten traditional modes of production and control of resources within their societies. For women, in particular, the Atlantic World significantly compromised and eventually much reduced their productive power and consequently their position within family and community.

Throughout the early modern British Atlantic World, workers struggled to come to terms with their position in a fast-changing world in which wealth inequality, social stratification, and labor were all conditioned by the rapidly expanding movement of people and goods. Glasgow's population shared experiences with others around the Atlantic World, including a process of physical displacement that involved the movements of hundreds of thousands of Scots not just physically but also mentally, for they found that familiar social systems and comforting beliefs ill suited their new positions and new expectations in new worlds. For example, the forced clearance and voluntary relocation of a large proportion of Scottish Highlanders combined to remove many people from a centuries-old system of land tenure and farming.[5] A small remnant remained on the land as crofters and tenant farmers, their position and privileges much reduced. Many more moved to urban centers, especially Glasgow. As wage laborers processing American crops and manufacturing other items, these workers were alienated from their traditional lives and cultures and constrained by the time-work discipline of manufacturing and industrialization. Others left Scotland altogether, destined for the Caribbean and mainland North America, where a great many became yeoman farmers. In short, from this one group of rural north Britons emerged a variety of new social, economic, and cultural groupings, all fashioned to varying degrees by the Atlantic World. With different relationships to the means of production, they would form different connections with other groups of the Atlantic World: a few came to identify themselves as planters and owners of men in the Caribbean, others as factors and merchants, still more as part of the vast North American group of yeoman farmers, and many as members of Britain's nascent urban proletariat.

How these different groups of Scots made sense of these experiences and how they interpreted their new social positions reveal the ways the Atlantic World provided cause and context for the coalescence of new classes and varying degrees of class consciousness. Those who remained on the land found that the feudalism suffered by their ancestors had been replaced by the equally harsh world of commercial agriculture and absentee landlords, and small crofters' associations began to develop to defend the interests of tenant farmers. Those who moved to the ports and cities of the British Isles became part of a new urban working class, keenly aware of both traditional popular rights and new rights fashioned and protected by wage laborers, yet held in check by the considerable power of their employers. For those who became yeoman farmers in the Americas, a keen sense of the rights accruing to land-owning farmers, however, meant that their existence became a lynchpin of their social and political identity.[6]

As they developed, these groups defined themselves in relation to other groups, struggling to protect existing rights and property and to secure more, all in the larger social context of culture, politics, religion, race, and so forth. Creating a complicated web of connections, the Atlantic World can reveal a great deal about the construction and experience of class in different locations and circumstances. Distinct class formulations and experiences coalesced in a very uneven fashion, jostling and competing within and without regions, and these interactions forced members of different groups to identify, articulate, and defend their interests. It is a story that is as much about consciousness and perception as it is about material reality: Scottish workers in Glasgow, yeoman farmers in Pennsylvania, wage laborers in New York City, and chattel slaves in South Carolina all came to think of themselves and their fellows in terms of their relationships with other groups, and how best they might protect and improve their situations. This chapter will explore the development of new class experiences and configurations in early modern Glasgow in the larger context of that city's participation in a fast-developing Atlantic World.

Approximately 7,000 people lived in early seventeenth-century Glasgow. Merchants dominated the community, but the craft guilds were a significant force, boasting 363 burgesses to the 214 of the merchants. By the end of the century, the population had more than doubled, for despite the restrictions of the Navigation Acts, Scots were beginning to trade with England's Atlantic colonies. Glasgow's first shipment of tobacco had arrived from Martinique in 1647, and two decades later the first of a growing number of sugarhouses began processing Caribbean sugar and distilling rum. New woolen manufactories soon followed, and the closing decades of the seventeenth century saw the development of Port Glasgow twenty miles down the Clyde, at which ships docked to carry European and American produce to and from Glasgow.[7]

During the century that followed, Scotland developed from the world's tenth to the world's fourth most urban nation.[8] In their tens of thousands rural Scots poured into Glasgow: by 1801, the city housed seventy-seven thousand people, and almost one-third of the population of the port of Greenock hailed from the Highlands.[9] The Act of Union (1707) had freed Scots from the restrictions of the Navigation Acts: tobacco, sugar, and later cotton began pouring into Glasgow, while refined and processed American goods and domestically created textiles and consumer goods poured out. The tobacco trade grew rapidly during the first quarter of the eighteenth century, with imports rising from two to four million pounds per annum between 1715 and 1725. After a brief hiatus, the trade increased enormously during the middle decades of the century, with tobacco imports rising from eight million pounds in 1741 to forty-seven million pounds in 1771.[10]

By the middle of the eighteenth century, tobacco accounted for almost half of all of Scotland's imports, and all but 2 percent of this trade entered the country through Glasgow's satellites at Greenock and Port Glasgow.[11] A relatively small group of Glasgow's mercantile families made huge profits, and intermarriage among them kept control of the tobacco trade and its profits relatively concentrated. The successes of the tobacco and subsequently the sugar trades in part resulted from the close relationships that developed between Glaswegian merchants and American planters. The merchants usually sent family members to the colonies as factors, who in turn developed close associations with planters and extended credit to them, tying the planters to Glasgow's merchants, and from whom they would often purchase manufactured goods.[12] The tobacco trade was, however, an uncertain one, for large profits one year might be replaced by significant losses in the next. All of these factors had a cumulative effect, and the enormous profits Glasgow's merchants earned, the vagaries of the tobacco trade, and the dependence of the planters on Glasgow's merchants for credit and manufactured goods all encouraged the city's merchants to diversify their business interests. Their capital was vital in the development of banking in Glasgow and its environs, and they bought huge areas of land, which brought social distinction, economic security, and local and national political power. As lords lieutenant, commissioners of supply, justices of the peace, and members of Parliament, Glasgow's mercantile elite dominated and all but monopolized political power in the city and surrounding countryside. They ruled Glasgow and much of the west of Scotland.[13]

Most significantly, these merchants invested heavily in local industry, and the foremost historian of Glasgow's tobacco lords found a "close correlation between the rise of tobacco commerce and the foundations of manufactories."[14] Not only did such investment and diversification protect their wealth, it also provided Glasgow's merchants with their own sources for the goods required by the American planters to whom they had extended credit. Merchants whose fortunes had been made in the American trade dominated entire industries, such as leather tanning, boot and shoe manufacturing, and iron production. To a slightly lesser extent, the expansion of coal mining (much of it now on local land owned by merchant families) and the textile industry, particularly linen manufacture, owed much to mercantile investment.[15] Especially during the first half of the eighteenth century, when very few Scots had access to the wealth necessary for the development of manufacturing and industry, the profits from Atlantic World trade and the needs and wants of American trading partners encouraged a small group of extremely wealthy Glaswegian merchants to invest heavily in local manufacturing. By no means were all of the manufactured goods sent by Glasgow's merchants to the

Caribbean, North America, Africa, and continental Europe Glasgow-made, but a growing number were, including such diverse items as hats, thread, fabric, leather goods such as saddles and shoes, and even ale and porter.[16]

The diversification of their interests insulated Glasgow's merchant elite against periodic interruptions of trade, most notably during the American War for Independence. More significantly, diversification massively expanded their political and economic power within Glasgow. As thousands of Highlanders and then later Irish migrants flooded into the city, the economic, political, and legal power of the mercantile elite enabled them to exercise a significant influence over the nature of that employment, the conditions of work, and thus the whole measure of the lives and experiences of the city's developing working class. However, the history of eighteenth- and early nineteenth-century Glasgow reveals that working-class life and culture was, at least to some degree, a product of negotiation. Despite the enormous political and economic power of employers to determine the conditions of employment and thus the very nature of work and the conditions of daily life, Glasgow's workers began to articulate their interests, drawing on traditional beliefs and practices but also on a larger Atlantic World context of popular rights. Very likely, the city's dependence upon trade and its ports encouraged the transmission of such ideas in printed and spoken form via the ships and seafarers who embodied the connections between the far-flung communities of Britain's Atlantic empire.[17]

For much of the eighteenth century, the rapid growth in Glasgow's population and manufacturing took place within a relatively small and concentrated urban area, with the River Clyde to the south and open fields never more than a few hundred years away. Until late in the century, wealthy merchants, skilled craftsmen, and poor laborers continued to live cheek by jowl, as illustrated by the early development of Cow Lane (later to become Queen Street) in the 1760s and 1770s. This was a new and relatively affluent development, which yet featured a mix of the homes and workplaces of merchants, skilled artisans, and their workers and dependents. John McCall, a merchant from Virginia, lived next to the stucco worker Thomas Clayton, who lived next to the wright John Wardrop, who in turn lived and worked next to the skinners John and Gavin Buego, whose property was adjacent to that of the coachmaker William Clark.[18] As late as 1750, the city consisted of only ten major streets, none of them paved, and it was only in 1776 that one of the first sidewalks was laid with flagstones, outside the Exchange on Argyle Street, for the express and exclusive use of the mercantile elite who gathered there to do business.[19]

Over time residential segregation increased as the wealthy built increasingly large mansions to the west of the medieval city, developing Virginia Street, Queen Street, and Buchanan Street. Consequently, the late eighteenth century saw an increasing concentration of poorer working Glaswegians in the oldest areas of the city, such as the High Street, Drygate, and Saltmarket, as landlords subdivided large tenements for the use of workers whose wages did not allow them access to better housing. However, while the wealthiest of merchants sought increased residential segregation, many of the smaller manufacturers continued to inhabit the tenements where they and their apprentices worked. On the outskirts of the city were a number of fast-growing communities of workers who lived in tied housing, from the textile workers of Pollokshaws to the coalminers of Calton and Barrowfield to the iron workers of Tollcross.[20]

The increasing concentration of population within Glasgow had serious consequences for Glasgow's workers. As textile production, dye-works, and tanneries expanded, pure water became scarce.[21] Fresh water supplies within the city were increasingly limited and often contaminated, and by the early nineteenth century over 60 percent of all deaths were the result of infectious diseases, with tuberculosis the largest single killer.[22] At the time of the American Revolution, a disused quarry lay at the edge of the city, on what would become West George Street, and it was the receptacle for much of the city's waste, including "the carcases of dead horses, dogs, and cats." Young children scavenged for bones to use as toys, and they tore into "the numerous putrid carcases" for "the finest maggots in the world," which they used for fishing.[23] Because people were living in increasingly concentrated quarters, with contaminated drinking water, and suffering from the malnutrition that was inevitable during periodic bouts of un- or underemployment, mortality rates in the city rose. Between 1783 and 1791, for example, children under the age of five accounted for 53.6 percent of the city's 12,757 recorded deaths.[24]

Relief of the poor became a larger and larger problem. In the early eighteenth century, those Glaswegians who were unable to provide for themselves received poor relief from the town council, the general session of the church, the incorporated trades, or the Merchant's House, each of which provided for those individuals for whom they were responsible. As the city grew, however, so too did poverty, destitution, and begging, and the early modern welfare system was overwhelmed and gave way to the town's hospital and a new almshouse, which together with the general session provided for the poor. A great deal of this poor relief was administered through the general session at the parish level, with only the worst cases of indigents and orphans being admitted to the hospital, wherein inmates were given new clothes, instructed in Christianity, taught basic literacy, and required to work as best they could. By the latter decades of the century, the hospital could no longer accommodate the ever-increasing number of truly indigent paupers. By 1774—with many city workers suffering because of the interruption of the American trade and an ensuing decline in local manufacturing—the institution was providing full meals or grain to those considered deserving of support but who could not be accommodated within.[25]

While the nature and conditions of work changed dramatically, and both wealth inequality and poverty grew, some historians have suggested that there exists little apparent evidence of social resentment or political opposition among Glasgow's eighteenth-century workers. This interpretation owes something to the religious and political climate of the era, and low-church Protestantism remained central to Glasgow's popular political culture. The city provided little popular support for the Jacobite rebellions of 1715 and 1745, and Glaswegians of all classes aligned themselves firmly with the Protestant succession.[26] Already membership in a British empire of trade fostered by the Hanoverian dynasty seemed integral to Glasgow's economic health, and neither tobacco merchants nor shoemakers believed that the restoration of the Stuarts would be beneficial. Furthermore, the republican ideology of the American Revolution and the egalitarianism of the French Revolution appeared to inspire relatively little political radicalism among Glasgow's workers, despite the rapidly occurring changes in their work and the growing wealth inequality visible in the city. Glaswegians were far more likely to gather under the conservative banner of "King and Country" than they were to support Thomas Paine, and civic officials organized large-scale celebrations of the monarch's birthday, with bell ringings, military parades, loyal toasts, and the burning of effigies of such radicals as Wilkes and Paine.[27]

As a result, historians have tended to argue that a combination of the economic and political power of employers and the relative conservatism of the workforce meant that worker consciousness and activism were a later-nineteenth-century phenomenon, which in Glasgow first appeared during the transformation of the textile industry to cotton, quickly resulting in the development of large-scale industries. With employers exercising more and more control over the conditions of employment and wages as well as funding and regulating civic poor relief, protest was a luxury that few appeared able to afford.[28] During the long eighteenth century, the city's skilled workers suffered a dramatic loss of control over admission to their crafts, their wages, and the traditional conditions of their employment, as newly arrived semi-skilled or unskilled workers performed more and more of the work fueling the city's growth. Consequently, living conditions declined, both for skilled workers and for the burgeoning population of semi-skilled and unskilled workers, most of whom had been displaced from their rural homes. The highly visible growth of wealth inequality must have been most apparent in the increasing concentration of the working population in crowded tenements with insufficient water and rising levels of disease and mortality.

Confronting such changes were some workers who sought to organize and protest, and for much of the century the Roman law origins of the Scottish legal systems allowed associations of artisans and workers to challenge wages and conditions in court. For while the legal system controlled wages and working hours, it also regulated prices, markets, and apprenticeships: the courts, in pursuit of the public good, the fair price, and the just wage held sway over both employees and employers.[29] However, as fast as Glasgow grew, so too did the traditional working relationships that had balanced the needs of employer and employee appear to deteriorate. Early in the century, masters had trained and been responsible for apprentices who lived with them, but by the end of the century larger-scale manufactories employed less-skilled workers who enjoyed none of the benefits of the traditional personal relationship with their master. Employers came to replace the master artisans who had enjoyed an intimate connection with their work and with the young men they trained for a professional career, and the gap between the interests of employer and worker widened.[30]

Tailoring provides one example of a craft that was directly transformed by Glasgow's growth in an Atlantic world context. Traditionally this was a small and highly skilled trade producing clothing to the specifications of the customer. By the end of the eighteenth century, however, "slop shops" employing large numbers of semi-skilled and unskilled workers mass-produced items of clothing for export to North America and the Caribbean, and, over time, for domestic consumption. The pace of change was slower in the shoe-making trade, though the trend was the same. In 1798, some eighty Glasgow shoemakers employed approximately six hundred journeymen, but throughout the second half of the eighteenth century, men such as James Dunlop had begun overseeing the mass production of cheap shoes by semi-skilled piece workers for export to the colonies: soon, these too were available domestically, undercutting the traditional artisans.[31]

The mercantile elite enjoyed a level of control over both the leather and the textile industries that approached dominance. At first the lack of water power prevented consolidation through the creation of large-scale water-powered spinning. As a result, Glasgow's traditional reliance on hand-loom weaving continued throughout the eighteenth century: in 1791, Glasgow's textile manufacturing was built upon the work of fifteen thousand looms in and around the city. According to the *Statistical Account*, each loom gave employment to an average of nine men, women, and children, whose labor ranged from picking the cotton to spinning and weaving to bleaching, printing, and dyeing.[32] Traditionally, manufacturers and merchants had controlled the complicated and expensive process of preparing flax, which was then distributed to thousands of men and women in and around Glasgow and beyond for spinning and weaving, after which the fabric was returned to the manufacturer for bleaching, printing, and dyeing. Over the course of the eighteenth century, the small independent spinners and weavers lost more and more of their independence as they became indebted to merchants, and thus tied to them for work, and more and more of their control over the conditions and price of that work.[33]

The changes in a wide array of occupations meant that by 1800 the word "tradesman" no longer referred exclusively to the most skilled craftsman but encompassed a range of workers including the least skilled, and the traditional path of an apprentice to journeyman, and for a few to the high status of master craftsman, had all but disappeared. Not surprisingly, then, there were workers who were deeply concerned about the erosion of artisans' control of access to their trade and production of goods. From the ranks of artisans emerged new journeymen's organizations. However, both national and local governments acted to limit the power of both traditional and new trade incorporations to control the employment of linen weavers, for example. Wages declined as more and more semi-skilled and unskilled workers entered the craft workforce. The enforced wage cuts of the 1780s prompted the first large-scale and violent expression of worker radicalism in and around the city, when thousands of weavers went out on strike and, in 1787, attacked the looms of those who continued to work. Angry strikers threw "stones, brickbats and other missile weapons" at troops who then fired on the crowd. Conditions worsened during the Napoleonic Wars, and over the following two decades weavers' incomes declined by two-thirds while food and other costs rose. Glaswegian and other weavers worked hard to enforce the traditional rights of the craft associations and guilds to turn to the courts for fair prices and wages, but the manufacturers refused to give way. Backed up by Parliament, which legislated against combinations of workers, the employers were empowered to set wages and conditions of employment.[34] Participation in Britain's Atlantic World of trade had created a financial and political elite with sufficient local and national influence and power to eradicate centuries-old workers' rights and privileges.

Glasgow's handloom weavers produced some political radicals who supported the Paginate ideology that in printed and spoken form was spreading around Britain's Atlantic World, and tradesmen were included among the members of the Glasgow Society for Burgh Reform who in 1792 supported "asserting and constitutionally establishing the rights of man."[35] Governmental repression kept most radical activity underground until a deep economic recession and the repressive governmental measures that culminated in the Peterloo Massacre of 1819 triggered widespread strikes in the west of Scotland and throughout Britain.[36]

However, politicized opposition could and did take other forms, as workers drew on an arsenal of weapons shared with others all over the Atlantic World. The late-eighteenth- and early-nineteenth-century wars with America and France hampered trade and manufacturing, bringing real suffering to the people of Glasgow. It was at such times that the conspicuous wealth and privilege of the manufacturers and employers who had most clearly benefited from imperial trade, and who had engineered the transformation of work and society at large, exposed them to the displeasure of Glasgow's workers. This can be seen, for example, in the case of a contingent of some five hundred "gentleman volunteers," an elite militia cavalry troop whose members furnished their own magnificent red and gold uniforms and beautiful horses during the 1790s. When war ended in 1802 the members paraded to, appropriately enough, the Merchants' Hall to return their arms, where they were met by a large crowd of workers. Many had been unemployed or suffered reduced wages and severe shortages of food, and they celebrated the end of the war while manifesting their resentment of employers who had suffered little by pelting "the volunteers as they came out of the hall with various ugly missiles . . . made more offensive by having been first submitted to the gutters."[37]

Similarly, crowds could manipulate and even take over such patriotic events as celebrations of the monarch's birthday. One celebration of George III's birthday at the dawn of the nineteenth century included the decoration of houses and carriages, a full military parade, and the drinking of loyal toasts by the city's magistrates, each one saluted by a volley of soldiers' musket fire. Later in the evening, however, the crowd took control of the streets and began building an enormous bonfire at the Cross. Soon such items as "hand and wheel barrows of all kinds, empty casks, loose doors and windows, shutters, articles of furniture, ladders, sign-boards, [and] pieces of builders' scaffolding" were being thrown by the crowd onto the fire. Revealingly, the laborers and workers celebrating their monarch's birthday were burning the tools and products of their own work: the late eighteenth and early nineteenth centuries were years of real hardship, and celebration could quickly turn to protest. Later in the evening, the crowd attempted to burn through the door to the prison, perhaps the clearest indication of an assault against civic authorities and the power of the law over workers, and as a result, the authorities ordered troops into the city, which they entered with bayonets fixed in order to clear the crowd.[38]

Even the city's youths challenged the wealth inequality and emerging social hierarchy of the city in their games. Robert Reid recalled winter snowball fights in the late eighteenth century, which took on new significance when "large parties of boys of tender age" gathered and called on their betters "to make obeisance to them on passing—the men to take off their hats, and the women to drop them a curtsey." Those who failed to comply were "unmercifully pelted with snow balls." These young boys grew up watching their parents living and working in more and more deferential relationships with employers and the city's mercantile elite, and they knew that similar lives awaited them: but on some winter days, with well-aimed snowballs, they could strike back.[39]

At the same time, artisans and members of the trades sought to affirm their status and their rights through annual processions. Despite the severe weakening of the trades, even in the early nineteenth century artisans proudly participated in annual processions featuring "the Deacons and Office-bearers of the different Crafts of the City, accompanied by the members of the several Incorporated trades." Their flags bore the emblems of their trades: the "masons displayed the plummet and the mallet; the wright, the saw and the plane; the smiths, the hammer; the fleshers, the cleaver; and the tailors, the shears, and so on."[40] More and more members of the crowds who watched these parades were unskilled or semi-skilled workers whose employment was undercutting the powers and privileges of the craft guilds and undermining their abilities to protect wages and working conditions. In such circumstances, these processions were less the celebrations of a century earlier than they were defiant shows of strength by weakened and embattled skilled artisans.

The moral economy of the crowd survived, even as the traditional role of Scottish courts in enforcing fair wages and just prices diminished. The "fearful time of dearth" in 1800 was so bad that many suffered like one Glaswegian handloom weaver and his family for whom "there was nothing in the house to eat, and they had little coals except what was on the fire. They went to bed supperless, and as they had nothing to eat thought it better to remain in bed instead of rising on Sunday morning."[41] Such depravation prompted a number of crowd actions, and "every Saturday night some meal-dealer's shop or other was gutted, and his provisions thrown to the starving people outside." Some merchants, judged to be hoarding food or charging unfair prices, were "put in bodily fear," as in the case of a merchant outside whose High Street store a crowd waited "with a halter fixed to the lamp-post opposite, ready to hang him had he come out—and ten to one they would have done it." Writing half-a-century later a commentator who had witnessed these proceedings condemned "the impunity with which the mob conducted their proceedings," not recognizing the legitimacy of a long-established right of the crowd in times of want.[42]

Glasgow's workers continued to enjoy preindustrial forms of popular entertainment throughout the eighteenth and even into the nineteenth centuries. Cock fighting and bare-fisted fighting drew large audiences, and large-scale chaotic games of football were as much popular riots as sporting events. However, a new world of time-work discipline and an ever more tightly controlled workforce resulted in the increasing regulation of even the pastimes of the city's workers, and by the early nineteenth century an official kept ball games and other riotous activities off Glasgow Green, the city's traditional playground.[43] More significantly, with the Police Act of 1800 the city's workers found themselves controlled at work and play by a professional police force organized and paid for by the civic authorities.[44]

Crowd actions, popular appropriation or hijacking of civic celebrations, bread riots and similar articulations of the moral economy of the crowd, and popular humiliation of members of the elite were all part of an Atlantic-wide popular political culture; its mores were spread in print and by word-of-mouth and thus belonged to a political culture of negotiation that was familiar to both activists and victims alike. Glasgow's newspapers reported, for example, the ways in which Bostonians had protested against the Stamp Act with effigies, a parade, the destruction of a building belonging to Andrew Oliver, the proposed stamp collector, and finally the destruction of the wealthy mercantile home of the Massachusetts Lieutenant Governor Thomas Hutchinson.[45] The rites, actions, and implicit social protests inherent in these activities were part of a transnational political culture that would have been entirely comprehensible to Glaswegian workers, who at times drew upon this shared discourse to articulate their own resentment of the oppressive rule of a local elite whose wealth such workers helped create.[46] Traditional forms of popular protest were politicized and radicalized by the political events of the second half of the eighteenth century, so that workers in Glasgow and indeed all around the British Atlantic World began experiencing and reacting to their situation in ways that demonstrated a new understanding of their class identity.

Like others all around the British Atlantic World, a rapidly growing population of workers in eighteenth- and early-nineteenth-century Glasgow experienced new kinds and conditions of employment. Merchants and manufacturers made wealthy by Atlantic trade possessed significant power over these employees and their work, but in the ways in which Glasgow's workers experienced, interpreted, and began reacting to their new world of work we can detect the glimmering of class. E. P. Thompson argued that when "people find themselves in a society structured in determined ways (crucially, but not exclusively, in productive relations), they experience exploitation (or the need to maintain power over those whom they exploit), they identify points of antagonistic interest, they commence to struggle around these issues and in the process of struggling they discover themselves as classes, they come to know this discovery as class-consciousness." Class happens, in other words, as "men and women *live* their productive relations, and as they *experience* their determinate situations, within 'the *ensemble* of the social relations,' with their inherited culture and expectations, and as they handle these experiences in cultural ways."[47]

Like Fernand Braudel's Mediterranean, the Atlantic World was a world of connections, a world in which people and goods moved between regions, countries, and continents. These connections led to the development and experience of clear and distinct class identities and interests, from the British working class to the North American class of yeoman farmers to the enslaved class of African Americans.[48] It is all too easy to think of the Atlantic World and of Atlantic crossings as fixed in time and space, rather than envisioning constant movement of people and goods, connections and reconnections. This movement informed the creation of classes all around the Atlantic World, albeit in different ways and with different rates of development of class creation and self-awareness. Although these interconnections can confuse and complicate, they may also inform and illuminate our understanding of class.

As the history of Glasgow demonstrates, class in the early modern Atlantic World developed out of the transformation of traditional social differentiation and organization into new and complex structures of inequality.

Mainland North America was far from immune to this process, despite the conviction of many American historians that class mattered more in Europe than in North America. The people of medieval Europe had experienced their lives as members of differentiated yet interdependent social orders or estates, which on occasion had appeared to be natural and virtually timeless. Of course, people did transcend these social orders, but with the demographic, economic, and social changes that swept through the sixteenth-, seventeenth-, and eighteenth-century British Isles, ideas about social position appeared far less certain than before.[49] As land ownership was consolidated and land usage transformed, large numbers of rural tenants and laborers left the land, either having been thrown off by those who sought to use the land differently or having chosen to seek better lives for themselves and their families elsewhere. In their tens and even hundreds of thousands, masterless men, women, and children traversed the countryside in search of work, often ending up in fast-growing towns and cities such as Glasgow, or in far distant colonies. At the same time, as commerce and colonial trade grew, manufacturing kept pace, and in towns and cities traditional craft hierarchies of master craftsmen, journeymen, and apprentices began to erode as wage labor became increasingly common. Ruling classes, too, were transformed, as medieval feudal lords were supplanted by landowners who were more focused upon growing crops, raising livestock, or in other ways utilizing the land in order to maximize profits, while in towns and cities, manufacturing and trade nurtured the development of mercantile capitalism and a new class of urban rulers.

The point here is a simple but significant one about how all manner of people, all around the Atlantic World, found themselves in new social positions with new social groups, a situation that required them to define and defend new interests, sometimes against powerful contending interests.[50] For many, the situation involved the possibility of change and progress, and ideologies of a rigid hierarchy of social orders and estates were necessarily recast. The people of the early modern Atlantic World were moving geographically and occupationally, experiencing new relationships with the means of production and developing new identities with others from a variety of backgrounds. Rather than defining themselves and their actions in terms of older social orders whose members had sought to protect their positions within a relatively fixed social structure, many men and women began to think about themselves in less rigid and quite revolutionary ways. As members of classes, acting in cooperative fashion, they might exercise more control over their situations, constantly defining and redefining their interests in relation to the members of other classes. It was a world of possibilities, wherein a manufacturing laborer in Glasgow or a tenant farmer in North Carolina thought about how to improve and even change a new and developing position. Their medieval ancestors had rarely gone beyond attempts to restore the status quo, but these folk were drawing on both traditional ideas and new ideologies of rights to change and improve their positions in the world.

In trying to comprehend how classes came into existence and how people came to identify themselves as members of a class with a shared class interest, many historians have followed Thompson's adaptation of the classic Marxist approach, arguing that class *experience* provided the historical mediation between productive relations and class consciousness.[51] In short, as distinct classes developed, they assumed shape and significance from the ways in which people combined in understanding and reacting to their situations. Pierre Bourdieu took this insight still further, broadening the Marxist concept of capital to include cultural and symbolic goods and asserting that class struggles are quite literally symbolic, for they are as much struggles over signs and symbols as over material reality.[52] However, historians of class interest and action in the seventeenth and eighteenth centuries—including Thompson—have often interpreted crowd actions and violence as defenses of popular rights and privileges, and thus as conservative reactions within a traditional environment of popular deference to elite rule. While these may be early movements toward class interest and action, historians have commonly seen them as predating real class and class consciousness.[53]

Nonetheless, although Glasgow's eighteenth-century artisans may have been defending "traditional" rights and methods they were doing so in new contexts, against the competing class interests of newly emerging groups or classes—the mercantile elite, manufacturers, and wage laborers. The result was a process of negotiation, wherein the mercantile elite, manufacturers and employers, artisans, and semi- and unskilled workers sought to protect and enhance their positions in a rapidly changing commercial environment. As Atlantic World historiography grows and develops, it is complicating our understanding of the history of class and suggesting that consciousness of class and class interest began to develop well before the advent of industrialization. It is becoming increasingly apparent that this early modern world was far more commercial and far more modern than historians once assumed.[54] From manufacturing workers in British cities to plantation slaves to yeoman farmers to artisans in North American seaport cities, groups of people in the Atlantic World were defining themselves in the ways in which they sought to improve existing and secure new social, economic, and political rights and privileges within a fast-developing international economy. Moreover, as these groups established normative patterns of behavior and political rhetoric in order to assert and defend their positions in society, they began to move toward class in ways that would form the basis for later, clearer expressions of class interest. Thus within the Atlantic World class identities were fast becoming a reality in quite significant ways. People were beginning to identify themselves as members of coherent groups within social structures of inequality, and they were employing this enhanced self-awareness to explain their material standards of living. In some cases, this entailed interpreting and reacting to the new forms of economic oppression and exploitation that they were suffering, from apprentices and journeymen facing an increasing use of wage labor by their employers to unskilled manufacturing workers.

Class and class consciousness can be realized only when folk become aware of their shared experiences and interests and then cooperate in order to advance. In the classic Marxist formulation, when "the worker co-operates in a planned way with others, he strips off the fetters of his individuality, and develops the capabilities of his species," and this is how class functions as the engine of human history, propelling humanity forward.[55] In examining these kinds of examples of shared experience and cooperative activity, we must follow Thompson in freeing ourselves of the assumptions of the ruling authorities of the Atlantic world, who saw and dismissed the activities of slaves, laborers, seafarers, and yeoman farmers as spontaneous, riotous, and criminal, with little meaning and even less legitimacy. As E. P. Thompson, Eric Hobsbawm, Peter Linebaugh, Marcus Rediker, Alfred Young, Eugene Genovese, and a host of others have shown, we can interpret such activities as assertions of class prerogatives and privileges and defenses of class rights in the "theatre of class hegemony and control."[56]

Within the complex and significantly modern societies of the Atlantic World, such cooperative activity transcended popular articulation of traditional and reactionary positions. The familiar images of self-sufficient farmers and autonomous tradesmen in independent workshops have given way to a more complex vision of Atlantic World societies of "ambitious and acquisitive settlers who pursued diverse commercial enterprises and accumulated consumer goods in a market society."[57] Thus, journeymen in port cities, urban laborers and seafarers, and yeoman farmers did not simply react conservatively against innovations threatening traditional work practices and popular rights. In addition, they were able to delineate and defend their interests in an Atlantic World market economy, a process that often involved defining themselves and their interests in class terms against the members and interests of other classes.

The development of the Atlantic World, with its massive movement of people and goods, and its transformation of work and accepted social hierarchies, played a pivotal role in undermining traditional conceptions of social orders and estates. As people came to terms with new worlds of work, production, and consumption, they combined in order to protect and improve their economic, political, and social positions. This is the experiential early process of class consciousness and activity. It was in the language and actions emerging from these interactions between the members of different groups that class identity and class consciousness took shape. By articulating their rights, their positions, and their demands, and then acting to achieve them, seafaring radicals, rebel slaves, protesting urban workers, and rebelling yeoman farmers began fashioning rudimentary class and class consciousness all around the Atlantic World. The Atlantic World could not create a unitary working class, but the social and economic transformations wrought by its movement of people and goods necessarily created many different classes in a variety of new contexts, featuring different social, economic, and political relationships.

Stratification and Class in Eastern Native America

Daniel K. Richter

The words *class* and *seventeenth-century Native North American* have perhaps never before been seen in the same sentence. Nor should they have been, if by *class* we evoke meanings familiar to Karl Marx, E. P. Thompson, or their successors. Clearly the economic, social, and cultural nexuses of inequality in Native America differed so profoundly from those of Western Europe that such meanings of class are irrelevant to the Indian societies of Eastern North America—at least until the eighteenth-century times and places discussed by Daniel Mandell in the next chapter. Yet if we are to understand the ways in which the emerging class formations of Western Europe interacted with Native American societies, both in the earliest stages of contact and over time, it is worthwhile to consider exactly what forms of inequality, hierarchy, and stratification did prevail in eastern North America in the era of European colonization.

These, too, are words seldom seen together. *Inequality, hierarchy,* and *stratification* fit uneasily in our ways of thinking about Native experiences. They usually enter the conversation, if at all, as consequences of European contact, as symptoms of cultural breakdown, as words loaded with negative moral freight, as things that had somehow to be *taught* to Indians. Nonetheless, scholarship now indicates that distinctive forms of economic, social, and political stratification—not edenic egalitarianism—were the norm among the agricultural peoples of eastern North America at the time of their first contacts with Europeans. An appreciation of that norm has profound consequences for understanding what came later.

As Karen Kupperman has suggested, when early European travelers and colonizers described Native American leaders as "kings," "lords," and "emperors," they knew what they were talking about. "In England," Kupperman observes, "aristocrats and monarchs, knowing that government rested more on honor and credit than on law or force, took care to surround themselves with visual emblems of magnificence . . . , presenting their persons in ways that affirmed their place atop the hierarchy." Such modes of presentation "were designed to convey ideas that mortal minds could not grasp directly; their desired effect was to evoke in the affirming audience a sense of wonder or awe." And nearly everywhere they looked, English travelers described Native leadership in ways that "echoed the language of English aristocratic self-presentation," convinced as they were that "Indians exhibited the same natural courtesy, virtue, and care for their reputations that characterized England's nobility."[1]

Indeed, linguistic, sartorial, and ceremonial markers of exalted status attached to hereditary Native leaders throughout most of eastern North America. The title of the Chesapeake Algonquian paramount chief Powhatan was *mananatowick*, which shares common linguistic roots with *manitou*, or "power." Algonquians of southern New England distinguished between "*ahtaskoaog* or 'principal men'" and "*missinnuok* or 'common people.'"[2] Mohawks set apart *rotiyanehr* (the term combines the concepts of "great" or "honored one" with "one who keeps the peace"). The Jesuit author Joseph-François Lafitau further distinguished (with different orthography) "*Roiander Gôa*, meaning 'noble par excellence,' from *gaïander*, the usual [Mohawk] word meaning nobility." In the Southeast, terms such as *mico* and "beloved man" carried similar connotations, while everywhere chiefs displayed their lofty status by wearing rare copper or shell ornaments on their bodies and living in communal houses that were larger, if not always more elaborate, then those of common folk.[3]

Few could match the trappings of the litter-borne, pearl-garlanded "Lady of Cofitachiqui," who met Hernando de Soto in 1539, or Powhatan's ritual storehouse guarded by "foure Images as Sentinels, one of a Dragon, another a Beare, the third like a Leopard, and the fourth like a giantlike man, all made evill favouredly, according to their best workemanship."[4] Nonetheless, there was no doubt about who was a member of the elite. "Although the chiefs have no mark of distinction and superiority so that, except in a few individual cases, they cannot be distinguished from the crowd by the honours due to be paid them, people do not fail to show always a certain respect for them," concluded Lafitau. "The councils assemble by their orders; they are held in their lodges unless there is a public lodge, like a town hall, reserved only for councils; business is transacted in their names; they preside over all sorts of meetings; they play a considerable role in feasts and community distributions; they are often given presents; and, finally, they have certain other prerogatives resulting from their preeminent status."[5] In some societies, these subtle patterns created a situation in which the clearest marker of social stratification was the *lack* of the forms of ostentatious display that Europeans found familiar. "The chiefs are generally the poorest among them," one seventeenth-century Dutch traveler along the Hudson River reported, "for instead of their receiving anything . . . , these Indian chiefs are made to give to the populace."[6]

For help in making sense of such characteristics of eastern Native American polities, it is useful to revisit the classificatory schemes developed in the 1960s by political anthropologists such as Elman R. Service and Morton H. Fried.[7] Their approach remains open to critique on any number of levels, and it would be particularly unhelpful to revive the evolutionary frameworks within which they worked.[8] However, as heuristic typologies that help us break out of vague moralizing about hierarchy and egalitarianism, the ideas of Service, Fried, and others, including the early Marshall Sahlins, remain useful.[9]

Service's now standard formulation (much criticized by those who nonetheless continue to use it) distinguishes four levels of "sociocultural integration": bands, tribes, chiefdoms, and states, with population size, sedentism, and modes of economic distribution as key determinants. His bands are small, mobile family groups of hunter-gatherers, with few political or social distinctions except those based on age and gender. His tribes are somewhat larger, semi-sedentary societies still organized mostly according to kinship, with virtually no economic differentiation, with exchange based on relatively equal patterns of reciprocity, and with collective leadership resting either in councils of equals or what other scholars would call "big men," whose status was temporary and achieved rather than hereditary or institutionalized. Service's chiefdoms, meanwhile, have considerably larger, permanently settled, populations—in the thousands rather than the hundreds—with a distinct hierarchy of kin groups, some of which possess hereditary chiefly offices invested with ceremonial and often sacred characteristics that set them apart from the generality of the population. Chiefly status is confirmed by—indeed rests upon—the power to redistribute valued resources to the community. As population continues to expand, presumably, such differences in power and status produce the seeds of the coercive inequalities associated with the state level of organization that Service does not explore in any detail.[10]

Fried's scheme emphasizes differential access to economic resources and to positions of status as the driving force behind four heuristic types that only partially coincide with those of Service: egalitarian, ranked, and stratified "societies" and "the state." Fried's egalitarian societies combine many features that Service associated with both bands and tribes. In this first type, goods "circulate" rather than accumulate, through reciprocal exchange, and much the same can be said of political leadership, which remains open to all those with the talents to achieve it. By contrast, for Fried, "a rank society is one in which positions of valued status are somehow limited so that not all those of sufficient talent to occupy such statuses actually achieve them." While the egalitarian circulation of many goods continues, "in rank society the major process of economic integration is redistribution, in which there is a characteristic flow of goods into and out from a finite center" at "the pinnacle of the rank hierarchy." In stratified societies, this kind of ranked rationing of political office is joined by similar "differential rights of access to basic resources . . . either directly (air, water, and food) or indirectly (things that cannot themselves be consumed but are required to obtain other things that are)." For Fried, "outstanding examples of the latter are land, raw materials for tools, water for irrigation, and materials to build a shelter." He did not explain how an elite group could actually achieve differential access to air (although perhaps this might make sense of various comments by Jesuit missionaries about their difficulty breathing in smoke-filled lodges), but Fried was very clear that his definition of stratification rests on hard material foundations that contain the seeds of the state. "It is usually unwise to treat as wealth such sumptuary marks of prestige as bird plumages, dentalium shells, or other paraphernalia of rank," he cautioned, "because that term conjures up a vision of universal exchangeability." Because "the marks of prestige cannot be used to acquire food or productive resources," the accumulation of them "does not convey any privileged claim to the strategic resources on which a society is based."[11]

There will be more on that point below, but for now it should be clear that, except for the hunter-gatherers of the far north and perhaps some of the small Algonquian-speaking communities that lived in estuarine environments in New England and the mid-Atlantic region, none of the major societies of eastern North America can accurately be described as "egalitarian," as "bands," or even, in Service's technical sense, as "tribes" (although Service himself, drawing on the secondary ethnographic literature of his day, so classified most of them).[12] Nearly every recent scholar of the Powhatans of the Chesapeake Bay insists that this formidable polity was not a "confederacy" but a "paramount chiefdom."[13] Stephen R. Potter drives home the same message for the broader Chesapeake region.[14] Kathleen Bragdon proposes that at least one of the three kinds of sociopolitical formations she has identified for southern

New England in the sixteenth and early seventeenth centuries comprised communities "best characterized as chiefdoms of marked social hierarchy and centralized leadership."[15] It might be added that—with their local community populations in the hundreds or thousands, with their at least seasonally permanent agricultural villages, with their redistributive economic systems, and with their clear patterns of hereditary, ritually charged office-holding—most Iroquoian- and Algonquian-speaking peoples of the Great Lakes region and nearly every society of the Southeast shared much with Service's category of chiefdoms, despite the fact that they often relied on collective rather than unitary leadership.[16] The term should no longer be confined, as it often has been, to the Mississippian societies that flourished before the year 1500.

And if "chiefdom" rather than "tribe" would appear to be the appropriate typological term in Service's vocabulary, at least "ranked," rather than "egalitarian," is the operative word in Fried's. The only matter in dispute would seem to be whether most eastern North American chiefdoms were also "stratified." Powhatan apparently controlled a considerable portion of the corn produced in his paramount chiefdom.[17] Algonquian chiefs in southern New England were repeatedly said to have collected "tribute," and elite Huron lineages evidently controlled particular trade routes from which they skimmed a form of taxation.[18] However, in none of these cases does the evidence convincingly support a definition of stratification based on differential access to basic resources that would satisfy Fried (or Marx or Thompson). Even for the prototypical eastern North American chiefdoms, the Mississippians, archaeologists remain deeply divided over the extent to which the lofty status of chiefs, and the mound-dominated ceremonial centers where they presided, extracted disproportionate basic resources from those of lower status and from subordinate villages.[19]

In the years since Service and Fried wrote, scholarship on chiefdoms has made it possible to resolve the apparent problem of the missing economic basis for stratification in the Native societies of eastern North America. As Timothy Earle notes, chiefdoms can emerge by multiple routes, only some of them involving the forms of differential access to resources Fried emphasized. Indeed, in global history, it may have been less common for chiefdoms to be based on the kind of control of vital commodities that Earle calls "staple finance" than on the mechanisms of "wealth finance" in what is often referred to as a "prestige-goods economy."[20]

As defined in a widely cited analysis of Iron-Age German chiefdoms by Susan Frankenstein and Michael Rowlands, "the specific economic characteristics of a prestige-goods system are dominated by the political advantage gained through exercising control over access to resources that can only be obtained through external trade." Prestige goods are anything but the basic utilitarian resources described by Fried. Instead, they are "wealth objects needed in social transactions."[21] The anthropologist Mary Helms explains that "prestige goods . . . may be crafted items acquired ready-made from geographically distant places or skillfully fashioned at home from materials— woods, clays, stones, metallic ores, paints—that are also derived from the outside world." Others "may be valued in their natural, unworked form as inherently endowed with qualitative worth—animal pelts, shells, feathers, and the like." In either case, they "constitute a type of inalienable wealth, meaning they are goods that cannot be conceptually separated from their place or condition of origin but always relate whoever possesses them to that place or condition." The social power of such goods comes from their irrevocable association with their source, often described as "ancestral beings—creator deities, culture-heroes, primordial powers—that are credited with having first created or crafted the world, its creatures, its peoples, and their cultural skills."[22] In other words, the prestige goods so central to the operation of chiefdoms are valued precisely *because* they cannot be exchanged for the more mundane goods on which Fried insisted stratification must be based. In a prestige-goods chiefdom, "political power is not directly linked to subsistence."[23] So Fried's "bird plumages, dentalium shells, or other paraphernalia of rank" turn out to be wealth after all.

Thus it would appear that rare items such as the crystals, minerals, shells, and mysteriously crafted ritual items that moved through the ancient trade routes of North America to be redistributed by chiefs undergirded a very real system of social and economic stratification—albeit one particularly fragile because it was dependent on external sources of supply that chiefs could not directly control.[24] As Mary Douglas and Baron Isherwood and many others have reminded us, the cultural meaning of goods is embedded in social and political relations; firm distinctions between prestige and subsistence goods may not just be hard to define but illusory.[25] If, as appears to have been the case with Cahokia and other Mississippian chiefdoms, the prestige goods controlled and redistributed by chiefs were embedded in rituals demonstrating power over agricultural fertility, they were no less the kind of resources necessary to sustain life than the land and tools Fried identified in more classically materialist contexts. As Thomas Emerson observes, "The ultimate symbols of [Cahokian] elite control may be represented by the presence of the exotic and beautifully crafted Earth Mother figurines at rural fertility temples—surely such items must have come into the local community via elite largess."[26] Similarly, if, as the Jesuit missionary Jean de Brébeuf said of the Hurons in the 1630s, "all their exertions, their labors, and their trading, concern[ed] almost entirely the amassing of something with which to honor the Dead," and if the funeral ceremonies on which "they lavished robes, axes, and Porcelain [wampum]" were considered vital to the power and welfare of the community, did not the elite chiefs who could control the trade in such goods enjoy privileged access to resources every bit as important as Powhatan's corn stores?[27]

If relationships of power—the "inalienable association [of goods] with their source"—remained central to redistribution in the prestige-goods economies of eastern North American chiefdoms, we need not necessarily engage in sterile debates over how, when, or if an initial trade in spiritually charged beads and copper became desacralized in a flood of glass, kettles, and axeheads.[28] The cultural functions of such items proved remarkably flexible over time. Copper kettles, for instance, began their careers in North America as prestige goods. Initially valued for their similarity to rare native copper and for the cultural associations of their red color, copper kettles were almost never used *as* kettles in the sixteenth and early seventeenth centuries but instead as raw material for all manner of Native-made objects such as gorgets, amulets, and beads that fit seamlessly into ancient patterns for the chiefly use and redistribution of prestige goods.[29] Yet, as Laurier Turgeon argues, as late as the 1670s, long after supplies of copper had dramatically expanded and earlier associations had slipped away, for the Native trading partners of New France, copper kettles remained something more than mere cooking and storage vessels. They were treasured items "hoarded inside the house, where they enhanced the decor," and "were taken off display only for special feasts" emphasizing communal and spiritual unity. Kettles assumed particular importance in mortuary rituals, as grave goods sent with the deceased into the next world.[30]

More significant—and more lasting than the literal interment of kettles as grave goods, which seems to have declined before the end of the seventeenth century—were the metaphoric uses of kettles that came to permeate eastern Native American discursive worlds. People spoke of hanging the kettle to welcome guests, of the kettle from which allies ate with one spoon, of the war kettle hung over the fire as a symbol of unity against one's enemies. "The copper kettle became the rallying point for individuals and groups, because its force of attraction was stronger than that of any other known object," Turgeon concludes. "Around the kettle people gathered for festivals of life and of death; around the kettle they reflected on the community and on what they wanted it to become; around it, too, they rekindled such hopes."[31]

"In the final analysis," says Turgeon, "the function of the kettle seems to have been more political than eschatological."[32] Unquestionably, kettles and other trade goods soon ceased to be spiritually charged prestige goods in the precise sense defined by Frankenstein and Rowlands. But the political function of goods endured. Leaders who controlled access to, and redistribution of, items from Europe continued to display their privileged "inalienable association with their source," a source no longer described as other-than-human, but no less vital to the material welfare of the community. How else are we to understand the boast of an Algonquin chief who told Brébeuf in the 1630s "that his body was hatchets" and "that the preservation of his person and of his Nation was the preservation of the hatchets, the kettles, and all the trade of the French, for the Hurons"? This relationship based on the control of goods, the chief proclaimed, made him "master of the French."[33] Mastery of the diplomatic connections that delivered crucial items (although not necessarily of the right to possess them) undergirded this vision of political power, and thus of a system of stratification based in the prestige-goods economy of Native American chiefdoms.

The forms of stratification outlined here remain obscured in the literature for many reasons, most of them fairly obvious. Service and especially Fried, who were dependent on twentieth-century ethnographic accounts and were locked in materialist evolutionary categories that rigidly distinguished prestige from subsistence goods, had relatively little to say about eastern North America. To the extent that they did examine historical sources and the secondary literature of their day, they found few hints that stratified chiefdoms, rather than egalitarian bands or ranked tribes, might have been the region's prevalent sociopolitical form. As Kupperman, Roy Harvey Pearce, Robert Berkhofer, Olive Patricia Dickason, Gordon Sayre, and countless other have demonstrated, the rhetorical imperative for European authors to contrast the "civilized" with the "savage," the "advanced" with the "primitive" has simply been too strong for the comments of those Europeans who actually saw the contrary with the own eyes to appear as anything other than misinformed idealistic oddities. And even when "savages" did appear to be "civil," they served more as "a living reproach to England" than as a depiction of living Native political orders.[34] Just as important, although less stressed in the literature, from the seventeenth to the twenty-first centuries, Native people themselves have wielded the image of "living reproach" to stress the great divide between supposedly egalitarian, voluntaristic, non-materialistic Indians and hierarchical, coercive, grasping Europeans.[35]

Yet, it was not all a matter of the triumph of literary trope and cultural imperative over accurate observation. From the 1630s onward, even the most careful European observers would have seen little evidence of social and economic stratification and hereditary political authority. Powhatan had died in 1618, and the chiefdom over which he had presided was smashed in wars with Virginia colonists that began in 1622 and resumed in 1644. No Chesapeake Native leader again would ever accurately be described "not onely as a King, but as halfe a God."[36] Much the same fate befell the chiefdoms of southern New England, where epidemics, new patterns of trade, and wars with Native and English colonial foes ensured that, as Neal Salisbury concludes, "in less than a generation, the world into which most surviving Indians had been born, and for which they had been prepared, had vanished."[37] In the meantime, epidemics, warfare, population resettlements, and, by the late seventeenth century, massive slave raiding so transformed the Mississippian-descended chiefdoms of the southeastern interior that, with the famous exception of the Natchez, few traces remained of the kinds of stratification witnessed by Soto's *entrada* in the previous century.[38] The transformation seems to be recalled in Cherokee traditions about the violent overthrow of a corrupt, oppressive priestly class known as the *Aní-Kutánî* and its replacement by a more egalitarian order.[39]

For the Iroquoian-speaking peoples of the northeastern interior, the forces undermining chiefly elites everywhere were only just beginning to be felt in 1636, when Brébeuf heard Hurons tell him that "formerly only worthy men were Captains, and so they were called *Enondecha*, the same name by which they call the Country. . . . But today they do not pay so much attention to the selection of their Captains; and so they no longer give them that name, although they still call them *atiwarontas, atiwanens, ondakhienhai,* 'big stones, the elders, the stay-at-homes.' "[40] The epidemics that killed at least half the Hurons and Iroquois and the wars those epidemics inspired, which would slaughter or resettle countless thousands of others, had already begun.[41] By the 1690s, when a Mohawk Iroquois spokesman claimed "that we have no forcing rules or laws amongst us," he was not just evoking an already standard trope of cultural difference but describing a reality in which what it meant to be a noble *rotiyanehr* had been profoundly altered.[42]

Yet more than just words such as *rotiyanehr* and pale reflections of "prerogatives resulting from . . . preeminent status" survived into the eighteenth-century world about which Lafitau wrote.[43] Although by his day the stratified chiefdoms of eastern North America had virtually ceased to exist, in at least three ways earlier indigenous patterns of stratification shaped later developments. First, one of the standard characteristics usually attributed to stratified chiefdoms is that they are inherently unstable political forms. Lacking a monopoly of force to defend its privileges, the elite depends for its status on a fragile ideological consensus at home and on equally fragile access to trade goods from abroad. Perched on a fine line between slipping "back" into less hierarchical forms or moving "forward" toward the coercive apparatus of a state, while "cycling" between periods of centralization and decentralization, chiefdoms are forever in flux—to the extent that Fried concluded that "stratified societies lacking political institutions of state level are almost impossible to find" in modern ethnography.[44]

Paradoxically, in this light, even at the point of catastrophic collapse, chiefdomship traditions may actually have provided an enduring set of political tools for dealing with massive change, for incorporating new peoples into reconfigured communities, for persistence through upheaval. As the anthropologist Patricia Rubertone observes, an understanding of the dynamic quality of chiefdoms suggests that, "rather than viewing these 'tribal' groups as remnants of population decline, social turmoil, and economic disruptions which many indeed experienced to varying degrees it might be more useful to consider their emergence as evidence of survival skills that were part of long-standing repertoires of experiences."[45]

This might prove a particularly useful way of looking at things in light of how studies of prestige-goods chiefdoms emphasize interactions with what Frankenstein and Rowlands call "external systems organised on different economic principles." The same chief whose status "depends on his controling external exchange of highest status goods . . . in turn acts as a dependant of an external system whose structure may be only vaguely comprehended."[46] In Frankenstein's and Rowlands's German example of the sixth century B.C.E., those mysterious differently organized systems were the commercial city-states of the ancient Mediterranean world who provided the prestige goods controlled by Central European chiefs. In eastern North America in the thirteenth century C.E., it is likely that emergent chiefdoms on the periphery of Mississippian influences were built on similar control of (or resistance to) prestige goods distributed from differently organized Cahokia, Moundville, and elsewhere.[47] In the mid-seventeenth century, the "systems organised on different economic principles" were European empires. Viewing eastern Native American societies as prestige-goods chiefdoms suggests that patterns of interaction with such systems may have had long precedents, even as the polities themselves altered almost beyond recognition.

Such continuities amid change suggest a second way in which a chiefdom model might provide fresh insights. The transformation of earlier forms of economic stratification and political leadership in the seventeenth century need not imply that the offices and cultural significance of hereditary chiefs disappeared as well, as the persistence to this day of hereditary chiefs among the Haudenosaunee Iroquois attests. The perdurability of league chiefs through the years—and the transformations of their roles from the noble *rotiyanehr* described by seventeenth-century missionaries, to the behind-the-scenes cultural integrators of the eighteenth century, to the "lords" whose offices were codified in writing at the end of the nineteenth, to the political activists many of them became in the twentieth—suggests the flexibility of chiefdomship's traditions.[48] In a parallel, but very different manner, the ways in which seventeenth- and eighteenth-century New England Algonquian sachems and people manipulated interpretations of hereditary claims to office to defend their lands and autonomy suggest that we have only begun to understand the importance of chiefdom traditions over time.[49] In many places, chieftainship endured and perhaps even grew in importance, even as chiefdoms themselves disappeared.

Third, an appreciation of Native societies as stratified chiefdoms revises our comprehension of economic transitions in the colonial era. Several scholars (including Mandell in this volume) have been exploring the complicated ways in which trade and trade goods, production, consumption in world markets, and encapsulation within a world capitalist system transformed Native life in the seventeenth and eighteenth centuries.[50] Clearly, new forms of economic stratification, of political power, of gender roles, of religious and ideological configurations were the result. Those transformations take on new colorations, however, when we try on for size the notion that stratified chiefdoms rather than egalitarian tribes were the starting point. Deeply rooted cultural patterns in which the material basis of stratification rested on redistribution rather than accumulation may have been one of the most important brakes on the corrosive consequences of engagement with European markets—indeed a far more powerful brake than could ever be accounted for by a model that assumes a starting point in egalitarian bands.

The case of Joseph Brant is instructive. Brant was not a hereditary civil chief but a war chief who emerged as the most prominent leader of the Mohawks allied with the British during the U.S. War of Independence. Scholars—most notably the anthropologist David Guldenzopf—have pointed to

him as a prime example of the new forms of possessive economic stratification that developed in Native communities during the late eighteenth century. According to claims filed with the British government after the war,
when the Mohawks lost their homes and became refugees at Niagara in 1779,
the Brant family compound—which, in keeping with the matrilineal descent
patterns of Haudenosaunee society, belonged to Joseph's mother and to his
sister Molly Brant—contained buildings worth £400 New York currency.
This was a substantial sum for any New Yorker and much larger than the
holdings of the majority of Mohawks whose claims were for less than £50.
Stocked with a complete array of eighteenth-century Atlantic consumer
goods, the main house had limestone foundations, a full cellar, plank floors,
and plastered walls, in contrast to the dirt-floored cabins in which most Mohawks lived in this post-longhouse period. Moreover, the Brant buildings
stood on private property that had evidently been purchased, like those of
several other elite Mohawks, from collective clan ownership. Joseph Brant's
total wealth of more than £1,100, especially when combined with his sister's
£1,200, dwarfed that of the three hereditary Mohawk chiefs who submitted
claims ranging from £30 to £102.[51]

These statistics, reinforced by archaeological investigations of the remains of the Brant house and similar findings for a handful of other war
chiefs, lead Guldenzopf rightly to conclude that "full blown internal economic inequalities with differential access to basic resources such as land,
dwellings and capital" had emerged among the Mohawks before the war and
were replicated when the refugees resettled at the Six Nations Reserve on the
Grand River in what is today Ontario, where Joseph Brant promptly built
himself a Georgian country house. But Guldenzopf's analysis also shows
how rooted these novel forms were in the older political-economic forms of
prestige-goods chiefdoms (although he does not use the term). Despite the
turn toward private land holding and accumulation of material goods,
Joseph Brant's power remained embedded in kin-based traditions of leadership. He was not a hereditary chief, but his sister Molly Brant was the most
influential Mohawk hereditary clan mother (as well as the widow of Sir
William Johnson, the British superintendent of Indian affairs), and the
Brant housing compound in the Mohawk Valley appears to have belonged
first to their mother and then to Molly, not Joseph. Just as important is the
source of the personal wealth of such families. The "wealthy warrior elite
and their female relatives," Guldenzopf concludes, "had achieved wealth because of their ability to manipulate the external colonial system" through
gifts, wages paid for military service, trading relationships, and marriage

ties—patterns originating in what otherwise would appear to be a long-gone prestige-goods economy.[52]

Finally, and perhaps most importantly, the political power of the Brant matrilineage depended substantially on the Brants' control of the external relationships that delivered material goods. At Niagara, Brant not only led effective raids on New York but also personally managed much of the distribution of British army provisions to the nearly four thousand Haudenosaunee men, women, and children who took refuge at Niagara when the Sullivan-Clinton campaign of 1779 had destroyed their homes. After the war, in 1786, he traveled to London to lobby successfully for the full payment of all Mohawk loyalist claims, to the tune of £15,000. At the Six Nations Reserve, he continued to play the redistributive role of chief, with lavish public feasts and with material rewards for his supporters. Most controversially, he also fought with the British government and with many of his own people for the right to sell substantial tracts of communal land to white purchasers. Yet even this most seemingly thorough embrace of private property was, as Brant and his supporters saw it, another example of a chief skillfully manipulating external connections to bring material benefits to his people. His plan was to use the proceeds of such sales to accumulate the principal of an annuity that would yield £5,000 in annual revenue for the reserve community.[53] Brant's "latter Days were sorely disturbed by the parties excited against him among his own People," eulogized his contemporary and fellow war chief John Norton. "This much however can be asserted in his favor, and proved by existing facts, that he obtained a much higher price for a few Townships of Land, which he disposed of in behalf of the Five Nations, than had ever been paid to the Aborigine of America." Norton calculated that, by selling 333,000 acres, Brant gained for his community an income equal to the annual annuity interest Seneca, Onondaga, and Cayuga chiefs had secured "from the United States for a Country containing about Fifteen Thousand Square Miles."[54]

However wealthy they may have been, however influenced by Euro-American patterns of gender, kinship, and capital accumulation, late eighteenth-century leaders such as Joseph Brant still had to bring home the goods on which their prestige among their people depended. In doing so, they drove home a message about the difference between Native American and European political economies and constructed a cultural identity that celebrated that difference. No Native person more effectively evoked the separation than the early nineteenth-century writer and activist William Apess. In his *Eulogy on King Philip* of 1836, among the many reasons offered to consider New England's King Philip a superior patriot to George Washington—indeed "the greatest man that was ever in America"—was that, when Philip's men faced their equivalent of the starving winter at Valley Forge, no one prospered while others went hungry. Instead, "when his men began to be in want of money, having a coat neatly wrought with wampampeag (i.e., Indian money), he cut it to pieces, and distributed it among all his chiefs and warriors."[55] The differences in cultural values embodied in Apess's story of chiefly distribution were very real, even if the specific tale might have been apocryphal. The egalitarian contrast grew from the very different modes of stratification that Native people and Euro-Americans had inherited.

3

Subaltern Indians, Race, and Class in Early America

Daniel R. Mandell

During the long eighteenth century, the distant and scattered English outposts in North America became linked provinces that played important roles within the sprawling British Empire. Those provinces developed mature societies, economies, and governments; their port towns and hinterlands enlarged their connections with other parts of the Atlantic World. Independence pulled those provinces out of the empire and increased their role in the Atlantic World, causing Euro-Americans to reshape their notions of nationhood. As part of this process, they renegotiated old categories of social status and shaped an ideology of race linked to that evolving class structure.

Entangled within that process were the surviving coastal Natives who lived along the interstices of the region's economy and culture, with communal and largely subsistence economies within and wage labor without.[1] As a modern market economy and new notions of class, nation, and race developed in the Revolutionary United States, the remaining Indian reserves attracted a noticeable number of blacks and whites, in part because such developments were partially neutralized in those communities. Many if not most Indians also left their reserves for long periods: men worked on the ships that carried goods and information around the Atlantic World, and women sold crafts and worked in white households. As these Natives became more integrated into the regional and world economies, and many married blacks and some whites, they were increasingly perceived as part of the undifferentiated people of color that became the lowest rank in the early republic. These Indians and their communities shed new light on the region's alienated socioeconomic classes. One might think of this as the emergence of the modern counterculture, in which Indians were, from the beginning of the world capitalist economy, both magnets for and symbols of the opposition to that system. This case study highlights how class embraces many aspects of life and culture as well as work and economic status, and how class and race are often linked in the history of the Atlantic World.

During their initial encounters, Eastern Woodland Indians sought to assimilate Europeans through diplomacy and by forging ties of kinship, a goal and tactics that reflected the Natives' social and political structures. European often called tribes "nations" and described sachems as monarchs, perceptions that reflected their own developing nation-states as well as the structure of many Native groups, as described by Daniel Richter's chapter in this book. When colonial leaders desired Native resources or assistance, they first tried to determine the boundaries and leaders of a particular community and then negotiated with those individuals as they would with fellow sovereigns. Competition between colonial powers and among Native peoples, plus European contempt for Native culture and land use, led Europeans to ignore those ideals and to regard Natives as barbarians. Moreover, while Europeans negotiated arrangements with Native leaders, thereby recognizing as well as transforming a tribe's sovereignty, they were not forging a relationship of equal nations.[2] Indeed, that pattern fits Immanuel Wallerstein's world systems structure, in which the core (capitals of colonial powers) dominates the periphery, which supplies labor and resources but receives relatively little.[3]

However, Natives largely managed to elude such relationships for centuries. While they participated in Atlantic trade, swapping furs and deerskins for consumer goods, they simultaneously resisted the developing capitalist world system. Goods that seemed relatively worthless to Europeans had high religious and social value to Native peoples, and Natives preferred to envision trade as a political and social relationship.[4] They were not alone: some elements of the old European class system resisted the transformations of the new capitalist economy, particularly in rapidly modernizing England. This is perhaps the deeper, structural way of understanding why Indian societies proved attractive to a noticeable number of colonists, whether deserters or captives.[5] English depictions of aboriginal cultures may have unintentionally provided a counterpoint to the often alienating pace of social and economic change.[6] Theories of world systems and of class need to account for groups who both participated in the capitalist economy *and* continued to resist its transformations. As we shall see, Indian enclaves within long-colonized areas of the United States would continue to attract such resistors and "dropouts."

Still, the larger view cannot be denied. Abstract monetary value in the capitalist economy flowed primarily to Europe. This relationship became formalized in eighteenth-century theories of mercantilism and also is described in modern world systems theory. Native peoples recognized this un-equal relationship when the *European* value of furs or deerskins dropped rel-ative to manufactured trade goods. The connection between economics and political power also became clear. The French crown sometimes subsidized trade with its Native allies in order to ensure increasingly needed military and diplomatic support, but where such alliances were no longer needed, particularly in areas where enough English or Dutch settlers lived, the colonists sought to subjugate neighboring Indians in order to feel more se-cure and to take more land. In Virginia, New Netherland, and New England, Native leaders often fought back ferociously. At that point, colonists found it necessary to negotiate with other Native groups to gain support or neutral-ity in the struggle.[7]

By 1700, Indian survivors within areas long settled by the English and Dutch no longer lived in sovereign groups. Some enclaves retained distinct territo-ries set aside in law, treaties, or deeds along the Chesapeake, in New Jersey, on Long Island, and in southern New England, and with those reserves they held onto a few shreds of their separate nationhood. They remained legally distinct, and in some cases provincial authorities treated with them in semi-diplomatic fashion. In Virginia, remnant Powhatan groups maintained their traditional social and political structures until the late eighteenth century, including significant roles for shamans; although Indians were supposed to be subject to the harsh provincial codes aimed at free blacks, the laws were rarely enforced among Natives. Lenni Lenapes (Delawares) retained many of their traditional rights by holding onto reserved land in New Jersey. Sim-ilar patterns existed in southern New England. Still, it was quite clear that their inhabitants were subjects of the provincial government and, through them, the English crown. By mid-century, provincial governments com-monly appointed guardians to manage Indian resources; these officials were often local gentry who had their own interests and were baffled by Native communities.[8]

  Indian reservations acted as buffers against many economic and cul-tural changes, including reliance on the Atlantic economy. Into the mid-eighteenth century, such reserves retained unusually rich holdings of timber, fish, and other assets. Even a century later, Mashpee was a paradise for fish-ing and one of the few places in southern New England where deer could still be found. Powhatan men continued to hunt and fish, not only for their fam-ilies but also for the neighboring gentry, and Powhatan women maintained slash-and-burn agriculture with common fields on their small reserves.

Lenni Lenapes held onto their traditional lands, creating separate towns and retaining seasonal economic migration between their villages, the Pine Barrens, and the coast. Montauketts on eastern Long Island guided colonial hunters and anglers through mysterious swamps.[9] True, a growing number of Indian men and women left their communities to become more active participants in the larger economy. Colonial interest in Native baskets and woodenware grew in significance in Virginia as well as New England.[10] Indians adopted cattle and other aspects of Anglo-American farming and began to build cabins and to fill homes with furniture and consumer goods.[11] However, such scattered and informal connections did not generate wholesale changes. While the Mohegan minister Samson Occom bound books and carved utensils for white customers, and farmed and kept livestock, he also lived in a wigwam, fished, and hunted, and his wife refused to speak English and dressed "mostly Indian."[12]

Still, Indian reservations also became reservoirs of cheap resources and labor. English settlements swamped once secluded Indian villages, transforming the region's ecology and compelling Indians to obtain capital for food and building materials.[13] Groups of Indians began to sell lumber and fish and to rent grazing land to colonial neighbors. Some worked as farm laborers or household domestics, or served as scouts or soldiers along the northern frontier. Indian men also became quickly involved in the emerging whaling industry, building on their hunting and whaling traditions. By the mid-eighteenth century, New England whalers were voyaging as far as the coast of Africa, and the trade was pulling many men out of coastal Indian communities.[14] While Indians had often gone to port towns to visit and do business, the rise of international whaling meant that a growing number went there to find work, becoming in the process part of the trans-Atlantic maritime world.

The lives of remnant Indians meshed increasingly with elements of the Atlantic economy: the international trade in colonial resources and crops; commoditization of land; and the development of a permanent wage-earning class, which in turn spawned a rootless proletariat. As Gail MacLeitch has pointed out, by the 1750s even Iroquois far from the coast were partially integrated into this economy, working as guides, soldiers, and laborers for colonists.[15] The class structure generated in the Atlantic economy ensnared coastal tribes more deeply. Nantucket merchants and sea captains manipulated Indian debts to force men onto ships, building the whaling industry that played a major role in the regional economy and the Atlantic World. Anglo-Americans also used many Indian children as servants, as parents indentured their children to cancel debt, because they could not support another mouth, or because indenture offered their children a way to adapt to the new culture.[16] In 1760, the Mashpee minister Gideon Hawley complained that "there is scarcely an Indian Boy among us not indetted to an English Master."[17] Virginians tried to acculturate surviving Powhatans primarily by turning them into laborers for colonial farmers, preferably beginning as indentured servants when children.[18] Indentured servitude remained common for Indian children until the mid-nineteenth century.[19]

Work and servitude with the colonists had significant consequences. The absence of Indian men renewed or increased the prominence of Indian women in their communities.[20] Since the English believed in corporal punishment and frequently whipped servants, Indians raised in English households may have inflicted that experience on *their* children, which would have been a significant change in Native childrearing. The large numbers of children raised in English households also played a significant role in the decline of Native languages, as English had become the dominant language in coastal Indian groups by the middle of the eighteenth century.[21] The literacy of Indians in New England actually declined, as masters were unlikely to teach their Indian servants—a definite handicap and "marker" of a servile class in a place where literacy was becoming a mark of citizenship and power.[22] Coastal Indians produced baskets, wooden implements, and other crafts in large amounts to trade for consumer goods, including not only tea, rum, and sugar, but also meat and medicine.

Because of these dynamics, Indians became part of the "lower sort" in British America. Their shifting social and economic circumstances—lack of capital, declining literacy, and dependence on masters—increasingly placed many Indians within the Anglo-American class system, leading authorities to regulate those outside reserves as members of the lowest social level rather than as tribal peoples.[23] Most "recognizable" Indians still lived within their ancestral communities and continued to hold a special legal status. Nevertheless, by serving as bound *and* wage laborers, subsistence *and* market workers, Indians generally represented a bridge between the past and future of labor in North America and the western world.

Part of this development was the intertwining of class and race in eighteenth-century North America and the blurring of distinctions between Indians and blacks.[24] Lieutenant Governor Thomas Hutchison of Massachusetts wrote in 1764, "We are too apt to consider the Indians as a race of beings by nature inferior to us, and born to servitude."[25] In Tidewater Virginia, surviving Indians "were considered to belong to a stratum below that of any Englishmen, along with free Negroes and African slaves."[26] Throughout the eighteenth-century colonies, as Indians began to live and work alongside African descendants, enslaved or free, Anglo-Americans increasingly lumped the two together in an underclass. Legislatures from New England to Georgia frequently linked Indians and blacks (and occasionally indentured whites) in restrictive laws.[27] Nearly every colony barred intermarriage between whites and Indians as well as blacks—and Massachusetts and Rhode Island added these laws in the 1780s after both states ended slavery. Whether indentured or "independent," Indians in colonial towns and cities often had no choice but to forge relationships with blacks and poorer whites who ignored the growing tide of racial prejudice. By the end of the Revolutionary War, Anglo-Americans increasingly viewed the remaining coastal Indians as part of an undifferentiated "people of color." This was the result of the emerging bichromatic ideology of racism, the high rate of intermarriage between Indians and African Americans, and new notions of the unchangeable nature of race.[28]

People of color became a permanent socioeconomic class forming the lowest strata in the infant United States.[29] Before the Revolution, Euro-Americans as well as Europeans saw citizenship and nationhood as derived from property and ancestry. They also divided society into two segments, gentlemen and ordinary men, or the few and the many, even as a strong middling class emerged.[30] The Revolution and the challenges of creating a new nation connected citizenship and nationhood to voluntary membership and republican ideology. Political conflicts between Republicans and Federalists made the change more acute. Republicans promised social and political equality for yeoman farmers and artisans, apparently ending class distinctions, but silently denied parity or citizenship to people of color, thereby connecting race and class in North America. In contrast, Federalist writers tended to see people of color as part of the general socioeconomic class structure, rather than a separate racial category. Yet, even their protests were more formal and theoretical than substantial.[31]

In response, Indian leaders struggled to distinguish themselves and their people, often (without any sense of irony) employing the language of race. In Virginia, while whites "wanted the Powhatans to merge with the bottom, non-white social strata," the Indians "became even more anxious to separate themselves" from those of African ancestry.[32] Among the Mohegans, Samson Occum sought to have a mulatto child dropped from the tribal register in 1789 to avoid "guinny [Guinea] Children" and other non-Indians from "tak-

ing root" among them. Occum and his Christian Indian allies had already established Brothertown, in Oneida territory, in an effort to forge a new Indian
nationhood that erased tribal distinctions and drew a deeper racial line.[33] In
1792, Gay Head's minister prepared a census to show that his people had little African blood.[34]

Behind the racist language, it is clear that Indian hostility toward blacks
formed from concerns about the perceptions of white men who held the reins
of power. Protests about race formed an important part of efforts by
Powhatans and Mohegans to impress magistrates with the existence of their
communities.[35] The conflicts also held nascent elements of class and gender
conflicts.[36] The creation of English-style farms by Samson Occum and his fol-
lowers led to complaints by other Mohegans that "they Take up more Land
than they have Right." Fifteen years later, a part of the tribe charged, "some
few there are that are stronger than others" will take all of the good land, "and
they will keep off the poor, weak, the halt and blind, and will take the dish
[lands] to themselves."[37] Other Indian communities experienced similar class
tensions expressed in racial terms. Around 1770, according to William Brown,
Narragansett men developed a "very bitter feeling" against blacks when large
numbers of women, including Brown's grandmother, married African American men "in order to change [their] mode of living. . . . The Indian
women[,] observing the colored men working for their wives, and living after
the manner of white people, in comfortable homes, felt anxious to change
their position in life."[38] In July 1788, some Mashpee men wrote of their fear
that "Negroes & English . . . will get away our Lands & all our Privileges in a
short time." Chappequiddick and Christiantown suffered conflicts at the turn
of the century "oweing to their Females Marying Negroes whom they did not
wish to have any right to their lands."[39] However, whites generally ignored or
dismissed these efforts by Indians to draw racial lines against blacks.

By 1800, surviving Indian communities reached an accommodation to
Anglo-American culture that resulted in informal landholding customs com-
bining aspects of their aboriginal ancestors and their white neighbors. The
best evidence remains from groups in southern New England that retained
landholding and management in common, but where those born into the
community could (regardless of ancestry) lay claim to and enclose land for
crops and pass it to their children. The lands of deceased proprietors who
lacked heirs reverted to the community, and any resident could cut firewood
and building timber from the commons, hunt game, fish, and take clams. In
addition, with the exception of the Mohegan and the Narragansett, women

could claim and hold land and vote as proprietors, which astonished visiting Anglo-American men.[40]

This landholding system discouraged innovations that involved more extensive or intensive farming, specialization, market risks, and profitability. Such changes were risky, required scarce capital and made entrepreneurs seem like selfish people violating community norms. This was particularly true since the reservation was a manifest symbol of the community: it held the community together and represented kinship, culture, and a sacred past.[41] Such habits and restrictions, according to Anglo-American observers, held progress at bay. These traditions were, ironically, upheld by state laws that barred the sale of Indian lands to outsiders. Legislatures also continued to appoint guardians to manage the finances and resources of Indian groups; these men usually leased out "surplus" pasture and sold timber to neighboring whites. Such arrangements provided a source of capital for community needs but also undercut the ability of Natives to expand their farming or other operations. Indians were also plagued by growing problems with poaching by neighboring whites, since the resources on the reserves were unusually plentiful and not valued as private goods.[42]

The Indians' mixed subsistence economy, featuring hunting *and* cattle, whaling *and* fishing, communal landholding *and* family allotments, and women holding land and voting, probably formed the greatest surviving boundary between Indian and Anglo-American cultures at the turn of the century. Surviving New England Indian stories underscore how community standards continued to condemn acquisition and the values of capitalism.[43] Gay Head's sale of clay from its famous cliffs shows how Indian groups managed to participate in the market economy without becoming part of it. Industries in eastern Massachusetts clamored for the clay to make into hearths, alum, or clay pipes, and by the early 1820s the community was selling at least 150 tons each year.[44] However, the Indians handled this connection to the regional and world economy in a traditional, communitarian manner. When a boat arrived to purchase a load of the clay, the Indians spread the word from neighbor to neighbor "for this clay is regarded as public property, and every inhabitant of Gay Head who is willing to dig and help load the ship receives a part of the profit."[45] All men earned the same, and women and children were given half; state officials at mid-century described these transactions as "almost realizing the wildest dreams of the communists."[46] Gay Head also refused to lease land on the reserve to whites who wished to build a factory to process the clay, "though tempting pecuniary advantages have been held out to induce them to make only some temporary arrangement."[47]

Since a market economy for capital and labor was emerging by 1800 in western and coastal Massachusetts, Native reserves acted as reservoirs of anti-market forces.[48] This enabled Indian communities to maintain a distinctive culture, including traditions that scorned individualism.[49] Perhaps as a result, a few reserves became refuges for poor whites and blacks from an increasingly uncertain, impersonal economy that (particularly for blacks recently freed and relegated to the lowest socioeconomic level) seemed a threat rather than an opportunity.[50] Mashpee, one of the largest surviving Indian communities, saw large numbers of immigrants after the Revolution, including a noticeable number of English, German, Irish, or African ancestry.[51] Decades later, a survey of Massachusetts Indians noted that mariners sometimes returned from long voyages with "foreign" shipmates of European or African descent who married Native women and stayed on the reserve.[52] While the presence of these whites and blacks in Indian communities became more apparent after the Revolution, this development may have been part of a much older effort among the lower sorts to find or create "alternative ways of life."[53]

Neighboring towns feared that Indian reserves were becoming asylums for miscreants who shared the Indians' sinful and unhealthy customs, such as refusing to save for the future, drinking too much rum, and "informal" marriages. In 1788, justices of the peace and selectmen of towns surrounding Mashpee told the legislature that the reserve threatened to become "a Receptacle of Thieves, vagabonds & Robbers."[54] In 1833, the Boston *Advocate* noted that Indian villages were "so many Alsatias, where the vagrant, the dissipated, and the felonious do congregate." Such concerns were also apparent where slavery rather than commerce dominated the economy. In Tidewater Virginia, local whites told the state assembly in 1784 and again in 1812 that the Gingaskin reserve served as "an Asylum for free Negroes and other disorderly persons," who trespassed and poached with impunity.[55] Thus, some whites and blacks joined Indians in what some today might call an underclass and found homes in Native reserves.

Movement in the other direction also forged this underclass as Indians and their "mixed" descendants continued to leave for work in the growing port cities as mariners, laborers, and domestics. As Simon Newman's chapter in this book shows, the dynamics of commerce in the Atlantic World similarly drew large numbers of Scottish Highlanders to Glasgow, reshaping their rural communities and cultures; many moved on to the Caribbean and mainland North America. After the Revolutionary War, a growing number of New England men, including Indians, became involved in the international deep-water whaling trade. In 1788, Mashpee elders complained that many of their young men remained in "foreign parts . . . having no attachments or Interests to call them home."[56] Two decades later, the English traveler Edward Kendall found only fifteen men and boys farming at Gay Head; the others were "at sea, in the [whaling] fisheries," which was "their favourite employ."[57] In 1861, a survey reported about 150 Indians from various tribes living in the whaling center of New Bedford; most were "looking forward to the time, more or less remote, when they shall return to the places of their nativity, finally to mingle their dust with that of their fathers."[58]

The industry became so large that masters and captains recruited men from many countries and backgrounds. Perhaps this is why Native men seemed increasingly to share aspects of the international maritime plebeian culture, although that behavior when exhibited by Indians was often depicted as part of their "savage" nature.[59] For example, a supposedly Indian characteristic was "improvidence," and many Indian whalers got themselves deeply into debt before leaving on a voyage.[60] However, this was actually part of the plebian subculture of whaling, which also involved the Indians' neighbors. Kendall described how many white men on Cape Cod spent all of their prospective wages before a whaling voyage, and that merchants and former whalers alike told him that only one in ten years did a man earn enough to pay his debts. As a result, whalers were often forced to go on the next voyage organized by creditors.[61]

Another seemingly universal aspect of the international maritime culture was heavy drinking and disorderly habits, although this was a growing problem generally in the United States by 1800. Of course, Indians were notorious for excessive drinking and violence, and such behavior by Native mariners could be perceived either as "traditional" or as part of being a sailor.[62] Regardless, it was clearly a problem for their vulnerable communities and families.[63] In 1838, as a wave of social reform swept a number of Indian enclaves, leaders in Gay Head asked the state to bar rum from their community. The tribe's many whale men on New Bedford ships often spent all of their wages on liquor, which they brought home and "dealt out freely to all their people who desire it . . . creating great suffering for the community."[64]

Not all Indians were whalers: like African Americans, Indians of both sexes continued to serve in Anglo-American households, some for wages and others as bound laborers. Montaukett men worked for money or goods at fence watching, tending livestock, or constructing rail fences.[65] John Avery wrote that Mashantucket Pequot women at the beginning of the nineteenth century "were often excellent servants in the household, and were more or less frequently employed by families" in Ledyard, Connecticut.[66] Whites did not perceive Indians as part of the regular labor market. In 1807, Timothy Dwight, the president of Yale, found that many Lantern Hill Pequots lived on farms in Stonington and worked for their rent rather than earning wages.[67] This marginal status extended to Euro-American gender norms. Around 1800, white farmers around Worcester County frequently gave hard cider to Hassanamisco Nipmuc Sarah Philips for her help. "In times of extra work she was considered a very desirable 'hand,' and the heaviest work was left for her to do."[68]

Those who lived in their ancestral communities continued to support themselves by subsistence farming, gathering, fishing, and hunting, even as they used reserves to produce crafts and food for the market. The few Indians who remained on the shrinking Montauk reserve after 1800, for example, maintained subsistence agriculture, raised some livestock, and obtained some capital or goods from neighboring whites by herding cattle, tending fences, and selling baskets, fish, and wild game.[69] An increasingly prominent aspect of Indian economies was the crafts trade. Native women discovered a growing demand among Anglo-American households for woven baskets, mats, and brooms, a demand stimulated, ironically, by the rising desire for order and cleanliness. Women and children gathered ash bark and other products from woods and swamps on their reserves or the interstices between towns and spent the long winters weaving. In the spring, women strapped their finished products to their backs and walked from village to village, expected and even welcomed by their white customers.[70]

Perhaps the most striking characteristic of Indian workers in the early republic was their transient life. One might be tempted to see such labor as a continuation of the mixed subsistence economies that distinguished aboriginal societies in southern New England.[71] Yet, Indians were not alone on the road. Growing numbers of men, women, and even whole families, of all ethnic and racial backgrounds, became transients in southern New England, probably most because of ill fortune, but many because they could not or did not want to take on newly structured forms of labor.[72] This tendency increased as New England industrialized.[73] Clearly, Indians shared many characteristics and interests with the new nation's emerging underclass.

Like many other white Americans, Dwight concluded that the only way to "improve" Indians was to imbue them with the civilized "*love of property.*" He also acknowledged in a sideways manner how others were attracted to "Indian" values by using the Pequots as an example to attack the ideas of the English socialist philosopher William Godwin, who saw freedom as the perfection of man. "Here the human race, as nearly as possible, are without the restraint of law, morals, or religion. At the same time, they are free in the fullest sense. No private individual possesses or exercises any power to control their conduct; and the government of Connecticut, either from despair of doing them any good, or from the unwillingness of its magistrates to execute law among these people, seems, in a manner which I cannot justify, to have resigned them to the dictates of their own passions and appetites."[74] But here again, Indians may not have been alone in their resistance to capitalism. Indeed, the continued indenturing and unpaid employment of Indians by some Anglo-Americans may be seen as part of their desire to keep the market economy at bay.[75]

Indians were keenly aware of their situation, even if they did not agree on a solution. In the 1830s, the Pequot Methodist minister and activist William Apess condemned anti-Indian prejudice and proposed (in addition to white repentance and enlightenment) that states should privatize Indian lands, noting that his people "are made to believe they are minors and have not the abilities given them from God to take care of themselves. . . . Their land is in common stock, and they have nothing to make them enterprising."[76] Few of his brethren agreed. Several decades later, when Massachusetts proposed "detribalizing" Indian groups in the state, the Mashpees proclaimed that such an action, with the dividing of the entire reserve and the end of restrictions on land sales to outsiders "would be a great disadvantage to us as a body. . . . We have prejudice to fight, and capital too."[77]

European outposts in North America developed as part of the Atlantic World and from the beginning involved Native peoples. They met and exchanged goods for food and furs, arranged land transactions or compensation, fought together and against each other, and met and sometimes married. These connections meant that they all experienced the gradual and uneven shifts of the market economy, which developed first in Europe and grew as it was fed by resources and people from elsewhere. Iroquois worked as traders, translators, and warriors; some traveled to Europe, and many ended up living far from their villages. Highland Scots moved to Glasgow; some then took ship to the West Indies or mainland North America. Enslaved Africans were brought from their continent; free or slave, large numbers traveled widely as mariners. But many resisted the disorienting transformation of the international market economy even as they labored for wages or participated in exchange networks. Sailors, dispossessed cottagers, and indentured laborers sought opportunities and places where they could regain power, community, and property. In North America, Native villages and tribes struggled to preserve the territories and sovereignty that sustained their autonomy; some chose to wage war when pressed too hard, as the Powhatans did in Virginia in 1622 and 1644, and the Wampanoags, Nipmucs, and Narragansetts did in New England in 1675.

During the eighteenth century, subaltern Indians developed deepening connections with North America's increasingly commercial economy. Men, women, and children became incorporated into the regional labor market, and whaling made them part of the international maritime proletariat. Exogamous marriages became more common, especially with men of African origins. As a result, Anglo-Americans increasingly viewed these Indians as part of a generalized people of color, treating and regulating them together in ways that set them apart as a plebian underclass. This underclass shared many characteristics: material culture, "Free-Will" Baptist or Methodist Christianity, unstable and temporary employment, and transience. Many Natives moved to the growing port cities, like the poor and displaced in Scotland, England, and other parts of the Atlantic World, seeking employment and social networks in the international maritime economy. These developments gained momentum after the Revolution, with the birth of a United States with its new sense of nationhood, newly distinguished core and periphery, nascent industrial movement, and infant class system.

At the same time, Indian communities maintained many aboriginal elements: their goal remained production primarily for subsistence with some surplus for trade, women continued to be able to claim and hold land, and the land remained within the community and could not be sold to outsiders. Men continued to hunt and fish on the reserve, again primarily for subsistence, although they also traded surpluses and skills. Resources could be sold and lands leased to whites, but alienation to outsiders was not permitted. As a result, Indian communities developed into reservoirs of non-market economies and social relations. They could not completely obstruct the individualistic marketplace and the emerging capitalist world system that accompanied it, but they limited and slowed its infiltration and, perhaps as a result, drew noticeable numbers of newcomers of African, English, German, and Scottish origin. The survival of such communities and their attraction to outsiders signifies the alienation of lower socioeconomic classes in the developing capitalistic economy. Surviving Indian tribes remained as islands of moral economy that attracted people at odds with the increasingly aggressive market economy.[78] As the United States expanded and destroyed the sovereignty of more distant tribes, those Natives would repeat this pattern of developing connections to the market economy while maintaining communal reserves and traditions.

Class Struggle in a West Indian Plantation Society

Natalie Zacek

In the summer of 1732, William Smith, the rector of St. John's Parish, Nevis, visited an acquaintance on the neighboring island of St. Kitts. In a letter to his friend Charles Mason, the Woodwardian Professor of Geology and a fellow of Trinity College, Cambridge, he described his thoughts and impressions as he and his host rode "through many Sugar Plantations, till we came to the thick Woods." These woodlands were ill suited to the cultivation of sugar, but, according to Smith, he and his friend "now and then . . . passed by a small Cotton Settlement, whose humble and temperate Possessor (Hermit like) lived by vertue of his own and three or four Slaves Labour." In previous letters, Smith had expressed his admiration for the luxurious and leisured way of life among the islands' great sugar magnates, but the small cotton cultivator was still more desirable to him. Such a man lived, according to John Milton,

with far truer Satisfaction, in his lonely Retirement, than can be found in stately
Palaces, or in the most extravagant and luxurious Cities, where
The noise of Riot ascends above their loftiest Towers
And Injury and Outrage: and when Night
Darkens the Streets, then wander forth the Sons
Of Belial flown with Insolence and Wine.[1]

Smith did not claim that Charlestown or Basseterre, the respective capitals of Nevis and St. Kitts, either boasted lofty towers or harbored Satan's offspring. However, it was evident to him that, even in islands that he repeatedly compared to tropical Edens, it was the small farmer, rather than the great planter, whose life approached the ideal in both sacred and secular terms.

This admittedly sentimental and clichéd depiction of the allegedly idyllic life of the independent cultivator, as opposed to that of the great planter,

appears at first glance to be a trivial and innocuous incident within an obscure work of eighteenth-century natural history. This vignette, however,
represented to Smith and to his metropolitan audience a lost opportunity, a
nobler resolution to the long-drawn-out and highly contentious process of
disposing of the Caribbean territories that Britain acquired from France at
the end of the War of the Spanish Succession. By valorizing the figure of the
"humble and temperate" small farmer, Smith presented a critique of metropolitan and colonial policymaking, which, he implied, had sacrificed the interests of the small farmer to those of the sugar magnate. This chapter
explores the lengthy debates about these newly acquired territories, and it il-
luminates the class dimension of the white population of the plantation
colonies of the first British Empire. Class has been the missing factor in the
historiography of the English colonies of the West Indies, largely due to the
adherence of many scholars to Edmund Morgan's influential thesis regarding
the work of racial difference in effacing class awareness in colonial British
American plantation society. Echoing Morgan, for example, Trevor Burnard
notes that in eighteenth-century Jamaica, "the first rule [of society] was a
presumption of white egalitarianism."[2] Careful analysis of the debate over
the "French lands," however, clarifies how eighteenth-century English West
Indian colonists (like the New Yorkers described in Simon Middleton's chapter in this book) defined themselves and others according to their positions
within the social and economic structures of their communities. In the
process, this definition influenced the lives of these communities.

By the terms of the Treaty of Utrecht (1713), France relinquished all of
the land it held in the Leeward island of St. Kitts (or, as it was then called, St.
Christopher's), bringing the entire island under British control for the first
time in its history as a European colony. The cession of these lands was a
source of delight to the metropole. For nearly a century, Britain and France
had uneasily shared the island. The colony's origin myth, or at least that deployed by its European inhabitants, held that the first French and English settlers had arrived on the island in 1625 on the very same day. Lacking "any
awareness of their [joint] arrivals," this "would cause between them a terrible
dispute, and a process which could not end otherwise, because the Island
would be divided between the two nations, and hunting, fishing, the volcano,
the salt ponds, and the meres would be held jointly."[3] The resulting pattern
of division, by which the English occupied the center of the island while the
French controlled both of its ends, would probably have proved less than
satisfactory even in a time of peace. But Anglo-French relations throughout
the late seventeenth and early eighteenth centuries were notably bellicose,

particularly during the 1660s and more or less continuously from 1689 to 1713. Anglo-French combat embroiled not only the lands and seas of Europe; it flared up thousands of miles away in the West Indies, where the two nations' colonies engaged in hostilities as their metropoles' proxies. St. Kitts was particularly vulnerable during these outbreaks of warfare: not only did it occupy the awkward position of a joint Anglo-French settlement, but its location to the leeward of Martinique, the locus of French power in the Caribbean, placed it directly in the pathway of French incursions. According to Richard Pares, this accident of geography made it inevitable that the island would "be lost or ruined again and again," an observation borne out by the anguish resonating throughout the settlers' repeated appeals to Parliament deploring the loss of their estates, slaves, and fortunes.[4] To force the French to cede all of their lands on the island would have been sweet revenge to the repeatedly dispossessed English Kittitian colonists.

However, the cession of the French lands was more than an opportunity to singe Louis XIV's beard; it was a great financial windfall as well. Although St. Kitts was economically underdeveloped at the beginning of the eighteenth century, especially in comparison with Barbados, its gently sloping terrain, generous annual rainfall, and rich volcanic soil were ideally suited to sugar cultivation, and French and English planters alike prided themselves on the superior quality of their product and the correspondingly high prices it commanded in European markets.[5] However, topographical factors limited the island's nascent sugar industry. As the French naval engineer Jacques Bellin pointed out, "Although St. Kitts is one of the largest of the Leeward islands, it is not one in which there is much valuable land . . . the centre is occupied by high mountains. . . . Therefore, only twenty-four thousand acres, or thirty-five thousand arpents [a French measure of land equivalent to 0.85 acres], can be valued as proper terrain for sugar culture."[6]

The lengthy debates over the optimal plan of distribution of the "French lands" developed within this nexus of profit and scarcity. As Noel Deerr, Richard Dunn, Richard Sheridan, and Sidney Mintz have demonstrated, sugar is a crop whose profitability rests upon economies of scale, and therefore it is most efficiently cultivated in vast plantations of hundreds or even thousands of acres.[7] From a purely economic standpoint, the best method by which to dispose of the newly acquired territories was to sell the lands to the highest bidders. Such a strategy would not only raise a significant sum of money for the crown, but would simultaneously allow St. Kitts's most successful planters to increase their landholdings. This, in turn, would, at least from Whitehall's perspective, empower the colony's most capable and best-

resourced landowners to expand their yields of sugar, rum, and related commodities to the utmost extent of the island's productive capacity. The financial rewards, for planters and crown alike, would be enormous.

The merits of such a plan appear obvious, and when one takes into
consideration the extent to which the great planters of the West Indies had
succeeded in asserting their influence in the metropole, through familial,
marital, political, and commercial connections, it might appear inevitable
that such a scheme would be the one adopted with respect to the ceded
lands. However, the issues of land distribution and its effects upon the social structure of the West Indian colonies were as important to concerns
over security and strategy as they were to those of economic gain. The struggle over the disposition of the French lands in St. Kitts was the result of
competing imperatives, in both colony and metropole, in relation to the nature and functions of colonial societies. At the most basic level, the question
was whether territorial security or economic productivity was the ultimate
goal of colonial settlement. As is evident in the chapters by Thomas
Humphrey, Simon Middleton, and Simon Newman, it was upon issues such
as these that ideas of class and rank in the colonial Atlantic world frequently
centered.

Land, in relation to its optimal use and distribution, and concern over its
scarcity, was a constant source of concern to European settlers in the West Indies. The Antiguan Samuel Martin's *Essay on Plantership*, the most widely
read tract among West Indian colonists on the subject of plantation agriculture, designated "Negroes, horses, and mules" as "the Nerves of a Plantation."
Yet Martin devoted twice as many pages in his *Essay* to "the Culture of various Soils" and "the best Method of cultivating Sugar-Canes" as he did to the
management of slaves and livestock.[8] The most pressing question related to
the ideal distribution of arable land in the West Indies was that of the consequences of the engrossment of such lands by a small class of wealthy planters.
A laissez-faire policy regarding land distribution would provide substantial
financial benefits to the metropole; rich planters would pay high prices to acquire new sugar lands from the crown, and greater production of sugar
would yield higher tax revenues to Whitehall. Yet by the end of the seventeenth century, colonial legislatures had begun to express anxiety about the
excessive concentration of land in the hands of a small elite. In 1698, for example, the Assembly of Antigua mandated that "no Plantation exceeding Six
Hundred Acres be granted" to any person because "the ingrossing of Land of
this Island has been one of the greatest Impediments to the well settling

thereof."[9] Two years later, the same island's Assembly was more specific in its complaints against engrossment:

Whereas Numbers of People are absolutely necessary to render a Place secure . . . and as nothing contributes more to the certainty of such Numbers, than the fixing small Free-holders in this Island . . . and whereas likewise the Avarice of some Men hath induced them under plausible Pretences to procure themselves large Tracts of Land, altogether inconsistent with their Capacity of settling the same . . . [all lands indebted to the common stock of the island for four or more years] shall be distributed in Parcels of Ten Acres, by the Governor, Council, and the Assembly . . . for the Encouragement of poor Settlers.[10]

The rhetoric of these acts emphasizes the validity and invalidity of patterns of land use. Engrossers of lands are criticized not for any perceived failure to increase the island's productivity, but for their "[in]Capacity of settling the same"—that is, their failure to people their lands, not with slaves, but with white laborers. Living as they did in a state of continual—and justified—anxiety regarding the threat of foreign attack, the islands' legislatures were convinced that "nothing can be a stronger or surer Defence to this Island, in Times of War and Invasion, than a sufficient Number of White People."[11] The assemblies attempted repeatedly from the late seventeenth through the mid-eighteenth centuries to increase the numbers of white settlers. The most common tactic was the passage of "deficiency laws" that levied stiff fines on planters who failed to employ a sufficient percentage of white workers among their labor forces and offered incentives to royal troops and other potential white colonists to settle permanently in the islands and to exert themselves in their defense. However, neither the carrot nor the stick achieved much in terms of increasing the population of white settlers in the island colonies.[12]

Such questions relating to the security of the Leewards, and the role of the white population in maintaining it, were rarely far from the minds of the islands' residents. They became particularly prominent during the War of the Spanish Succession, when an unexpected French attack devastated the islands in 1706, resulting in the destruction of many settlements and estates and the displacement of a significant number of whites and slaves alike. Colonial administrators, who hoped to deflect blame for the disasters, pointed fingers at various local culprits. Lieutenant Governor Walter Hamilton wrote from St. Kitts to the Council of Trade and Plantations, "praying your Lordships to belev that I did what was possible to be done for" the crown. However,

the Assembly would doe nothing for the preservation of the Island. . . . Had the people throwne up such trenches as I press'd them to doe, and the Windward and Basseterre officers done theire duty, I might have hoped (at least) to have preserved from
Godding Gutt to Brimstoane Hill, with Sandy-Poynt Towne and division, from being
destroyed by the enimy.[13]

Hamilton's memorandum laid the responsibility for this debacle
squarely at the feet of St. Kitts's planter elite. In his eyes, the Assembly had
done "nothing for the preservation of the Island, nay, were soe infatuated that
they would not beleve there was any such thing as three French men of warr
in the French Islands, and much less any designe to attack any of her
Majestie's an hour before the enemy's fleet appeared."[14] This apparent care-
lessness was compounded by selfishness and treachery, as when "the two
Capts. William and John Kitt and Capt. Chr. Stoddard began to mutiny and
threatened to leave their post, and would go to their wives and children,
which they did." This selfish action "was the cause that the pass at Godding
Gut fell into the enemies hands and of the subsequent destruction of plantations and Sandy Point," and which led a court martial to decide "that the
prisoners had been guilty of a high misdemeanor, and that they loose their
Commissions."[15] A Mr. Stanley reported similar examples of selfish behavior
by members of the local elite of Nevis, stating that, when he and his neighbors took shelter in the local redoubt, the "Deodand," they

mett some of our Grandy Men . . . which ought to have joined with us or fought, but
thought better to Secure themselves with wives & Children in this Safe retreat, where
we was to fight it to the very stumps. But as the Devill and some of our Grandy men
would have it . . . wen the Enemy march'd boldly up to us; and by the strength of the
place we had ten to one against them; We Surrender'd the place and Island in great
hurry without fireing a Gun. . . . I would not have you be too forward in defending
the Behaviour of some of our Grandees, for they do not deserve it, and time will tell
you who they are, though now you would little suspect them.[16]

In the autumn of 1706, a few months after he had arrived to take up his
commission as governor and commander-in-chief of the Leeward Islands,
Daniel Parke made explicit the connection he observed between the islands'
military weakness and the concentration of land in the hands of a few. In his
view, "Nevis was a rich little Island, but there are but few people, the Island
was devided amongst a few rich men that had a vast number of slaves, and
hardly any common people, but a few that lived in the town [Charlestown];
when I muster'd them, I could not gett 200 into the field." According to
Parke,

Coll. Codrington took the same method to ruin St. Kitts, that is, he granted all the French land to rich men that only sent some Negroes to plant the land, by wch. means the Island was not one whit the stronger; those grants are now out, and the Assembly have addressed me to give no grants but to the inhabitants of the Island, or to those that will be obliged to come and settle here, wch. method I take; and encourage all the poor people I can to come and settle here, by giving them grants of land.[17]

Parke refers here to grants made by Codrington of the lands temporarily ceded by the French during the hostilities of the late 1680s and early 1690s. In a subsequent dispatch to the Council of Trade and Plantations, he presented several examples of large tracts of land having been granted to people of influence in the islands and in England, with little apparent oversight or concern regarding their failure to populate them sufficiently with white laborers.[18] Parke claimed that "Mr. Clayton of Leverpool has got a grant for two Plantations in the French ground from my Lord Treasurer, by wch. he ruins two poor people that had it granted per [former governor] Sir Wm. Matthews . . . my Lady Russell and Stapleton had each of them above 200 negroes, and not one white man on their Plantation; Col. Codrington has 400 negroes on one Plantation, and but one white man." The only significant defense of the islands was presented by the royal regiment stationed there, but "the men in 5 year [were] but once cloathed and yt. so scandalously, it is a shame to see them, so yt. what little pay the soldier receives, he is forced to buy cloathes wth. it, or go naked; if the Coll. was obliged to be wth. them, he would be ashamed to see his men in such a condition as they are; no surgion wth. them nor anything else that is fitting for them."[19] In Parke's opinion, no advantage was to be gained "to have it [the Leewards] full of Negroes belonging to merchants in England and rich men in Antigua, they are only a temptation to the enemy and no strength."[20] Unlimited concentration of land in the hands of a few, many of whom were absentees, was bad for the crown, the island, and the majority of the white inhabitants, all of whom suffered from the lack of internal security brought about by a small population of whites. The latter resulted from limited opportunities for poor white migrants to secure farmlands or even employment as overseers. Instead, elite families such as the Russells, Stapletons, and Codringtons dominated the land and "breed up their Negroes to all manner of trades and make overseers of them; by this means they have drove all the poor from them."[21] Parke's critique of these "rich men" was undoubtedly influenced by his ongoing conflict with his most prosperous and assertive colonial subjects, a clash that ended with his murder at these men's hands in December 1710. Nonetheless, his critique is insightful in its connection of the concentration of land in the hands of the few and the constant challenge of defending the colony from foreign attack or slave uprising.

The situation of the Leeward Islands was, to English eyes at least, far more promising in 1713 than it had been in the past quarter-century. Victory over the French not only appeared not only to bring national glory but seemed to herald the beginning of a new era for colonization and commerce. As Margaret Rouse-Jones has pointed out, the constant threat—and, often, reality—of French attack had kept these islands, and particularly St. Kitts, in a "frontier" state.[22] The cession of the French lands provided new opportunities for territorial and commercial expansion in the expectation of peace. Leaders such as Hamilton and Parke recognized that the root of these islands' problems lay in the excessive concentration of land in the hands of a few, some of whom were absentees, and most of whom appeared to be unconcerned about strengthening the islands' security, or even abiding by the dictates of the local legislatures in maintaining a sufficient percentage of whites among their labor forces. The acquisition of the French lands could be seen as a felicitous opportunity for the imperial and colonial governments to work together in order to consciously create a white yeoman class, one that would presumably express its gratitude for such concessions by committing itself wholeheartedly to the defense of the island and the interests of its long-term economic and social development.[23]

Yet it would be almost two decades before the question of the French lands of St. Kitts was entirely resolved, and when consensus finally was reached over disposition of these lands, it would neither address security concerns nor attempt to bring about a realignment of class interests. Instead, in 1726 the lands were put up for sale to the highest bidder, with the only stipulation against engrossment being that no single tract could contain more than two hundred acres.[24] How did such a situation come about? By examining the lengthy and sometimes tortuous path that led from the Treaty of Utrecht to the completion of the land sale process in 1728, we can see the nature and extent of the involvement of a wide variety of players in this game, and simultaneously we can chart the collision of clashing imperatives in imperial policy.

Historians frequently employ the dynamic of "push" and "pull"—negative and positive factors—when analyzing the motivations of historical actors. These polarities are particularly useful in examining the process of distribution of the French lands in St. Kitts, as in this instance we can map these factors onto the several class-based interests that were at stake in this process. For the wealthy planters of St. Kitts, significant "pull" factors existed, which encouraged them to assert their perceived right to purchase the lands acquired by the Treaty of Utrecht. In conjunction with the planters of Nevis, they had throughout the last decades of the seventeenth century and the first of the eighteenth lamented loudly and publicly their sufferings at the hands of the French, and the devastation the attackers had wrought upon their estates and finances.[25] These "Poor distressed Planters" had deluged Parliament with petitions describing the depredations they had suffered and requesting redress, in pursuit of which they employed rhetoric that cast them as the natural leaders of any attempts to restore the islands' fortunes. They depicted themselves as representing "many Hundred Families of very industrious and useful People," of the sort ideally suited to rebuilding their societies. They also warned Parliament that, should they despair of succor and leave the Leewards to seek opportunities elsewhere, French settlers would move onto their former lands and would pose a hazard to the entire sugar trade of England, "with all its advantages."[26] If Parliament did nothing to ameliorate their distress,

there is much greater Reason to apprehend a Total Desertion of the Inhabitants, than any Vigorous Efforts towards a Resettlement; for that above Nine Parts in Ten of the said Inhabitants are by this fatal Stroke reduced to the extremest Poverty and Want; and the few who are in any Circumstances of Resettling, never think of doing it in Ruined and Deserted Islands. Since therefore a speedy Settlement of the said Islands will be a considerable Benefit to the Nation, and in a few Years Repay with good Interest what shall be advanced towards the effecting thereof, the Petitioners do humbly hope, that the Comfortable Re-establishment of so many Industrious Useful Subjects, will also have its due Weight, and appear a Generous Charity worthy of an English Parliament.[27]

The petitioners' rhetorical strategy was simple but effective. In their formulation, they who had suffered most at the hands of the French, that is, the prosperous planters, rather than the struggling small farmers or landless men, had the most to lose in terms of real and personal property. Indeed, this fact might have partly excused the actions of the court-martialed Stoddard and the two Kitts, who as captains in the local militia would have been men of some property and might have placed protection of their estates over loyalty to their community. Within an economy of restitution, the great planters' previous efforts to enrich themselves, settling and improving the island and thus benefiting the crown, should be rewarded not only with financial redress, but also with the opportunity to employ some of this deserved largesse in the purchase of the lands surrendered by their former enemies.

The "Poor distressed Planters" would eventually succeed in attaining both of their goals, but some years would pass between the financial remuneration and the opportunity to use these funds in land purchases. Their claims that "the Damage of the said Inhabitants and Traders [had been] of 500,000 *l*. Sterling and upwards" and that Britain "will lose at least 150,000 *l*. Sterling yearly, whilst the said Islands continue in the present Ruinous Condition" appear to have struck Parliament as hyperbolic. Nevertheless, it "was Resolv'd, that a Sum not exceeding 103,003 *l*.11 *s*.4 *d*. be granted for the Use of such Sufferers of Nevis and St. Christophers," and "That for Making good the same, Debentures be made out, and delivered to the Sufferers with Interest."[28] This was an enormous sum in the context of early Georgian England, amounting to approximately twenty million pounds in modern currency. A metropole that made such a huge grant had a very strong incentive to ensure that the colony would be able to make swift recompense for such generosity.[29]

One might expect, as the "Sufferers" did, that the release of these debentures would allow them to purchase lands from the ceded territories and begin the process of re-establishing themselves. However, they were not the only group to lay claim to the French lands. Although "the French" as an imperial power had been forced to abandon the island, "the French" as individuals had not all followed suit. The majority of French settlers "removed from thence into their other islands," resettling in Martinique, Saint Domingue, and elsewhere in the Caribbean basin. Yet a significant number of French colonists petitioned the English crown to allow them to retain their landholdings in St. Kitts based on their alleged English sympathies or on their victimization by their own countrymen because of their Huguenot beliefs.[30] The widow Elizabeth Renoult made a "humble Peticon" to retain her husband's "Considerable Estate" because "he was of the Protestant Religion . . . and did . . . Swear Allegiance to the [English] Crown." Alletta de la Coussaye requested that she and her children be granted her father Captain Vandelbourg's two-hundred-acre plantation in Capisterre since he had suffered persecution by the French authorities because of his Huguenot sympathies.[31] The English commentator John Campbell, writing at the end of a later Anglo-French conflict, noted that "it is certain that some of the best [French] families remained" on the island.[32]

The anonymous author of "The Case of the Sufferers of Nevis and St. Christophers" made a marginal note that the act that authorized the payment of £103,000 to the "Sufferers" "pass'd in the same Session with the South-Sea Act."[33] This was not the only moment in which the fates of the Kittitian planters and the South Sea Company would be intertwined. Although the company's troubles would not peak until early in the following decade, by 1714 it had already accumulated significant losses; it was with the hope of recouping these losses that the company's directors added their names to the list of those who hoped to be given grants out of the French lands. Perhaps not surprisingly, this plan aroused tremendous opposition among the English planters. Planters granted temporary possession over French plantations prior to Utrecht were understandably reluctant to relinquish these estates, particularly in favor of the company.[34] Some of the Kittitians were quite likely men of financial sophistication and thus accustomed to the machinations of the "stockjobbing trade," but they were adamant that it was "those who had settled and cultivated" the lands who ought to retain the title to them, and they succeeded in urging Parliament to reject this project.[35]

We have seen how "pull" factors encouraged St. Kitts's stratum of wealthy and established planters to see the "French lands" as their rightful property. Not only would these lands serve as their recompense for the losses they had suffered in the course of the war, but these planters were by their own lights the obvious candidates to make use of the land in a way that would both enrich themselves and yield profits to the metropole. However, what sort of "push" or "pull" factors existed for the poorer sort of white settlers? To what extent did they attempt to ensure that at least some of the French lands accrued to them? Moreover, how much importance did the apparent need to develop a yeoman class, for reasons of security, exert in the face of the desire for profit among planters and politicians alike?

To examine the second question first, it was immediately evident to informed observers that it was only by selling the French lands to the highest bidders that England might reap immediate profit from the Kittitian windfall. Considering how expensive the War of the Spanish Succession had been for the crown, and the extent of the difficulties the nation's finances experienced in the first quarter of the eighteenth century (as epitomized by the attempt to reduce the national debt via the South Sea Company), it would have been remarkable had anyone but the most farsighted imperial administrator supported a policy of creating a yeoman class by setting aside large segments of the newly acquired territory for the use of poorer islanders. The bare facts were that it was only the great planters who "had the resources and the confidence to rebuild . . . [and they] bought this land in large lots at prices that no small man could match."[36]

A response to the first question is rather more complex, but what is perhaps most significant in this matter is the innately unstable and challenging position of the poorer sort of whites in the sugar plantation societies of the eighteenth-century British Caribbean. As the work of Peter Linebaugh, and of many of the scholars in this collection, has rendered in vivid terms, the lives of the poor were inherently very difficult on the material level. However, in the eighteenth-century Anglo-American world, poverty denoted the lack of daily necessities rather than just luxuries. At the same time that poor people experienced hunger, cold, or ill health, they also lived in a society in which "law was central to ruling-class authority, replacing in some respects the role formerly played by religion."[37] The poor were not simply people who had fewer possessions or lesser amounts of land or money in comparison to others; they were "the poor," a group seen as "other," as homogeneous, and, frequently, as dangerous. Although the white social hierarchy of the Leeward Islands developed slowly in comparison with that of Barbados, perhaps the prototypical sugar colony, by the beginning of the eighteenth century Leeward planters already believed they had reason to view their poorer fellow white settlers with a degree of suspicion. We should treat with some caution Hilary Beckles's claim that indentured servants and other poor whites, particularly those who, like many of those who went to St. Kitts, were of Irish extraction, were "black men in white skins" who felt a strong affinity for and frequently made common cause with free and enslaved people of color. Nevertheless, the early colonial history of the English Caribbean shows that poor whites often saw their interests as diverging substantively from those of the wealthy planters, and that in certain circumstances, including slave rebellions or foreign attacks, their allegiance to the English imperial project could not be taken for granted. Looking back into seventeenth-century Kittitian history, we can see a trope developing of the innate alterity and untrustworthiness of poor whites, who are depicted variously as attempting to betray the island to the Spaniards, making common cause with disaffected slaves, and crossing the boundary into French territory in order to attend religious services with the Jesuits.[38]

The great planters of the island were not entirely unsympathetic to the difficulties encountered by poor whites. Accounts of the French invasions frequently mention the valiant attempts of "small" men to defend the island. Throughout the Leewards, tavern licensing was used as an informal kind of poor relief, by which men who had been disabled "in the Service of this Island," or their relicts, would be granted a license to keep a tavern, an occupation that generally provided at least a bare living.[39] In an act of 1728, the St. Kitts Assembly decreed that if more than one head of livestock were brought to be sold for meat at one of the island's established public markets, a market clerk was charged to "cut up a Side of one in Pieces, not exceeding six Pounds, for the Use of the poorer Sort of People; and if but one, then a Quarter to be cut up in such Pieces . . . and that the same . . . can be taken off by the said poor People."[40] But if the poor were not necessarily persecuted or ignored within the island's society, they were nonetheless marginal people, literally, as those who succeeded in acquiring land had settled along the coast or in the hills, in lands ill-suited to sugar cultivation, and also figuratively, in that they lacked sufficient acreage or income to hold office or even to vote for their alleged betters. This marginality forestalled them from taking on the positive economic and social attributes associated with yeoman farmers and relegated them to the status of the poor, whether "deserving" or otherwise.

As far as the great majority of the men of influence in both metropole and colony could see, the proper business of a settlement such as St. Kitts was the enrichment of the mother country, and it would achieve this goal almost exclusively through the cultivation, refining, and sale of sugar, that rich man's crop. Although some prescient observers might—and did—express their concerns about the island's failure to develop the sort of white yeomanry that could be called upon to defend the settlement against foreign attack or slave insurrection, the fact remained that such people were not viewed as economically useful in times of peace—which, after all, greatly outnumbered moments of conflict—and that there seemed to be much potential profit to be lost and very little to be gained by great planters passing up the opportunity to acquire more acreage for sugar cultivation in order to allow less privileged men to use such lands for their own farms. Reverend Smith's idyllic picture of the small cotton farm, "whose humble and temperate Possessor (Hermit like) lived by vertue of his own and three or four Slaves Labour," may have exerted a sentimental appeal among the chattering classes of Georgian London, but it is unlikely to have affected many Kittitians similarly. The wealthy planters would have seen the "Hermit" as, at best, economically and socially superfluous, while actual small farmers, recognizing the degree of marginalization they would suffer, were far more likely to take their chances in a "good poor man's country" on the western marches of a North American mainland colony such as Pennsylvania or Virginia than they were to leap at any opportunity to struggle for subsistence in a society moving ever closer toward plantocracy. The decision to sacrifice the creation of a yeoman class to the demands of sugar monoculture was not inevitable, but given the relative strength of the competing interests, it could easily be seen to have been overdetermined.

In terms of the generation of revenue, the policy of selling off the French lands to the highest bidders was very successful. By 1727, the former French territories were so prosperous and well settled that the Assembly chose to incorporate them into the island's political structure by allowing

them to send representatives to the Assembly, placing them on the same foot-
ing as the longer-established parishes that had been under English rule for
over a century.[41] The Assembly's rationale for passing this legislation is re-
vealing:

Whereas his Majesty's Subjects, now inhabiting the late French Part of this Island, are
equal, if not superior to the Inhabitants of the English Part, both in Number and in
Property, and yield a greater Revenue to His Majesty, and contribute more largely to
the Taxes, and other Publick Expences of this Island; it is therefore but just and reasonable that they should have a Share in the Legislature of the Island, and the Privilege of choosing an equal Number of Representatives in the Assembly.[42]

In the five decades separating the Treaty of Utrecht from that of Paris,
which brought the Seven Years' War to an end, St. Kitts was, relative to its size,
the richest colony in the British empire.[43] Its leading citizens were less the
"great tangled cousinry," in Bernard Bailyn's phrase, of the colonial Chesapeake than a sort of extended family club, in which the greatest planters held
the highest elective and appointive offices, and 80 percent of those who possessed two hundred or more acres of land occupied seats on the governing
council.[44] Meanwhile, with the exception of the occasional "Hermit" of the
sort so admired by Reverend Smith, the majority of the lesser whites were
impoverished and landless, living primarily in Basseterre's "Irish Town,"
which by the 1730s was known as a locale of "Robberies, and other Disorders."[45] As the population of small farmers continued to drop, and their
lands were engrossed by such "Grandy-Men" as the Phippses and Cunning-
hams, Willetts and Millses, the colony became ever more dependent upon the
imperial system for imports by which to feed both slaves and masters and for
royal troops to maintain security.[46]

The prominent historian Richard Dunn's claim that St. Kitts, like the
rest of the English settlements in the West Indies, was a "social failure" does
not quite capture reality. Instead, as Margaret Rouse-Jones argues (and I con-
cur), the St. Kitts society that evolved and flourished between 1713 and 1763
reflected the values and beliefs of its creators—its ruling class.[47] These interpretations have perplexed historians of colonial British America since Carl
Becker first theorized many decades ago about the difference between "home
rule and who rules at home." As other chapters in this book make clear, the
subject of class and class struggle remains an essential yet understudied element of the history of the Atlantic World.

5

Class at an African Commercial Enclave

Ty M. Reese

In 1766, as Cape Coast and its West African hinterland experienced a famine that entailed a six-fold increase in the price of corn, the free "natives . . . suffered severely." However, slaves owned by British trading companies endured even worse misery, "afford[ing] the most piteous examples that can be conceived." An unusually severe rainy season, accompanied by "violent gusts of wind," followed the food crisis, destroying the British fort at Sekondi and weakening Cape Coast Castle, which was operated by the Company of Merchants Trading to Africa (CMTA). Even though "constantly employed" and "allowed liquor as usual for working in their own hours," the CMTA's slaves continued to go hungry. Rather than supply the necessities of life directly to its bondpeople, the CMTA customarily paid them in trade goods, which slaves would then barter for food. However, in this crisis, those commodities no longer covered the cost of subsistence. The British governor blamed the problem on the increasing availability of "luxury" items on the coast and the consequent decline in their value. To solve the problem, Governor Hippisley recommended increasing company slave wages 25 percent because of the increasing "luxury" of the coast; however, the wages were still to be paid in commodities. With hindsight, it is clear that the predicament of the company's slaves resulted, in part, from the way that labor was organized and how workers (both bound and free) were paid and able to feed (or not feed) themselves.[1]

To maintain the infrastructure of Britain's Gold Coast slave trade, the CMTA required considerably more labor than just the slaves it owned. Officials knew, though, that it was difficult to obtain free laborers who would work effectively, since they "receive very little encouragement by words, nor are they the least attentive to promises in [the] future," and because "the present now is what they look upon." An example of the coastal labor problems occurred when Governor John Hippisley negotiated with Cudjoe Caboceer, the leader of the town, to hire fifty free laborers. They were "idle and saucy enough," Hippisley complained, but "if they don't work they shall however receive no pay."[2] At the end of the year, after Hippisley succumbed to disease, the new governor, Gilbert Petrie, discharged "all the free labourers that were furnished by Cudjoe Caboceer." Initially, "they behaved tolerably well," Petrie noted, "but at last grew so excessively lazy, that to keep them all at work, would have constantly employed the under-surveyor and near as many company slaves as there were free labourers." Ironically, when Petrie settled with the supposedly free workers, Cudjoe "showed by appropriating the whole to himself, that they were [instead] his slaves."[3]

This episode illustrates several issues concerning the nature of labor and of class relations at Cape Coast specifically and in the Atlantic World in general. Employers consistently tried to organize labor in ways that would advantage themselves (and their class), whether by purchasing slaves and servants or by hiring workers for wages. However, the systems designed by the wealthier classes often broke down. Sometimes, as in Cudjoe's manipulation of the CMTA, other people in positions of authority won the struggle to define and control labor. At other times, workers were able to negotiate or to force more favorable terms. Like wealthy elites, laboring people sought to advance their own interests. In Cape Coast, free and unfree African workers used strikes, demands for gifts, and bargaining for wages to improve their positions. The various classes found themselves in different situations and conditions across the Atlantic World, but the struggles among them still shared many similarities.[4]

This chapter analyzes the various labor systems utilized by the CMTA and the conditions of employment and slavery at Cape Coast as a way to explore the operation of class in this enclave and to shed light on its place in the larger Atlantic World. West African seaboard peoples, unlike many of their Native American counterparts, maintained a dominant position in dealing with Europeans for centuries. While Cape Coast societies (somewhat akin to American Natives discussed by Daniel Richter in this volume) were often highly stratified, more than just the elites benefited from participation in the Atlantic economy. Instead, a broad segment of Cape Coast society were able to "eat" from the European presence. The concept of "eating" referred, in part, to the ability of Africans to share in the profit arising from interaction with Europeans. According to local traditions, the consumption of presents (or *dashees*) provided by Europeans was considered a form of eating in which most societal members engaged.[5]

Free West African coastal workers thus enjoyed a decided advantage over their counterparts in many other areas of the Atlantic World, since they usually worked to obtain luxury goods rather than necessities. Employees hired by the CMTA continued to engage in traditional means of subsistence by fishing and agriculture; they did not fall dependent on company jobs to feed themselves. At Cape Coast, the Fetu (the local sovereigns and part of the coastal Fante confederation that controlled much of the Gold Coast Atlantic trade) allowed the presence of the British in part because it provided opportunities for many people in their society. In their tenuous positions as tenants in the eighteenth century, the CMTA belonged to an intricate coastal system involving the struggle among local elites, ethnic conflicts, various systems of labor, and African customs that reinforced the dependent status of Europeans. These all reminded Europeans who wielded the most power in the region and often drained them of resources eaten by coastal peoples.

While the position of laborers in Cape Coast differed somewhat from those in other regions of the Atlantic World, similarities still existed. Cape Coast laborers defined themselves through their work, negotiated with their employers, played a vital role in the development of the Atlantic economy by maintaining the coastal commercial infrastructure, and found ways (often through pilfering) to supplement their incomes. By acquiring luxury items, laborers redefined their status while simultaneously challenging the traditional divisions that existed within Cape Coast society. Within this process, they worked to protect and expand their position. As in other areas of the Atlantic World, both clear and muted distinctions existed between free and unfree labor at Cape Coast. The desire to eat united all workers, even as their status as locals or outsiders occasionally divided them. Free laborers, such as the indigenous canoemen, continued their traditional means of subsistence while using company employment to gain access to a global assortment of commodities that supplemented and improved their status within Cape Coast society.

However, company slaves—considered to be interlopers similar to the English at Cape Coast—occupied a much different position. As outsiders, they did not share as readily in the consumption of goods brought by Europeans, nor did they produce their own food. Still, several factors enhanced their ability to negotiate (when compared with bondpeople in many other parts of the Atlantic World). The CMTA desperately required their labor in order to make the company profitable. In addition, the CMTA also lacked the power to punish its slaves or to sell them off the coast. Company slaves seized these advantages. They successfully negotiated (if sometimes tacitly) to set hours of employment, to establish holidays, to receive liquor from the company during working times, and to be paid wages (in commodities) rather than be supplied with shelter and food. These slaves enjoyed a similarly advantageous position as bondpeople in the northern regions of the new United States. As those states phased out slavery in the late eighteenth and early nineteenth centuries, usually forbidding the sale of slaves outside of the region, black Americans bargained with their owners for better conditions or even to secure their freedom.[6]

The limitation of the sources makes it impossible to conclude with certainty whether these laborers developed a unified class identity or envisioned themselves as belonging to a larger regional or Atlantic World working class. Still, some evidence suggests that individual laborers recognized how they fit within larger groups. Institutions in the local community encouraged people to construct their identities around their work. For example, seven *asafo* companies—patrilineal organizations that pursued military, social, and political goals—existed in the Cape Coast. With the long-term European presence in the area, these indigenous associations expanded their power and popularity, providing local laborers even greater opportunities to distinguish themselves as employees distinct from the managers of the CMTA. In addition, the labor systems at Cape Coast resembled those in much of the Atlantic World, and workers in all of these areas often responded to comparable situations in analogous fashions. In 1786, for instance, CMTA slaves expropriated an extraordinary amount of rum while transporting it from ship to shore in their canoes. In one sense, they were merely adhering to the long-standing custom of transferring "spilled property" from owners to workers that occurred in ports across the Atlantic World.[7]

Cape Coast laborers fit well into Peter Linebaugh's and Marcus Rediker's conception of an Atlantic proletariat. These Africans workers not only contributed to the development of the Atlantic World through their toil, but, like laborers in Europe and the Americas, they pursued their own goals and developed their own identities through work, struggle, and negotiation. At the same time, West African coastal workers illustrate that the Atlantic proletariat was far from cohesive; rather, as Simon Newman argues in this book, regional and local variations were numerous. As in much of the Atlantic World, various systems of labor existed side by side at Cape Coast. Free and bound laborers usually interacted on a daily basis, often blurring the distinction between freedom and slavery for many West African workers.[8]

In the wider Atlantic World, decisions about which labor system to utilize depended on a host of factors, ranging from disease, to climate, to the availability of workers, to the price of hiring or enslaving people. The recent emphasis on the history of the Atlantic World has deepened our understanding of both workers and labor systems, although scholars still avoid studying labor in West Africa, dismissing the region as merely an exporter of slaves. However, the flow of commodities through the region, the unity and the divisions among workers, the relationship between locals and strangers, along with the motivations, desires, and prejudices of Cape Coast residents describe and define not only a single commercial center but also countless trade enclaves throughout the Atlantic World.

Like other Atlantic ports, Cape Coast depended upon an array of skilled and unskilled laborers to insure the flow of commodities in and out of the port. At Cape Coast, the most important, and united, group of African laborers were the coastal canoemen. Before the arrival of Europeans, Cape Coast was a fishing village. As the European tenancy became permanent, it developed into an important trade and administrative center. As Cape Coast became a trade enclave, the traditional modes of production, fishing and agriculture, remained the source of livelihood for most of its inhabitants. While the slave trade is sometimes viewed as only profitable for a small, elite minority of West African society (who directly participated in the buying and selling of slaves), the canoemen of Cape Coast found in the European presence an opportunity to supplement their incomes and gain access to desirable commodities. European slavers and the CMTA hired canoemen to carry goods from ship to shore and slaves from shore to ship. The labor of the coastal canoemen therefore served a vital role in the success and expansion of the slave trade.[9]

The CMTA also paid canoemen to carry the annual supplies from the supply ship to shore and then from Cape Coast to the company's various outlying forts. The company's coastal enterprise depended upon these goods to protect and expand England's slave trade, and any loss created enormous problems. The movement of goods was the canoemen's most important job, but it was not their sole job. When the supply ship *Basnet* arrived in June 1755, for instance, the canoemen unloaded it in three days. Governor Thomas Melvil then sent the company's slaves to Anomabu to unload supplies needed to construct the fort there.[10] The canoemen likewise played a vital role in conveying information and delivering messages, correspondence, presents, and people along the coast and inland rivers. When hired by slavers, of course, they carried not only consumer goods to shore but also human beings to slave ships.

The cohesiveness of the Cape Coast canoemen, coupled with their clear understanding of their relationship with the CMTA, allowed them effectively to exploit the European presence sanctioned by their rulers. For example, in 1754 the Anomabu canoemen refused to work unless they received higher wages. Tellingly, the strike occurred when the canoemen were transporting lavish *dashees* from the CMTA to the wealthy elite, designed to persuade local powerful men to permit the company to construct a new fort.[11] Clearly, the canoemen wanted to eat some themselves. Such wage disputes were common. Like most employers in the Atlantic World, the company tried to minimize the pay of free workers, usually through negotiations to establish fixed rates. The canoemen bargained hard, not only for higher wages but also by demanding their own *dashees* before departing on long trips. This gift, separate from wages, provided another chance for laborers to eat.[12]

Their labor provided canoemen access to the commodities of the slave trade. Like the New Yorkers discussed in the chapter by Simon Middleton, West African canoemen defended traditional rights and privileges that increased their access to these goods. The most important customary perquisite, and one found throughout the Atlantic World, entailed their entitlement to any good that spilled into their canoe. This practice developed even further at Cape Coast, since canoemen were largely unsupervised except when loading or unloading their crafts. When the company hired *bomboys* (supervisors) to oversee the "launching, drawing and landing of canoes," the African *bomboys* habitually looked the other way.[13] Recognizing the problem, during the summer of 1780, the company's council decided to hire a European *bomboy* to stop the canoemen from "embezzlement."[14] Another major problem for the company—which the canoemen knew and exploited—was that the CMTA, as an interloper in Africa, lacked the sole authority to discipline its workers. The company must first bring the issue to the local palaver system, which would cost considerable time and money, and it might well lose the case.[15] Over time, the power of the CMTA and Europeans began to increase along the coast. In 1805, the CMTA independently tried eighteen canoemen from Accra (a city about one hundred miles west of Cape Coast Castle) for stealing one hundred pounds of gunpowder. Finding them guilty, the company sold many of the canoemen to cover the cost of the gunpowder and levied an additional £60 fine.[16]

The canoemen's willingness to work for wages provides insight into the widespread consequences of the slave trade on West Africa.[17] The canoemen desired access to the commodities flowing into the coast and found ways, mainly through employment, to acquire these goods. The canoemen expected to consume many of the same commodities as the local elite and, in the process, they slowly challenged the coastal patron-client system. Their employment illustrates how the process operated, as well as how trade goods linked the entire world and goods from India ended up in the hands of African workers. Adhering to regulations by the British government, the CMTA paid all coastal costs in commodities. The CMTA typically paid canoemen in alcohol, tobacco, and textiles; these three items represented the most easily exchangeable and desirable goods on the Gold Coast. In 1764, for example, 45 canoemen unloaded the supply ship *Charming Beckie* in 200 trips. For their labor, the canoemen received an average of thirteen shillings each, paid in brandy and Indian textiles, including *negannepauts*, *bejutapauts*, and *tapseils*.[18] A year later, 43 canoemen made 220 trips to unload the *Ruby*, receiving about fourteen shillings each in brandy and textiles for their labor.[19] During April 1769, the company paid 174 canoemen £69 in twelve ells of cloth and fourteen *soot romauls* (handkerchiefs) for their journeys to the British factories dotting the Gold Coast: Anomabu, Accra, Sekondi, Komenda, Tantumquerry, and Dixcove. The distance between Cape Coast and these outer forts determined the wages paid.[20] Canoemen also supplemented their pay with *dashees*; after unloading the *Basnet*, they received 17.5 gallons of brandy.[21]

Local skilled (and unskilled) African laborers constituted another group of wage laborers who worked for Europeans. The company employed these laborers somewhat reluctantly but out of necessity since workers, especially those with necessary skills, were so difficult to obtain. Tropical diseases and the image of Africa as the "white man's graveyard" discouraged most European artisans from migrating to Cape Coast. The CMTA also came to believe that Africans were the only people biologically capable of working in local conditions. Soon after his arrival, Governor Melvil reported that "the white laborers are almost all sick, I never expected much good from 'em for this is not country for Europeans to work in the sun, even though they are sober men." In that same year, the difficulties of construction at the fort in Anomabu caused Mr. Apperley to observe:

These white men which I have at present that are not artificers (which is four) are useless for me as no white man can work at laborer work in this country. The white bricklayers can work but five hours a day and the blacks seven hours in the day. The sun being so extremely hot here; as I find the black bricklayers are the people I am to depend on for building the fort, out of the 23 men slaves Captain Bruce brought [from] Gambia, I've made twelve bricklayers, three carpenters and three smiths.[22]

The CMTA tried unsuccessfully to solve its labor needs by hiring "crimps," who acquired laborers (sometimes in a shady fashion) off the streets of London and Liverpool, then shipped them to the company in West Africa. They received meager wages in alcohol and tobacco, which they bartered for rations. Most of these men died, as much from diseases such as malaria and yellow fever as from the hard work in unfamiliar hot and humid conditions. Local African laborers, better nourished and with more resistance to the diseases (which most had contracted and gained immunity from in childhood), did not suffer similar rates of mortality. Officials of the CMTA recognized that they needed to obtain labor locally, but they were caught in a dilemma. "As to company slaves," Governor William Mutter commented, "it would undoubtedly be necessary to have a supply of them, but till they could be procured [mainly paid for], free labourers might be hired, and they would come full as cheap as company slaves, but then they must not be relied upon entirely, for if they once saw you could not proceed without their assistance, extravagant wages and insolent behavior, would in spite of the greatest indulgences, knock all our schemes in the head."[23]

At Cape Coast—as in some other parts of the Atlantic World—free labor was sometimes cheaper then slave labor because workers could be hired and fired as necessity dictated. The governor and council, who were familiar with Cape Coast's conditions, understood these advantages. The African Committee in London, however, viewed slavery as the most desirable labor system for the CMTA. All of them worried, though, that their free and unfree laborers might realize their extreme importance to the business endeavor and use that knowledge to their own advantage. They were right to be concerned.

The size of the Cape Coast labor supply varied, depending on the season and on local events such as celebrations and palavers. During a labor shortage in 1762, Governor Thomas Bell saw "an absolute necessity to hire some freemen as labourers to help carry on our great building." He paid them four *ackies* in trade goods per month, the same wage as a company slave.[24] In 1766, heavy rains weakened the castle, causing Governor Hippisley to describe it as "rotted," "damaged," and "sinking into the ground." Hippisley lacked sufficient company slaves and could not hire any free labor to repair the castle. The labor shortage continued in 1767, when Governor Gilbert Petrie reported that "neither a bricklayer or carpenter can be spared without obstructing in a great degree the important and necessary work of rebuilding this castle."[25]

For the company, African wage labor played a vital role in maintaining the coastal infrastructure that it oversaw and protected. One crucial problem was that the structures the CMTA inherited from the Royal African Company were decrepit; the first twenty years of CMTA control was a period of continual rebuilding and improvement. In the 1750s, the problem of labor hindered the plans of Governor Thomas Melvil and of Apperley. Both desperately needed bricklayers and carpenters; for Apperley, the hospitalization of seven African bricklayers and one African carpenter stopped construction at Anomabu.[26] The continuous construction necessitated a constant supply of building materials, especially timber, bricks, and lime. Obtaining timber was the responsibility of the sawyers, who, by tradition, controlled the rights to timber and used it to their own advantage in negotiating with the company.

The CMTA's "Diary of Employment" for 1777 illustrates the use of free coastal labor. On one day in July, the company employed eleven bricklayers, seven carpenters, four sawyers, five smiths, three armorers, four coopers, nine artificer boys, seventeen male laborers, thirty-two female workers, and six stone blowers. Throughout 1777 and 1778, the number of employees remained relatively constant, with the majority being bricklayers and both male and female laborers. The company employed women as unskilled labor, reflecting that in West Africa physical labor was not the exclusive domain of men.[27]

Another group who possessed the ability to eat was the growing Eurafrican population, whose mixed racial heritage permitted them access to important and permanent positions. Many were soldiers. In 1774, Governor Mill enlisted twelve Eurafrican military men into the garrison, whom he regarded as the "fittest for this climate." Mill preferred them as soldiers to the CMTA's tradition of crimping and indenting men in London, most of whom quickly died of tropic diseases in Africa.[28] The African Committee disagreed, however, ordering that only three-quarters of the military should be Eurafrican.[29] Importantly, though, these soldiers received the same pay as did whites: £27 coast money annually.[30] Eurafricans also served in other capacities, like William Norman, who was hired as a carpenter for £36 annually.[31] A handful of Eurafricans received a European education, subsequently finding employment as artificers, factors, and writers, affording them better pay and greater authority in the company.

As noted above, free labor provided a cheap but sometimes disruptive labor source, and the company often utilized unfree labor in the form of company slaves. Like free laborers, company slaves maintained the infrastructure of England's slave trade. One problem for the company was that the British Parliament prohibited it from selling its slaves off of the coast. This provided company slaves some room to maneuver and at least limited opportunities to eat in the same fashion as did free laborers. While the company's account books maintained distinctions between free and slave labor, the company, like many other employers in the Atlantic World, utilized slaves for the same tasks performed by free workers, and their hours of work seem to have been identical. One important distinction is that company slaves received a subsistence wage in the form of trade goods, which they then were expected to barter for food. This created a precarious situation (as described in the vignette at the beginning of this chapter) for company slaves when prices of the necessities of life increased.

In recent decades the study of slavery, especially within the plantation complex in the Americas, has greatly enriched and expanded our understanding of various versions of this labor system. However, local African slavery has too often been omitted from research about the Atlantic World. One important system of West African slavery was company slaves who fit into Suzanne Miers's and Igor Kopytoff's conception that their outsider status contributed to their marginality.[32] While the company defined their slaves as chattel, the system of company slavery was a hybrid of slavery in the Americas and in Africa as well as wage labor. While the CMTA owned its slaves, for example, these workers still enjoyed various rights that protected their position.

The CMTA's coastal position provided access to local slave markets, yet the company, like many others in the Atlantic World, preferred to import people from other areas. Local slaves created too many problems, in part because they might appeal to the local African elite for protection, in part because they might more easily disappear into neighboring communities, which they knew well. The CMTA tried to obtain its slaves from Gambia because officials believed they were better, more easily managed workers. In 1764, Governor Mutter requested that the African Committee allow him to purchase fifty or sixty such slaves. He wanted to teach most of them to be bricklayers, carpenters, and smiths—the type of workers necessary to reconstruct the company's crumbling infrastructure. Indeed, Mutter even hinted at the possibility of sending the Gambians to Britain for training.[33]

The company's purchase of Gambian slaves created problems in Cape Coast, since it introduced outsiders into the community and exacerbated ethnic tensions with the local Fetu and Fante people. It strained relations among unfree and free laborers as well, since the former were seen as interlopers while the latter usually came from neighboring villages. Slaves owned by the company formed one of the seven *asafo* organizations in Cape Coast, and their Brofu-Mba association clearly marked them as outsiders. In August 1772, during a local celebration, the company's slaves and the town's soldiers fought openly. By official accounts, the slaves had stolen some valuables and insulted one of the local women. Conflicts between Lower Town (where slaves may have enjoyed full citizenship) and Upper Town in Cape Coast were widespread. Not surprisingly, company slaves usually sided with Lower Town in their quarrels with Upper Town. In December 1779, a serious brawl erupted between the two towns. When the female and children slaves of the company sought protection in the castle, it had to be closed.[34]

The company slaves, like wage laborers, repaired and strengthened the castle in the 1760s, as the CMTA hoped (incorrectly, as it turned out) that its formidable appearance would awe local people and prevent them from attacking the fort.[35] During the summer of 1765, company slaves rebuilt several walls and then "pave[d] the spur" to prevent a new water tank from being destroyed by the rain.[36] Three years later, Governor Petrie commended the slaves on their excellent work on the castle, singling out three hard-working carpenters. This was an important time to strengthen the castle since it appeared that the Asante and Fante would soon go to war.[37] Company slaves also performed other tasks, of course. Because of the scarcity of skilled laborers, the CMTA used unskilled slaves to substitute for skilled labor when possible. When Apperley supervised the construction of the new fort at Anomabu, for example, he ordered company slaves to gather stones for construction rather than sidetrack bricklayers engaged in other projects.[38] Governor Mutter explained that the company hired free labor only when it lacked sufficient slaves to carry out the work, although the company's endemic underfunding usually prohibited it from buying all the workers it required.[39]

Company slaves lived either in the castle or in town, and they received a subsistence wage in the form of commodities. The CMTA's financial records reveal how the system operated both for the owners and for the slaves. From January to mid-August 1770, the company distributed 571 gallons of rum and 506 fathoms of tobacco to slaves, at a total cost of £412. This amounted to substantially less than what was paid to white servants (£725), but more than the cost of hiring free canoemen and laborers (£114), repairing the fort (£377), providing *dashees* (£94), and paying ground rent and water customs (£4).[40] The problem with this subsistence wage system occurred when the prices of local foods rose and when, because of increasing importation, the prices of rum and tobacco fell. For January to March 1780, the company paid its slaves £357 in twenty and one-third *halfsays* (wool textiles), 368 gallons of brandy, 437 fathoms of tobacco, 9/32 ounces of gold, and one *brawl* (cotton cloth manufactured in both India and Manchester).[41] One last example of the cost of slaves is recorded in the *Report of Cape Coast Castle for 1770–76*. In this seven-year period, the company spent £145,450, with over £20,622 on company slaves. Many of the slaves were unfit to work due to illness, worms, pregnancy, or advanced age. Without slaves, the castle would have ceased to function, since they carried water, cleaned the apartments, tended the garden, and cooked meals. Of course, the bondpeople had little individual choice except to participate in supporting the Atlantic slave system.[42]

This study demonstrates the differences and similarities between class relations in Cape Coast and in many other areas of the Atlantic World. Affluent classes, whether in Africa, Europe, or the Americas, realized that the control of labor was often the key to their individual and to their class success. They organized labor along a spectrum from bound to free, depending on a web of local surroundings and the international environment. At Cape Coast, in contrast to their dealings with most of the American Natives, the British found themselves in a dependent status for centuries. In their efforts to organize laborers, whether free or slave, Europeans were largely subservient to the authority of the local elites.

Workers also claimed their own power. They made it clear that it was a "perquisite belonging to them at every fort" to be employed by the company, and they adamantly protected this customary privilege. It was one of many rights, including those over firewood and timber, that benefited coastal laborers.[43] They took advantage of the CMTA's desperate need for labor and its inability to discipline its workers or to peddle recalcitrant slaves into the Atlantic slave trade. Canoemen and artisans who continued to produce their own food and who earned money primarily to obtain luxury goods were in a strong position to deal with white employers. Both bound and free workers consequently were able to bargain hard with the CMTA to enhance their working conditions and to increase their pay.

A Class Struggle in New York?

Simon Middleton

In April 1689 news of the Glorious Revolution in Europe and the overthrow of the Dominion of New England in Boston reached New York City, prompting fears of a pro-Stuart backlash and a renewed war with the French and Indians to the north. Francis Nicholson, the province's unpopular lieutenant governor, and his council of leading merchants met in the fort to consider the city's situation and its restless population. In Suffolk County, Long Island, militiamen mustered and marched on the city intent upon defending their "English nation's liberties and properties from Popery and Slavery."[1] To quell the unrest and prepare for a possible French attack, Nicholson ordered the city's militia to supplement the guard at the fort and commence repairs on the dilapidated defenses. In the weeks that followed, delays in the work prompted suspicions concerning the lieutenant governor's commitment to defend New York. Beginning on the evening of May 30, a series of confrontations between Nicholson, the militia, and the inhabitants culminated with a row during which the lieutenant governor allegedly manhandled a respected militia officer and threatened to fire the town. Soon after, Mayor Stephen van Cortlandt later recounted, "We heard the drums beat and the Towne full of noise, and seeing the people rise and run together in armes . . . in ½ hour's time the fort full of men . . . [and] no word could be heard but they were sold betrayed and to be murdered, [and] it was time to look for themselves."[2] Thus began the only full-scale revolt in the history of New York City prior to the era of the American Revolution, which historians have named Leisler's Rebellion for the merchant and zealous Calvinist who emerged as its leader.

The sources concerning the breakdown in authority that led to the New York revolt are well known and well studied. While there has been broad agreement concerning the major protagonists and the course of events that led to the collapse of royal rule, interpretations differ concerning the rebels' motives for seizing the fort and then backing the Leislerian administration of the city for the ensuing eighteen months. An earlier generation of scholars emphasized class conflicts arising from economic discontents created by a decade of declining trade, rising taxes, and the engrossing of urban wealth by a well-connected merchant elite.[3] In his study of 1953, Jerome Reich credited the rebels with a struggle against a colonial aristocracy that figured in the development of popular rights and participatory democracy in New York.[4] Elements of this view of the rebellion, as a contest pitting poor and beleaguered colonists against wealthy and arrogant leaders, and the challenge it implied to political and economic inequalities linger on in some accounts.[5]

In the intervening decades, however, others have been more skeptical of economic and socially-leveling motives. From the outset the rebels characterized their resistance as a *defensive* action, intended to save the city from the evil designs of local papist conspirators and their French allies, and for William and Mary and the Protestant cause. The rebels' demands were conservative not radical: they aimed to preserve rather than alter the state; as they saw it, to sustain rather than challenge legitimate authority. Their primary objective was the restoration of "Loyall and faithfull persons fit for Government" and a return to what they considered a just administration and civic harmony. It is true that the majority of well-to-do merchants joined the anti-Leislerian opposition. But when popular violence erupted, the rebels targeted suspected conspirators rather than simply men of property who could be found on both sides.[6] If a class interpretation of the outbreak of the revolt rests on rebel antipathies grounded in economic inequalities and discontent with social hierarchy, then Leisler's Rebellion was clearly a different kind of struggle. Accordingly, other accounts have viewed events in terms of familial and ethnoreligious ends: disputes among elite merchant families in pursuit of power and prestige; Dutch and English antagonisms arising out of the transition to English rule and the struggle in 1683 to secure a chartered provincial government; a townspeople's war in defense of municipal autonomy in the style of Baltic city-states and the Hanseatic League; and, finally, a preemptive strike by ardent Calvinists and admirers of William of Orange in support of the "one true religion" of the Protestant church.[7]

Each of these explanations has its merits, not least because they clarify the varied motives that colored different rebels' behavior. The most convincing interpretations look beyond the situation in post-conquest New York and locate the revolt within its proper, Atlantic World context. Only one study directly addresses the schism that divided the majority of townspeople from the majority of prominent city merchants, which it attributes to Dutch and English ethnic animosity. However, in recent years this assessment has been brought into question by scholars who have stressed the protean and unstable character of contemporary ethnic identities.[8] Consequently, one of the costs of our greater understanding of the motives of different constituencies has been a diminishing sense of what united the majority of the city's middling and poorer residents against New York's political and mercantile elite. This is the stark social division that struck earlier commentators as indicative of class antagonism and which no amount of historiographical revision can obscure. The interpretive challenge of Leisler's Rebellion, then, is to relate the clearer sense we now have of rebel motives to the demonstrable cleavage of the city into two rival camps, with the vast majority of ordinary inhabitants on one side and the city's merchant elite on the other. In response to this challenge, this chapter argues, we need to reconsider the class dimension of the revolt. To do so, we first have to ponder the relationship between social power and economic culture in this specific early modern context.

In keeping with other essays in this book, this chapter conceives of class as a social relationship that exists wherever and whenever individuals share structural positions in connection to the opportunities and constraints that develop in response to processes of production and accumulation. In this sense, class relations reflect two kinds of inequalities, in material conditions and in social power, and the maintenance of these inequalities either consciously or unconsciously by dominant groups, ideas, and cultural arrangements. The notion of social power employed here implies more than the force exerted by one class over another to attain its particular ends. In its broadest sense, social power is expressed in the assumptions and normativity—the givenness if you will —that instills a sense of order in human relations. It is manifest as much in the needs and loyalties it nurtures as in the aspirations and behavior it forecloses and condemns. As such social power is best conceived not as a linear imposition by which one group drives another toward an objective, but more as a field of relationships that pull as much they push men and women into social and cultural arrangements with particular economic outcomes. This field of relationships is constantly under scrutiny—contested, negotiated, and rarely if ever static. To understand the class dimension of the New York City Revolt, then, we have to investigate not only the antagonisms that develop within processes of production and accumulation, but also the character of contemporary social power and the sense of security and unanimity it fostered prior to the fractures and resentments that provoked the revolt.

As a first step, we should broaden our idea of the economy and the meaning of economic activity beyond their usual association with self-interested commercial exchange. This association reflects a tendency to impose a reductionist reading of individual behavior as driven by desire for gain and to eschew the "thicker" cultural readings of market activity that historians have applied so productively to other areas of social life, ranging from popular beliefs to family relations. Thus while we have a great deal of useful information on commercial cycles, imperial regulations, and the importance of furs and plantation products in the Atlantic trade, our understanding of the symbolic meaning of early modern exchange relations remains limited by neoclassical liberal assumptions regarding the ambitions for gain that are presumed to drive "rational" economic actors. It is from this perspective that it is tempting to characterize the revolt as a struggle between haves and have-nots, in terms recognizable to the modern eye. But as a growing body of work suggests, there is much to be learned by considering the ways in which the meaning of what seem familiar notions, such as interest, rights, credit, or privilege, have changed over time.[9] With this in mind, and looking beyond the perspective of an ahistorical *homo economicus*, one begins to discern the contradictions between individual actions and community ideals that fostered dissatisfaction and ultimately the revolt.

In early New York City, debates concerning market relations and the economy were bound up with considerations of community safety and prosperity, and with claims for local privileges and liberties whose distribution was rationalized as the means to an orderly moral and social end. These privileges and liberties afforded their holders public status and commercial advantages and were sometimes referred to as rights, but only in the sense that they were exercised with or by right and in accordance with what were presumed to be widely accepted standards of rectitude.[10] The public character and function of these rights meant that they were always accompanied by duties that obliged holders to employ their preferential faculties in the service of the common good. Thus, city carters enjoyed a monopoly of the local carrying trade but agreed to behave in a civil manner and work for regulated rates. In this fashion the burden of public obligations was mitigated by the benefit of public acknowledgment. In addition to providing individuals with a justifiable (or rightful) claim to employment and acts that they were under an obligation to perform, privileges and liberties granted holders a concomitant right to what others were obliged to render unto them. City carters invoked this right when they petitioned the city for increased rates for hire and for the exclusion of unregistered carriers from the trade. Most importantly of all, inasmuch as these particularistic privileges and liberties served to check the scope of authoritarian governance, they also served as a symbolic guarantee of fundamental rights to liberty, property, and freedom of conscience. Thus, attacks on local privileges and liberties were construed as indicative of potentially more sinister arbitrary tendencies and designs within the government. Appreciating the level of anxiety and suspicion provoked by threats, whether real or imagined, to urban privileges and liberties is essential to our understanding the fears that prompted middling New Yorkers to seize the fort.

These public debates concerning individual and community privileges and rights echoed the priorities of an Old World political culture centered on republican, civic, and customary norms familiar to the residents of New York City who hailed from diverse European states, but principally England and the Dutch Republic.[11] At the center of this political culture lay a concept of liberty that differentiated between free subjects and slaves based on the formers' capacity for self-government, and which tied the political condition of both to the fortunes of the communities within which they lived. Individual and community liberty depended on the freedom of citizens to act according to their own will and to be governed by their representatives. Releasing free citizens from the dread of arbitrary power and the likelihood of unlawful seizure of property this liberty also provided an incentive for civic virtue. Free men aimed to undertake great deeds and to gather fortunes for themselves and the greater glory of the state. Unfortunately, liberty was a fragile and much coveted faculty and free subjects did not have to be subjected to daily, tyrannical depredations before their freedom was imperiled. Instead, the liberty of free subjects was endangered whenever elements in government assumed discretionary or arbitrary powers and, disregarding individual and community rights and their representatives, governed without regard for customary and constitutional convention. In these circumstances, free subjects could rapidly find themselves drawn under a slavish form of government characterized by corruption, sycophancy, and tyranny: citizens would be required to cultivate servile habits in order to survive—to dissemble, conspire, and grovel; the once prosperous and harmonious community would collapse amid misery, rancor, and division.

Civic leadership in seventeenth-century New York City fell to members of a merchant oligarchy who were distinguished by their personal wealth, family connections, and contacts in the expanding Atlantic trade. These merchant leaders occupied a delicate position. As burgomasters and *schepens*, and after 1675 mayors and aldermen, they oversaw the regulation and quality control of trade and the orderly administration of civic life. In this capacity, they lobbied, successfully, for city interests and for the authority to distribute municipal franchises and privileges to local residents and artisans, who worked for themselves and in the interests of the common good. As magistrates and holders of municipal office and commissions in the militia, leading city merchants claimed and commonly enjoyed deference to their authority by ordinary citizens who valued the certainty and harmony of market relations and the protection afforded their homes, property, commerce, and privileges. This commitment to local rights and community interests enabled the infamously polyglot community to transcend national and ethnic differences and bind together residents who hailed from disparate origins. However, as international shippers of colonial products and importers of European commodities, city merchants also earned their increasingly prosperous livings by supplying the inhabitants with consumer and trade goods. Their struggles on behalf of municipal rights were driven, at least in part, by their determination to profit from the community they governed. Moreover, inasmuch as municipal ordinances and the distribution of privileges provided for the organization of local production and exchange, these same ordinances and privileges could also become the focus of class antagonisms if manipulated, or perceived to be manipulated, by merchant leaders in their own rather than the city's interests.

However, there is a big difference between the class antagonism cultivated by perceived administrative injustices and the collapse of authority that led to revolt. It was more than grumbling dissatisfaction that led city inhabitants to overturn a government that had heretofore afforded them status and security in an uncertain and frequently dangerous colonial world. What turned class antagonism into the rampant fear that precipitated the revolt was the construction the inhabitants placed upon their leaders' actions in the uncertain months following the Glorious Revolution. After years of niggling disputes over the provisions of local privileges and rights, economic difficulties, and the apparent reluctance of civic and imperial governors to secure the town from French and Indian attack, the townspeople could bear their situation no longer. Even now, however, the rebels did not set out to turn the world upside down. Instead, they sought a fair-minded government that could restore the balance of interests and obligations that characterized the city's earlier years. It was here, in the justification and limits set upon the rebellion, that religious motivations and, in particular, the spasm of anti-popery sentiment that swept the city played its part. Anti-popery flourished in New York City because, as in other times and places in the seventeenth-century Protestant world, it served to justify and guide the rebels in their actions. By reducing the city's woes to a single and easily intelligible force—the pope and his conspiratorial agents—and by legitimating resistance to royal rule, anti-popery provided for the defense of individual and community rights while holding out the prospect of a return to harmonious civic life once the evil and designing papist forces had been removed.[12]

Thanks to the continuing renaissance in North American Dutch studies, we now know a great deal more about early communities in New Amsterdam and wider New Netherland.[13] Settled in the 1620s as an outpost of the West India Company's far-flung empire, New Netherland was governed by quasi-martial law administered by a director general and his handpicked council. However, the failure of New Netherland to prosper over the ensuing two decades prompted the company to give up its trade monopoly in an effort to attract private merchants and stimulate commerce. Beginning in 1649 a merchant pressure group conducted a successful campaign against the company for the establishment of a municipal government that would administer trade and civic life according to Dutch practice and in the residential interest.[14] The merchants sought what they "consider[ed] to be the mother of population, good Privileges and Exemptions": in particular, recognition of New Amsterdam's staple right as the major provincial port, the authority to limit the activities of non-resident traders who competed with residents for Indian furs, and a day-to-day administrative role in the town. The merchants were undoubtedly motivated by their desire for greater influence over the export of furs and tobacco and the importation of supplies and trade goods. However, to justify their case they drew on republican political arguments, declaring that they held their "privileges to be the same, harmonizing in every respect with those of the Netherlands."[15] In the absence of such privileges, New Amsterdam's leaders feared "the establishment of an Arbitrary Government among us," and likened their condition to that of slaves living under the company's tyrannical power.[16]

By 1653, the residents had their municipal government and a board of merchant burgomasters and schepens took charge of the school, the docks, and a newly established public weigh-house. Thereafter they added incrementally to their administrative remit. In 1657, this municipal order was formalized with the introduction of the burgher right that differentiated between the rulers (30 or so "great burghers") and the ruled (some 240 "lesser burghers"). All burghers were required to establish residence by owning or renting real property. This granted holders the freedom of the city and the privilege of engaging in local commerce. Lesser burghers swore to obey local laws, pay taxes, work on public projects, serve in the militia, and show due "respect and reverence" to the city's merchant leaders.[17] In return, they were protected from seizure of their goods for debt and shared in exclusive access to the handicraft and retail trades. Tradesmen who were burghers—including butchers, bakers, porters, tavern keepers, and coopers—also secured additional trade privileges and bore supplementary duties depending on their occupation. All traders settled their differences in court according to the Roman-Dutch law and standards of equity established through arbitration and in reference to local practices.[18]

Following the conquest of 1664, the newly installed English governors relied on local Dutch merchants to administer trade. Leaving the municipal government and court intact, the new authorities also bolstered the city's privileges. The administration of artisanal trades continued as before: city bakers, butchers, and porters sought refinements of privileges secured during the Dutch era, and new groups, such as the carters, secured protection for their trade and assumed civic duties ranging from garbage collection to fire prevention. The respect shown by the conquerors for the established civic order affirmed the promise of the liberal surrender terms and appeared to auger a non-despotic English administration, thereby providing for a harmonious transition within the town.[19] In the ensuing decade, leading city traders capitalized on the grant of a monopoly on the upriver trade between the city and Albany and amassed considerable fortunes, doubling their share of urban wealth while the proportion held by the middling and lower sort fell precipitously.[20] Circumstances worsened for ordinary residents and committed Calvinists following the third and final Anglo-Dutch War and the arrival of Edmund Andros as governor in 1674. Andros adopted a more intrusive approach, requiring the use of English in court and intervening in the affairs of the Dutch Reformed Church, thereby earning the enmity of an ultra-orthodox minority led by the wealthy German merchant and church deacon, Jacob Leisler. Thereafter, the governor drew leading Dutch, and subsequently English, merchants into partnership in a colony-wide rationalization of trade designed to increase provincial revenues.[21] City merchants secured regulated or de facto monopolies over the export of flour and bread to the West Indies and the importation of rum and trade goods to the colony.[22]

The restructuring of provincial government and trade anticipated the later and more ambitious Dominion of New England and sent shock waves through local and regional economies, making the merchant administration unpopular with provincial farmers and traders. In June 1680, for example, the deputies from Elizabeth Town, New Jersey, "held an argument of neare two houres, pleading their rights and privileges" with the governor, but to no avail.[23] While a handful of leading families capitalized on the governor's program, the fortunes of most did not improve. In the late 1670s, provincial trade entered a period of decline that lasted up to and beyond the revolt of 1689.[24] Of course, periods of dearth and glaring inequalities of wealth were hardly unusual in the seventeenth-century Atlantic World. What mattered for the playing out of subsequent events was not only the severity of the inequalities but also the way in which they were perceived and discussed. In particular, the manner in which the republican principles underpinning the establishment of New Amsterdam and the undertakings given (and expectations raised) following the conquest appeared increasingly at odds with the prosperity enjoyed by an *arriviste* group of city merchants during a time of dearth and want for many. As conditions worsened, city residents suspected the prosperity of a well-connected few. When the Labadist Jasper Danckaerts visited New York in 1679 he met residents who remembered the days of New Netherland fondly and spoke disdainfully of city merchants who "charged so dreadfully dear for what the common man had to buy from them that he could hardly ever pay them off and remained like a child in their debt and consequently their slave." Moreover, Danckaerts reported, "It is considered at New York a great treasure and liberty, not to be indebted to the merchants for any one who is will never be able to pay them."[25]

By the early 1680s the negative perception of merchant leaders as, in Danckaerts's terms, "if not worse at least usurers and cheats" prompted fears concerning the municipal administration. The ordinances and regulations that had once provided for civic order and served as guarantees of individual and community liberty were subject to increasingly suspicious scrutiny.[26] When the authorities ordered the tanners and their foul-smelling pits out of the city, shoemakers suspected a plan to restrict their access to leather and undermine local production, thereby requiring residents to purchase more expensive imported shoes.[27] When city coopers endeavored to protect their livelihoods and ensure the quality of local workmanship, they were hauled before a court of inquiry, fined, and those serving as municipal barrel inspectors were summarily dismissed.[28] When city carters refused to work at regulated rates, they were also dismissed en masse and only readmitted following their public apologies and upon punitive terms and conditions against which they were still petitioning a decade later.[29] Previous historians have examined these protests individually, as demonstrations of discontent by local tradesmen intent on shoring up their declining fortunes. However, considered collectively and in the context of the delicately balanced deferential order proposed here, the rumor mongering, work stoppages, and organized petitions for respect of trade privileges bespeak an appeal by the broad, middling section of the local community that civic leaders ignored at their peril.

In the mid-1680s a combination of crop failures, the outbreak of war in Europe, and the removal of the provincial administration to Boston following the creation of the Dominion of New England further depressed city trade. Some chose to quit the colony, and according to the Catholic governor Thomas Dongan—who arrived in 1683 to assume the post vacated by Andros following his recall to London—those who remained were "generaly of a turbulent disposition." In 1685, these turbulent residents were joined by some three hundred or so Huguenot refugees who arrived in the city as fugitives from the atrocities committed against French Protestants following the revocation of the Edict of Nantes.[30] In sublime disdain for the province's abject condition and the Huguenots' tales of bloody repression that had brought anti-popery pots to the boil, Dongan introduced new taxes, settled lavish manorial estates on favored supporters, and elevated his Catholic co-religionists to positions of authority within the provincial government. It was in this context that the crisis provoked by the Glorious Revolution in England provided for the transformation of disparate demonstrations of disaffection with the merchants' administration of urban trade and civic affairs into a collective defense of the city from popery and slavery. In so doing a revolt inspired and united by its opposition to a rapacious class of merchant "grandees" delivered massive popular support to a cadre of orthodox Calvinists whose zealous and uncompromising doctrinal stance had previously ensured that they remained on the margins of the city's political life.

In closing, reconsidering the class dimension of New York's revolt in 1689 requires us to consider not only the inhabitants' experience of hard and uncertain times in the years leading up to 1689, but also the manner in which they construed these experiences through available linguistic and cultural resources. The economic misery and insecurities surrounding the fear of French attack mattered, but so did the fact that in seeking an explanation for their woes the rebels drew upon languages of protest and resistance centered on civic privileges and anti-popery whose themes and linkages were developed in response to other struggles in other times and places. Rather than mere verbalizations stimulated by a collective experience of worsening conditions, these languages of privileges and anti-popery had their own structure, logic, and history. The first constituted an overt and frequently noisy element of local politics elsewhere in the colonies and across seventeenth-century England and the Dutch Republic.[31] Derived from republican and civic-humanist sources, it encouraged New Yorkers to consider the status of their civic privileges as critical indicators of the integrity and intentions of local government and of the security of their rights to liberty and property. The second was a religious language, in the English tradition intimately connected to the language of republicanism, that ranged far beyond questions of doctrine and church government to encompass all manner of negative characteristics attributed to Catholics and their "papist" fellow travelers, thereby explaining the source of the evil that afflicted the city and providing a rationale for justifiable resistance. Such was the prominence of anti-popery in theological and popular circles between the era of the Dutch Revolt and the Glorious Revolution that its effects were still discernible in the antipathy toward Catholics in the nineteenth and twentieth centuries.

These languages of protest and resistance that united the majority of ordinary city residents behind the seizure of the fort and Leisler's administration also connected their rebellion to similar struggles in the early modern Atlantic World. Although the details of particular disputes varied from place to place, the status and function of local privileges as an aspect of individual and group property critical to material well-being and their symbolic significance as guarantors of fundamental rights were familiar to rural and urban communities across early modern Europe and the Atlantic World. As other chapters in this book demonstrate, concerns for similar local and customary practices and perquisites informed class negotiations and struggles from the dockyards of Glasgow to the shores of West Africa. Also familiar in Protestant northern Europe and the wider Atlantic World was the association of anti-popery with anti-Spanish sentiment evident in the polyglot New Yorkers' denunciation of their merchant leaders as "grandees"—a pejorative designation that invoked the tyrannical rule of Spanish colonial overlords and which was echoed by small planters in their struggle against the "Grandy Men" on St. Kitts, as Natalie Zacek discusses in her chapter in this book. Reconsidered in this fashion, New York's revolt becomes less a parochial spat reflecting discontents peculiar to a particular time and place and more a chapter in the unfolding drama of struggle throughout the emerging Atlantic World. In this tussle, a class of men and women who depended upon the security of transplanted notions of local rights and privileges for their survival found themselves grappling with a coalescing group of merchants, landlords, and royal officials who were intent upon using the machinery of the infant military-fiscal English state to strike down these idiosyncratic and inconvenient obstructions to their expropriation and accumulation of resources and wealth in the Americas.

7

Middle-Class Formation in Eighteenth-Century North America

Konstantin Dierks

The editorial board of *Time Magazine* has been selecting a "Man of the Year" since 1927; in 1969 it selected not an emblematic individual but a symbolic social group, whom it called "The Middle Americans." The choice was an unusual one, yet the editorial board struggled less to justify the aptness of its selection than to describe who comprised this nebulous group. They were "defined as much by what they are not as by what they are." "Middle Americans" were *not* "the poor or the rich"; they *were* "a vast, unorganized fraternity bound together by a roughly similar way of seeing things." How could such a shapeless social group come to personify an entire year in the cultural life of an imperial nation in the thick of a war in Viet Nam and a civil rights movement at home? "Middle Americans," the magazine intoned, "physically and ideologically inhabit the battleground of change." A loose amalgam of racial but especially class identity, they seemed not a force propelling change, so much as one reacting to it—reacting against every perceived manifestation of turbulence in the 1960s, whether black militancy, foreign war, generational tension, rising taxes, or declining "morals." Largely sympathetic to their plight, the magazine granted "Middle Americans" the victim status for which they hungered.[1]

However ridiculous this instance of cultural swaddling may now seem, it nevertheless reminds us of a once-powerful analytic move: to conjure up the cultural figure of the middle class and to locate it within a *battleground* of historical change. No matter how shapeless in reality, the *cultural figure* of the middle class was nevertheless commonly used for much of the twentieth century to explain the march of history. In the 1930s, for instance, some scholars sought to explain the rise of fascism in Italy and Nazism in Germany through the bitter resentments of the middle class.[2] In the 1950s, both triumphalist and cautionary scholars attributed the newfound global dominance of the United States to the predominance of its middle class.[3] Ironically, *Time Magazine* in 1969 may have helped usher in a real decline of the middle class in the United States,[4] although the concern here is less with the relative standing of the middle class than with the explanatory power it has been, and can be, accorded.

Refocusing on the eighteenth-century Anglophone Atlantic World, this chapter seeks not to claim the origins of a middle class for that era, but instead to interrogate contemporary understandings of the process of historical change in relation to the "middling sort." In eighteenth-century print culture circulating on both sides of the Anglophone Atlantic World, authors of several new genres of technical literature (that is, literature that taught skills) presented the "middling sort" as a cultural figure within an Atlantic economy, an economy growing increasingly commercialized as well as reliant on the practice of letter writing. Like scholars in the 1930s and again in the 1950s, and similar to the editorial board of *Time Magazine* in 1969, technical authors of the early eighteenth century sought to explain not how change had happened in the past, but how change *was happening* in the present. The energies of the ever-shapeless middle class served as a means to clarify broader historical transformations, whether the rise of Italian fascism in the 1930s, the rise of global dominance by the United States in the 1950s, the election of President Richard Nixon in 1968, or the commercialization of an Atlantic economy in the early eighteenth century. For watchful authors living in all of these eras, historical change could not be explained *without* invoking the middle class.

Yet this analytic move—explaining an interval of historical change through the energies of the middle class—no longer holds the sway it once had. Since the 1980s, historians concerned with either class or capitalism have encountered vigorous theoretical challenges that question the very concept of class, never mind the existence of a middle class.[5] Class identity has been especially charged with being too fissured by competing identities such as gender and race to be of any analytic value in explaining historical change.[6] (The fall of class analysis has meant the rise of race as the new central trope of North American history since the 1980s.) One spirited defense of the concept of class among Early Americanists has emanated from Seth Rockman, who argued that it is impossible to explain the power relations of capitalism without the concept of class. Still, he conceded that it is also impossible to explain such inequalities *solely* through the concept of class, that is, without using the concepts of race and gender as well. Rockman thus deftly sought to move the triad of race, gender, and class away from an unproductive zero-sum game, a competition that the concept of class has been losing miserably, so that the phenomenon of capitalism has too often been removed from historical scrutiny since the 1980s.[7]

This chapter proposes a different strategy for reviving the concept of class, one focused not, à la Rockman, on material structures of inequality, but instead on discursive processes of historical explanation. One might account for our variant strategies simply by our differing objects of analysis: the early nineteenth-century working class in Rockman's case, the early eighteenth-century middle class in mine.[8] In both cases there has been another challenge to class analysis, this one gentler because from the inside, questioning not the concept of class itself, but the appropriate threshold for class consciousness. Some historians of the middle class raise the bar for class consciousness high and see voluntary associations or political organizations as the crucial indicators.[9] Others set the bar lower and see cultural values and styles as fundamental to class formation.[10] One lesson of this ongoing debate, though, is that there was no single origin for the "middle class" in the Atlantic World. Indeed a broad scholarly consensus grants that a middle strata of society has existed in Europe since the twelfth century and in the North and South American colonies since the sixteenth century. Yet the fact of economic position is inadequate to explain when, how, and why middle-class identity was imagined to be a force driving historical change. The activation of class identity fluctuates over time—sometimes class identity is quiescent and goes unnoticed, yet other times it becomes salient—as *Time Magazine* insisted in 1969, and as authors of technical literature urged in the early eighteenth century. Modes of class identity likewise vary—sometimes cultural life, other times political life may be the means to activate class identity. In this book, the chapters by Andrew Schocket and Lawrence Peskin emphasize institution building, for instance, whereas the chapters by Jennifer Goloboy and Susan Branson stress the circulation of values. Hence, the most useful premise for research would be to examine the varied historical specificity of class formation, rather than try to pinpoint a single theoretical template that purports to explain class formation in all times and all places. Beyond this, however, the ultimate goal is to interrogate those eras when class identity supposedly inhabited a battleground of historical change—when the energies of the middle class apparently drove a broader historical transformation. In other words, the ultimate analytic prize is not class formation in some real sense, but the historical transformations that the activation of class identity was at times imagined to propel.

Middle-class identity achieved a new plateau of cultural salience in the early eighteenth century in England and its North American colonies, as articulated in several genres of technical books teaching the skills of arithmetic, accounting, penmanship, law, business, spelling, and letter writing. In England the authors of this technical literature gave a sudden concerted attention to their social audience, while in the North American colonies such books were avidly reprinted for the first time.[11] Both of these separate phenomena deserve scrutiny for us to decipher the cultural mission animating this efflorescence of technical literature on both sides of the Atlantic in the early eighteenth century. The historian should not merely seek references to a "middle class" in such technical literature because one would not expect the construction of a "middle class" to be the explicit cultural project of these books.[12] Instead, most crucial was how the books represented social space, cultural change, and personal agency. In addressing these dimensions of life, did the books activate class identity or some other kind of identity? If it was class identity, in what ways was it activated? Of highest priority is to historicize the concept of agency, precisely because it can facilitate a sufficiently flexible analysis that matches the variable activation of identities such as class, gender, or race. Once we detach agency from a facile association with free will or subaltern resistance, we can treat it as a set of both stated and unstated notions about possibilities and constraints for taking action in the world. Then we can begin to give agency a history of its own.[13] Furthermore, we can then decipher the cultural projects undertaken in the past that had the effect of activating people in the middle stratum of society. If such projects were not explicitly about the formation of a "middle class," what were they actually about?

Keeping this conceptual framework in mind—notions of agency, and activations of identity—can sharpen our analysis of the many new technical books about arithmetic, accounting, penmanship, law, business, spelling, and letter writing.[14] Such books first became available in England in the mid-sixteenth century, but it was in the late seventeenth century when the number of competing imprints began to multiply dramatically. In 1684, the author of *The Merchant's Dayly Companion* offered a historical explanation to justify the publication of another new business manual, an explanation hinging upon a new sense of modernity in the era. He detected, for instance, a growing use of domestic and overseas postal service—"now so prodigiously great" compared to "our Ancestors days"—as one of many signs of visible change in English life necessitating the cultivation of technical expertise in the writing of letters and the handling of documents.[15] To many authors mastery of technical skills did seem a matter of necessity in the face of a commercializing economy. "Whoever would be a Man of Business, must be a Man of Correspondence," insisted the author of a business training manual in 1716.[16] Just as authors deemed technical skills such as letter writing as crucial to the capacity of middling young men, so did they deem business to be crucial to the capacity of the English nation in the late seventeenth century. "England is properly a Nation of Trade," proclaimed an anonymous author in 1684.[17] For authors of a variety of technical books, these were the two intertwined measures of English modernity by the early eighteenth century: a core workforce highly skilled in literacy and numeracy, and a nation highly effective in both domestic and overseas trade.

Equally notable for technical authors was the fact that the social audience of their books moved from background to foreground. The titles of these books might still mention a given technical skill, but increasingly they trumpeted the social audience seeking mastery of that skill—especially clerks, scriveners, tradesmen, and the like. These occupations were strictly male domains, as can be seen in titles such as *The Young Man's Companion,*[18] *The Young Secretary's Guide,*[19] and *The Instructor, or Young Man's Best Companion.*[20] At the confluence of so many genres, so many imprints, and so many editions appearing in the late seventeenth and early eighteenth centuries was a concerted identification and activation of a loose strata in English and colonial Anglo-American society—middling young men. This did not amount to an explicit rhetoric or comprehensive vision of the "middle class" per se, but neither was it simply an inert position in the economic structure. All this new technical literature issued a call to identification, and to action.

There was a mission spurring the call to action. What was new and energizing in the world was a social constituency of young middling men finding themselves newly involved in a commercializing economy ("Business in Merchandize" and "Trade"), newly interacting with their social superiors ("Persons of Quality"), newly investing in literacy and knowledge ("as well Tradesmen, Farmers, Husbandmen, as Young Gentlemen, Ladies, and others, that can Read and Write"), and newly included in the audience of technical books ("all Ranks and Conditions of People" and "all Capacities").[21] This aura of inclusiveness was extended to newly literate tradesmen and farmers, but no thought was given to those men (and women) who were not literate, rendering the cavalier language of universalism ("all") more rhetorical than real. The aim of these books was to absorb a strata of middling young men into a world of literacy and numeracy and business and decorum and duty, a strata we could retrospectively label the lower middle class. For instance, a business manual from 1699 listed the following A-C trades: "apothecary, attorney, baker, barber, bayliff, brasier, blacksmith, bricklayer, butcher, bookbinder, chyrugeon, carpenter, carrier, carver, chandler, cheesemonger, clock-maker, cloothier, collier, coomb-maker, confectioner, cook, coppersmith, coach-man, currier, cutler, cordwainer. . . ."[22] The list goes on and on in this vein, sketching a social milieu weighted toward those in the service rather than the patronage end of a commercializing economy.

Although addressed to middling young men, these books remained remarkably preoccupied with the top of the social hierarchy. "In directing your Letters you must be very wary," one letter manual warned in 1713, "for a little mistake may give disgust and spoil all, especially with those of the higher Rank."[23] In this obsession with the social elite, colonial imprints seemed the most surreal. Even a colonial letter manual that claimed in 1748 to be "better adapted to these American colonies, than any other Book of the like Kind" nonetheless devoted several pages to detailed instructions on how to write letters to rarefied "Persons of Quality": king and queen, prince and princess, duke and duchess, marquis and marchioness, earl, viscount, baron, and their consorts, knight and lady, mayor, justice of the peace, and esquire.[24] Of course, the colonies contained almost none of such people who stood perched at the apex of the social hierarchy in faraway England.[25] Meanwhile, colonial letter manuals offered almost no guidance on how to address people lower down the social scale, the very kinds of people who did predominate in the colonies. These manuals were certainly marketed to such middling folk, aiming to benefit young men who would not mind identifying themselves as possessing "ordinary Learning & Capacity," but they were designed to guide such young men in their potential interactions with social superiors.[26] At the same time, colonial editors of English books treated horizontal interactions with "Persons of other Ranks" with the same briskness and flippancy as English authors: "you may dignifie them with Master or Mistress, according as your Humour suits you."[27]

So, this new technical literature of the late seventeenth and early eighteenth centuries did articulate an explicit cultural project—to help literate young middling men pursuing service occupations to navigate a commercializing economy and an elite social realm with which they were already intersecting, but which was nonetheless new to them and thus fraught with uncertainty. The books devoted many pages to the mastery of an array of technical skills, but they offered no systematic image of how the economy worked or what the social order looked like. Such a significant blind spot betrays the early and experimental moment of these books, which were reaching toward something they did not fully apprehend or comprehend, indeed reaching toward something that was still undergoing development in the early eighteenth century—a commercial Atlantic economy. The cultural mission was not to construct a complete "middle class" per se, but it was clearly to activate an identity that can only be interpreted as class identity. This is not to say that other identity categories were not invoked—gender certainly was—but that such other identities did not carry the same burden of purposefulness and activation that class identity did, at least in these genres of technical literature, in the early eighteenth century.[28] This mission was still too inchoate to amount to a full-fledged cultural style or political program— which are the thresholds of class formation favored by historians—but it would begin the process of identifying and activating a social constituency that would ultimately contribute mightily to the commercialization of the economy in England and its North American colonies.[29] Appreciating both the energy and the uncertainty voiced in the technical literature enables us to narrate the story of this commercialization not merely in terms of people's reaction to it. This reactive stance is often how historians narrate the "great awakening" and "consumer revolution," as unhappy or happy reactions to a commercialized economy that already existed.[30] Instead, we can move toward narrating the early eighteenth century in terms of an intertwined process of commercialization and consumerism, and in terms of the action (rather than reaction) of people, even if those people did not know precisely what they were generating, or what the outcome would eventually be.

However, we should avoid narrating history purely through the stated purposes of people in the past. We also need to interrogate what people left buried within assumption, myopia, or foreclosure. In this way, scholars can discern not only stated cultural projects undertaken by people in the past, but also unstated cultural work enacted by people even as they concentrated their aims and energies on specific purposes. Indeed, that unstated cultural work was crucial in providing the discursive framing around cultural projects, and it helps us register an image of the middling sort in the early eighteenth century standing innocently apart from any social disruption, conflict, or inequality.

For all its filigree detail, the technical literature of the early eighteenth century omitted much. The many technical books articulated a new in-between social space—a commercializing economy that lured young middling men some distance away from their families and communities and into contact with the social elite. The novelty and challenge of the situation came not only from mastering technical skills, but also from an alertness to old imperatives of family duty as well as new imperatives of social decorum. For instance, the 1748 edition of *The American Instructor* featured not only detailed instructions about penmanship and accounting, but also sample letters home from nephew to uncle and from brother to sister.[31] Yet the technical books portrayed no ambition for young middling men to emulate the social elite, only to master protocols of deference whenever young middling men interacted with the elite. The elite remained apart and above. At the same time, almost no thought was given to the lower ranks of society, never mind any effort to distance middling young men from them. The lower sort was mostly unmentioned and invisible. In other words, the technical books articulated no sense either of social competition among middling young men, or of social conflict with people higher or lower on the social scale. There were no boundaries to be enforced or to be crossed.[32] The higher ranks were securely higher, the lower ranks were vaguely lower, and the middling ranks would remain middling even after technical skills were mastered and a service occupation was secured. All this placidity was certainly not the stated cultural project of the technical books, but it was the cultural work they did in the early eighteenth century—to leave both the fact and the principle of social hierarchy unchallenged.

This image of social inertia connects, in turn, to a peculiar sense of cultural change. The technical books voiced neither resentment toward former disempowerment nor hope for future empowerment on behalf of young middling men. Instead, novelty and challenge came paradoxically from the already-ness of the situation—from the immediacy of already being involved in a commercializing economy, already interacting with social superiors, already investing in literacy and knowledge. There was no sense of any dramatic or pressing process of historical transformation, only of a vaguely new and slightly unfamiliar circumstance that presented modest opportunities and provoked mild anxieties. "In every thing be circumspect and cautious to please," the author of *The Young Secretary's Guide* exhorted in 1713, "that you may have your Expectations answered."[33] Here and everywhere in the technical literature the stakes were made to seem relatively low, more episodic than structural. In turn, no significant impact was expected from the actions of the middling young men beyond occupying their economic niche, tending service skills, satisfying family duty, and not offending their social superiors. Failure to meet these expectations might cause them to lose their access to and place in the commercializing economy, but the fortunes of that economy were not dependent upon anyone's individual mastery or any group's collective participation. Even if the young man might not personally "thrive in the World" (more rather low stakes), "Trade and Traffick" would apparently simply go on, just as the social hierarchy would apparently simply carry forward, both somewhere safely beyond the scope of human intervention.[34] This too was the unstated cultural work done by the technical books—to activate young middling men, yet to make almost nothing in the world contingent upon their activity—no success, no jeopardy, no harmony, and no conflict.

This image of historical inertia raises the vital question of personal agency. The technical literature of the early eighteenth century encouraged young middling men to step forward into a slightly mysterious social space between family and social elite and to apply due skill, decorum, and duty, enabling them to fit into an already happening cultural change. Yet these steps and actions were repeatedly presented as "necessary Expedients," as a baseline of expectation apart from any exercise of choice or expression of desire.[35] All this talk of necessity entailed limited ambition, limited empowerment, and limited impact. The books afforded young middling men the prospect of new technical skills, but not any claim to effective power over others. They afforded social access, but not any claim to authority. They afforded protocols of deference, but not any claim to social superiority. Moreover, they afforded self-improvement, but not any claim to benefiting society. Indeed, this set of limited effects amounted to a cultural premium upon "agency" rather than "power." The distinction between these two concepts is critical—"agency" involves an ability alongside an imperative to accomplish personal goals in the world, without thought to broader dynamics of domination or resistance in society, the purview of "power." This, then, was more unstated cultural work done by the technical literature, so that the activation of class identity in the early eighteenth century was enacted through an attention to horizontal social linkages, not vertical conflicts; an attention to cultural participation, not transformation; and an attention to limited agency, not arrant instrumental power. It would be a privilege of the middle class—in contrast to people we might consider subaltern—to become activated without a perception that any power was at stake in their ambitions or endeavors. All this did not amount to a *battleground* of historical change, yet young middling men remained the key cultural figures represented in the new technical literature of the early eighteenth century. In advancing an image of a commercializing Atlantic economy, the authors of the new technical books at the same time depicted the transformation of the economy as eerily without social disruption, conflict, or inequality.

Furthermore, it would be the good fortune of the middle class ultimately to effect far more than it would aim for, at least in this early moment of the eighteenth century. Looking forward from the appearance of the first new breed of technical books in England in the 1680s, vast material consequences had increasingly pervaded everyday life on both sides of the Atlantic by the 1760s. These included attending and staffing innumerable schools; making, selling, and buying books, stationery supplies, and desks; and incessant writing, conveying, and reading letters, manuscripts, and documents. The components of that material culture extended beyond the Atlantic World to a global economy. Unknown to consumers, writing quills, for instance, could come to North America all the way from Germany or Hudson Bay; writing ink included ingredients from Syria and Sudan; sealing wax derived from shellac from India.[36] The technical literature not only promoted a new and distinctive cultural and social thrust for middling young men but also contributed to a new and decisive historical juncture in the formation of a thickening consumer culture and communications infrastructure in the early eighteenth century.[37] Middling young men noted opportunities and cultivated them; they stepped some way into social spaces; they embraced a measure of cultural change; they claimed a bit of personal agency; they reinforced the social hierarchy. Above all, they commercialized the transatlantic economy, not only staffing but also patronizing an array of business services. The ranks of the middling sort filled up with new occupations, the commercial landscape filled up with new businesses (schools, printshops, bookshops, paper mills, furniture shops, post offices, and so forth), and households and workplaces filled up with new consumer goods, in both England and the colonies in the first half of the eighteenth century.

All this activity in print, commercial, and consumer culture comprised an interval in the history of a middle class marked by an increasingly purposeful economic and cultural life, if not political consciousness. Yet all of this historical change emanated from only one cultural domain—technical books related to epistolary culture and the management of documents—where class identity seemed to become salient and activated in the early eighteenth century. There were many other domains of life in the Atlantic World where class identity was not so salient in this same era.[38] However, some notion of personal agency is always embedded in whatever identity category may be salient, which testifies to the utility of agency as an analytic concept across identity categories. Were there commonalities, then, across cultural domains? Was the primacy of personal agency and social participation—as opposed to instrumental power and domination—unique to the arena of letter writing, or unique to class identity, or unique to the middle class, or unique to the eighteenth century?

8

Business Friendships and Individualism in a Mercantile Class of Citizens in Charleston

Jennifer L. Goloboy

In 1809, Charles Machin was robbed by his business partner. Nearly destitute, lacking even a winter coat, Machin fell into a state of melancholy. While he was in this condition, his friend William Parker discovered him.

[Parker] expostulated with me, on my want of firmness, to which I listened a, a mere statute [*sic*] unable to speak. His arguments were impressive and his noble Soul expanded when he pourtrayed to me the situation of others, far worse than mine. I felt its force and as if posessed of new life, springing from my seat I was caught in his embrace and in the fervency of the Strongest Affection he clasped me to that heart, which knew how to beat in simpathy for the distresses of another. And with a Soul too large to inhabit so small a space, he vowed Eternal Friendship. With the enthusiasm of men bewildered, whos hearts were ready to burst from thier narrow limits, we embraced each other, the warmth of which was sensibly felt. And as if the same feeling possessed each Soul, our acknowledgements were expressed by the grasp of Friendship.[1]

Parker then gave Machin the money he needed to cover his debts. Today this reminiscence might seem unusual, overwrought, and unintentionally erotic. But Machin's initial desperation would have been understood by his contemporaries. He lived in an era nearly without institutional safety nets, even for men who had once been economically comfortable. Parker, we are meant to understand, saved Machin from privation and possibly imprisonment. Machin's memoir was shaped not only by the Romantic language of sympathy, but also by the real and omnipresent danger lurking for middle-class entrepreneurs. Friendship and family provided security in an unstable world.

Many merchants in the eighteenth- and early nineteenth-century Atlantic

World built friendships as strong as Parker's and Machin's for sound business reasons. They fostered personal connections to secure reliable business partners and to find assistance in times of trouble. Within a century, however, matters and perceptions changed considerably. By the late nineteenth century, merchants often envisioned themselves (and other members of their class) as self-made. They sensed a dog-eat-dog work world composed of hostile competitors, among whom only the independent-minded could prosper. They thought they had created their own success, without the assistance of patrons or family members.

The letters of merchants in Charleston, South Carolina suggest how conditions in Revolutionary America and the new nation helped to shape the ethos of the middling sort.[2] The men in this study would not have characterized themselves as "middle class," since the term was not commonly used in the eighteenth and early nineteenth centuries. Yet, they often described themselves as a separate "class of citizens," and they frequently embraced values that would come to be identified with the middle class.[3] They believed in working hard and deferring pleasure in the hope that they would earn enough to educate their children and retire comfortably. They passed along similar ideals to their children, teaching them to be useful members of society. Often religious, they still emphasized self-control and self-restraint rather than religious enthusiasm.[4]

As products of a post-Malthusian world, the mercantile class of citizens acknowledged few limits on their capacity to become rich, and, accordingly, they spent considerable money on fashionable clothing and houses.[5] Nevertheless, the historian Margaret Hunt is correct to emphasize the limits of middle-class ambition.[6] While many of the merchants lived luxuriously, they rarely perceived themselves as men of leisure or seldom allowed their children to escape the world of work. Even many of the wealthiest men, such as Henry Laurens and Christopher Fitzsimons, ensured that their sons received educations enabling them to support themselves. The merchants' perceptions about their economic condition shaped their definition of themselves and of their business partners and other class members. If they worked hard enough in their youth and manhood, and if fate did not turn against them, they would earn a retirement of independence and leisure. Laziness, lack of skill, or pure bad luck would doom them to a lifetime of work. They adopted the ethos that seemed most likely to protect them.[7]

Some Revolutionary-era merchants, as Andrew Schocket argues in the following chapter, moved into the economic elite—deeply influenced by British merchants—where they wielded considerable regional and even international authority. However, it is also fruitful to consider merchants as a status group operating in the social realm (to use Max Weber's insight) rather than solely as a class wielding economic power.[8] Charleston's merchants knew they stood far above the "lower sort" of workers, slaves, and servants on the socioeconomic ladder. Still, judging themselves by British standards, they realized they did not qualify as true "gentlemen." Real gentlemen did not fear that an unstable marketplace would make them unable to care for their children; real gentlemen gave their children a classical rather than a practical education; real gentlemen usually did not even have an occupation. Values, not political or economic influence, made these men bourgeois.[9] The passage of their letters across the ocean reminds us that middle-class culture was created transnationally, throughout the Atlantic World.

Historians have demonstrated that economic transformations between 1750 and 1850 shaped the development of middle-class culture. Stuart Blumin examined how middle-class work became a matter of the "head" not the "hands." Richard Bushman found that the dropping prices of luxury goods introduced gentility and refinement to the middle class. Mary Ryan traced the ideology of separate spheres to the removal of women from economic participation.[10] As Lisa Norling has pointed out, the nineteenth-century economy became increasingly impersonal as it developed.[11] In Charleston specifically and North America more broadly, economic development made business friendships less necessary, creating the conditions and encouraging the evolution of middle-class ideals of individualism.

Colonial South Carolina was a triumph of mercantilism.[12] Carolinians grew rice and indigo—both crops that could not be grown in Britain—and bought British manufactured goods. Between 1768 and 1772, rice composed 64 percent of the average annual value of goods exported from South Carolina, indigo 25 percent, deerskins 4 percent, and naval stores 1 percent.[13]

In order to service this thriving economy, colonial Charleston developed a large mercantile community. As R. C. Nash found, there were an unusually large number of commission merchants in Charleston, compared to northern colonial ports, where merchants tended to trade on their own accounts. Commission merchants bought and sold goods on request for a commission.[14] Commission merchants thus faced the problems of locating clients and then persuading those clients to do business with them rather than their competitors. Merchants first attracted clients by demonstrating their superior access to information. Ingratiating letters sailed across the Atlantic, promising that their senders were active correspondents who knew Charleston and its related markets well. Francis Clayton wrote a prospective customer, "If you Should think fit to Employ us You may always depend on the Earliest notice of any Change in the State of our markets or Whatever we imagin'd would be Conducive to your Interest." Clayton added, "We have also Connections in the West-Indies & all along the Continent wehich propperly Cultivated will occasion us at all times in some measure to be acquainted with the State of Trade in Both."[15]

Clayton and his peers obtained their information primarily from private individuals. They exchanged letters describing the state of trade with friendly merchants in other ports. They discussed rainfall and the progress of the crops with planters in the backcountry. They sought out politicians to hear rumors of tariff increases. The men with the broadest networks of informants had the best knowledge of how to trade.

But becoming a successful eighteenth-century merchant meant more than providing the most accurate information to clients. Merchants built strong networks of vertical and horizontal friendships that provided emotional satisfaction to all parties. Merchants' letters reveal a world of mutual obligation and encouragement. Young men learned to seek out patrons and to reward these patrons with respect. Clayton's letters, and those of his partner, Robert Hogg, reflect the responsibilities of novice merchants toward the elders who had helped them. As one of them wrote to a man who had found a dry goods supplier for them, "it is the Inclination of every good man to Encourage these Beginners who if they are Fortunate will Suceed them in Generosity of Temper by that means they will Continue to Bless the human Species—these [illegible] a great many years after they have gone to Enjoy the Reward of it—I wish I may prove Such a one for the Exercise of yours."[16] Older merchants supported younger ones and were eventually replaced by them. The younger men knew they could never possibly repay their elders but could only help the men who followed them.

As young men established themselves within the mercantile community, they continued to cultivate mercantile friendships. Sociability became an increasingly important tool for them, partly replacing the deference they had used in their younger days. Men chatted about politics, religion, and family life. The Charlestonian Josiah Smith was delighted to find that his ideas on education corresponded so exactly with those of his friend, the Londoner William Manning: "am pleasd to find that your Sentiments & mine Coincide in placing Our Sons under the Care of Honest Clergymen, in Order that their morals may be the more properly directed & Securd them." Smith even found meaning in the fact that the number of children in each family was identical; that was another sign that his values corresponded with Manning's.[17]

The merchants also frequently wrote about their personal aspirations. Their letters reveal a shared understanding of man's goals. These were family men, who justified their hard work and attention to business in terms of their duties to their dependents: wives, children, and other needy relatives. Men who were slow to start a family were jovially mocked by their peers.[18] For years, David Lamb teased Robert Henderson for remaining unmarried. When Henderson finally did marry, Lamb said that it was time for Henderson to start having children, or as he put it, "many feet may [you] manufacture for Childrens Stockings."[19] Lamb revealed his vision of the ideal mercantile family when he added, "I hope you will remember it is now late in the day with you & so make a good use of your time, I expect soon now to have my sons in the Counting House with me, I hope you have one on the Stocks [that is, "in stock"] by this time but should that not be the case I hope you will not despair but always keep in mind that I was five years married before I got any thing."[20] Lamb envisioned sons to follow him in business, and to eventually replace him in the family hierarchy. He hoped that Henderson would have the same comfort.

Mature merchants revealed their own weakness and fragility around each other in ways that they could not with the women of their families. In this sense, the letters James Hamilton received from his friends Zephaniah Kingsley and John Couper were far more intimate than the ones he received from his wife, Isabella. As Kingsley wrote to Hamilton in 1805:

This last year has been a period of Misfortunes so much so, that I allmost despair of ever accomplishing the wished for object of independance which seemed to be sometimes within my reach & then again totally to disappear: By experience I have learnt that fortune is neither to be won by prudence nor industry & have only to thank God that ambition the attendant of health has not yet deserted me & keeps hurrying me on like a Soldier in hopes of victory; yet well aware that if not soon obtained that period must come when nature will relax the Springs and leave me distanced in the course.[21]

Kingsley was not desperate, but he was weary of his endless economic struggles. In Hamilton, he felt that he had a sympathetic ear. Success tantalized Kingsley, lying just out of reach. He felt that the pursuit of wealth dehumanized him, turning him into a machine with its springs winding down. At the same time, it masculinized him, filling him with martial virtue. This was the essence of a man's struggle, he felt: to win security and financial independence for his family before time defeated him.

Compare Kingsley's letter to Isabella's response to James's fear of failure, also written in 1805. James was concerned that a hurricane and financial mismanagement by a trusted agent had injured the family's fortunes. Isabella restated her gratitude for whatever material wealth her husband saw fit to provide to her. "I feel no mortifications in regard to myself my dear Mr. H. I have always been provided for far beyond any thing I had a Right to expect and am not affraid of the future, pleased and happy with each other, I could live contented in that little Hut on St Simons [the location of the family's plantation] for ever if Necessary." Isabella then abruptly changed tone within the same sentence, reminding her husband that she was not the only member of the family under his care.

But my Child, that is the sore place, my Father & Mother are very anxious to keep her, it seem'd to be making up for my leaving them in the prospect of having the charge of her, and I think it will be most prudent untill we are settled give me your Opinion candidly as for my feellings I must put them out of the question, little Isabella I must place at School here with your approbation, I cannot give up the charge I have taken of her.[22]

Isabella's reassuring comments must have been heartening to her husband but also a little intimidating. Because she was dependent upon him, she would not allow her husband to show signs of weakness. Her words served as a reminder of how many people needed him to be a good provider, beginning with his wife, and including his nieces and nephews, such as little Isabella. The roles of men and women within the family were too distinct for any real fellow feeling. Isabella could not sympathize; she could only flatter. Only another man could truly understand the difficulties of the mercantile world.

George Nelson's letters reveal what might be called the male world of love and ritual before the War of 1812.[23] Unmarried, he rarely had any contact with women, except during his awkward attempts to find a wife. Nelson rationalized his lack of romantic success: "as to me geting Married it is true we have a many very fine Ladies here some of which I have the pleasure of being acquainted with but you know old birds must not be caught with chaff."[24] Nelson did not have much emotional satisfaction from his family life. He generally treated his relatives as dependants rather than as equals. Most of his family was much poorer and less educated than he; he sent them money and even a dictionary in the hopes that it would make their letters more intelligible.[25]

Nelson's closest relationships were with other male merchants. He man-

aged to make his fortune in the turbulent 1790s by investing in the new nation's government securities, but many of his friends were not so lucky. A series of letters reveals how his friend Samuel Bellamy (or Ballamy) slowly slid
into failure. Finally, Nelson made Bellamy a rather generous offer, akin to
that made by William Parker at the start of this chapter: "if it should so happen that your affairs should be past recovery you must come & live with me
I am sorry here you make your Self so unhappy there are people in much
worse Situation then you are you see you have neither wife nor family have a
good heart."[26] At times, it must have seemed to men like Nelson that wife and
family were nothing but a burden; the true, emotional life was lived with
other men.

Mobile to the point of rootlessness, merchants traveled throughout the
Atlantic World in the pursuit of their fortunes. Between 1784 and 1798,
George Nelson lived in Charleston, Philadelphia, New York, and London.[27]
Zephaniah Kingsley, who was born in Bristol, England, became a citizen, in
succession, of the United States, Denmark, Spain, and once again the United
States.[28] As they traveled, men such as Nelson and Kingsley gained new correspondents among the mercantile community. Using shared experiences to
sustain long-distance business friendships, merchants reinforced transatlantic similarities in middle-class culture. These men helped insure that
middle-class culture was a child of the Atlantic World.

Despite the success of the Charleston merchants, the eighteenth-
century economy remained underdeveloped. As the historian Margaret Hunt
wrote,

One of the reasons it is so difficult to recapture the ethos of the early modern trader
is that it is hard for many people to conceive of families engaged in investing capital
in the absence of most forms of property insurance, health insurance, credit bureaus,
generally agreed-upon and highly systematized methods of securing debts, and bodies of law, including bankruptcy law, that assume a quite remarkable separation between personal or family property and business assets and liabilities.[29]

Essentially, Charleston's merchants, like the English businessmen and women
whom Hunt analyzed, were engaged in partnerships that were unlimitedly li-
able for all debts, with very few institutionalized forms of protection. (Ma-
rine insurance was the major exception to this principle.) There were few
nonpolitical institutions of any sort to assist merchants.[30] Corporations were
rare and generally designed to promote public good rather than private interests. Given the value merchants placed on being good providers for their
families, they believed this was a risky state of affairs.

TABLE 1. VALUE OF RICE AND COTTON EXPORTED FROM CHARLESTON, 1829–1831

Year	Value of Rice	Value of Cotton	Total Value of Exports	% Value of Rice	% Value of Cotton
1829	1,667,256	5,708,656	7,510,506	22	76
1830	1,172,195	6,293,927	7,618,819	15	83
1831	1,218,859	4,885,431	6,266,233	19	78

Source: William Ogilby, "Answers to the Foregoing Queries by His Majesty's Consul at Charleston, South Carolina," William Ogilby Report, University of South Carolina. All values are in U.S. dollars.

The clatter and hiss of mills sounded from Manchester to Massachusetts; in the early nineteenth century, cotton was the raw material that powered the Industrial Revolution. For a brief period before soil exhaustion set in, South Carolina was at the center of North American cotton production. In 1811, 50 percent of the cotton grown in the United States came from South Carolina.[31] The British consul William Ogilby calculated the value of cotton and rice exported from Charleston from 1829 through 1831 (see table 1). For all three years, cotton was over 76 percent of the value of all exports. Rice had been an average of 64 percent of the value of exports from 1768 through 1772.[32] Cotton had supplanted rice as Charleston's most valuable export.

How did the rise of the cotton trade affect the way business was done in Charleston? When the wealthy colonial merchant Henry Laurens wrote his clients and partners before the Revolution, he tried to estimate how much rice had been exported and how much still remained in the country. He wrote a business partner that "exports exceed 90,000 Barrels therefore there cannot be a vast quantity in the Country." Laurens probably would have been able to obtain export data; a local newspaper intermittently published trade statistics before the Revolution.[33] However, he typically avoided quantifying the rice supply in his letters. For example, he explained that the supply of rice was temporarily low because "the Rice Factors, altho the Crop of Rice is very large, begin to stop some parcels from coming & to Store others that does come to Market." In this letter, he did not estimate the size of the crop of rice or compare the amount shipped with the amount shipped in previous years.[34] R. C. Nash has pointed out that Europeans typically bought rice only when there were crop failures in Europe.[35] There was no use in comparing demand one year with the demand of previous years, because it fluctuated freely. Laurens made sure that his clients knew about the situation in South

Carolina, but he did not believe that a stream of statistics would make his information any more credible to his clients.

Letters from after the War of 1812 emphasize quantifiable information. Lewis Trapmann, a locally prominent merchant who served as consul from Prussia, heard about rumors in Liverpool suggesting that the supply of cotton would be inadequate for the year's needs.[36] Trapmann argued that the supply would be adequate, and he backed his assertion with statistics:[37]

Estimate of the Supply of Cottons for 1829/30—

Gulf of Mexico	460,000
Georgia & So. Carolina	380,000
No. Carolina & Virginia	70,000
	910,000
Probable distribution	
Home consumption	120,000
France & Contt. of Europe	230,000
Great Britain	560,000
	910,000

While it is suspicious that Trapmann's supply and demand tally up exactly, his attempt at estimating the need for cotton represents an advance beyond what could have been done when rice was South Carolina's preeminent crop. Cotton went to a specific number of factories in Europe and North America; rice was purchased by a varying number of merchants to supply countries where the crops had failed. Henry Laurens needed to know about how much rice was left in the backcountry because a shrunken supply would increase price. He needed to know whether factors had really run out of rice, or whether they were just temporarily holding rice back from the market. Men who sold cotton, like Trapmann, needed to know the supply of cotton for an additional reason—they could estimate the total demand for cotton. Accurate quantification was more useful once demand was known, and therefore cotton impelled the Charleston merchants to adopt statistical analysis.

Since what Charleston's merchants knew could be readily displayed as data, there was no reason for them to write individual letters to each client. Information about the cotton crop was sent to clients in a form that was increasingly quantified and far more impersonal than the information about colonial-era rice or Napoleonic War-era crops had been. What merchants after the War of 1812 sent to clients was often merely a preprinted sheet with a short, impersonal letter referring to the client's own business scribbled on the flyleaf. Typically, these preprinted sheets reported the size of the cotton and rice crops exported to date, comparing them with the amount exported the previous year, and estimating the stock on hand. Vincent Nolte, a merchant based in New Orleans, claimed that he, in 1818, was the first to publish such statements.[38] However, European firms had issued preprinted circulars before Nolte did.[39] Firms in Charleston commonly mailed printed proprietary analysis by the 1820s.[40] Later, anonymously compiled statements were publicly available.[41] Even more detailed statements, including the news from Liverpool, could be purchased in the 1830s from a Charleston newspaper publisher.[42] Merchants did not even have to pretend that they were doing the majority of their own research.

Emphasizing the quantifiable was a trend that extended beyond Charleston.[43] As Patricia Cline Cohen has discussed, rising numeracy reached a point in the 1790s when the collection of statistics seemed to be a laudable enterprise. Since the sixteenth century, Cohen noted, men had believed that "whatever was quantifiable was objective, in the sense that it existed apart from any imposition of taste or moral judgment on the part of the viewer."[44] After the War of 1812, Charleston's merchants sent statistic-enriched, often preprinted letters because they wished to appear objective, unbiased, and detached. Henry Laurens and his pre-Revolutionary cohorts, in contrast, eschewed statistics because they wished to give their correspondents the sense that they were receiving personal service from men who had inside information. They alluded, mysteriously, to letters from correspondents informing them of political decisions affecting trade, and to friends in the backcountry who would let them know about the state of the crops. Both the colonial and the nineteenth-century merchants attempted to allure their clients with the accuracy of their information. In the colonial world, good information was perceived as secret, hidden, and achieved through superior personal networks. In the nineteenth-century world, good information was perceived as public, precise, and untainted by personal opinion.

After the War of 1812, references to politics, family, and other masculine interests grow more infrequent, as do comments on the importance of friendship and the reciprocal obligations between merchants. When John Longsdon arrived in Charleston in 1819, he wrote a letter to an acquaintance and possible trading partner in England, much as Francis Clayton had done in 1763. But while Clayton promised his correspondent personal attention and the benefits of Clayton's broad network of friends, Longsdon merely offered a generic bundle of data. As he wrote to the firm McConnel and Kennedy, "I have the pleasure to commence the transmission of advices to you concerning the State of this market for Cottons—which will be continued from time to time without any other assumption than that you may perhaps at some future period see it desirable to order purchases in this market, and favor me with a share of your correspondence."[45] Longsdon's tone is dry and emotionless, rather than cheerfully ingratiating, as was Clayton's. It is not clear what, if anything, differentiated Longsdon from any other correspondent McConnel and Kennedy might have in Charleston. Longsdon could offer neither personal attachment nor personalized service.

Even merchants who were friendly generally separated private correspondence from their business letters. Frederick Smith, for example, knew the proprietors of Ogden and Ferguson fairly well. Letters from his firm, Gourdin and Smith, were as dry as those from any other firm. For example, Smith wrote Ogden and Ferguson while on his honeymoon tour, discussing a cholera epidemic in New York: "It is indeed consolatory that the ravages of the pestilence should, with so few exceptions, be confined to the intemperate & profligate; still more is it gratifying that every individual in your part of the world whose friendship I can claim, should so far have escaped."[46] While this letter is certainly not as intimate as those exchanged by Nelson and Ballamy, it goes beyond the world of business into an affirmation of presumably shared beliefs, including the common idea that the degenerate were more prone to contract cholera.[47] Gourdin and Smith's letters to Ogden and Ferguson were restricted to business commentary. A letter written before Smith left for his trip demonstrates the common tone: "Yesterday the letters by the 16 Feby packet came to hand, which have caused an advance in Uplands here—Today several sales were made for France of not decidedly prime at 11 cts—& good fair cannot be had under 10 1/2—English buyers keep aloof, but there is a great disposition to purchase which is checked only by the advance in prices."[48]

It would certainly be wrong to argue that friendship ever disappeared from Charleston merchants' business relationships. Rather, during this period, changes in the level of information publicly available made a new model of business relationship possible. This new style, unlike that of the previous century, did not root commerce in a network of deep personal relationships. As information became more publicly available, nineteenth-century merchants could more readily separate their business interactions from their friendships. Merchants could deal in new markets where they had no personal connections, and they could switch customers without regard to personal loyalty.

As Konstantin Dierks argues in his chapter in this book, the middle class often did not articulate the transformations it was undergoing. To see how

Charleston's merchants might have interpreted the declining necessity of business friendship, we can turn to contemporary business manuals. An instructive comparison might be made between John Hill's *The Young Secretary's Guide: or, A Speedy Help to Learning* (1750) and *The Complete American Letter-Writer, and Best Companion for the Young Man of Business* (1807). The earlier book is organized into categories such as letters of advice, letters of recommendation, and letters of congratulation, and so on. The author mentions letters of business in the introduction but does not label any as such in the body of the text. In practice, Hill's categories contain both business and personal letters. Within the individual letters, economic and social information are often combined. For example, a letter labeled "A Letter of Advice to a Friend" is really a business letter informing a friend of the state of business in a certain town. The writer informs the reader that he has enclosed a newspaper giving the state of local trade, and that he has heard that the reader's business in London is going well. In the middle of the letter, the writer adds, "Our Friends are in a perfect Fruition of Health, and kindly present (especially such as I have had lately the Opportunity to converse withal) their Love and kind Respects to you, and your good Lady."[49] In this letter, business emerges from a network of friendship. This handbook taught its readers to combine business and personal sociability in their letters.

The later book argues for a much more rigorous separation between business and personal life, and it models business letters carefully stripped of personal content. *The Complete American Letter-Writer* is divided into two sections, "Letters on Merchandize and Trade" and "Familiar Letters on Interesting Subjects," reflecting the author's view that letters on trade should, in general, lack familiarity. A letter similar to the one described above is purportedly from a man in Albany writing to a childhood friend now settled in New York, asking to be sent goods from the city. What is striking is what is missing from the letter. The writer offers no information on the status of trade in Albany. The offering of information was no longer part of the currency of friendship, reflecting the greater collection and public release of trade statistics. The letter suggests that neither man is living in his native city. Therefore, it is not surprising that the writer omits references to the health of mutual friends in Albany. Much more startling is how little the writer says about either man's circumstances: "I have heard of your success in New-York, and it is with pleasure that I can assure you that I am comfortably settled here."[50] The writer does not even send his best wishes to his old friend's wife, which would have been an unconscionable omission earlier.

In general, the later manual is far more concerned with the need to avoid bad company than the need to cultivate friendships. Several letters addressed to young men refer to the fragility of a merchant's reputation, which is the source of his credit, and warn them from acquiring alluring yet debased acquaintances.[51] A letter purportedly from an uncle to his nephew states,

In the first place . . . I would advise you to be *industrious*.
In the second place, *frugal* and *attentive*.
In the third place, be *choice of your company*: for on your company must depend your character; upon your character will depend your credit; and upon your credit will depend your fortune.[52]

What emerges from these letters is a transition to the ideal of the self-made man. Earlier merchants learned to become adept at cultivating friendships that were both economic and social in nature. Later merchants learned that success was found through diligence and hard work; friendships were a dangerous distraction from business.

The business revolution thus transformed how middle-class men saw the market. For an eighteenth-century merchant, Dame Fortune may have been cruel and arbitrary, but the market was made up of friends. The nineteenth-century image of the market was a lonely, alienating place, made up of deceitful strangers. Nevertheless, both of these images were flawed. Business friendships may have been stronger in the colonial period, but the marketplace in general was more disorganized, providing few protections for individual businessmen. The early nineteenth century was a period of rapid institutional development. For example, banking came to Charleston in the early 1790s.[53] Technically public in nature, banks often still relied on private relationships to function.[54]

Historians of the nineteenth century have often believed the bourgeoisie was inherently made up of self-seeking individuals whose natural tendencies created a liberal political and economic sphere. Stuart Blumin argued that the middle class "binds itself together as a social group in part through the common embrace of an ideology of social atomism." Debby Applegate referred to the "fiercely individualistic ideology that seems to characterize the middle class."[55] This argument is appealing because we are thus able to blame the rise of the nineteenth-century middle class for the fragmentation of our own society, our ability to forget how tied we are to the rest of humanity, and our short-sightedness about our duties to posterity. But if the middle class was always individualistic, Machin, Parker, and their eighteenth-century peers seem not to have been notified.

Our colleagues in Britain have used gender theory to remind us that the ideal of independence was a delusion. As Davidoff and Hall wrote, "Middle-class men who sought to be 'someone,' to count as individuals because of their wealth, their power to command, or their capacity to influence people, were, in fact, embedded in networks of familial and female support which underpinned their rise to public prominence."[56] We could similarly argue that their ability to see themselves as self-made men rested on nineteenth-century economic development, and on institutions created by the middle class.

The dream of being "self-made" became more important in the early republic. Nevertheless, the men of the nineteenth-century middle class were not individualists; had they been, society would have dissolved. Their social networks were less personal and more institution-based than those of their predecessors yet remained equally powerful. The "ideology of social atomism," as Blumin called it, bore little relationship to the lived experience of the nineteenth-century middle class.

Corporations and the Coalescence of an Elite Class in Philadelphia

Andrew M. Schocket

Nearly all the historical literature focusing on class struggles and negotiation has analyzed working class formation; that on the Atlantic World is no different. However, working people were not the only ones increasingly conscious of class. The chapters in this book by Konstantin Dierks, Susan Branson, and Jennifer Goloboy that analyze the evolution of middle-class sensibilities, culture, and friendship testify to the growing scholarly interest in the middling sort's emergence into a self-aware bourgeoisie constructed as much or more through conscious self-conception and the shaping of a middle-class discourse than through economic differentiation. Nonetheless, amid the instability of the early modern Atlantic rim, members of elites were at least as concerned with class formation and class interests as were their less well-off neighbors. Indeed, like most privileged people in all times and places, the small groups at the top of the social and economic ladders of the late eighteenth-century Atlantic World tended to be more cohesive in the pursuit of class interests and more articulate in their definition of class than those whose hands could not reach the higher rungs. Furthermore, those elites gained or kept their high position precisely because of their ability to leverage broad access to natural resources, to finished goods, to others' free or coerced labor, to information, and to capital from around the Atlantic littoral. To examine the transatlantic context of one elite group's efforts at class formation sheds light onto local class relations, the formation of a transatlantic wealthy class, and the coalition of an Atlantic World elite in the midst of revolutionary convulsion.

Historians studying the early United States have long debated the extent to which the American Revolution upended colonial elites and inhibited these groups' ability to reassert themselves economically and politically in the wake of the American Revolution.[1] In the new northern states, various groups of rich men competed with alliances of artisans and farmers over the political and economic power that had been mostly the province of powerful urban cliques under British rule. Scholars investigating early national politics as well as early national elites have noted how small coteries of men in the various states worked to use their economic leverage and to revise the new political structures (especially state and national government) to recover some degree of the political power they had lost during the Revolution.[2] While such studies constantly note that many of the men most active in this reactionary project greatly admired Britain and its institutions, they have not done enough to illuminate the ways that a few small groups of Anglo-Americans adopted British know-how and benefited from British capital in their efforts to solidify their economic position and to regain some modicum of the influence they had lost.[3] Transatlantic flows of capital and information were integral to the formation of Philadelphia's wealthy, corporate class at the end of the eighteenth century. By placing a subset of Philadelphia's post-Revolutionary merchant and legal elite into a greater Atlantic context, we can better delineate the process through which that elite aimed to reassert its power and authority.

At the close of the American Revolution, few in the Atlantic World were more concerned with their precarious economic, political, and social class status than Philadelphia's wealthy merchants, lawyers, and gentlemen. Because many of the wealthier merchants had been loyalists or perceived loyalists, the ones who stayed after the Revolution held a precarious position. Though they had managed to help wrest their own sovereignty away from Britain, they now constituted a typical post-colonial elite, negotiating an area between a greater world they aspired to join and the domestic conditions they schemed to dominate. A small group of elite Philadelphians chose a European vehicle to ensure class stability and to claim continued economic and political dominance. Influenced by British writings on and examples of corporations, especially in banking and internal improvement, some Philadelphia merchants initially saw the business corporation as a convenient legal, financial, and institutional structure to provide services such as banking and insurance and to foster the construction and administration of infrastructure such as internal improvements. Soon, however, the small community of corporate insiders, disappointed and frightened by their limited influence over state politics, used the corporation to wrest control over much of economic policy and transportation policy from the state, insulating decision making from what they perceived as the fickle and unreliable (read: overly democratic) Pennsylvania legislature. The cohesion of Philadelphia's post-

Revolutionary elite economic class can only be understood in the context of the Atlantic World, and the consideration of this elite class can further elucidate the greater theater of the Atlantic World's class struggles.

When historians of the United States think about chartered business corporations in the context of the Atlantic World, colonial joint-stock companies or monopolistic trading concerns are what initially come to mind, yet neither had much to do with the early republic. Granted charters by the crown, these institutions offered a financial, legal, and administrative framework for large, long-term projects that monarchs would not or could not undertake for themselves but nonetheless perceived to be in their interests. Settlement corporations, such as the Virginia Company and the Massachusetts Bay Company, conjure mental images of John Smith whipping lazy Virginians into shape, John Winthrop clenching his teeth at any signs of dissent, and frustrated English investors using their worthless stock certificates as scrap paper. Such corporations—at least in their original form and purpose—were for the most part long gone by the Revolutionary era.[4] Trading companies marched on. One trading corporation—the British East India Company—claimed to have lost track of several crates of tea in the Boston harbor in 1773, and along with other British, Dutch, and French trading companies it continued to compete with North American merchants for some time. Beyond those institutions, Early Euro-Americanists tend to have vague conceptions of the Bank of England; the common perception of historians is that the business corporation was "an all-but-moribund institution in late eighteenth-century England"[5] and North American corporate law and practice was a "homegrown product," constructed "with scant borrowing from, or even knowledge of, English law."[6] Such is the heritage of business historians and legal historians long on North American exceptionalism and Yankee ingenuity but short on rigorous analysis of close parallels between North American business corporations and their European forbears.[7] For these historians, European corporations represented a feudal holdover swept away by the American Revolution.

Nothing could be further from the truth. Not only were business corporations such as banks and internal improvement companies among the most innovative economic institutions in eighteenth-century Britain, but also they served as direct models for early Anglo-American corporate efforts.[8] In the decades following the American Revolution, the use of the British corporate form and an influx of British capital invested in corporations played central roles in the formation of an North American elite economic class and its subsequent consolidation of capital and of influence over economic development.

Philadelphia was the epicenter of this transatlantic migration of capital and of methods to organize it. After the America Revolution, elite Philadelphians turned to a tried-and-true British device, the corporation, to solve their credit and money supply problems—a solution far longer established but less innovative than their colonial fiat money and land bank schemes had been. Philadelphians founded the nation's first bank, the Bank of North America, controlled the first and second Banks of the United States, and established seven other corporate banks in the area. Not only did the banks loan money, but also they issued currency, thereby alleviating both the cash and the credit crunch—exactly the functions performed by some British corporate banks. Philadelphians founded incorporated insurance companies to distribute risk and to provide investment capital—exactly the functions performed by the British incorporated insurance companies. Philadelphians established internal navigation companies for direct profit and to speculate in land, and eventually mining—exactly the functions performed by the British incorporated canal companies. Through their control over such institutions, a coterie of elite Philadelphians consolidated their control over crucial economic policies in Philadelphia and beyond.

Not surprisingly, it was an elite Philadelphian in 1789 (the ubiquitous Benjamin Franklin) who pointed out that, even with the establishment of the new federal government, "in this world nothing can be said to be certain, except death and taxes."[9] In the 1780s, the Quaker City's wealthier residents had plenty of reasons to be nervous: Pennsylvania's most radical of state constitutions, unrest in the commonwealth's western reaches, unseemly egalitarianism in Philadelphia's streets and taverns, the breakup of many family fortunes in the Revolution, an influx of new merchants, the economic dislocations of the Revolution and its aftermath, competition with merchants in New York and Baltimore, and the usual risks of Atlantic World commerce. More than merely political or economic, such challenges threatened the position of elite Philadelphians as individuals and as a class.

Just as Philadelphia's well-to-do still followed British fashion and literature, they took their financial cues from Britain even after the American Revolution. The most successful London merchants diversified their portfolios once they had made their fortunes in Atlantic commerce. The plantations, landed estates, and corporate investments these merchants bought held distinct advantages over transatlantic trade. The combination of steady incomes and ease of management allowed such men to provide long-term financial security for their families.[10] Rather than spending all their days in counting houses and coffee houses, their children could devote their careers to more prestigious cultural and political pursuits. If elite Philadelphians could find stable, easily managed investments close to home, they too could retire and ensure their families' continued prominence.

Compounding the enduring personal challenges of building dynasties, the founding and growth of the new nation entailed novel sets of problems for the greater Philadelphia community. The chronic shortage of money for the growing economy remained a source of complaint. Like specie, flexible credit could be difficult to acquire. With an economy growing in both relative and absolute terms, currency and credit were short for merchants and their debtors. Philadelphians also faced the typical late eighteenth-century North American urban challenge of gaining access to a sprawling hinterland exploding in population and productivity. Beyond a day's ride of the fall lines of major rivers, the hinterland suffered from access that was restricted by poor road quality, and the bulkiness of most agricultural products rendered the cost of transportation to market prohibitive—a particularly unsettling prospect to the many wealthy Philadelphians neck-deep in land speculation. Both farmers and city merchants started to demand new artificial inland navigations that would "secure the grand objects of conveying the products of the interior country to the metropolis, and returning with the imports or manufactures of the latter."[11]

Colonial British Americans had improvised solutions to these problems with mixed success. To deal with the lack of currency, various colonial governments founded land banks or issued fiat currency. The former allowed farmers to mortgage their land to the government, which issued notes up front for the loan; these notes circulated as cash. The latter consisted of paper currency issued with the promise that the state would back its value (thus "fiat"). In general, farmers and artisans whose business was local favored these solutions to currency shortages, while urban-based international merchants whose customers were overseas abhorred the notes, which held little value in long-distance commerce. Long after the Revolution, both these devices—especially land banks—would be proposed repeatedly, especially by agrarian interests.[12]

In contrast to these institutions that were derived in North America, a particular group of Quaker City men who confronted these problems was increasingly inclined to look to Britain for solutions. A subsection of Philadelphia's economic elite, these Philadelphians tended to be among provisioner merchants whose primary profits came from exporting grain, men such as Thomas Fitzsimons, Robert Morris, Thomas Willing, and William Bingham. This central core of men was joined by a smattering of other merchants, lawyers, and others depending upon the nature of subsequent corporate ventures. Wealthy men of every stripe speculated in land and so provided a broad base of support for the first internal improvement projects. The solicitor James Wilson, the instrument maker David Rittenhouse, and the College of Pennsylvania professor William Smith all joined the rush. The majority of this group had been Anglicans, and the core came from several interconnected family circles that included the Allens, the Willings, the Binghams, and a few other well-established clans.[13]

Ironically, the city's business community became even more closely enmeshed with the British economy and the men who ran it during the 1780s than it had been before the American Revolution.[14] During the war, many disaffected and loyalist Philadelphia merchants fled to Britain, from which they conducted business with former associates who remained in North America. Despite that migration, between 1774 and 1785, the number of merchants operating out of Philadelphia actually increased by 60 percent, with most of the new merchants hailing from Britain, Holland, and France.[15] These men brought not only capital but also connections to business associates all over the Atlantic World.[16] Meanwhile, both Philadelphian and British mercantile firms saw the end of hostilities between the two nations as an opportunity to reopen old trading ties or to create new ones. British merchants sent sons, nephews, trusted clerks, or junior partners westward to drum up business in North American port cities.[17] These connections typified the reintegration and even intensification of Anglo-American trade after the Revolution. Not coincidentally, the Philadelphia men most central to this transoceanic economic integration also would be most active in early corporations: for example, the two sons of Francis Baring, the founder of London's House of Baring, would marry the daughters of William Bingham, who not only facilitated the Barings' land speculations at great personal profit, but also wrote the bylaws of the Bank of North America.[18]

The strengthened ties between communities on opposite sides of the North Atlantic fostered a greater exchange of information on all sorts of business opportunities. Philadelphians saw, read, and heard about in and from Britain a host of institutions—banks and canal companies—that integrated a national economy while providing for regional development. Furthermore, they had witnessed the profitability of those British corporations that administered banks and internal navigation. Many Americans read the London-based *Gentleman's Magazine*, which displayed the prices of British corporate stocks, and they were familiar with the popular British title *Every Man His Own Broker: or, A Guide to Exchange-Alley, in Which the Nature of the Several Funds, Vulgarly Called the Stocks, Is Clearly Explained*, which went through at least half a dozen editions during the eighteenth century.[19] Well-read Philadelphians could easily observe that over the long term, bank and internal navigation company stocks rose gradually and issued regular dividends without demanding any input of time on the part of the majority of investors.

No corporation held greater respect in the eyes of many moneyed Philadelphians—especially Robert Morris and William Bingham—than the Bank of England. Incorporated in 1694, its charter provided for ownership in hundreds of shares that private investors snapped up; the institution then used its capital to purchase large blocks of government securities at comparatively low interest rates. Thus, it allowed the crown to continue to finance and fight its expensive wars while minimizing the necessity of rapid tax spikes. For their part, stockholders expected steady profits, receiving annual dividends ranging from 4.5 to 9 percent every year from its founding through the end of the eighteenth century.[20] Though these returns could be lower than the going rate for money-lending—the general standard was 6 percent a year, though often went higher—bank investors were assured that the crown would pay up because of its ability to raise tax revenue.[21] Meanwhile, the company's governing board and major stockholders became a powerful financial and political influence. The Bank of England provided stability for its patrons on several levels: for government budgeting especially in wartime, for a financial community wary of high government debt, for investors, and even for those concerned about potential political unrest, all of which were on the minds of Quaker City businessmen.

Well-read Philadelphia merchants, especially those who had emigrated from Scotland, were also familiar with Scottish banking practices. The Scottish example held great attraction for Philadelphia merchants because Scotland had faced some of the same problems as the United States, such as a lack of local currency, a negative balance of trade, and inadequate credit facilities.[22] The Bank of Scotland performed functions similar to those of its English counterpart, but unlike the Bank of England, the Bank of Scotland did not acquire full monopoly status as part of its charter. Also unlike the Bank of England, Scottish corporate banks opened branches and issued notes as low as shillings and pence, thereby greatly supplementing the general money supply.[23] The Scottish system served as a prototype for banks chartered in Pennsylvania. State banks, just like the Bank of North America and the Bank of the United States, resulted from a transatlantic pollination.[24]

Although banks were among the most prominent British corporations, the most abundant proliferation of eighteenth-century British business corporations occurred in inland navigation. In 1759, the duke of Bridgewater made the first of several applications to Parliament for the right to connect his coal estate in Worley to Manchester with a canal, a spectacularly successful twenty-nine mile project begun in 1760 and partially opened to traffic in 1761. "The utility and profits of it were soon perceived by a discerning and trading people," wrote John Phillips, in an account known to late eighteenth-century North American readers, "and a number of applications immediately made to Parliament for different acts."[25] From the 1760s through the 1790s, Parliament issued eighty-three charters for internal navigations.[26] Many were successful business concerns, especially those that connected coal-mining regions with growing urban areas. Britain's growing internal navigation network provided local economic growth and national economic integration.

Collectively, British corporations enabled the mobilization of large pools of capital, the stabilization of state and individual finances, a solid money supply, and better transportation. From the perspective of Philadelphians such as Thomas Willing, these constituted enviable and necessary ingredients of orderly economic expansion. Both individually and aggregately, the Quaker City elite faced the exact problems that British corporations seemed designed to address. Philadelphia's moneyed men yearned for control over state fiscal and economic policy, the city's continued economic growth, personal financial security, and the general economic stability that, in their minds, underlay social and political stability. Businessmen tend to turn to established methods to solve new problems; Philadelphia's men of commerce were no exception.[27] Hence, they instinctively moved to establish economic institutions along the British model.

It was a model they knew and from which Robert Morris, William Bingham, Thomas Willing, and their associates borrowed heavily in their founding of the first U.S. business corporation—the Bank of North America—and subsequent corporate banks. In name, in form, and in operation, Philadelphia-based banks closely followed British precedent, beginning with remarkable similarities in their charters. British bank charters dictated that a majority of electors was required in order to amend company bylaws, that the companies' governor, lieutenant governor, and directors were to be elected annually during a specified one-month time frame, that the directors must be English (or, in the case of Scotland's banks, Scottish) subjects, and that a majority of directors constituted a quorum for official business.[28] The charters of the Bank of North America and the Bank of Pennsylvania also stipulated that bylaws be amended by a majority of electors, that the president and directors be elected annually in a specific time frame, that directors be citizens of the United States—or in the case of the Bank of Pennsylvania, residents of the state—and that a majority of directors were required for a quorum.[29] They raised capital in similar ways, as well; both British and North American banks issued a limited number of shares, set a maximum for individuals' initial investment, and collected their capital through subscription. They even operated under comparable limitations, including charter-mandated capital ceilings, the condition that company boards could only issue dividends out of profits while preserving the paid-in capital, and prohibitions against engaging in any other trade. Moreover, once Philadelphia was home to several banks, company officers met to coordinate money policy in much the same way as their Scottish counterparts did.[30] Philadelphia's bankers clearly mimicked British bankers through their adoption of such similar methods and structures.

Although merely cribbing from British examples when founding banks, Philadelphia's first corporate boosters engaged in a more interactive transatlantic process when it came to establishing canal companies. The famed canal mania of 1791–94, during which a frantic Parliament chartered sixty-one internal improvement corporations, was not limited to Britain: state legislatures established the first wave of canal corporations in the new nation during exactly the same period, suggesting that the canal craze was actually a transatlantic phenomenon.[31] British writers and readers followed North American internal improvement developments: John Phillip's magnum opus, *A General History of Inland Navigation*, which was published in London in 1792, included a section titled "North America" that described several canals in progress, including the Philadelphia-area projects.[32] Just as in banking, North American knowledge and modeling of British internal navigation corporations was widespread and detailed. North America's most complete treatise on internal navigation during the 1790s, written by William Smith and published in Philadelphia in 1795, included long passages quoted directly from the introduction of a popular British book that promoted several incorporated British canal efforts and from other works that became standard references for both British and North American internal improvement boosters.[33]

Philadelphians put this knowledge into practice the best they could. In 1766, the English canal booster Richard Whitworth published a pamphlet that could be read as a manual for the organization of a bid to secure financing and a charter for an internal navigation company, and indeed, most British efforts to create internal improvement companies followed Whitworth's blueprint. His suggestions typified organizers' efforts: advertise widely, explaining where the proposed canal would go and announcing a time and place for interested parties to meet; have meetings at multiple locations to drum up financial and political support; have the attendees sign a solicitor-composed petition to charter the company; ask for subscriptions to pay for the solicitor and other costs associated with the charter legislation process, the money for which would be returned upon successful application; generate subscriptions for backing the actual project; get local landholders and merchants to sign a sympathetic petition; finally, apply to Parliament.[34] Whitworth even included language for the various petitions and meeting resolutions.

Philadelphia-area project boosters followed suit, from the first two projects in 1791 through the 1820s, in much the same manner. They advertised in newspapers the meetings they were holding along the proposed route, drew up subscriptions and petitions, had a lawyer among their numbers to draw up a charter, and campaigned in the area for political support in the form of sympathetic petitions and financial support in the form of subscription shares. The language and structure of early internal improvement company charters in the Philadelphia area also echoed that of their British counterparts. Just like corporate banks, canal companies on both sides of the Atlantic provided for the annual election of directors to ensure the will of the stockholders, graduated voting systems designed to limit the influence of large stockholders, and lengthy sections devoted to the adjudication of disputes between the companies and the owners of lands through which the canals would flow. Philadelphia-area project boosters did the same, using nearly identical methods.[35] Rather than an example of Yankee ingenuity, the North American corporation resulted from a close mimicking of British institutions.

Some Pennsylvanians explicitly acknowledged North American corporate founders' intellectual debts to their British colleagues. By necessity, such admissions were extremely rare: having just thrown off the British imperial yoke, few people in the new nation beyond corporate boosters wanted to adopt British institutions so soon after the Revolution. Nonetheless, there were occasional signs. In an anonymous pamphlet touting the benefits of incorporating the Bank of North America, one writer argued that "similar causes to those, which in the reign of William the Third, occasioned the necessity of erecting the bank of England, now exist in this country," and that like the Bank of England, the proposed Bank of North America "is formed on such principles, as must place it on a secure and permanent basis."[36] When explaining banking operations to aspiring Boston bankers, Thomas Willing, the first president of the Bank of North America, privately admitted that "accident alone threw in our way, even the form, of an English Bank Bill."[37] Later observers could be more frank. As a governor of Pennsylvania pointed out in 1814, specifically referring to the Bank of England, "The principles of that institution are substantially those adopted in all the banking establishments of the United States." Indeed, he argued that "British institutions and practices [contained] the principles which have generally been adopted as the basis of every branch of financial policy in the United States."[38]

The Philadelphians most active in copying British corporations did so both in banking and in internal navigation. Many of the same men involved in the founding of the Bank of North America were also instrumental in the establishment of Philadelphia-area improvements. Robert Morris was at the center of a group that included men who sat on the boards of more than one of these institutions. Morris's corporate coterie included William Bingham, who wrote the bylaws of the Bank of North America and served on the board of the Susquehanna and Schuylkill Canal Navigation Company and a score of others.[39] They cemented the institutional connection through the bank's later ownership of canal company shares.[40] Thus began a pattern of interlocking directories that created a dense web of Philadelphia corporate connections, one that further solidified elite economic and social ties. As measured by similarities between the Dance Assembly—perhaps Philadelphia's most exclusive social organization—and the composition of corporate boards, membership in the corporate world became increasingly synonymous with membership in Philadelphia's dominant elite in the first decades of the nineteenth century. This was class solidarity in the making.

That coalescence did not occur in a vacuum. The borrowing of British corporate practice further integrated the United States into the Atlantic economy beyond the adoption of similar institutions. Indeed, the Bank of America's original establishment was possible only because of a sudden influx of specie from Cuba to the bank that ensured it would be able to meet its first obligations.[41] In addition, through the creation of legal entities featuring partible ownership, the incorporation of North American banks allowed foreigners to buy stock in U.S. business ventures. One Philadelphia broker informed a Caribbean correspondent anxious to buy bank stock that shareholding in the Bank of North America "is but small and Ch[ie]fly owned in Europe & our Monied men here," although other banks' stocks were somewhat more readily available.[42] Nonetheless, it was an opportunity that wealthy British investors did not pass up: by 1803, they owned over $34 million in the stock of state banks and the Bank of the United States.[43] The British would also invest heavily in North American internal navigation projects once the Erie Canal's spectacular success seemed to bode so well for such endeavors. Meanwhile, corporate officers in the United States borrowed more than money, also continuing to adopt new British financial methods including the use of preferred stock (also known as preference shares) to raise money from reluctant investors.[44] Such common efforts showed their ultimate fruition in the development of railroad technologies and corporations on both sides of the Atlantic in the 1820s and 1830s.

The foundation of business corporations, along with their transatlantic ties, contributed significantly to the coalescence of elite Philadelphia in the early republic and its further interconnection with the European economic elite. Heavy European investment provided an economic underpinning of Philadelphia's upper crust. Bank founders, including Robert Morris, Thomas Willing, and William Bingham, explicitly stated that Bank of North America shares would sell at the high price of $400 to limit shareholding to monied men, thereby both admitting a sense of elite solidarity and limiting the opportunity of bank stock ownership to the rich. With bank stocks quickly rising to over $500, and with the average Philadelphian only possessing around $630 in total property, the opportunities for most Quaker City residents to share in the benefits of stockholding were slim at best.[45] In a tellingly self-conscious yet exquisitely self-absorbed manner, the bank's supporters shamelessly counted themselves as "the most respectable characters amongst us."[46] Because wealthy Philadelphians always had first crack at buying bank stock, subsequent European purchases of stock entailed a large transfer of money across the Atlantic into the hands of Quaker City's well-off. Continued transatlantic interest in bank stocks meant that the establishment of every new corporate Philadelphia bank would result in the flow of capital from wealthy Europeans to their Philadelphia counterparts. In turn, the banks' ability to draw investment provided confidence in the banks and gave them adequate assets to lend confidently. The steady dividends provided the steady income that elite Philadelphians had craved for so long, ensuring family economic stability; the practice of establishing stock-owning trusts for widows and children testified to such motivations. Furthermore, lending policy ensured that well-to-do and well-connected merchants had access to banking capital to bolster their fortunes and to weather the inevitable vicissitudes of transatlantic and continental commerce.[47] The establishment of corporate banks in the United States, then, functioned exactly how their founders intended: as a transatlantic investment on the part of Europeans to benefit and solidify some of Philadelphia's richest families.

Corporations also became a vehicle for elite control over a large swath of Pennsylvania's economic policy to tilt it further toward an elite corporate agenda. Philadelphia merchants already knew that a dearth of reliable currency could spark not only economic dislocation but also social unrest, and they soon decided that the Pennsylvania legislature could not be trusted to look out for the interests of big creditors or to follow the currency policies favored by Quaker City creditors and land speculators—that is, Philadelphians with capital to invest.[48] If anything, economic problems resulted in increased unrest after the Revolution, escalating into a rash of road-closing and court-closing demonstrations in rural Pennsylvania during the 1780s.[49] Pennsylvania's radical constitution of 1776 guaranteed nearly universal white male suffrage, meaning that Philadelphia merchants could not rely on the state-house to enforce unpopular measures limiting money supply. Unlike in the colonial period, rich Philadelphians no longer controlled the Pennsylvania legislature and could not expect the legislature to enact economic policies to their liking.[50] However, their ability to leverage their capital to establish corporations was the result of an implicit negotiation of power in which elite influence waned in electoral politics but remained—and perhaps even grew—over decisions on money supply, credit, and internal improvement.

One might expect that Philadelphia's corporate founders would generally be Federalists—politically conservative and culturally Anglophilic—and for the most part, they were. But with the founding of internal improvement corporations and especially the Bank of Pennsylvania, Philadelphia's corporate community eventually expanded to include more dry goods merchants, that is, merchants who mostly sold imported goods, and numerous Republicans. Tellingly, Federalist-dominated banks tended to loan to Federalists, and Republican-dominated banks tended to loan to Republicans. But corporate insiders did not let these differences of political philosophy and lending practices divide them on class matters. Rather, they joined together to collaborate on issues that crossed party lines but hardened class divisions.

Philadelphia's corporate men used British models to enact economic policies that furthered their class interests. The Scottish system of incorporated banks that allowed the mercantile community to control and regulate currency and credit constituted an exemplary such model. In scheduled meetings, representatives of Scotland's three incorporated banks gathered to coordinate issuing and lending policy.[51] In their efforts to keep note issues at conservative levels, they prevented general inflation, always the bane of those who are net creditors, such as the Philadelphia merchant community. Just as importantly, these meetings allowed bank officials, rather than public authorities, to decide how many banknotes they would issue, when, and most importantly, to whom, thus ensuring that corporate men could provide capital to their friends and associates. By 1810, top officers of Philadelphia banks agreed to form "a Confidential Committee, to confer together, and enter into such regulations, & make such arrangements, as may appear to them, best calculated for the general good."[52] Not surprisingly, they assumed that the "general good" happened to coincide with their own interests. Through the establishment of their own corporate financial institutions and their collusion similar to Scottish bankers, Philadelphia corporate associates exerted tremendous influence over issues such as money supply and credit availability that, before and immediately after the American Revolution, had been in the hands of the Pennsylvania legislature. This coordination was not limited to banks: it extended to internal improvement projects, as well. The dense interlocking of corporate boards allowed a close community of several hundred families great leverage over what projects would get capital and how much. Control over routing for internal improvement projects ensured that the metropolitan interests of Philadelphia merchants and speculators often came ahead of those who lived on or near potential turnpikes and canals. In sum, Philadelphia's small urban elite used European institutions and capital to consolidate control over state economic policy and regional economic development. This allowed corporate officers to leverage corporate capital to further their class interests, firmly planting themselves permanently at the pinnacle of Pennsylvania's political and economic landscape.

Consideration of the founding of North American business corporations in the context of the Atlantic World further complicates our understanding both of class formation and of the American Revolution. By adopting a cis-Atlantic viewpoint—that is, by placing early North American corporations and their founders in the Atlantic World that they so consciously inhabited—we can better illuminate both local and Atlantic World phenomena.[53] Whether the American Revolution was about home rule or about who ruled at home, the adoption of British corporations showed that, decades later, the Revolution in all its Atlantic World dimensions may have run its course. The founding of business corporations in the new nation confirmed national independence and provided for economic structures that fostered regional and national integration, but it also further integrated the United States in the Atlantic World and kept it in Britain's economic orbit. As Lord Sheffield pointed out in 1784, in terms of commerce "Great Britain will lose few of the advantages she possessed before these States become independent, and with prudent management she will have as much of their trade as it will be her interest to wish for, without any expence for civil establishment or protection."[54] In addition, the transatlantic flows of ideas and capital as represented through corporations clearly provided the means for corporate insiders, their associates, and their families to consolidate their control over post-Revolutionary America. By the 1820s, corporate officers were scrambling to dodge the charge "that the incorporation of the monied interest already sufficiently powerful of itself, was but the creation of odious aristocracies, hostile to the spirit of free government, and subversive of the rights and liberties of the people."[55] Those monied interests and odious aristocracies were the result of Atlantic World cooperation between elites on both sides of the pond. In an economic sense, then, the American Revolution was no revolution: at best, it was an American Interregnum.

Ultimately, just as many chapters in this book emphasize the need to consider the Atlantic World through the lens of class, this particular episode in class formation in late eighteenth-century Philadelphia echoes Simon Newman's argument that we can only understand class formation in any given site if we take into account its Atlantic World context. This is true not only for the elites that either emerged or entrenched themselves because of transatlantic connections. We also must continue to remind ourselves that local class-imbued negotiations over labor, natural resources, culture, and language were all but scenes in the greater theater of the Atlantic World. If we do so, then the project of which this book is just a beginning will offer far greater insights into the Atlantic World of the eighteenth century and the global world of the twenty-first.

Class, Discourse, and Industrialization in the New American Republic

Lawrence A. Peskin

In the half century from the Revolutionary crisis to the 1820s, the conception of class by urban residents of the new nation underwent an important transformation. In the Revolutionary era, perhaps informed by philosophers such as David Hume, urban Americans frequently thought of class in terms of the three great economic orders—commerce, manufacturing, and agriculture.[1] The parades marking ratification of the Constitution held in all of the new nation's big cities in 1788 reflected this conception. Paraders celebrating the Constitution organized themselves by occupational orders—merchants, artisans, and even farmers from nearby rural areas. Each of these orders had its own hierarchies. Merchants stood at the head of the commercial order, with clerks and waterfront laborers beneath them. Artisans were further subdivided into trades, and some, such as silversmiths, were commonly understood to be higher in status than others, such as shoemakers. Furthermore, within each trade, masters stood at the top of the hierarchy, while journeymen, apprentices, and common laborers occupied subordinate positions. In agricultural America, this hierarchy took the form of masters of a different sort who stood above yeoman farmers, slaves, and other laborers.

By thinking about their social order in this way, Americans were able to integrate seemingly contradictory notions of class relations marked by hierarchy and deference on the one hand, and, on the other, a conception of class distinguished by cooperation of the three roughly equivalent orders. Thus, while the actual urban society contained wide disparities in wealth and social status, particular members of the society were at least as likely to identify with one of the three great economic orders as with a class position that cut across the economic orders to unite workers or masters or middling sorts. In this way, the late colonial city markedly diverged from more modern, industrial notions of cross-cutting class distinctions constituting broad upper, middle, and lower strata.

It was not until 1827 or so that urban Americans began to favor the more modern conception of class. In its broad outlines, the story of this transformation is an old one, dating back at least to Marx and rewritten in various forms by many subsequent generations of historians. Most of these scholars, although not all, have imposed modern definitions of class structure in their analysis of these events, providing teleological stories of one kind or another. The linguistic turn that was nascent in earlier sociocultural theorists such as Max Weber[2] and his intellectual descendent, E. P. Thompson, and that later rose to prominence along with the rise of postmodern philosophy and literary criticism has prompted historians such as Sean Wilentz in the United States and Gareth Stedman Jones in the United Kingdom to re-create these historical actors' languages of class rather than imposing historians' own vocabulary (often derived from Marx). Examining what historical figures said about class creates an enigma; for by speaking and thinking about their world, these historical actors were also redefining the way in which they and their contemporaries thought about class relations and, therefore, in a real sense changing the nature of those relations. Therefore, in studying their language we are investigating both the vocabulary used to understand class transformation and one of the means by which class relations were actually constructed.

Nonetheless, the changing economy drove both the modifications in class structure and the transformations in language used to express it. While the worldwide market revolution caused all three of the sectors of the American economy to grow—commerce, agriculture, and manufacturing—the emergence of the United States out of colonial dependency caused manufacturing to undergo the most radical transformation. While some areas, particularly New England, did develop small manufacturing sectors, and all of the urban areas contained good numbers of artisans who primarily served the local market, most colonial Americans had little interest in manufacturing, and imperial regulations often prohibited it. With the end of the Revolution and the end of imperial rule, the manufacturing sector would begin to grow very rapidly. During these years, the first short-lived American factories were constructed. But perhaps more important, artisanal and household manufacturing grew very rapidly as thousands of new craftsmen arrived in the cities and, in some areas, farm families produced twice as many domestic manufactures as in the prewar years.[3]

Language and ideas also played a part in this transformation. The postwar depression and the glut of British manufactured goods hardly made this the most economically propitious period to enter into manufacturing. However, patriotic motives induced many Americans to call on their compatriots to redirect the American economy away from the old colonial condition. Manufacturing boosters lost few opportunities to repeat (sometimes nearly ad infinitum) a small core of ideas clothed in a recognizable vocabulary of key words and phrases. Their starting point was a mercantilist macroeconomic analysis, based on the idea that nations were locked in economic combat over scarce resources and that success would be revealed by a positive balance of trade. Following from this premise, they concluded that nations, and especially their governments, must take action to promote economic independence and self-sufficiency as a means of stemming the outflow of cash to commercial competitors; hence, the need to develop domestic manufactures. Most important, they believed that it was imperative for government policy, in the argot of the day, to "protect and encourage manufactures," meaning there was a need for protective tariffs and various other means of encouraging manufacturing. Finally, they denied that their nation should depend solely on manufacturing or any single economic endeavor, but the three great sectors should be evenly balanced in what they often called a "harmony of interests." While it would be foolish to argue that this discourse alone caused economic and social change, it nevertheless was an important factor helping to shape the way in which groups and individuals reacted to changing market forces, thereby helping to determine the contours of the postcolonial economic system.

This pro-manufacturing discourse originated with urban artisans during the Revolutionary crisis. They quickly realized that friction with the mother country could become an opportunity to expand American manufacturing. Their success in the Revolution further politicized artisans, who led the fight for tariff protection in the immediate postwar years. This politicization also helped artisans to define themselves as a coherent, dynamic order, if not quite as a class in the modern sense. Thus, pro-manufacturing discourse can be viewed alongside artisan republicanism; small producer ideology; ethnic, racial, and gender identity; and other political-cultural currents as an important ingredient in worker culture.

By stimulating interest in American manufacturing, the Revolution gave new importance to the manufacturing sector at the same time that it stimulated conflict between artisans and merchants. During the Revolutionary crisis, the perceived unfairness of the Stamp Act, Townshend Duties, and Coercive Acts prompted economic protests against imperial authorities that often targeted English manufactures. These actions generally were accompanied by a healthy dose of pro-manufacturing rhetoric. Nonimportation, probably the highest profile activity, specifically boycotted British manufactures. It was intended primarily as a temporary strategy to coerce Whitehall into relaxing the offensive acts, but of necessity it also stimulated the domestic manufacturing sector as a means of offering replacements for the English goods that were temporarily excluded from the American market. Entrepreneurs created small manufactories. Learned societies such as the American Philosophical Society and the New York Society for Promoting Arts, Agriculture, and Oeconomy backed innovative manufacturing experiments and offered prizes to creators of new products. Civic groups in Boston, Philadelphia, and New York founded textile-making projects. Philadelphia fire companies urged their members not to eat lamb in order to facilitate "the increase of our woolen manufactories" nor drink foreign beer in order to "encourage the breweries of Pennsylvania." Even Harvard College's graduating class pledged to "take their degrees next commencement dress'd altogether in the manufactures of this country."[4]

All of these projects needed support from members of the public in their roles as consumers, producers, and traders. As a result, the public sphere was flooded with pro-manufacturing rhetoric ranging from speeches at town meetings to proclamations from fire companies, to prospectuses for publicly funded manufactories, to Benjamin Rush's speech at the opening of Philadelphia's American Manufactory, in which he declared, "A people who are entirely dependent upon foreigners for food or clothes must always be subject to them." Even newspaper advertisements employed this rhetoric. Daniel Mause hoped Pennsylvanians would encourage his new stocking manufactory "at a time when AMERICA calls for the endeavours of her sons." A Massachusetts fish hook manufacturer boosted of "render[ing] this country an essential service by establishing a manufacture necessary to its prosperity." And the New York Paper Manufactory urged "all of those who have the welfare of the country at heart" to sell them rags to be used as raw materials in making paper.[5] In this way, entrepreneurs sought to link patriotism and manufacturing together in the popular consciousness.

Pro-manufacturing rhetoric was most pronounced in the larger seaports because they were the centers where foreign goods were bought and distributed and where many domestic goods were manufactured. Urban merchants led the nonimportation movement due to their function as importers and exporters as well as their general preeminence in urban society.

However, if nonimportation were to succeed as a popular program, merchants needed the support of artisans. Artisans were extremely obliging, and in making the cause their own they began to emerge into the urban public sphere as a politicized group whose support was now indispensable to political elites. In this sense nonimportation and the pro-manufacturing rhetoric of the day turned the artisans into a self-conscious and powerful political order. However, artisans occupied a difficult position in urban society. On the one hand, they could see themselves as proudly independent free people constituting the vital manufacturing sector. On the other hand, most of them were clearly subordinate to the merchant elite in both wealth and status. Furthermore, most were also economically dependent upon merchant patrons. Their prominence in the Revolutionary crisis would prove to be an opportunity for them to assert their independence and their dignity.

Merchants supported nonimportation and pro-manufacturing efforts as instruments to force the British government to roll back its colonial policy to the pre-1763 status quo. But for artisans, pro-manufacturing efforts became an end in themselves. Clearly, this approach was not in the best interests of merchants who, after all, profited greatly by importing manufactures. These opposing conceptions of the pro-manufacturing movement came into conflict at key periods in the Revolutionary crisis. During the fight against the Townshend Duties, New York mechanics showed their distrust of the merchants' nonimportation resolutions by publishing their own resolves, including their intention to "make known such importers or retailers as shall refuse to unite in maintaining and obtaining the liberties of their country" by breaking the boycott. In passing such resolves, artisans were implying that the merchants, who had just passed their own resolutions pledging to abide by nonimportation, could not be fully trusted but rather must be policed by the mechanics. Similarly, when Philadelphia merchants appeared to be lessening their commitment to nonimportation in 1770, that city's mechanics threatened to boycott any who backed down from the agreement.[6] In 1774, following passage of the three coercive acts, mechanics in Philadelphia and New York pushed occasionally reluctant merchants to institute and abide by nonimportation.[7] In announcing their support for nonimportation in this militant fashion, urban artisans were declaring their political independence from the merchants, at the same time that they were declaring themselves equal to all other men.

Artisans continued to be politically active once the war was won. Calling themselves artisans, mechanics, manufacturers, or tradesmen—anything to distinguish themselves from the merchants—they formed committees in all the major cities.[8] Most often, these umbrella groups consisted of representatives from all the mechanical trades. They occasionally also included grocers, chandlers, and other small retail merchants. At war's end, these groups complained very publicly that British merchants and Loyalists at home were conspiring to keep America dependent on her former "mother" by flooding the market with cheap British manufactures. In New York the "Whig Mechanics, Grocers, Retailers and Tavern Keepers" complained that former Loyalists, "obnoxious characters, avowed enemies to our constitution and laws," monopolized business in that city with the assistance of aldermen who continued to sell them trading licenses as a way to augment the city's coffers. In Philadelphia Robert Porter told a large meeting of "mechanics and manufacturers" that, despite the outcome of the war, Great Britain intended to reenslave America by "destroy[ing] without the possibility of redemption, the trade and manufactures of America."[9]

All the mechanic committees agreed that the way to protect Americans from these threats was through tariffs on manufactures. Such tariffs would keep out the offending goods while giving domestic manufactures room to flourish. The campaign for protection reached high tide in 1785, when Boston's Committee of Tradesmen and Manufacturers coordinated a national push for tariffs. At least two of the six leaders of this committee had been Sons of Liberty. They drew on their wartime experience as patriot leaders when they decided to write to mechanics throughout the new republic to encourage them to lobby their state governments for protection. They hoped that in addition to gaining tariffs, their movement would help to encourage "the exchange of the produce and manufactures" of the new states, and they envisioned a day when "the northern states might furnish many articles of manufactures which are now imported from Europe, and in return might receive those supplies peculiar to the growth of the southern."[10] In other words, they were working to create an independent national market based on northern manufactures and southern raw materials.

The Bostonians' campaign was remarkably successful. Their letter received widespread publicity in all the major cities and mechanics in those places often sent copies on to their counterparts in smaller towns.[11] In Boston and Philadelphia, mechanics attending public meetings pushed merchants toward more protectionist stances much as they had a decade earlier during nonimportation.[12] As a result, the states with the three largest cities—Massachusetts, New York, and Pennsylvania—all passed tariffs that year. Pennsylvania's act was described as a measure to "encourage and protect the manufactures of this state," and the preamble expressed gratitude to the state's "artizans and mechanicks" for supplying articles "without which the [American Revolution] could not have been carried on." The Massachusetts act also declared that its purpose was to encourage domestic manufactures.[13]

This legislation was a triumph for the mechanics' committees. Over the course of just two decades, urban artisans had grown to become an important political force. Protectionist, pro-manufacturing discourse brought them together, and protection of manufactures remained their most important goal throughout this period. By 1785, they had moved beyond local politics to create a national network of protectionist committees. Still, it would be very premature to interpret this activity as class consciousness in the modern sense. The mechanic committees did not envision a world divided into workers and capitalists. The variety of labels they gave to their organizations—the General Society of *Mechanics* and *Tradesmen* of the City of New York, the Philadelphia Committee of *Manufacturers* and *Mechanics*, the Boston Association of *Tradesmen* and *Manufacturers*—cautions against describing them as a working class. Rather, they defined themselves as members of the group that manufactures things, a set that could include apprentices, journeymen, small masters, and wealthy manufacturers. By so doing, they continued to accept the old conception of a tripartite society of manufacturers, merchants, and farmers as well as traditional notions of craft hierarchy. While it is quite likely that these traditional notions—harkening back to European craft guilds—were largely an imagined tradition in North America, where historians have recently argued that relations between artisan masters and underlings were far more modern and exploitative and far less communal than this tradition would suggest, they nonetheless continued to be an important part of the colonial artisans' intellectual world.[14] Furthermore, this nostalgic view of artisanal life would serve to paper over actual conflicts of interest within the manufacturing sector during the coming decades.

After the Revolution, the pleasant prospect of tariff protection and economic growth brought new people and new tensions into the manufacturing sector. Most notably, a more monied group of businessmen became interested. For lack of a better term we can label these individuals merchant-manufacturers; that is, they were men grounded primarily in the world of finance who found the moment a propitious one to invest in manufacturing projects. The lack of a better term is important here because it reflects the fact that these individuals did not necessarily appear to be sui generis at the time. Rather, they blended well with master mechanics who owned large establishments and were often known as "manufacturers" themselves. For roughly the two decades between the late 1780s and the late 1800s, the similarities between mechanics and manufacturers—both members of the manufacturing sector—outweighed the differences. One of the important factors that masked potential conflicts of interest was their shared use of pro-manufacturing rhetoric.

One source of optimism for both groups was the new federal Constitution. Mechanics expected the Constitution to create a more energetic government capable of implementing their economic vision. An observer of the Baltimore ratification parade reported that the mechanics, "anticipating, under the new government, an increase of their different manufactures from the operation of uniform duties on similar articles imported into the United States[,] vied with each other in their preparation." In Philadelphia an observer noted, "The patriot enjoyed a complete triumph, whether the objects of his patriotism were the security of liberty, the establishment of law, *the protection of manufactures*, or the extension of science in his country." The slogans emblazoned in the banners carried by many groups of mechanics clearly reflected their protectionist positions. New York's ship joiners predicted, "This federal ship will our commerce revive/and merchants and shipwrights and joiners shall thrive." And that city's leather craftsmen marched under the slogan, "Americans encourage your own manufactures." Philadelphia's weavers prayed, "May government protect us," while nearby the whip and cane makers declared, "Let us encourage our own manufactures." Baltimore's silversmiths and watchmakers declared, "No importation and we shall live," while just ahead of them in the parade line the blacksmiths' and nailers' banner rhymed, "While industry prevails/We need no foreign nails."[15] That the parades' purpose was to celebrate the new government underlined the assumption that these groups looked to *government action* to protect domestic manufacturing.

Once the federal government was established, urban mechanics from Baltimore to Boston immediately began a second national protectionist campaign along the lines of their effort in 1785. Writing to the Bostonians, the New Yorkers explained the importance of cooperation: "When our views, like our interests are combined and concentrated, our petitions to the federal legislature, will assume the tone and complexion of the public wishes and will have a proportionate weight and influence."[16] Mechanic committees in Boston, New York, Philadelphia, and Baltimore soon drafted petitions to Congress that articulated their protectionist positions with the now familiar pro-manufacturing language. Reviving the theme of economic independence, the Bostonians noted that "the citizens of these states conceive the object of their independence but half obtained" until manufactures "are established on a permanent and extensive basis by the legislative acts of the Federal Government." The New Yorkers, fearing that the flood of imported goods would recolonize them, complained that "their country, having gained the form of liberty had left in the hands of their enemies the instruments of oppression, and the spirit to exercise it." The Baltimoreans prayed that America would "see and pursue her true interest, becoming independent in fact as well as in name" and that "the encouragement and protection of American manufactures will claim the earliest attention of the supreme Legislature of the nation." They added, "It is an universally acknowledged truth, that the United States contain within their limits, resources amply sufficient to enable them to become a great manufacturing country, and only want the patronage and support of a wise, energetic government."[17]

It was at this time that merchant-manufacturers stepped in, founding so-called manufacturing societies in all the major cities.[18] Members of Philadelphia's manufacturing society, the Pennsylvania Society for the Encouragement of Manufactures and the Useful Arts, literally joined the mechanics' parade, marching together as a unit in that city's constitutional ratification procession. They occupied a rather anomalous position in the line of march, between the farmers and the infantry and about three floats ahead of the first mechanics. This position well reflects the nature of the manufacturing society itself. It had much in common with the mechanic trades marching nearby. Riding in the float was a well-known master calico printer named Joseph Hewes along with his printing machine and his family. Behind the float marched one hundred weavers and a group of cotton card makers. All of this symbolism comported well with older notions of mechanics organized by trade and producing in a household environment. However, at the front of the manufacturing society's display marched the organization's managers, the men who had invested in its stock and the committee that managed its manufacturing fund. In other words, this was the beginning of an industrial corporation led (literally) by financial experts and shareholders rather than skilled mechanics. In addition, the float itself contained several pieces of automated machinery operated by trained workers, including one woman, rather than by traditional craftsmen. A nineteenth- or twentieth-century observer might well have viewed in this spectacle the first step in the proletarianization of the workers.

The expertise of the manufacturing societies' leaders tended toward financial matters rather than mechanical or technical skills. They quickly incorporated and began selling stock to the public. A core of merchants invested heavily in several of these projects. Some, like the Connecticut Manufacturing Society, produced little more than hot air and speculation as investors expected to get rich from rising stock prices without ever manufacturing a thing. But others did indeed create new textile manufactories that were way stations between European proto-industrial manufactories and modern factories. Like proto-industrial projects, they hired many out workers, often women, as spinners. However, like more modern factories, they employed a number of weavers and other workers in factory buildings stocked with new, innovative machinery.[19] Despite significant capital investments, they rarely had much success, and they all collapsed within a few years. Nonetheless, the manufacturing societies were the crucible of a new class of industrial capitalists. Before they had become an economically viable species, these men began to anticipate the new world ahead made possible by political independence and the European Industrial Revolution. Before there was anything approaching a factory system in the new nation, they pronounced themselves industrialists.

In so doing, they used language that was strikingly similar to that employed by pro-manufacturing mechanics since the Revolution. The members of Philadelphia's manufacturing society marched in the ratification parade with a banner proclaiming, "May the Union government protect the manufactures of America," a slogan nearly identical to those carried by many mechanic trades. The planners of the Boston manufacturing society deplored the "ruinous expense" incurred in "unnecessary importations" of foreign manufactures just as protectionist mechanics had for almost three decades. Referring to these same importations, Samuel Miles of the Philadelphia society noted, "We feel an hourly diminution of our wealth, and the support of our labourers is becoming precarious and difficult."[20] Like the mechanics of 1785, the merchant-manufacturers also saw manufacturing as one part of a national market freed from dependency on European imports. The New Yorkers observed: "This state produces the raw materials of flax, hemp and wool; the southern states produce considerable quantities of cotton, and if those raw materials can be manufactured amongst ourselves, it will keep the money in constant circulation at home, as well as furnish employment to a vast number of people, and train up our youths to habits of industry."[21] In short, a vibrant manufacturing sector could link together the three great orders—manufacturing, agriculture, and trade—at the same time that it forged new and increased economic bonds between the former colonies.

There are a few scattered suggestions in the record that some mechanics were resentful of merchant "speculators" entering manufacturing. The conflict surrounding Alexander Hamilton's Society for Establishing Useful

Manufactures in the early 1790s is a good example. As a quasi-governmental entity, the SUM was much larger and better capitalized than earlier private manufacturing ventures. Consequently, it engendered more hostility. Opponents were less concerned about the prospect of new factories than they were about the size and influence of this particular project. A Connecticut mechanic complained that Congress was "building large manufactories at the expense of government, which will create an influx of wares to our detriment . . . [and] take business out of the hands of those already engaged in the arts." George Logan, the president of the Germantown Society for Domestic Manufacturing, complained that the SUM would reduce those "who are personally engaged in manufactures" to poverty.[22] An SUM supporter responded that the conflict merely reflected a misunderstanding over Hamilton's definition of the term "manufacturing establishments." This term, he explained, "clearly meant every manufacturing establishment, great or small, owned by one or many persons."[23] His point, in other words, was that Hamilton intended to encourage *all* forms of manufacturing, not only the massive project on the Passaic River.

While it is debatable whether that was really Hamilton's intent, the larger point is that the conflict over the SUM was neither a debate over the desirability of manufacturing per se nor a clash between industrialists and laborers. Rather it was an internecine squabble within the manufacturing sector over the rules of competition. Small producers feared that the SUM would create monopolies that would edge them out of business while SUM supporters either believed there would be plenty of profits for everyone or secretly hoped to run the smaller producers out of business. Whichever the reality, both groups continued to share the same goal of increasing the manufacturing sector and both continued to speak of the necessity of government encouragement for manufactures. Manufacturers, whether wealthy merchants or poor mechanics, continued to think of themselves as members of the same order, a mindset that was certainly facilitated by their shared promanufacturing vocabulary.

The Associated Mechanics and Manufacturers of Massachusetts, founded in 1795, offers a good example of the continuing rhetorical connections between mechanics and merchant-manufacturers. This organization's official name proclaimed the unity of mechanics and manufacturers. In addition, although the group was more commonly known as the Massachusetts Mechanic Association, many members were no longer traditional mechanics but were rather, as Gary Kornblith has noted, closer to being profit-oriented businessmen than communally oriented artisans. Their constitution stipu-

lated that members be either a "master workman," a "proprietor of a manufactory, or a superintendent thereof." Traditionally trained master craftsmen
were initially the largest of these groups, but manufactory owners without
craft training were also a significant contingent. At this stage, however, their
establishments were fairly traditional—an axe manufactory, a chair manufactory, a large blacksmith shop—using hand labor rather than mechanized
processes.[24] Moreover, as late as 1800, the Massachusetts Mechanics Association led a traditional parade to mourn George Washington's death, in which
mechanics were organized by craft much as they had been in 1788.[25] Thus, the
Massachusetts Mechanic Association continued to occupy the middle
ground between traditional mechanics and industrial capitalists.

At a gathering in 1810, members of the Massachusetts Mechanic Association
performed a song about "the plough, loom and chisel, with commerce combined" in order to show the harmony of interests among agriculture, commerce, and manufacturing.[26] However, by this date, manufacturing was
beginning to be defined by jennies, mules, spindles, and other forms of automated machinery rather than by hand looms and chisels in many parts of the
northeastern United States. Nevertheless, even by the late 1820s, when industrialization was well underway in many places, distinctions between more
traditional mechanics and emerging industrial capitalists remained surprisingly blurred. An important cause of this confusion was the piecemeal nature
of American industrialization. While areas such as Baltimore, the Merrimack
River Valley, and upstate New York underwent classic industrial revolutions
involving relatively large factories that were owned by well-capitalized (and
often incorporated) industrialists and contained modern machinery run by
wage workers, other areas followed different paths. In cities such as New York
and Boston large traditional manufacturing establishments such as sugar re-
fineries and rope walks proliferated, but due to lack of water power, automated textile factories were rare. In many rural areas farm families continued
to make homespun and produce other domestic manufactures. Many trades
such as carpentry and blacksmithing continued to be practiced by traditional
craftsmen throughout the United States. In short, to be a "manufacturer" in
rural Virginia meant something very different than in Lowell, Massachusetts
or in New York City.

   This blurring was greatly enhanced by pro-manufacturing rhetoric that
did little to define exactly which form of manufacturing it was promoting.
This definitional vagueness resulted from several factors. Perhaps most obviously, it reflected the reality of a transitional period in which manufacturing

took on many guises and therefore meant different things to different people. Even within a single group, such as the Massachusetts Mechanic Association, manufacturing continued to be defined in terms of traditional crafts by industrialists who were often building large, nontraditional establishments. That many industrial capitalists continued to define themselves as mechanics was, therefore, not entirely sinister; in a sense it was a natural outgrowth of traditional ways of thought that understood all manufacturers to be part of a cohesive, organic economic order. However, increasingly in the 1810s and 1820s, as manufacturing corporations grew larger and industrial capitalists became more prominent, the rhetorical emphasis on the essential unity of the manufacturing sector became more and more self-serving.

It would sometimes be good business for industrialists to describe themselves as mechanics. Ever since the Revolution mechanics had held a cherished place in the popular imagination as the small producers who had once made political independence possible by their contributions to nonimportation and who were now making economic independence a reality in their workshops. Manufacturing promoters struck this note continually and with much success. Merchants and moneymen were far less popular—often viewed as sharpers, speculators, and purveyors of decadent luxuries.[27]

The mechanics banks of the 1810s offer an excellent example of how merchant-manufacturers sometimes appropriated the mechanics' popularity. Such institutions emerged in all of the major cities between 1806 and 1814 as a means of providing credit to cash-starved entrepreneurs intent on founding new manufacturing establishments.[28] Many of their initial supporters envisioned them as populist institutions designed to free small producers from the merchants' clutches. "It has been said," wrote one proponent of Baltimore's Mechanics Bank, "that all the banks at present . . . are sources of great grievance and machines of oppression to mechanics, and that this [bank] has been instituted to remedy this evil." Another wrote, "We want a bank established and conducted on fair principles that will protect the industrious mechanic, the honest retailer, the prudent dealer, from the nefarious bunch of harpies and shavers that infest our city." In Philadelphia, supporters of the Farmers' and Mechanics' Bank pledged "to advance the interests of agriculture, manufactures and the mechanic arts" and "to repress the practice of usury."[29] Such populist assertions could be useful to bank founders who invariably sought support from state legislatures in the form of corporate charters. Legislators who might feel uncomfortable pledging state support to "usurers" or "harpies and shavers" could feel better (and more secure electorally) about making credit available to virtuous mechanics.

The projectors of these banks were well aware of this advantage. According to Joseph Buckingham of the Massachusetts Mechanic Association, the founders of Boston's Manufacturers and Mechanics Bank were "certain gentlemen [who] had petitioned the Legislature for a bank charter" and supposed that "the influence of the mechanic interest, if enlisted in their behalf, might be useful in aid of their project."[30] Many mechanics, however, were uncomfortable with this strategy. They feared that merchants were merely using them in a new way. These fears seemed realized when, despite protestations to the contrary, the banks' boards of directors came to be dominated by men who clearly were not small producers. The charter of Baltimore's bank required directors to be "practical mechanics or manufacturers," but in actuality very few were mechanics in the traditional sense. Instead, most directorial candidates were large manufacturers, and, four (two architects and two flour merchants) were hardly manufacturers at all. The New York bank required only four of its seven directors to be "actually engaged in the mechanical profession," and most were large employers with political aspirations.[31]

As a result, traditional mechanics and the directors of the "mechanics banks" soon came into conflict. In Baltimore, a group of mechanics tried to pursue a more populist vision of the bank, calling for directors to be "practical mechanics, artificers or handicraftsmen" rather than merely "practical mechanics or manufacturers" as stipulated by a second, ultimately victorious group, which sought to include merchant-manufacturers as well as traditional craftsmen. There followed a very acrimonious election for directors of the new bank in which at least seven separate slates were put forward. Participants in the election made class-based appeals to the extent that some candidates were implied to be better friends to mechanics than others were. In one case, mechanics were warned to "be on your guard . . . to put in such men as Directors to the Mechanics Bank of Baltimore, as you know to be favorable to our interest."[32] There was similar conflict in New York. That city's General Society of Mechanics and Tradesmen, which was controlled by master mechanics, originally led the campaign to incorporate a mechanics' bank. Yet, once the bank gained incorporation, members of the GSMT feared that its directors were trying to take control away from them. Conflict became so intense that one of the bank's directors apparently got into a physical altercation with a GSMT member, while the directors accused the GSMT of treating them with "contempt" and "rudeness."[33]

Emphasizing the unity of the manufacturing sector could also serve to undermine internal class conflict. Larger manufacturers made some effort to insure loyalty by emphasizing consensus within the manufacturing sector.

Philadelphia's Manufacturers' and Mechanics' Dinner is a good example. Intended as an annual celebration but held for only two years (1808–9), this event was the brainchild of Philadelphia's nascent industrialists, men who promoted new-style manufacturing and often owned their own manufactories.[34] The annual dinner was a tribute to Philadelphia's rapidly growing manufacturing sector. In his 1809 oration, the chemical manufacturer, statistician, and physician Adam Seybert lauded the many manufacturing projects managed by the dinner's directors, most of whom were large-scale manufacturers. References to mechanics were much rarer. Presumably, Seybert had them in mind when he discussed the "improvements of machines" toward the end of his speech. Americans, Seybert affirmed, "have exhibited many proofs of their skill" in machine making. If this was his homage to mechanics, Seybert seems to have been thinking of them more as what contemporaries might term "mechanicians" than as traditional mechanics.[35] They were the technical experts who made the new factory machinery run rather than the small, independent master craftsman whose shop had long been a neighborhood fixture. These newer sorts of mechanics were, of course, vital to the smooth operation of Seybert's and his colleagues' factories. The mechanics were well aware of their importance and not above threatening to take their expertise elsewhere if not properly compensated.[36] The Manufacturers' and Mechanics' Dinner may be seen as a form of non-pecuniary compensation that afforded mechanics a measure of social recognition and public praise. The dinner's planners also offered mechanics a measure of healthcare through a "mechanics fund" to "provide for the indigence or infirmity" of workers and their families. In return, they hoped mechanics would transfer their sense of craft unity from the disintegrating trades to the emerging industrial capitalists.

Manufacturing benefited significantly from Jefferson's embargo, Madison's nonintercourse, and the unintentional protection from foreign imports provided by the War of 1812. Once the war ended, however, protectionists feared that the resumption of trade would threaten the new factories constructed in these years much as the glut of British goods following the Revolution had eroded American manufacturing and wreaked economic havoc. Consequently, a new cohort of protectionist committees launched very public campaigns for tariffs in 1816, 1820, 1824, and, most importantly, 1828 using language and arguments similar to the earlier groups. With the collapse of the Federalist Party, which generally opposed tariff protection, and the growing influence of northern industrialists, they won all of these battles except the fight for the 1820 tariff. The leaders of these campaigns created dozens of ad-hoc committees sponsoring probably hundreds of public meetings throughout the United States, nearly all of which submitted protectionist petitions to Congress. All of this activity culminated in the large and influential Harrisburg Convention of 1827, at which protectionists laid the groundwork for the tariff of 1828.[37]

The very names of many of these committees—"agriculturalists and manufacturers," or "wool growers and manufacturers"—proclaimed what the Massachusetts Mechanic Association had once described as the unity of the plough and the loom. They also signaled the end of the mechanics' long dominance of American protectionism: virtually no committees of mechanics sent pro-tariff petitions to Washington during this period, and some, such as the Tallow Chandlers and Soap Boilers of Boston, opposed the 1824 tariff. Indeed the protectionist citizens of Middleton, Connecticut declared, "Most of your memorialists have no personal interest in manufacturing establishments."[38] Few of the delegates to the Harrisburg Convention in 1827 were manufacturers, although many were politicians who hoped to protect home markets. The few who were involved in manufacturing were wealthy industrialists such as Abbot Lawrence of Massachusetts, Francis McLean of Connecticut, David Wilkinson of Rhode Island, and Edward Gray of Maryland.[39] Mathew Carey, a wealthy printer and leading manufacturing promoter, observed that the protectionist network of this period was dominated by rich capitalists, many with $50,000 to $150,000 invested in manufactures.[40] Industrial and political elites were again appropriating the pro-manufacturing rhetoric of the mechanics while taking advantage of the vague term "manufacture" to benefit from the popularity of supposedly virtuous producers. Even Martin Van Buren got into the act, declaring himself a "wool producer" at a protectionist meeting in Albany, presumably alluding to sheep on the farm land he owned.[41]

Meanwhile, the people who actually did the work of industrial production were beginning to eschew the protectionist movement. Beginning in the late 1820s, mechanics and other workers began forming new societies in which, as producers and employees, they differentiated themselves from industrial capitalists whom they viewed as consumers and employers. The Working Men's Republican Political Association of Penn Township, Pennsylvania identified "two distinct classes, the rich and the poor; the oppressor and the oppressed; those that live by their own labour, and they that live by the labour of others. . . ." George Henry Evans, the editor of *Working Man's Advocate*, preferred to distinguish between "the *useful* and *useless* classes."[42] The nomenclature of the new organizations—the Working Men's Party, the

Farmers' and Mechanics' Society of Stark County, the Association of Working People of New Castle County, the New England Association of Farmers, Mechanics and Other Workingmen, and many others—was notable for the absence of "manufacturers." The old understanding that society was composed of the manufacturing, farming, and commercial orders was giving way to a more modern conception of class. Although many workers still identified themselves as farmers or mechanics, the sudden emergence of "workingmen" as an important category signaled the beginning of a conscious self-definition as workers rather than employers and, therefore, the emergence of a modern working class.

To be sure, workers were still uncertain who exactly belonged to this group. George Henry Evans included small employers if their work was "useful." Small employers, including master workmen, were also included in the New England Association of Farmers, Mechanics, and Other Workingmen. Philadelphia's *Mechanics' Free Press* editorialized, "If an employer superintends his own business (still more if he works with his own hands) he is a working man and has an interest on the side of the remuneration of labour. . . ."[43] Still, the fundamental opposition was now workers versus bosses rather than manufacturers versus other economic sectors.

Tariff protection was far less important for these workingmen than it had been for earlier mechanics. A labor radical such as Thomas Skidmore could still write, "Society is as much a compact to consume the productions of each other's industry in total exclusion of the foreigner as it is for the common defense against the attacks of the common enemy." But excluding the foreigner and his goods, while perhaps still desirable, was now rather low on workers' lists of priorities. The most important issue for workingmen's organizations was probably the ten-hour day, followed by lack of access to education, harsh debtor laws, and the imposition of militia service. At the same time, according to one historian, "most if not all of the *bona fide* organizations of the Working Men's party appear to have been opposed to protection." The *Mechanics Free Press* complained that "of all others, tariff protected manufacturers are most prone to reduce the wages of their workmen."[44] In short, workers were now more anxious to be protected from their own employers and the state than from foreign imports. Rather than agitate for tariff protection, members of Philadelphia's Mechanics' Union hoped to provide "each other mutual protection from oppression," and their leader, Thomas Heighton, called for an end to "the fostering wing of legislative protection" that allowed bosses to accumulate "their annual millions from the toils and labours of the operative classes."[45]

Thus, while the pro-manufacturing discourse of patriotic economic independence through the harmony of interests would live on for many years in the ebb and flow of continuing tariff battles and the writings of political economists such as Henry C. Carey, those who worked with their hands would no longer dominate it. It would be transformed from an important component of late eighteenth-century worker culture into a shibboleth of first Whiggish and then Republican industrialists. Rhetoric that once helped unite the manufacturing sector now divided the working class from the capitalists. But, another hallmark of this discourse, the emphasis on production as a virtuous pursuit, would continue to blur class lines, perhaps up to the present, as industrialists and factory workers, farmers and day laborers, even academics, all claimed to belong to the ranks of the productive workers.

Sex and Other Middle-Class Pastimes in the Life of Ann Carson

Susan Branson

In 1816 a respectable, middle-class woman named Ann Baker Carson attempted to kidnap the governor of Pennsylvania. Why she performed such a daring deed is a tale of the nineteenth-century world turned upside down and inside out. Carson related her version of the crime in her memoir, the *History of the Celebrated Mrs. Ann Carson* (1822).[1] The events described in the *History*, though unusual, are accurate. Newspaper accounts, trial transcripts, and letters corroborate Carson's tale. Yet it is Carson's interpretation of those facts, an interpretation that cannot be verified, that offers a rich source of information about emerging class identity in the nineteenth century. A memoir is a unique opportunity for someone to shape or create an identity. The author can say anything she wants, any way she wants, about herself, including who she believes herself to be (or at any rate, who she wants the reader to believe her to be). Ann Carson was bound by certain facts that were common knowledge, such as her parents' occupation, and her own occupation, education, and friendships. Carson could not change these things about herself. But how she represented these circumstances and events to her readers—her consciousness of audience, her intentions, and her assumptions about society—all provide an uncommon perspective on North America's developing middle class and women's place within it.

Her social and economic background placed her squarely within that segment of Euro-American society that promoted a new sense of refinement and adherence to the gendered behavior dictated by the ideology of separate spheres. Carson's father, Thomas Baker, was a ship's captain employed by various Philadelphia shipping firms who kept his family in genteel comfort. He sent his daughters, including Ann, who was born in 1785, to some of the first female academies in Philadelphia. But a reversal of fortune in the late 1790s compelled the Bakers to marry off their fifteen-year-old daughter to one of her father's fellow officers, thirty-nine-year-old Captain John Carson. Carson was the son of the well-known Philadelphia physician John Carson. The captain's income and social status should have kept Ann in the comfortable middle-class world she knew.[2]

But the captain was an alcoholic who could not consistently fulfill his financial obligations. At Ann Carson's insistence, in 1812 he sailed off to the East Indies. In October 1815, believing that the captain was dead (having not heard from him in three years), Ann Carson married Richard Smith, a handsome but penniless young Irishman several years younger than she. But the captain was alive and well. He returned to Philadelphia a few months after Carson's marriage to Smith. Upon discovering his wife bigamously married, Captain Carson threatened to divorce her. Before legal action was taken by any of the parties concerned, Richard Smith shot and killed Captain Carson. Smith was convicted of murder and sentenced to die. Ann Carson was tried as an accessory to murder, but no clear evidence surfaced to substantiate the indictment. Carson was acquitted. Though there were mitigating circumstances in Smith's situation, including Captain Carson's threats to kill Smith, the governor of Pennsylvania refused to grant a pardon. Carson, as she explained in her memoir, then chose the only means she believed left to her: she acquainted herself with "the fraternity of desperadoes, who keep civilized society in bodily fear for either life or property."[3] Having planned to kidnap the governor and force him to release her condemned lover, Carson accompanied two armed men to the vicinity of Selinsgrove, Governor Snyder's estate near Lancaster. But once her plan was discovered, Snyder's friend John Binns wrote to the governor, warning him of Carson's plot:

The infernal Fiend who has caused the murder of her husband and the violent death of him she called her husband is raging with madness and has put all upon the cast of the die. . . . Do this or do anything else your judgment may direct to guard you against this enraged Tygress [*sic*] for a time. . . . I beseech you to guard against all the machinations of this Fiend of Hell for a little while and all will be over.[4]

Carson and her men were apprehended as they neared the vicinity of the governor's residence.

Richard Smith's execution proceeded as scheduled, and Carson stood trial for attempted kidnapping. She was acquitted of all charges. But the two trials and her attempts to free Richard Smith left her heavily in debt. She lacked financial resources to begin a new business and she had lost the credibility to elicit assistance from former friends and acquaintances. Even her family turned against her. According to Carson, her brothers-in-law were chiefly to blame for bringing her to trial and had prejudiced her sisters and many of her friends against her. According to Carson, "I was hunted, like a hare pursued by the hounds, from respectable society." As a result, Carson chose "to initiate [herself] among that class of people who set *law, justice,* and forms, at defiance." The life of a respectable, but impoverished woman held no appeal. Among criminals, in contrast, she believed she could preserve the material comforts she was accustomed to. This life was not without its risks, however. She was arrested in Maryland on a robbery charge and identified by Maryland's attorney general as the "celebrated Mrs. Carson of Philadelphia, a lady whose talents when united with outlaws, such as she is at present connected with, renders her a dangerous inhabitant to any state."[5] Carson was nevertheless declared innocent of the charges but ordered to leave Baltimore. Soon after this she was convicted for receiving stolen money in February 1821 and served eleven months in the Philadelphia penitentiary. After her release in January 1822, Carson determined to write and publish her story. The *History of the Celebrated Mrs. Ann Carson* is more than just a tell-all, name-all apology for an outrageous crime. It offers readers a window on the values and self-identity of the developing middle class in the new nation. Carson's *History* helps us see who they are by drawing a boundary around their likes and dislikes, fears and aspirations—some of which were shared with members of other social and economic groups.[6]

Identification and description of this segment of society that in the early nineteenth century was becoming culturally, economically, and socially dominant has challenged historians for some time. What exactly *was* the middle class? Being in the middle implies both a lower and an upper stratum. A very basic, economic distinction identifies the middle class as a group who needs to generate income through some kind of occupation. They are distinguished from the lower class because the middle class does possess some form of property—real estate, stock in trade, or professional credentials—that exempt them from manual labor.[7] Although this situation had existed in Europe and North America since at least the early modern era, the advent of industrial capitalism in the early nineteenth century began to crystallize these categories, making it more difficult for individuals to transcend one category to a higher one (and perhaps also facilitating the descent from above to below).

However, economic classification is only one of a variety of ways of locating the class position of a group or an individual. As Konstantin Dierks remarks elsewhere in this volume, culture or politics can also be the "means to activate class identity."[8] One mode of social organization may be of more use than another, depending on the time, place, and circumstances under investigation. The attributes associated with the middle class were not confined to the group of people who can be defined as such merely through either their wealth or their relationship to a means of production. As John Seed has said, "The specificity of context is crucial; which middle class, in what particular local or regional economy, shaped by what kinds of relations to other social classes, at what specific historical moment? Class, then, is not a matter only of this or that aspect of a group—size of income, type of occupation, life-style or whatever—but a shifting totality of social relations."[9] To be a member of the middle class in the early nineteenth-century United States meant one needed to possess material attributes: money, dress, and education, but also certain values and beliefs. Ann Carson's memoir takes inventory for us of many of these middle-class traits.

The middle class shared certain values with those beneath and above, and they appropriated certain behavior and prejudices from those above them on the economic and social scale. The middle class consciously sought to exclude those below from association or identification with themselves, as well to condemn some of the practices of those further up the social and economic scale.[10] It was this exclusion and criticism of social and economic inferiors that Carson used to identify individuals and groups who were not of her class. The comments she makes about behavior, dress, education, and speech—all markers that distinguished class—show us what was important to Carson and her readers.

The middle class developed its sensibility against a background of dramatic economic, social, cultural, and political circumstances in the late eighteenth and early nineteenth centuries. The proletarianization of workers pushed some individuals economically downward and kept others at the bottom. Yet this same transformation provided others with new relationships to the marketplace and allowed them to attain a measure of affluence that had not been available to them before. Economic forces facilitated the rise of artisans to merchants, bankers, or professionals. In many families, such as the Bakers and the Carsons, this happened in one generation. Ann Baker Carson's grandfather was a house carpenter in Britain. Ann's father, after coming to North America, served as an officer under Stephen Decatur's command during the Revolution. By the time of Ann's birth in 1785, he captained ships for a Philadelphia merchant and was able to keep his family "in a style suitable to his rank and fortune."[11] John Carson's grandfather was a barber who was able to educate his sons as professionals. Carson's father became a wealthy Philadelphia doctor who in turn provided his son with the means to become, as Ann's father was, a well-to-do ship's captain in the West India trade.[12]

The fortunes of another Philadelphia artisan family, the Merediths, exemplified these rapid economic and, equally importantly, domestic transformations. Jonathan Meredith, a successful tanner, began his career in the 1770s living above his shop. By the time he retired at the turn of the century, he had moved his residence away from the tannery and built several new homes in the city as rental properties and investments. Rather than training under their father in preparation to take over his business, Meredith's sons attended university and became professional men.[13] The Merediths were also at the vanguard of changing domestic relationships. Jonathan's wife, Elizabeth, contributed to the family's achievement of economic affluence and the opportunity for their children to become professionals and entrepreneurs rather than artisans. Elizabeth Meredith kept the tannery's books, supervised apprentices, and cared for boarders and her household. Meredith's daughters did none of these things. Instead, they attended the Philadelphia Young Ladies' Academy and socialized with other young men and women from middling and elite families. They married businessmen who did not expect their wives to contribute to the family income.[14]

A new set of social values concerning the activities and responsibilities of wives and mothers shaped the training, education, and expectations of such women. Elizabeth Meredith's life and work revolved around the family economy. Her daughters' did not. Meredith's daughter-in-law, Gertrude, was the wife of the president of the Schuylkill Bank and a founding member of the Pennsylvania Academy of Fine Arts. She ran her household and supervised her servants. Gertrude Meredith defined her domestic role as that of "an *attentive* wife, and a *good* mother—herein consists my ambition—I feel no other—it is the only pursuit I delight to labor in."[15] Gertrude Meredith was also very conscious of her own class status. She articulated this awareness through her comments on those she deemed her inferiors. After meeting a young woman who had married above her class, Meredith was thankful to have been "born a lady . . . I could scarcely keep from assuring her that I was fully sensible of her elevation and considered her now quite my equal." And she dissuaded her husband from sending their son to Mr. Brown's school on the grounds that it was made up of "little rag tags and bob tails," rather than boys of their own social station.[16] Thus through behavior, manners, and opinions, this class of men and women has left the modern observer with sufficient information to assess what was important to them, who they judged as belonging to their own class, and who they judged as *not* belonging. Their schooling, memberships in civic organizations and reform societies, and their literary interests illuminate their values.

Racism and nativism were common traits in white, native-born North Americans of all classes. But an antipathy to petty producers, the valuing of education and refinement, and an emphasis placed on individual responsibility, achievement, sentimentality, and maternalism were the ideals perhaps most directly associated with, and to a certain extent formulated by, the middle class itself.[17] Ann Carson used her *History* to confirm these values. Though Carson did not share Meredith's prosperity, she did embrace Meredith's values, beliefs, and prejudices. Hence, Carson's work is more than just a narrative of the events of a colorful life. It is a vade mecum to the social and cultural attitudes and ambitions of the North American middle class in the early nineteenth century.

Carson designed the form as well as the content of her narrative to appeal to her audience. As a literary text, the *History* would have been both familiar and enticing to an early nineteenth-century reader. An exposé of a scandalous series of events, Carson's book was a precursor to the fiction (in the form of dime novels) and nonfiction (penny papers such as the New York *Sun* and *Herald*) that attracted scores of antebellum readers.[18] The *History*, written soon after Carson's release from prison in 1822 on a house robbery charge, is a deliberately crafted document intended to entertain, shock, instruct, and gratify. In this regard, it belongs to the tradition of the "true-crime" story: narratives related by criminals themselves. There were many early North American gallows-side confessions and accounts readily available from the numerous booksellers and circulating libraries in Philadelphia and other cities of the eastern seaboard.[19] Carson had a rich body of crime narratives to draw on as she constructed the *History*. An immediate precursor to Carson's memoir was the *Sketch of the Life of the Notorious Stephen Burroughs* (Hanover, New Hampshire, 1798). Burroughs argued to his readers that his character put him at odds with social conventions and legal authority, insisting that his behavior was justified by circumstances. Carson explained her activities in a similar manner. She also followed Burroughs's lead by turning the tables on the legal system and its representatives: Burroughs apparently "regularly challenged the motives of his persecutors and the fairness of the legal proceedings undertaken against him."[20] Carson did likewise. This may have been merely Carson's denial of any wrongdoing, an interpretation of the law's pursuit as unjustified malice, rather than a reasonable attempt to curb illegal activities. Nevertheless, it must have been hard for readers to see a pistol-packing woman with accomplices, on her way to kidnap a governor, as innocent.

The *History*'s plot weaves together themes of duty, love, and betrayal—typical elements in popular eighteenth- and nineteenth-century sentimental fiction. In structure, style, and content, it closely follows the prescriptions of this literary genre, giving a twist to the tradition of crime narrative. This explains part of the appeal of her story to middle-class readers, who reveled in sentimental fiction such as *The Power of Sympathy*, *Charlotte Temple*, and *The Coquette*. These three books were among the most popular novels of the early republic, and they were all based on real-life scandals. Carson's autobiography was one step closer to reality than such stories, but it clearly shared many characteristics with these fictional depictions of actual events.[21]

Carson's *History* contains fainting spells, lovers' vows, duels, and drama. But it is also chock-full of attitudes and opinions that identify Carson's class. She wrote with pride of herself as a working woman, satisfied that she was "a useful and active member of society."[22] She recounted one occasion when her "spirit was aroused" when she heard a rather arrogant colonel from Virginia disparage a storekeeper. Carson haughtily replied to the colonel, "Hold, sir, I am but a *store-keeper*."[23] However, this pride came at a price: because Captain Carson had failed to provide the home and financial support she expected, Carson became the family's chief breadwinner. With china her husband procured on an earlier Asian trip, Carson opened a shop. She valued the financial independence her work brought her. Through her own efforts, she daily increased her little capital and added to her stock in trade. Later she made trips to Boston and New York to obtain supplies.[24] When the embargo, and then the War of 1812, curtailed the import trade, Carson resourcefully turned to supplying clothes for the military. She and her mother employed several women to do this. Though forced out of her expected domestic role, Carson's depiction of herself as a hard worker, and her self-praise for her ability to provide for her family, reflected the values of readers who themselves had made the jump from wage earner to independent producer. Ann Carson would have drawn the sympathy of her readers in her record of the downward spiral of her family's fortune: her husband was increasingly handicapped by his alcoholism, and Ann took over as head of the household. "He pursued this ill line of conduct for some time, till my patience was nearly exhausted; and, irritated by his imposition, in not only forbearing to make any provision for his family, but depending totally on me, I therefore gravely inquired one day, what he intended to do in future for his living? Adding, I could not afford to support him in idleness and daily intoxication." Like the early nineteenth-century merchants in Charleston discussed in Jennifer Goloboy's chapter, Ann Carson believed in the power of her own abilities to overcome adverse circumstances (such as a ne'er-do-well spouse) and to achieve economic success and financial security.[25] At least this is the way she portrayed herself. In fact, Carson's business acumen was not quite so sharp. In 1811, she asked the wealthy Philadelphia merchant Stephen Girard for a $1,000 loan in order to purchase more chinaware (she had overextended her credit with the local china wholesalers). Sometime thereafter, perhaps because Girard did not give her the loan, Carson spent time in the Prune Street debtor's prison.[26] The truth of her business affairs, and especially her dependence on generous cash infusions from other people, clashed with Carson's self-image of strength, initiative, and talent. Carson sought admiration, not contempt, from her readers.

Perhaps the more tenuous her grasp on middle-class status became, the more intent she was to distinguish herself from mechanics and shopkeepers "whose ideas soared not beyond the art of making money."[27] She claimed to place a different value on work than did these crass dwellers in the marketplace. The people she criticized valued the making of money for its own sake—as an end rather than a means to an end. Carson, in contrast, positioned herself as a genteel provider who worked out of necessity; she claimed, "[I] valued [money] for its utility alone, and was anxious only for sufficient to answer my purposes; this my store produced."[28] This was largely a distinction without a difference of course. Carson sought to retain for herself (and in the eyes of her readers) her status as a genteel middle-class woman. Her slide down the economic ladder robbed her of many of the outward markers of her class. Her words and her demeanor were the only means left with which she could prove her status.

Carson defined her class identity in part by her distinction between manual and nonmanual occupations. She disparagingly referred to an ignorant farmer as "Mr. Ploughshare" and deliberately contrasted the uncouth behavior of a plasterer whom she called a "man of mortar" and "Mr. Lath and Plaster" to the "civility" of a merchant "gentleman."[29] According to Carson, the judge who presided over her trial in February 1821 was unqualified for his station because of his profession. He was "a man of weak and superficial understanding." He lacked sufficient education to fill such an important civic role because he had spent his life "toiling for bread" as a hatter.[30] Carson was even less satisfied with the jurors, "men from the lowest grades of society, apparently ignorant and uninformed, consequently the slaves of prejudice."[31] She was not alone in her opinion. For example, in a short story published in the *Weekly Magazine of Original Essays*, "The Plague of the Learned Wife," a tradesman complains that his wife reads too much and bothers him with reading aloud passages containing "hard words." Her "bookish" interests also mean that she is of no help to him in his business. From the husband's point of view, there seems little to be gained from studying books: "According to my notion now, neither tradesmen, nor tradesmen's wives, nor any body belonging to them, have any business to talk like *skolards*."[32] This humorous mocking of the willful ignorance of tradesmen suggests a tacit understanding among the *Weekly Magazine*'s readership that education was one of the attributes that separated them from their economic and social inferiors.

Nor did Carson spare women in her class distinctions. She condemned those who failed to meet her standards of "politeness and feminine delicacy," such as two "witless" women she encountered on a boat ride from New York to Philadelphia: "One of these curious ladies was the wife of a grocer in Kensington, of the genuine Camptown breed and manners; ignorant as the tawdry finery with which she was profusely loaded; yet purse-proud, and wrapped in self-consequence."[33] The woman's manners and clothes indicated she was of a lower class. Her husband's occupation, though superficially similar to Carson's, was not by itself a marker of class. Acquisition of wealth was not a sufficient condition for middle-class membership—much depended upon what one did with it. Carson, though a storekeeper, had education and manners that distinguished her from the grocer's wife.

Indeed, Carson's notion of class, not surprisingly, had little to do with economics. She defended her middle-class identity despite her fall from prosperity. Although one needed to be raised in a family in which affluence could provide the means to acquire education and proper training, even without an income to support a genteel lifestyle, individuals such as Carson could indicate their class origins. According to Carson, many of her partners in crime came from "families of the first distinction, who, having squandered their patrimony, resort to illegal means to replenish their empty pockets, to procure those indulgences they have been accustomed to."[34] These men and women dressed, spoke, and behaved like middle-class North Americans. They did not forego the clothes, style, or living conditions they were used to. This situation highlighted one of the increasing dangers of urban life: the business, social class, and legitimacy of a stranger could not be known from her outward appearance. Carson and others used this anonymity to their advantage. With the proper clothes, manner, and sufficient amount of money, criminals could "pass" in respectable society; they preyed on others by exploiting social conventions and expectations.[35] As C. Dallett Hemphill has noted, manners were "gate-keeping devices to serve the cause of social exclusivity" for the middle and upper classes. There is no better example of this in

Carson's narrative than her social call on Dolly Madison. Carson looked, talked, and behaved like a middle-class woman and therefore gained access to the president's wife.[36]

The importance of clothing to maintain a middle-class identity is also highlighted by Carson's reaction to being forced to wear prison clothes, an act that removed the outward vestiges of her social standing. The prison authorities allowed her to wear some of her own things, and they put her in charge of selecting and repairing the female prisoners' wardrobe. Among the many criticisms Carson leveled at her fellow inmates was their inability to repair their clothes. She put this down to the women being "generally [from] the lowest grades of society, scarce one removed from Hottentots." Carson took it upon herself "to civilize and bring into some kind of order" these untidy individuals. To her surprise (but not to ours), she recalled, "Many of them hated me for the care I manifested for them, toiling all day to keep them decent and comfortable."[37]

Another reason for Carson's low opinion of her fellow inmates was the fact that a large number of them were black.[38] Most white nineteenth-century North Americans shared Carson's racism. Although Carson employed a black woman and talked fondly of the "faithful servant" whom Richard Smith had "emancipated from the horrors of slavery," her contact with black prisoners in the Walnut Street jail evoked virulent comments and behavior.[39] She was particularly disgusted by the dining arrangements. Carson complained that the women were seated "promiscuously, without any distinction of age or color." She watched as her fellow inmates caught their meat "in their fingers, and gnaw[ed] it like dogs, no knives or forks being then allowed them."[40] Carson refused to sit at a table with black women and asked to have them removed. Though she did not get her wish, Carson was able to persuade her jailers to force the women to sit at the lower end of the table. And she was repulsed by the religious hypocrisy of the black prisoners, whom Carson perceived as merely attempting to ingratiate themselves with visitors by "affect[ing] to feel the powers of religion to so violent a degree, that persons in their immediate vicinity were endangered by the surprising feats of agility they performed." Carson also complained that these women gave off "a noisome effluvia."[41]

Carson's unapologetic depiction of these women as coarse, dissimulating, and smelly may disgust the modern reader, but an early nineteenth-century white, middle-class reader would have agreed with Carson's opinions. For example, Carson related the following episode to exonerate herself from rumors that she was cruel: "In my walk from the prison to the court house, my sister Sarah Hutton in company, an impertinent black woman insulted me as I passed. Sarah having a parasol in her hand, struck her a smart blow in the face with it, and report has ever said that I beat a poor black woman unmercifully for only looking at me." Hitting a defenseless woman without provocation was wrong, but smartly cracking a social and racial inferior was not.[42]

In addition to racial prejudice, the *History* evokes religious and nativistic antipathies. Anyone not white, Anglo-Saxon, and Protestant was the target for Carson's spleen. The Catholics she encountered were written off as untrustworthy because they were "like the greater part of the ignorant Irish of that persuasion, *priest-ridden*."[43] She disparagingly commented on the greed, corruption, and incompetence of the politicians and members of the legal profession of immigrant origin. Carson claimed that the prosecuting attorney at her kidnapping trial, an Irishman, was drunk in the courtroom. Carson reserved the lion's share of her condemnation for Governor Snyder, of whom she noted, "Some of Simon Snyder's friends have said that he would have suffered death rather than commit an act derogatory to his dignity as governor; but those persons should have remembered that he was of mean spirit, and low [and immigrant] origin." Nor did she spare Snyder's wife. This "would-be fine lad[y]," whose conduct Carson complained was no better than that of servant girls, "ought to have been better educated, have more spirit, dignity, and respect for the office of her husband."[44] Carson was explicit about the motivations for the *History*'s publication: to exonerate herself from the malicious rumors about her character, and to make money.[45] Inflammatory comments like those about Snyder and his wife may well have been included for their shock (and money-making) value. But they may also have helped readers distinguish Carson's status from those beneath her.

The *History* works hard to justify Carson's class position despite the fact that she violated its norms. What she told readers she did have were refinement, delicacy, education, sensibility, morality (of sorts), and maternal feelings—all characteristics cultivated and valued by the middle class. Her robust racial and ethnic prejudices, and her disparaging remarks about artisans and the pretensions of their wives, would all have struck a chord with her readers. The *History* is also framed by assumptions about the private and public duties and obligations of men and women: Carson weighed her expectations of marriage and family life against the ideology of separate spheres. Though a series of circumstances denied her economic stability and a secure, affective family life, she nonetheless championed the values embraced by many of her readers. If anything, Carson proved how much she believed in these ideals when she exposed the deficiencies in her own family and the failure of first her father and then her husband as family providers.

Carson articulated a middle-class point of view, but whether such an audience enjoyed her work is unknown. In some ways, Carson was an equal opportunity offender. The *History* would certainly have titillated, but also affronted, a good many readers. The newspaper editor John Binns was among those who despised Carson's book. In his scathing review of it in the *Democratic Press*, he warned readers: "It is a reproach to our police that such a book is publicly advertised and sold in our city. Its details of crime, however glossed over, are calculated injuriously to effect [*sic*] the morals of young people."[46]

Carson's portrayal of herself as a victim was intended to justify her descent into the criminal world, but her abandonment of middle-class virtues—such as marriage and a legal means of earning a living—would have been condemned by the very people with whom Carson sought to identify herself. Comfortably situated men and women may have found unsettling Carson's account of the precarious circumstances that propelled her into financial distress and ultimately crime. Could they, too, lose their possessions and position in the blink of an eye? Or would her readers have felt self-congratulatory, assured that their lawful behavior, prudence, and self-control would save them from a similar fate?

Ann Carson was engaged in the project of positioning her class identity, and in the process she aids us in uncovering the boundaries of the early nineteenth-century middle class. Class position depends upon a degree of earning power. That earning power in turn maintains a certain level of material status: living quarters, dress, food, entertainment, education. In other words, commodities and consumption matter as much as production. Despite their "tawdry finery" as Carson described it, the Camptown ladies (and Governor Snyder's wife) were not middle class. They dressed differently, spoke differently, and behaved differently than Carson; they might have had more money than she did, but they did not do the right things with it.[47]

The fact that so many others claimed some of the same values as the middle class should not surprise us. After all, who would claim *not* to be honest, virtuous, and hardworking? But did they supervise others or labor with their own hands? Could they write a business letter? Did they know how to pour tea? Did they call their evening meal "dinner" or "tea"? These traits helped define middle classness in the early nineteenth century. Many of these characteristics no longer define the twenty-first-century middle-class person, but this mutability reinforces Seed's argument for paying careful attention to historical context. This is the value of Ann Carson's memoir—it helps us pinpoint the totality of class identity for her time and place.

Leases and the Laboring Classes in Revolutionary America

Thomas J. Humphrey

In April 1767, William Lowry leased approximately eighty unimproved acres for two lives, his life and that of his wife, Elizabeth, from Robert Livingston, Jr., the proprietor of Livingston Manor. He agreed to deliver annually a rent of twenty-five *schepples* of wheat, roughly fifteen bushels, and four "fatt hens" to the Livingstons' "Mansion House." Lowry also arranged to labor one day per year for the manor lord; clear at least two acres every year; build a barn; plant an orchard of one hundred apple trees; fence in the lot; maintain the roads near his leasehold; pay all taxes and assessments; pay six shillings per year to support a Protestant minister; and offer the manor lord the first chance to buy any produce the tenant may want to sell. Although tenants could never sell the land they rented, they could sell the improvements they made to the leasehold. If Lowry decided to sell the improvements, he had to clear the sale with Livingston, who would take as much as one-half the sale price. After paying off any debts to the landlord, the tenant would receive whatever remained.[1]

William Lowry was hardly unique. Over the course of the Revolutionary period, thousands of people moved into the American countryside without the capital necessary to buy land and became tenants.[2] In New York's northern Hudson Valley, for example, between 1769 and 1785 at least twenty-one hundred people signed leases for land on Rensselaerswyck, an estate of one million acres, and more moved onto the estate before the end of the century. One might expect such increases in the Hudson Valley, where tenancy predominated, but tenancy spread into western New York too. William Cooper prospered by making land available on credit. He offered tenants good land and long mortgages. While the land ultimately reverted to the farmers, Cooper had to act as landlord during the mortgage period, regularly pressing farmers to pay off their debts. And tenants moved onto the medium and smaller estates that dotted parts of Delaware, Schoharie, Ulster, Sullivan, and Greene Counties, and the Mohawk and Susquehanna Valleys.[3] Nor was the growth of tenancy specific to New York in the Revolutionary era. Tenancy thrived in parts of Maryland, Pennsylvania, New Jersey, South Carolina, Virginia, and even Massachusetts.[4]

The growth of land tenancy was critical to class formation. While few historians would deny that capitalism and industrialization in the nineteenth and twentieth centuries produced deleterious, class exploitative relationships, historians such as Gordon S. Wood have contended that "no classes in this modern sense yet existed" in early America. In so arguing, Wood and like-minded historians have created a kind of declension narrative for colonial America and capitalism in which they describe a glorious preindustrial past followed by the rise of democratic capitalism replete with class struggle, which, circularly, demonstrates both the strength of capitalism and the power of democracy. People only waged class conflict, they continue, because society was democratic enough to allow it and because people believed that they too could strike it rich. The Revolution acted as the tipping point. Samuel P. Huntington, however, reinterpreted for non-industrial societies Karl Marx's general theme that people in industrial societies divided over their relationship to capital—the goods integral to survival, profit, and the reproduction of surplus. He concluded that in agrarian societies such as early America property not capital served as the means of production. Of course, in early America, property took on two forms. Plantation owners relied on one kind of property, enslaved Africans, to extract agricultural raw materials from the other kind of property, land. Thus, in early America, people were separated according to their relationship to land, slaves, or both.[5]

In many respects, Huntington was rephrasing what John Locke had written nearly three hundred years before. In his *Two Treatises of Government*, Locke noted that labor on the land had given some men living in early modern England "a Right to Property." Some of these men subsequently obtained secure possession of "the Property which Labour and Industry began" through a "Compact and Agreement." For Locke, that "Compact," a paper title derived from a political authority, was the ultimate proof of legitimate ownership of property. In England at the time, however, some men owned property while many others did not and those who owned it were trying to legitimate their growing power in England and, specifically, in relationship to the monarchy. Viewed in that light, Locke's writings may be seen as a way propertied men justified their political power. For Locke, as for other enlightened thinkers, independent men owned property and were, as a result, best suited and most capable of ruling an ordered society. These men were least likely to use politics for personal gains. The opposite was also true: Men who did not own property were dependent and were more likely to use whatever political power they had at their disposal to better their economic conditions. According to Locke, men without property were best ruled by those men who owned it.[6]

Although a definition of class that divides groups primarily by their relationship to property and power may be helpful and instructive, it best serves as a starting point. People's relationship to the means of production in early America served as the basis for the common experiences and conditions that enabled them to see shared interests, experiences, goals, friends, and antagonists. These commonalities often emerged, and emerge, out of the formal and informal patterns of social, religious, and cultural behavior that characterized everyday life. Individuals drew on these commonalities—their shared relationship to property and power and their common experiences—to form themselves into a class. When they bonded over these similarities and used them to overcome, or at least to set aside, their dissimilarities while they pursued their common interests, they acted as a class. Class, then, is more than a relationship to the means of production. While based on people's relationship to property and power, class grows out of everyday human interactions spurred by similar lived experiences.[7]

Several chapters in this collection illustrate how people's relationship to property and power shaped their lives and daily interactions. Specifically, this and the following two chapters show how elite Americans exercised the political and social power they acquired by virtue of their property to structure the lives and deaths of poorer people in their communities. At the same time, these three chapters demonstrate how lower-class Americans struggled to make the best of societal conditions that were working against them. Gabriele Gottlieb, for example, demonstrates that capital punishment had a distinct class nature from 1750 to 1800, much as it does today. In fact, political elites reserved the power of life and death for themselves, and they used it to sanction their legitimate claim to authority. However elites applied it, poor people suffered the ultimate punishment far more often than wealthier people did. The stark differences in the fates suffered by people of different classes suggest that punishment, even for the same crime, depended on one's class. Similarly, Sharon Sundue reveals how political and social elites used the system of pauper apprenticeships to preserve class distinctions. Pauper apprentices were rarely taught a skill. Instead, they were simply an alternative form of unskilled labor that incipient industrialists relied on for production.

By the second decade of the nineteenth century, justices in Massachusetts were questioning the legitimacy of these arrangements but only if they threatened to degrade the child. If not, the contract stood, however cruel.

Pauper apprenticeships and Hudson Valley tenants contradict the conclusions of historians such as Paul A. Gilje and Howard B. Rock, who suggest that capitalism and industrialization created opportunities through exploitative relationships and that laborers in the post-Revolutionary United States were freer after they escaped the labor contracts that had bound and inhibited them in the precapitalist world. The burgeoning democratic capitalism of the new marketplace of the early republic "inevitably altered the world of the mechanic" in cities because "larger capital requirements made it more difficult for [journeymen] to become masters." For Gilje and Rock, the flirtatious girl, the rowdy male, the striking sailor, the upstart journeyman, the newly freed black, and even the new hardships they faced, were all products of the country and of the democratic capitalist society that emerged out of the Revolution. In the new United States, economic individualism and political individualism fed each other, and democracy and capitalism went hand in hand.[8]

These chapters also build on the work by historians such as Gary Nash and Billy G. Smith, among others, who have quite effectively shown the persistence of poverty and class-based power structures throughout the eighteenth century. For these historians, class formation and poverty were not products of either capitalism or changing relationships between craftsmen and journeymen inspired by the Revolution. Class bonds formed out of relationships to the means of production, material condition, race, and shared backgrounds and experiences. The Revolution may have affected the rhetoric of these processes but the motives behind them came from somewhere else. In this book, for example, Konstantin Dierks describes how a middle and upper class formed around a literature prescribing certain behavior. Moreover, while she outlines how onerous contracts shaped the lives of poor boys, Sharon Sundue likewise demonstrates how wealthier parents delayed their sons' entry into the workforce by keeping them in school, an advantage obviously not available to poor people. Much of this literature, however, focuses on urban workers and the urban experiential processes of class formation. However, the present chapter follows the advice Simon P. Newman gives in this book to look to the countryside, to farmers, to see class in early America.[9]

Newman's call for sharper studies of class formation in the countryside highlights how historians of rural America have focused primarily on freehold farmers during the Revolution. In doing so, they have linked republicanism and citizenship in the emerging country to owning a freehold, making republicanism dependant on an idealized community of freehold farmers. In that interpretation, the American Revolution becomes a changing force that propelled an independent yeomanry to the forefront of the emerging post-Revolutionary society. Thus, in the generation after the Revolution, yeoman farmers, either as members of a squatters' republic or as the mainstay of a republic of small farmers, flexed their political power enough to facilitate the rise of Jeffersonian leaders.[10]

Thomas Jefferson gave these historians plenty of reasons for that enthusiastic historical perspective. Jefferson and fellow Revolutionaries combined property ownership with citizenship to form a building block for political and economic autonomy in the new nation. Jefferson was a particular proponent of freeholders. In his *Notes on the State of Virginia*, he exhorted that the people "who labour in the earth are the chosen people of God." "Corruption of morals in the mass of cultivators," he continued, "is a phœnomenon of which no age nor nation has furnished an example." Quite fittingly, for Jefferson, these sons of the soil made the best rulers.[11]

Revolutionaries such as Jefferson highlighted the relationship between economic autonomy and political independence in large part because they based their authority in the new country on the connection.[12] Once they secured their brand of authority, Revolutionaries sought to expand their economic endeavors to implement the political independence they had recently won. To accomplish these goals, they had to outline the political institutions necessary for the full development of capitalism.[13] But that transition came at an ironic price. While the Revolution guaranteed the political liberty of a greater number of men in the new nation, fewer and fewer of them possessed the economic wherewithal to increase their capital resources and, thus, to succeed in national and international markets. To compete in these markets, in the first two decades of the nineteenth century, manufacturers and businessmen began freeing up available capital by cutting labor costs. Some hired day laborers instead of apprentices and journeymen. Others hired poor children. Sharon Sundue describes how that shift changed the lives of poorer children. The shift to wage labor resulted in a widening gap between employers and their employees, and it reduced laborers to commodities, turning workers into components in the process of production. In the democratic capitalist United States, laborers became labor and struggled to hold on to their autonomy. For those few people with capital, or access to it, the post-Revolutionary world offered expanding opportunities and greater access to political power; for those many people without it, post-Revolutionary society promised declining prospects.[14]

The impressive growth of tenancy in the Revolutionary era illustrates what was happening everywhere under capitalist development. More and more people, from artisans to dock workers to tenants, found themselves displaced from the means of production and pushed closer and closer to the edge of subsistence. This kind of class formation began before the Revolution as people with similar relationships to property grew increasingly aware of their shared position and common political and economic goals. But after the Revolution, the transition to capitalism accelerated and widened social gaps.

In the late colonial period, thousands of people like William Lowry moved into New York's northern Hudson Valley on the promise of good land for cheap and became tenants. Although several smaller estates dotted the valley, Livingston Manor and Rensselaerswyck dominated the region. The number of tenant households on Livingston Manor, an estate of 160,000 acres, increased from 50 in 1715 to approximately 460 by 1776, although unimproved land was still available. The number of tenant households on Rensselaerswyck exploded from 82 in 1714 to approximately 1,150 in 1776. There was plenty of room for more on the million-acre estate. Like William Lowry, most of these tenants promised to pay rent on time, to remit fees for services such as grinding grain or milling lumber, to offer any surplus goods to the landlord before going to market, and to remain peaceful. Any tenant who violated the conditions of the lease could face eviction. In return, lessees expected landlords to keep the peace and to grant them some latitude when circumstances kept them from paying rent.[15]

The two items common to every lease, the size of the lot and the amount of rent, varied considerably.[16] On Livingston Manor, approximately 90 percent of tenants rented between 60 and 160 acres; the average leasehold contained 112 acres. On Rensselaerswyck, nearly 90 percent of tenants leased between 75 and 180 acres, while the average tenant on that manor leased approximately 139 acres.[17] Once tenants made their lots productive, landlords expected them to begin paying rent according to the stipulations of their leases. Landlords generally expected tenants to pay between 10 and 20 percent of their total wheat production in rent, making wheat the dominant crop in the region. By the end of the colonial period, most landlords had moved away from defining rent in terms of a percentage of the crop and asked tenants to deliver a specific number of bushels of wheat per acre rented. The tactic enabled landlords to regularize their income and gave tenants the chance to plant their fields to meet their household needs and rent requirements. The

Van Rensselaers, however, did not calculate rent rates so precisely until the middle of the century. Early in the century, they required tenants to pay 10 percent of their wheat production in rent, but they raised rates in the 1760s when they determined that tenants should pay between ten to twelve bushels of wheat per one hundred acres. Similarly, by the late 1750s, the Livingstons required each tenant to pay approximately fifteen bushels of wheat per one hundred acres, making their rents the highest in the Hudson Valley.[18]

In any given year in the late colonial period, landlords collected enough rent to make them comfortable, if not rich. The Van Rensselaers, for example, collected one-half to two-thirds of the rent due and received, on average, between 750 and 1,400 bushels of wheat per year, which equaled between £260 and £490. They also collected a small mountain of other goods and services that must be added. Each tenant agreed to work one or two days per year on the manor to maintain fences and roads and to perform other odd jobs such as fixing tools or repairing the manor lord's house. Some tenants paid off part of their rent by laboring for the manor lord. All that labor had value. On the eve of the Revolution, the Van Rensselaers received approximately one thousand total days of labor from tenants, which was worth roughly £1,200.[19]

The Livingstons fared better. In the twenty-five years before the Revolution, they usually collected two-thirds to three-quarters of the rent due. Rent collection varied dramatically from year to year. In 1756, for example, Robert R. Livingston collected 1,450 bushels of wheat, worth approximately £365, from his tenants on Clermont, the southern part of the manor. Three years later, he collected 2,100 bushels of wheat worth roughly £735. In both years, he took in another £100 worth of hogs, hens, and labor. Such returns prompted Livingston to boast, "[It was not] improbable that I may be absolute [the] Richest Man" in all of New York.[20] His sentiment was more fact than swagger. From 1767 through 1775, tenants on Livingston Manor delivered an average of 3,443 bushels of wheat per year worth approximately £1,200 and provided another £500 in goods and services. In the last decade of the colonial period, the Livingstons earned approximately £1,700 per year in rent.[21]

Rent filled landlords' pockets, but they collected other fees that increased their incomes. Most landlords usually collected one-quarter of the first sale of the improvements a tenant made to his leasehold, and then one-eighth of all future sales. These quarter-sales fees, like rent, demonstrated to tenants that landlords ultimately controlled the land and reaped the biggest reward from it. Moreover, the stipulation gave landlords the chance to reject an undesirable person. In 1763, for example, John Robinson arranged to sell the improvements he had made to his leasehold to Johan Barhart Koens for £90. Robert Livingston, Jr., approved the deal only after he reviewed Koens's reputation. The landlord then collected the £90 from Koens, took £30 of it to cover the quarter-sales fee and Robinson's outstanding debts, and gave Robinson the remaining £60.[22]

Many landlords also restricted tenants' market activities by creating and then maintaining a monopoly over the services that tenant farmers needed. Tenants needed mills to grind their grain or to mill their lumber and stores for trading. Most landlords took advantage of those needs and stipulated that tenants mill their grain and lumber at facilities landlords owned. Some tenants invariably found the landlord's stores and mills convenient, but others hoped to find better prices and services off the manor and so chafed at the restrictions. The Van Rensselaers owned seven saw mills and three gristmills, which they rented to tenants. Robert Van Deusen, for example, paid a flat fee to run a gristmill. He earned money by charging tenants a small portion of the grain he ground for them, usually 10 percent. The Van Rensselaers paid, too, but only after Van Deusen milled one hundred bushels of wheat per year for them at no charge.[23] Although the Livingstons had built and improved their mills to meet the demands of the growing tenant population, Robert Livingston, Jr., worried that his family was losing money because they did not have enough of them. In 1765, he urged his family to build new mills "as fast as [they] could" to meet growing demands. The Livingstons charged tenants a tenth of whatever they milled for the service, so, even if the Livingstons milled only half of the approximately 48,000 bushels of wheat tenants produced annually from 1767 to 1775, they received nearly 2,400 bushels of wheat in fees, equaling roughly £840 in additional income per year.[24]

Rent, quarter-sales, and fees added up, and they made landlords some of the richest colonists. Conservatively, over the last ten years of the colonial period, the Van Rensselaers earned approximately £2,500 to £2,700 per year in goods and services from their tenants. Over the same period, the Livingstons took in roughly £2,500 worth of agricultural goods and services from their tenants.

Landlords turned that agricultural produce into merchant capital in the Atlantic market. How they did so demonstrates the importance of Hudson Valley grain and produce to transatlantic trade. In 1766, for example, the Livingstons shipped the flour ground from tenants' grain to Jamaica and Curacao, where agents working for and with the Livingstons traded it for European textiles, Jamaican molasses, olive oil, and oysters. The Livingstons' ships then carried these goods back to New York City and Albany, where the Livingstons and other merchants sold them to the region's more affluent customers and, less often, to tenants. Walter Livingston recounted a similar trade pattern the following year. Again, ships carried flour and lumber from Albany to New York City to Pensacola and, finally, to New Orleans, where merchants traded similar goods for barrels of cod, mackerel, and gun powder in addition to crates of Spanish handkerchiefs, Bermuda potatoes, chocolate, capers, cotton, and sugar.[25]

Landlords retained their position in that trade network in part by limiting tenants' market activities. Most of the leases issued by the Livingstons and Van Rensselaers usually required tenants to shop and trade at stores landlords owned and give landlords the first chance to buy surplus agricultural produce. Both maximized the movement of agricultural goods from tenants to landlords and inhibited tenants from trading off the manor. If tenants lacked the goods to trade at the stores or the cash to buy what they needed, landlords offered them credit. But when tenants used that credit to buy the goods they needed to survive, especially while they made their leaseholds productive, they went further into debt to their landlords. In 1749, Solomon Schutt, for example, signed a lease for land on Livingston Manor. The new tenant agreed "to grind his grain for own use on the Lessor's mill" and to "give the Lessor and his heirs the preemption of all grains and other Produce of the farm . . . Except what Leasees may want for his own Consumption & use in his family." Schutt signed a standardized lease that the Livingstons continued to use for the rest of the century. The Van Rensselaers required their tenants to agree to similar stipulations.[26]

Northern Hudson Valley landlords accumulated tenants' agricultural produce, sold it in the transatlantic market, and grew rich. They may not have been the wealthiest men or families in the British colonies, a title likely held by Caribbean sugar planters, but they were as wealthy as any group of men on the mainland, and landlords were fantastically wealthier than their tenants. In 1779, the estate claimed by Stephen Van Rensselaer's heirs (he died in 1769) was valued at approximately £19,000. John Van Rensselaer's portion of his family's land was valued at £10,000. Combined, the family's holdings totaled £29,000, roughly 110 times the value of the realty leased by an average tenant on Rensselaerswyck. Similarly, while the average tenant on Livingston Manor lived on realty valued at £127, Robert Livingston, Jr., owned real estate assessed at £30,000, or 240 times greater.[27]

Tenants could never aspire to the riches of their landlords, but they could at least hope to live like their freehold neighbors. And, in many cases, they did. Tenants and freeholders usually lived on similarly sized lots, and they had improved roughly the same proportion of their land. Not surprisingly, they lived on similarly valued lots. The average freeholder in the Hudson Valley owned land rated at approximately £228. Freeholders living in the neighboring regions of Kinderhook and Halfmoon, near Livingston Manor, owned lots worth £194 and £144 respectively, only a bit more valuable than the average leasehold on the manor. Some freeholders and a few tenants lived quite well. Some tenants even owned property off their leaseholds, while some wealthier tenants organized a dinner club to emulate the habits and lavish lives of their richer landlord neighbors. But, to be sure, these better off tenants were a minority. Most tenants and freeholders in the region lived uncomfortably close to the edge of subsistence and struggled to survive under sometimes harsh and oftentimes unforgiving conditions. Moreover, living like a freeholder, or even becoming one, hardly guaranteed unbridled material success or unshackled market participation. Participation in markets likely depended on networks of kin, friends, social obligations, and proximity, and, in a region dominated by landlords, freeholders in the Hudson Valley, like tenants, may have found their endeavors restricted or compromised too.[28]

These comparisons, however, also obscure fundamental class differences between freeholders and tenants. Although all farmers lived only a bad harvest or two away from poverty and they all struggled to produce enough for the household, tenants shouldered the additional burden of rent. They had to support their families and to provide a portion of the landlord's income. Worse, tenants quickly found themselves entangled in a web of debt to their landlords that inhibited their future endeavors. Landlords, after all, made certain that they, not tenants, reaped the long-term wealth and profits from tenants' labor because the land and any improvements tenants made to it—all of it—inevitably returned to the landlord. More significantly, landlords and freeholders, on one side, and tenants, on the other, related to property differently. Landlords may have owned far more property than yeomen, but they both owned land. Simply put, tenants did not. This bears repeating: tenants did not own the land they occupied and improved.

While the War for Independence threw the manorial economy and landlordism into turmoil as landlords' Revolutionary choices put their estates in jeopardy, it did little to alter what had become the traditional distribution of property and power in the Hudson Valley. The acreage owned by landlords in the southern Hudson Valley decreased significantly when

Revolutionaries sold off the estates of landlords turned Loyalists, and manor lords who became Revolutionaries faced mounting anti-landlord sentiment and threats to their estates from both the British and insurgent tenants. The state legislature further eroded landlordism by outlawing primogeniture, entail, and any existing feudal tenures. Despite these attacks on manorialism, the Van Rensselaers and the Livingstons held fast to their Hudson Valley estates. They did so by obtaining powerful seats in a state and federal political system they designed to inhibit the government's ability to attack property rights. After the Revolution, newly available land in the west eased tensions in the Hudson Valley by offering dissatisfied people the chance to start over, but not everybody moved. Many preferred to take their chances with landlords and stay on land they had worked for years rather than pit themselves against antagonistic Indians and roaming bands of British soldiers.[29]

Wealthier men, however, moved into western New York and established new estates beyond the Hudson and Mohawk Valleys. New proprietors, like Hudson Valley landlords, aspired to generate income from people working on their land. James Duane, for example, had accumulated approximately thirty thousand acres northwest of Albany before the Revolution. The land remained relatively unoccupied until after the war, when he began filling it with nearly 250 tenants. Similarly, William Cooper launched his estate and town roughly fifty miles west of Albany after the Revolution. Cooper mortgaged the land to settlers, but he acted as a landlord while the farmers paid off their debts. Even long-time landlords started new estates on the frontier, but they did not necessarily administer them the same way they operated their Hudson Valley estates. Chancellor Robert Livingston administered his family's Hudson Valley estate as his predecessors had. He was more willing to operate as a speculator in western New York, where he bought and then sold land to finance new endeavors. Livingston used some of that money to fund Robert Fulton's experiments that led to the steamship *Clermont*, which was named for a portion of the Livingstons' estate.[30]

Livingston invested in these ventures to offset declines in rent returns during the Revolutionary period. During the war, rent returns for Livingston Manor had decreased significantly, but every manor lord watched as rent payments declined. Rent returns on all the manors declined during the war. The amount of wheat paid to the Livingstons, for example, dropped from a high of approximately 3,680 bushels in 1774 to a low of 1,342 bushels in 1779, far below even the worst year in the decade before independence. Although that number started to increase slowly after 1779, the Livingstons did not

reach prewar income levels until the mid-1780s. The Van Rensselaers experienced similar declines.[31]

While landlords' incomes increased after the war in part because they
expanded their endeavors, rent returns increased because migrants began
moving onto the uninhabited regions of Livingston Manor and Rensselaerswyck. Like people who took leases before the Revolution, postwar migrants
sought good land at low rates, and landlords obliged with long, developmen-
tal leases, fairly good land, and comparatively low rent. In fact, the Livingstons and Van Rensselaers issued the same printed leases after the
Revolution that they had used before it. The Livingstons, for example, gathered up unused leases, scratched out any references to the king, Parliament,
or Britain and inserted more appropriate Revolutionary dates and references.
These new, post-Revolutionary tenants paid higher rent than earlier tenants—rent on Rensselaerswyck, for example, rose from roughly ten to thirteen bushels of wheat per one hundred acres—but they agreed to the same
stipulations. Like their predecessors, most postwar migrants who became
tenants did so because they did not have the money to buy a freehold. While
some of these migrants moved onto leaseholds vacated during the war, others took unimproved lots. In the roughly two decades after the Revolution,
the population of Livingston Manor increased from approximately 4,600
people to nearly 7,400. The same thing happened on Rensselaerswyck, but
more dramatically. Between 1779 and the end of the century, approximately
3,300 new tenants signed leases for land in the western and northern portions
of the manor.[32]

Some of these new tenants, and some older ones, may have erroneously
believed they could sell their improvements as one might sell a freehold, or
they thought, again incorrectly, they might eventually pay off the land and
get freehold title to it. If so, they were mistaken. The Van Rensselaers never
intended, and the leases did not imply, that tenants would ever own their
leaseholds. When Stephen Van Rensselaer flatly refused to get rid of the
quarter-sales stipulations after the Revolution, many tenants simply ignored
it. Reeve Huston rightly points out that "for the next three generations, many
tenants simply neglected to inform the manor office when they sold their
farms." The landlord or his agent would have assuredly learned that a new
tenant was paying rent, but the responsibility of informing the landlord of
the sale was the old tenant's. The Van Rensselaers could not justifiably pros-
ecute new tenants for violating the lease. In a survey of 768 leases that matured in the last twenty years of the eighteenth century, only 45 percent, 348,
changed hands with the landlord's knowledge. The rest, 55 percent, either

remained with the heirs of the original lessee, or the tenant or heirs sold off the improvements without telling the Van Rensselaers.[33]

Selling their improvements without telling their landlord was only one kind of tenant resistance. James C. Scott has theorized that this kind of resistance demonstrates that exploited people rarely if ever completely consented to their exploitation. Instead, they resisted it. Some tenants, for example, probably refused to grind their grain or mill their lumber at mills owned by the manor lords. Others failed to pay rent, some because they could not and others because they would not. Finally, some tenants resisted tenancy and landlordism more aggressively. Even though landlords ultimately held the upper hand in the relationship, unruly and rebellious tenants likely utilized these acts of noncompliance as a way to negotiate for more power, agency, or both in a region dominated by landlords.[34]

In 1747, tenants resisted the Livingstons' attempt to fleece them by offering less than the market value for wheat. The incident started when Philip Livingston ordered Peter DeWitt, who operated one of the stores on Livingston Manor, to offer tenants only 3s per bushel of wheat when the market price was 3s 3p. Tenants who had regularly traded at the store also knew the going market price for wheat and refused to sell. Livingston retaliated by threatening to evict them. The tenants again balked, threatening to let their wheat rot rather than be cheated. The manor lord finally gave in and bought the wheat at market price. The Livingstons, however, simply gave up one kind of swindle for another. In the 1750s, another store operator, Charles DeWitt, boasted that he sold earthenware to tenants for at least a 70 percent profit, and at a far higher price than tenants could have bought it off the manor.[35]

Tenants resisted landlordism more overtly and more regularly by refusing to pay rent, the activity that epitomized the landlord-tenant relationship. While many tenants could not pay rent because they suffered during the war, many other tenants took advantage of the chaos of war to stop paying rent. During the war, Stephen Van Rensselaer and his family watched anxiously as rent returns plummeted, but they expected them to rebound once the war moved out of the Hudson Valley in the late 1770s. They were disappointed. Rent returns increased slightly, but they did not return to prewar levels as fast as the Van Rensselaers had hoped. By the time Stephen Van Rensselaer became manor lord in 1785, he felt it necessary to compel delinquent tenants to pay what they owed. In fact, on the day of his twenty-first birthday, when he officially took over as manor lord, Van Rensselaer warned delinquent tenants that if they did not pay up, he was going to sue them. While he worried about collecting what tenants already owed him, Van Rensselaer was as worried about future debts. He knew that many people who had signed leases in the late 1770s and 1780s had not started paying rent when their leases matured and might not ever pay unless forced to. Some of these tenants, however, clearly could not pay. They had not made their farms productive, or they had not recovered from the war yet. While these tenants bothered Van Rensselaer, he was far more concerned with those tenants who flatly refused to pay. Regardless of how often or seriously he threatened them, these dissidents rebuked him at every turn, and the new manor lord spent the ensuing decade hounding them.[36]

By the early 1790s, Van Rensselaer's hard tactics started paying off and tenants were settling their debts. Although rent payments fluctuated for the rest of the century, Van Rensselaer usually collected approximately three-quarters of the rent due and his income skyrocketed. In 1792, for example, Van Rensselaer received 13,925 bushels of wheat (worth approximately £4,800), 2,226 fowls, and 550 days of labor from his tenants. The following year, he received 14,893 bushels of wheat, 2,362 hens, and 581 days of labor from his tenants. Four years later, in 1797, his income rose to 25,216 bushels of wheat, 4,342 hens, and 1,075 days of labor from tenants. Even though he collected only a portion of the rent owed to him from 1792 to 1797, usually roughly one-half to three-quarters, Van Rensselaer's income rose from approximately £4,800 to £8,000. Despite these returns, unpredictable weather and poor crops conspired to keep tenants from paying rent regularly, and most continued to owe a year or two in back rent. Van Rensselaer, like other manor lords, was usually willing to overlook these problems if a tenant otherwise paid rent consistently.[37]

Philip Schuyler tried a less onerous approach to encourage recalcitrant tenants to pay rent. Although Van Rensselaer met with limited success, Schuyler's attempts to get tenants to pay led to murder. Schuyler managed the part of Claverack that belonged to his wife, Catherine, the daughter of John Van Rensselaer. The region contained the notoriously unruly towns of Hillsdale (formerly Nobletown) and Spencertown, where, according to Schuyler, many of the tenants in the region had not paid rent since the war; others had not paid in decades, if ever. By the time Schuyler called on them to pay their back rent, it was plain that many of these tenants intended never to pay rent again. To Schuyler's credit, he recognized the limited potential for earning profits from these tenants, so he offered them two choices. Any tenants who wanted to stay on the land they had improved could buy it from him for 18s per acre with a five-year mortgage and the cancellation of all back rent. Those tenants who could not afford to buy their land could eradicate all rent in arrears by paying one year's rent. Schuyler considered these conditions gracious because they resembled, and in many ways bettered, the stipulations put on tenants who bought land confiscated from Loyalists in the southern valley. Thus, he believed that most of the disgruntled people would take the deal. He was wrong; most refused to pay him anything for land that they thought should be theirs anyhow.[38]

Angered at such open refusal, Schuyler decided to take stronger measures. In the middle of October 1791, Schuyler directed the deputy sheriff of Columbia County to appraise John Arnold's farm, to evict Arnold and his family, and to auction the improvements they had made to the land. Arnold had not paid rent in years, if ever, and had emerged as a notorious rioter and a known leader of rural insurgents. When the deputy sheriff arrived at Arnold's farm, he noticed that many of the local inhabitants had already "assembled and with threats deterred the deputy" from following Schuyler's orders. A few days later, the sheriff, Cornelious Hogeboom, visited Arnold's farm with his relative Stephen Hogeboom, who as a county judge. While these men waited for another deputy to deliver the eviction papers, disgruntled rural people began congregating ominously in nearby woods. The sheriff and his party wisely tried to leave, but Arnold, incensed that his farm was being sold from under his feet, drew his pistol and fired into the air. At the signal, thirty to forty men with painted faced rushed from the woods and chased the sheriff and his companions.[39]

The rioters rode and ran around the clearing, shouting at the sheriff and his posse and shooting their guns into the air in the hopes of convincing the sheriff and his men from selling Arnold's farm. The maneuver worked, and the sheriff and his posse began to disperse. John Arnold and Thomas Southward, however, had far more sinister motives. They trapped the sheriff and Southward shot him in the chest, killing him. Stephen Hogeboom and the other men retreated to the nearby town of Hudson, where they organized a posse to capture the rioters, most of whom had retreated to Peter Showerman's farm. Hot on the rioters' heels, the posse captured thirteen men, who were later charged with felonious rioting and second-degree murder. It took the posse weeks to ferret Arnold out of his hiding place, and the posse captured Southward at much the same time. The court charged Arnold with rioting, but it charged Southward with capital murder, indicating that he and not Arnold had shot the sheriff. Four rioters, however, escaped capture by boarding a boat headed for Nova Scotia, the primary destination for the rural lower sort who had sided with the British during the Revolution. They chose resistance, violence, and then migration to Canada over living as subordinates in a manipulative socioeconomic relationship.[40]

A study of landlord-tenant relationships in the northern Hudson Valley reveals the exploitative nature of tenancy in the eighteenth century. In addition, it demonstrates that comparisons of an exploitative post-Revolutionary capitalist economy with a paternalist precapitalist colonial past can no longer stand. Tenancy was always exploitative, and it remained so until the system collapsed in the 1840s. Throughout it all, landlords prospered by profitably expropriating and then selling the agricultural goods produced by their tenants. They turned their economic standing into authority by creating and maintaining gross inequalities in access to, and use of, property, markets, and power. In New York's northern Hudson Valley, independence for some depended on suppressing the liberties of others.

Although this chapter explores various conditions of tenancy and highlights the growing number of tenants who lived in the countryside during the Revolutionary period, it also hints at a more complex understanding of the Revolution. If independence, or happiness for Jefferson, depended on the ownership of property, and most reasonable men of the time presumed that it did, the increasing number of tenants raises complex questions regarding the politically radical nature of the Revolution. What could independence based on property ownership mean to those people throughout the countryside who did not own the land they inhabited and improved? The answers to those questions and concerns will encourage historians to reexamine the Revolution, the society that waged it, and the nation that emerged from it. More than that, I hope they will persuade historians to abandon a strictly top-down approach, to define independence more inclusively rather than less, and to incorporate the ways local events and groups of lower-sort Americans shaped a radical revolution of their own.

Finally, this chapter and those by Gottlieb and Sundue demonstrate how people's relationships to property and power shaped people's lived experiences during the Revolutionary period. Taken together, they illustrate the power of analyzing history through the lens of class and class struggle. While some historians have described class formation in the Revolutionary era, many of whom have contributed to this book, they have heretofore only succeeded in pressing the authors of the master narrative, which largely ignores class and class struggle, to alter their stories slightly or, worse, to add another box for "the poor" on the margins. That perspective, the legitimacy of it, can no longer be ignored. This book acts as a clarion call for dismantling the prevailing top-down, American-exceptionalist narrative that dominates the literature. In its place, we can construct a far more inclusive narrative that questions the legitimacy of the polarization of wealth and power inherent in democratic capitalism, and that incorporates the stories of, among, others, prisoners, pauper apprentices, and tenants.

13

Class and Capital Punishment in Early Urban North America

Gabriele Gottlieb

In 1769, Dolly and Liverpoole were burned at the stake on the green in front of the Charleston workhouse. Dolly was convicted of poisoning her mistress's child and attempting the same on her master. Liverpoole, a "negro doctor," supplied the poison. Four years later, twenty-one-year-old Levi Ames, condemned for burglary, "was turned off just at four o'clock" in front of a "vast concourse of people, who attended this awful scene, supposed to consist of seven or eight thousand people." In 1789, five "wheelbarrow men"—convicts sentenced to public labor—were hanged in Philadelphia. They had escaped from prison and killed a person while burglarizing a house.[1] These offenders numbered among the more than two hundred people who were executed in Boston, Philadelphia, and Charleston during the second half of the eighteenth century. Most were young, poor, and male (although a few were women). Many had knocked about the Atlantic World, mostly working as slaves, sailors, soldiers, laborers, and artisans. All were hanged, gibbeted, shot, or burned at the stake.

The nature of criminality and situations in which officials deal out the harshest punishment of execution reveal a great deal about every society. The activities defined as "criminal," the manner in which lawbreakers are treated, and the vigor with which certain infractions are prosecuted reflect what communities (or at least those exercising authority) value most or prize least. Crimes against property (such as burglary), for example, suggest something different about a society than do crimes against people (such as assault). The characteristics of the executed likewise reflect the class that wields power. In early North America, the white lower classes and black people were much more likely than merchants or ministers to be put to death for their misdeeds. In addition, most of the capital offenses involved crimes against property.

An execution was meant not only to achieve retribution and justice but also to maintain social control over poorer classes by wealthier groups. Authorities applied it to restrain the behavior and actions of working people, whether bound or free. Local conditions in early urban centers, especially the ways in which the labor force was organized, shaped the application of the death penalty: the higher the proportion of forced labor, the higher the execution rate. Reflecting the social control aspect of the death penalty, officials in Boston, Philadelphia, and Charleston (the three cities considered in this chapter) designed execution rituals that would build community cohesion and uphold social order. Judges and juries used capital punishment more frequently in times of crisis, either perceived or real, while its implementation tended to decline in moments of relative social tranquility. A relatively high number of executions occurred in the mid-1780s, for example, when many laboring people in the newly independent nation experienced extreme economic hardship, unemployment, and poverty. Shays's Rebellion intensified the fear of social upheaval and threats to property among the country's ruling elites. An expanded use of the death penalty enabled them to maintain and strengthen the power and authority of their class.[2]

The protection of property likewise was vital in capital cases. In nearly two-thirds of the cases in the second half of the eighteenth century, officials executed people for offenses against property.[3] The percentages of executions for property crimes were especially high immediately after the Revolutionary War: 95 percent in Boston; 67 percent in Philadelphia; and 69 percent in Charleston. As Thomas Humphrey argues in the previous chapter, power and authority in the newly founded nation relied on the relationship between economic autonomy and political independence. How to discipline labor—free or bound—and how to protect private property thus became a dominant agenda of the courts.

In the late morning hours of May 9, 1800, the pirates Peter Lacroix, Joseph Baker, and Joseph Berouse, dressed in white and accompanied by two ministers, were "brought from the prison by civil officers, and conducted in a cart to Market-street wharf." After winding their way past curious crowds in Philadelphia's streets, they stepped into a boat to be conveyed to the place of execution, an island in the city's harbor. Arriving "at the fatal spot, the prisoners kneeled down, and after some time spent in prayer, . . . they were prepared for the conclusion of the awful scene." Before they were "launched into eternity, in the view of an immense concourse of spectators, who crouded the wharfs and the shipping," all three asked "the world to forgive them." An hour after the hanging, "their bodies were put into coffins and buried near the gallows."[4]

This scene exemplifies the basic structure of the execution spectacle in early North America: the "parade of death" from the prison to the place of execution; the presence of civil and religious officials; the address of the crowd by the condemned; and the burial in an unmarked and eventually unknown grave.[5] Execution days were the pinnacles of capital punishment, demonstrating ultimate state power—the taking of a human life—in a carefully staged ceremony in front of a large crowd. Authorities designed the day's lessons to build community cohesion and to reinforce principles of social discipline and morality. Even when authorities pardoned condemned people, the reprieve frequently (and purposefully) arrived only after they stood for a while with a rope around their necks. In May 1764, for example, William Autenreith, John Williams, and John Benson reached the place of execution in Philadelphia together. Benson was pardoned, but not until "the others were turned off, having gone through all the Solemnity of that dismal Scene, being blind folded, tied up, as he imagined, and about to step into Eternity" with the others.[6] Waiting to the last moment provided authorities with the "benefits" of the ritual of punishment without the deadly end, turning a moment of ultimate state power into one of mercy and forgiveness. The relationship between executions and pardons is essential in understanding the functioning of capital punishment. As the historian Douglas Hay argued about criminal law in eighteenth-century England, it was one of the ruling class's chief ideological instruments, embodying "majesty, justice, and mercy." Its effectiveness lay in its inconsistency, including its frequent pardons, mitigation by juries, and reductions of sentences to lower penalties.[7] Criminal law in British North America, especially concerning the death penalty, functioned in a similar fashion, allowing authorities to prevent or counter possible community opposition to an execution and to present the representatives of the state as merciful and forgiving.

In the eyes of authorities and of those who wrote about the spectacle of death, the behavior of the condemned was the central aspect of an execution, since the day's "success" could rise and fall with that moment. Officials expected the condemned to address the assembled crowd by confessing to a sinful life, warning spectators against making similar mistakes, and confirming the fairness of the death sentence. In 1752, for example, John Webster "made no confession till he was under the Gallows," but he then admitted to several robberies in the Philadelphia area. Two decades later, Smart (first name unknown) confessed while standing with a rope around his neck that he was "guilty of the Murder and Robbery . . . and acknowledged the Justice of his Sentence." In 1788, William Rogers, who was about to be hanged for piracy, declared under the gallows that he "only hoped that his unhappy fate would produce the effect of deterring others from committing similar offenses."[8]

At times, such last minute declarations and confessions created more anxiety and discomfort among authorities and spectators rather than the hoped-for tranquility and safety meant to follow a confirmation of state power. When Robin, a South Carolina slave, was gibbeted for the murder of his master in 1754, "till within an Hour before he expired, [he] constantly declared his Innocence; but at last confessed." Robin stated "that he himself had perpetrated the Murder" but "at the same Time disclosed [a] Scene equally shocking"—a conspiracy among several slaves. Robin and eight other slaves apparently had planned "the Murder of two other Gentlemen in Beaufort" and then "they were to have taken a Schooner" to get to St. Augustine in Florida.[9]

Declarations of innocence or the mocking of the execution ritual also seriously undermined the authorities' claim of legitimacy and justice in taking a human life. Richard Wheldon, who was executed for burglary in 1753, steadfastly "declared himself innocent of the Fact for which he was to suffer."[10] Sally Arder, who was hanged for murder in 1795, "persisted to the last in declaring herself to be innocent of the crime for which she suffered, and forgave those whom she said had been the cause of her unjust condemnation."[11] While standing under the gallows in Philadelphia, "One-Armed" Tom Robinson, who was hanged for highway robbery in 1784, confessed "he was the man who had committed the rape and murder of a young woman on the Gray's ferry road" several years earlier. He boasted that he watched the execution of an innocent man for that crime while he "picked a drover's pocket of a large sum of money." After his declaration of guilt, Tom continued to mock the spectacle, turning to Peter Brown, one of his accomplices, and asking him with a smile, "Don't you think after we get there (pointing downwards) we can manage to bilk the Old Fellow and get out again?"[12]

Officials worried about more than the behavior of the condemned. The crowd's emotions and actions were likewise beyond the control of officials and difficult to predict. On many occasions, authorities ordered local militia or other troops to accompany the death parade and to be present at the gallows.[13] A poem written a few days before the execution of Levi Ames for burglary in 1773 expressed concerns about the crowd's possible behavior at the gallows:

See! round the Prison how they Throng
From every Quarter pour;
Some mourn with sympathizing Tongue
The ruder Rabble roar.[14]

Often, the spectacle evoked empathy and pity from the crowd. When two young men were hanged in South Carolina for stealing horses, "their contrite behavior . . . drew tears from the eyes of most spectators."[15] At the executions of Thomas Rogers and James Harvey in 1787, "the heart-rending sight of four young men"—two of them were pardoned—"preparing to bid adieu to time and mortal life, occasioned most spectators to shed tears." Despite this obvious affection for the condemned, and perhaps reflective of tensions against the wealthy, "some hardened offenders picked several gentlemen's pockets."[16]

Some executions met with open resistance by members of the community. In 1756, the hanging of Owen Syllavan had to be postponed twice in New York; the first time was "for the Want of a Hangman" and the second resulted from "the Gallows being cut down on Friday Night by Persons unknown."[17] In Albany in 1773, John Wall and two other counterfeiters escaped and, after being recaptured, barricaded themselves in prison. Their execution required that "the Militia and the whole City [be put] under Arms."[18] When John Dixon was hanged for burglary in 1784, "a considerable number, chiefly of the populace, manifested their doubts and dissatisfaction concerning the lawfulness of the intended execution," announcing "that it would be a murderous bloody deed."[19] Moreover, an execution did not necessarily mean the end to resistance. In Chester County, Pennsylvania, "some infatuated adherents of the noted James Fitzpatrick, lately executed . . . for highway robbery, have killed the horses, and set fire to a hay stack of Mr. McAfee," who had captured Fitzpatrick.[20]

The ritual of capital punishment displayed shaped early North American culture beyond the execution day itself. E. P. Thompson, describing gentry-plebian relations in eighteenth-century England as a "societal field-of-force," noted that the symbolic expressions of power and protest were of enormous importance. Execution days represented a moment when rulers asserted their control. However, the poorer classes, using the same rituals, often engaged in a countertheater of "ridicule or outrage against the symbolism of authority."[21] The gallows were a significant representation of power in urban North America as well, and they attracted threats and mocking by North American crowds, especially during the turbulence of the Revolution and the creation of a new nation.

Popular protests often imitated closely the culture of punishment displayed on an execution day, including the parade of death. In August 1765 during the Stamp Act controversy, a "considerable Number of People" assembled in Annapolis, Maryland, "to shew their Detestation of, and Abhorrence to, some late tremendous Attacks on LIBERTY," hanging a local official in effigy:

> They curiously dressed up the Figure of a Man, which they placed in a One Horse Cart, Malefactor-like, with some Sheets of Paper in his Hands before his Face: In that Manner they paraded through the Streets. . . . When they proceeded to the Hill, and after giving it the MOSAIC LAW, at the Whipping Post, placed it in the Pillory; from whence they took it and hanged it to a Gibbet . . . and then set Fire to a Tar Barrel underneath, and burnt it . . . By the Many significant Nods of the Head, while in the Cart, it may be said to have gone off very penitently.[22]

Similar protests occurred in other major cities. In Boston, on August 14, 1765, "a Great Number of people assembled at Deacon Elliotts Corner . . . to see the Stamp Officer hung in Effigy, with a Libel on the Breast, on Deacon Elliot's tree & along side him a Boot stuffed with representation, which represented the Devil coming out of Burk."[23] Some crowds combined tarring and feathering with a "visit" to Boston's gallows. On January 25, 1774, John Malcom was put "into a Cart" and the people "Tarr'd & feathered him." They then carried him "thro' the principal Streets of this Town with a halter about him, from thence to the Gallows & Returned thro' the Main Street making Great Noise & Huzzaing."[24] In 1766, during a confrontation between the local stamp officer Henry Van Schaak and a popular crowd in Albany, New York, someone posted a note on Van Schaak's door to meet with the Sons of Liberty. Underneath the note, another piece of paper was pinned on the door, displaying "gallows with a figure drawn in imitation of a man hanging" with the words "The just fate of a traytor."[25]

These episodes demonstrate that the lessons of capital punishment and the symbolism of the theater of death were understood and exploited by all classes in early North America. While the state literally used its ultimate power to take life, the popular classes employed the ritual of punishment to threaten although rarely to kill local officials. Hanging and burning effigies of people in power suggested a vision of a social order turned on its head, with the powerful on bottom and the marginalized on top. During the protest leading up to the Revolution, crowd actions targeted British officials primarily (although not exclusively). Gatherings of people employed similar protests against American elites in the early years of the new nation. Ironically, some of the wealthy Revolutionary leaders who may have supported hanging British officials in effigy subsequently found models of themselves swinging from the popular gallows. In March 1790, for example, six effigies appeared in Charleston, two in place of a statute of William Pitt that had been "removed from his old place of residence." The other four dummies, "said to represent some of the Delegates of Congress, whose political principles did not coincide in opinion with the freemen of Charleston" were, telling, placed "before the Exchange" that symbolized the rich and powerful residents of the city.[26]

Even as authorities in Boston, Philadelphia, and Charleston used executions as a common means to exert the hegemony of the ruling classes, local differences and variations over time characterized capital punishment in the three Atlantic ports. Based on both the absolute and the per capita rate, Boston executed fewer people than did Philadelphia or Charleston.[27] Boston's authorities did not put any criminals to death during the War for Independence, distinguishing them from officials in the other two cities. In the 1790s, advocates of prison reform and the abolishment of the death penalty successfully halted executions in Philadelphia for a decade, even as executions elsewhere rose.[28] The race of the executed was more important in Charleston, where the death penalty, both legal and extra-legal, helped to support slavery as well as to keep lower-class whites in line. Charleston also stands out for a higher number of women who suffered execution. White females drew mercy from officials in New England and the mid-Atlantic that black women did not enjoy in the South Carolina port.

Twenty-one men and two women went to the gallows or faced the firing squad in Boston during the second half of the eighteenth century. While six of the executions occurred during the third quarter of the eighteenth century, none took place during the American Revolution. More unified across the classes than Philadelphia and Charleston in their resistance to Britain and owing to the city's evacuation, Boston may have perceived little advantage in using capital punishment during the war. Executions increased dramatically in the five years following the war, as class tensions grew out of the severe economic depression in the region.[29]

Besides being primarily male, Boston's executed were relatively young (an average age of twenty-six) and mostly poor. Their occupations placed them among the lower classes. There were ten laborers, five mariners, two soldiers, a bricklayer, and a slave. The race of people put to death is more difficult to determine since it is often not specified in the records. Judging from the available evidence, three-quarters were white and one-quarter were people of color.[30]

Many of the condemned were transients who had seen a good deal of the Atlantic World. John Bailey, who was hanged for burglary in 1790, was born free in New York. At the age of six, he boarded a ship and began a (short) lifetime of traveling around the Atlantic, sailing to St. Lucia, Ireland, and Liverpool. He arrived in Boston and bound himself "apprentice to Mr. *Joseph Homberry*, tailor-chandler," but he soon ran away and was shortly after sentenced to death at the age of nineteen.[31] Born in France, John Baptist Collins became a cooper's apprentice in Holland at the age of sixteen. Collins may have been sold to the East India Company, since his "Master . . . makes a Practice of sel[ling] them [slaves] for Soldiers or Sailors [to the] *East India Company.*" According to his dying confession, Collins had sailed to the East Indies and had also spent some time at the Cape of Good Hope. On one voyage, he met his accused accomplices, Emanuel Furtado from Portugal, and Augustus Palacha from Italy. In 1794, all three were executed for murder and piracy, allegedly committed on a voyage to Boston.[32]

Rich and powerful Bostonians, not surprisingly, were concerned with protecting private property. Thus, offenses against materials goods were most frequently the cause for a death sentence and subsequent execution. Fourteen people were found guilty of property crimes, and three others for a combination of personal and property offenses. Four people were executed for murder, while two soldiers died by a firing squad for their military misconduct (see fig. 1).

The protection of property as a priority in capital cases is likewise reflected in the prosecution patterns in the Boston's Superior Court of the Judicature.[33] Of the 715 cases prosecuted between 1750 and 1794, 74 percent involved property crimes and 13 percent concerned personal crimes such as murder and assault. Conviction rates further confirm the significance of property in criminal cases: 80 percent of defendants in cases involving property offenses were found guilty, but only 46 percent were convicted in cases involving a personal crime. Of the 48 murder charges, the court convicted only 11 defendants, most for manslaughter. Just 3 cases resulted in death sentences. By contrast, 15 of 191 accusations for a capital property crime such as burglary, robbery, and counterfeiting resulted in the defendant's condemnation, and 11 of those eventually ended in death. Once condemned of a capital crime, defendants rarely survived: 78 percent of them ended their lives on the gallows.

Philadelphia's officials executed nearly five times more people than did

FIG. 1. PROPORTION OF EXECUTIONS IN BOSTON BY NATURE OF CRIME, 1750–1800

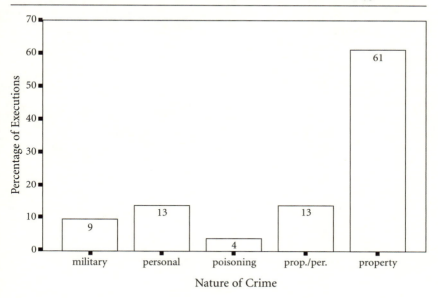

Boston's authorities during the second half of the eighteenth century. Ninety-seven men and two women suffered death by hanging or by firing squad. The number of deaths varied between one and four each year in the late colonial period, but the number increased dramatically during the Revolutionary War, when forty-one people were slain. Nineteen more people died between 1784 and 1789, when a moratorium on capital sentences began. Another three Philadelphians lost their lives in 1800, when issuing the death penalty resumed.[34]

Condemned Philadelphians resembled condemned Bostonians: they were disproportionately male, young, white, and poor. Their age averaged twenty-six, and most were in their early twenties when they participated in the parade of death. Officials identified five of the executed as "black" or "mulatto," and the remainder mostly likely hailed from Euro-American backgrounds.[35] Of the thirty-five people with known occupations, there were ten soldiers, nine laborers, six servants, five artisans, three mariners, and two slaves. Most of these men and women undoubtedly were poor, living at or below subsistence. They drifted in an out of the city's underground economy, "supporting themselves and Family," according to one account,

FIG. 2. PROPORTION OF EXECUTIONS IN PHILADELPHIA BY NATURE OF CRIME, 1750–1800

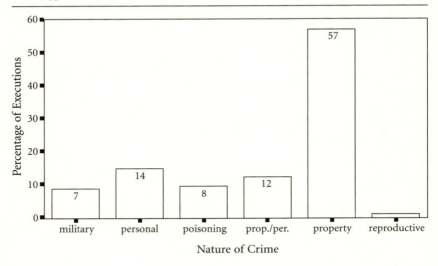

"chiefly by Pilfering and stealing for many Years."[36] If they were like other poorer Philadelphians, they were haunted by the specter of poverty and frequently were pushed onto the public and private charity rolls. At times, they relied on illegal activities to obtain the necessities of life. Still, two affluent Quaker artisans, a miller and a carpenter, were hanged as traitors during the Revolution, while a doctor and a tavern owner also experienced the same fate.[37]

Executions for property crimes were frequent in Philadelphia (see fig. 2), as they accounted for two-thirds of the offenses. Unlike in Boston, political transgressions were also important, accounting for one of every nine executions. The prevalence of property crimes among executions in Philadelphia is duplicated in the records of the Superior Court; two-thirds of those cases involved property damage.[38] The justice system once again supported the values of wealthier people—the ones most likely to be concerned with the protection of property—by threatening those types of indiscretions with death.

Contradicting the idea that slaves were relatively well protected from execution by the state because they were private property, most of the people executed in Charleston were black bondpeople. Race was vital to the decisions about whom to execute in Charleston, since slavery was so central to southern society. Maintaining racial order overlapped with controlling the lower classes in general, whether black or white. Authorities hung or burned nearly one hundred people in Charleston during the second half of the eighteenth century. The number of executions was elevated at mid-century when paranoia about slaves supposedly poisoning their masters swept the region. Of the thirty-eight people killed between 1750 and 1775, twenty-five of them were bondpeople, including two doctors. Another was a free, black, ship pilot who was hanged and burned for aiding runaways. Capital punishment seemingly declined during the Revolutionary War, although the sources are too inadequate to be certain.[39] Still, several factors might account for authorities' resolve to take fewer lives of people in bondage. The chaos of war may have encouraged a shift of power from established institutions such as courts to individual masters in disciplining slaves. Moreover, the threat (and reality) of slave rebellion loomed large in slave owners' minds. Harsh and excessive punishment of slaves in these circumstances might have triggered even greater resistance to bondage.[40]

Fully half of the executions in the second half of the eighteenth century occurred in the 1780s. The proportion of white people who suffered the ultimate penalty increased significantly during those years, perhaps because officials and wealthier South Carolinians wanted to pass a message along to free whites in the newly independent country. The slave revolution in St. Domingue beginning in the early 1790s once again intensified the fear of a similar bloody event in the southern states. Eighteen slaves were killed by the government during that decade. In 1797, for example, two slaves, Jean Louis and Figaro, and a free black person were hanged, having been accused of planning "to set fire to the city as they had formerly done in St. Domingo."[41]

As in Boston and Philadelphia, bound and working-class Charlestonians numbered disproportionately among those whom the state put to death. They included forty-nine slaves (including two doctors), ten individuals engaged in the maritime trades, eight sailors, three soldiers, one captain, and a ship's pilot. In contrast to the other two cities, though, females accounted for one out of every ten of the executed. Charleston's authorities obviously had fewer qualms about condemning women as long as they were black.[42]

As in the other two port cities, officials in Charleston singled out misdeeds

Fig. 3. Proportion of Executions in Charleston by Nature of Crime, 1750–1800

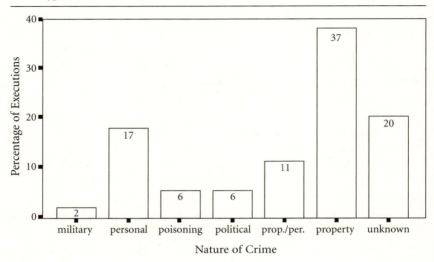

against property as being especially deserving of capital punishment (see fig. 3). In addition, South Carolina's planters and authorities relied on the death penalty to control the workers they owned. Since slaves belonged to their masters, owners might have objected to the financial losses incurred by an execution. Recognizing the interests of slave owners, the state softened the blow by financially reimbursing them for slaves condemned to death.

Of course, owners also inflicted the death penalty on their slaves without observing the niceties of law, thereby laying bare the terror and violence central to the control of bound laborers. Hector St. John de Crèvecoeur's comments capture one such shocking event. On his way to a dinner party at a plantation near Charleston, he passed "a negro, suspended in a cage, and left there to expire." Crèvecoeur recorded his horror:

I shudder when I recollect that the birds had already picked out his eyes, his cheek bones were bare; his arms had been attacked in several places, and his body seemed covered with a multitude of wounds. From the edges of the hollow sockets and from the lacerations with which he was disfigured, the blood slowly dropped, and tinged the ground beneath. . . . The living spectre, though deprived of his eyes, could still distinctively hear, and begged me to give him some water to allay his thirst.

After Crèvecoeur reached the plantation, the owner explained that the "the laws of self-preservation rendered such executions necessary."[43] How many slaves fell victim to such extralegal capital punishment in the name of "self-preservation" will never be known.

Capital punishment was intricately entwined with class and race in early urban North America (much like it is in our own times). The protection of property was a major goal of the judicial system, to the extent that most people put to death by the state were killed for crimes against property rather than against other humans. The lower classes, both free and bound, bore the brunt of the hangman's noose. Laborers, sailors, servants, slaves, transients, and young adults were the most vulnerable. From the perspective of wealthier citizens in power, it was precisely those lower sort who required discipline. To make the point more forcefully, officials designed elaborate execution-day rituals, demonstrating their authority both to give life by pardon and, more importantly, to take human life by violence.

Class Stratification and Children's Work in Post-Revolutionary Urban America

Sharon Braslaw Sundue

Early in the 1790s, a fourteen-year-old servant named Benjamin Hannis recognized an opportunity to run away from his mistress, Catherine Keppele, and he took it. Benjamin was unlucky; he was recaptured, and authorities committed him to jail, no doubt regarding the circumstances as rather unremarkable. But Hannis's case was appealed to the state supreme court, where the justices declared Benjamin's indenture void, concluding remarkably that no parent or guardian under any circumstances could make his child a servant in Pennsylvania.[1] Historians typically cite this case to analyze the changing meaning of child custody at the turn of end of the eighteenth century.[2] Court debates in this case also reveal attitudes toward child training and nurture at a moment when North Americans placed new emphasis on education to train citizens for the responsibility of political consent.[3] Justice Bradford, for one, explained that an indenture "by which the infant is bound to serve, and not to learn any trade, occupation, or labour, cannot be supported upon the principles of common law, nor by the express words of any statute."[4]

Bradford faced the tricky task of accounting for the "custom of the country," which had tolerated the servitude of minors for nearly two centuries. Ignoring history, Bradford argued that such "instances" had not been "general." All of the early laws had referred exclusively "to imported servants only" and thus were merely "founded on necessity." In his opinion, "no such necessity existed as to the children who were already in the province." In fact, Bradford implied a youthful servant would be "in a very degraded situation," "a species of property, holding a middle rank between slaves and freemen."[5]

Bradford and the other justices left open the possibility that for certain "classes" of children, servitude could be justified in terms of "necessity." Justice James Shippen agreed that a parent could not transfer the right to his children's personal service "for money paid to himself" but argued that he might transfer that right and "may possibly bind them as servants" "where the covenants appear on the face of them to be beneficial to the child." The "beneficial" labor contracts he referred to applied primarily to "poor and indigent" children, who by virtue of involuntary indenture, would be saved from "being bought up meanly, and in habits of idleness and vice."[6] The judges did not elaborate what "beneficial" training for the poorest children would require; did revolutionary concern for education extend to their indentures as well? The actual magnitude of change needs to be tested by considering the vocational experiences of children at the bottom end of the social scale. What actually happened to poor children in the post-Revolutionary period? Was there, in fact, a new concern for their vocational education?

This chapter compares efforts to "train" poor children in the aftermath of the War of Independence in three North American cities: Boston, Charleston, and Philadelphia. By analyzing vocational education, it explores a key mechanism Weber identified as constructing social class boundaries, both economically and culturally.[7] Elite efforts to afford the poor an education were also an important indicator of their desire to institutionalize status differences. In recent years, there has been a resurgence of research on the kind of instruction provided to poor children in the guise of pauper apprenticeship during the late colonial and early national periods.[8] Ruth Herndon argued that pauper apprenticeship was "profoundly conservative," preserving status distinctions based on class, gender, and race.[9] This chapter builds on that insight, highlighting the ways in which the administration of poor relief and the construction of race and class intersected in a profoundly *local* way. It argues that poor children's access to more than basic education was contingent on particular local demands for labor, and that it intersected with the desire of elites to perpetuate specific social hierarchies.[10] Differences in efforts to train poor children thus underscore the disparate impact of class, race, and gender in late eighteenth-century North America.[11]

In Boston in the postwar period, elites followed the colonial model for training the children of the poor, relying upon the publicly administered apprenticeship system. In fact, the city's Overseers of the Poor placed children in involuntary apprenticeships throughout the war, with only a brief hiatus. Placement during the war years reflected wartime disruption in Boston; the overseers sent most poor boys and girls outside of the city. In fact, they apprenticed fewer than one-quarter of the girls and just one boy to Boston residents. The plurality found themselves sent west, to rural communities in Worcester, Franklin, Hampshire, and Hampden Counties.[12] In fact, it seems that the desire of the city overseers to place these children perfectly complemented farmers' demands for young labor—boys in particular; as sons left family farms in order to serve in the war, farm laborers had become scarce.[13]

Boston's poor children were a cheap alternative, with indentures promising years of continuous service. Moreover, the Overseers of the Poor were happy to meet that demand, providing forty Massachusetts farmers with almost 90 percent of the boys, officially apprenticing them to learn the trade of "husbandry."[14] Indentures legally required that masters teach boys and girls to read, write, and cypher, though the overseers made no provisions to ensure that these clauses were enforced.[15] Given the chaotic state of public education in Massachusetts in the postwar years, these children did not seem to have had any greater access to formal schooling than they would have had if they had remained in Boston, which lacked any kind of public primary schools prior to 1818. For example, Spencer, Massachusetts, the destination of at least four of the apprentices, only kept school in a handful of its ten districts.[16]

After the conclusion of the war, we might predict that the overseers would revert to the prewar pattern of placing girls in apprenticeships as domestic servants with Boston's merchants, and boys with the city artisans. But they did not. For the next decade, overseers would place only a handful of the boys in the kind of low-status craft apprenticeships with masters who had preferred to use these cheap young laborers prior to the war. These artisans had difficulty attracting other workers, be they voluntary apprentices or the city's growing number of free, adult wage laborers, themselves drawn from the city's growing group of poor residents.

Instead, they continued to send most boys west to work as farm laborers, primarily in the farming communities in Worcester County and the Connecticut River Valley. The overseers and the boys' employers appear to have been so satisfied with this new pattern of placement that it only intensified over time: the number of poor boys employed in husbandry rose to more than 80 percent in the first years of the nineteenth century.[17] During the same period, the number of girls sent west also remained consistently high, stabilizing at about 70 percent of the total number bound by the mid-1790s.

An examination of the families employing these children helps to explain the new pattern of placement. For the most part, these children were bound to men like Paul Mandell of Hardwick after the war.[18] Beginning in 1771, he took both nine-year-old Ann Allen and five-year-old Sarah Lewis into his home; little George Forbis and eleven-year-old William Warren joined them in the next two years. Four years later, two more children joined the group: eleven-year-old Lydia Baker and six-year-old Abraham Remick; less than a year later, another two children were bound to him. "Squire Mandell," as he was known locally, was one of his town's wealthiest citizens, the owner of a very "valuable farm" in excess of seventy-two improved acres who offered nearly continuous public service.[19] While not all of the masters were quite so illustrious or took nearly as many poor apprentices, the majority were wealthy landowners who would have required significant supplies of farm labor and household help and who were particularly hard hit by the exodus of young men from the community during the war years.[20]

These men continued to take the city's impoverished young people to work on their estates and around their households, signifying a continued demand for young cheap labor after the war. These farmers were on the cusp of a movement to intensify agricultural production and increase the level of market exchange in the late eighteenth and early nineteenth centuries by diversifying production, particularly on larger farms.[21] Farmers also increasingly focused on livestock production because the return on the labor investment was particularly high. And the care of livestock was a responsibility that was well suited for the underutilized labor of young boys and girls.

Rural families also stepped up small-scale household production in the decades following independence to supplement their agricultural production.[22] Women were particularly important producers of cheese, yarn, and textiles, all exchanged locally.[23] This work necessarily took time away from other routine household tasks; women could only devote time to it when they had the help of daughters, young female relatives, or neighbors. In their absence, Boston's poor girls would do in a pinch. The region's elite, whose own daughters were likely enrolled in full-time academies, would also find themselves in need of female domestic servants; thus, Elizabeth McCullough and Elizabeth Bennet found themselves working in the homes of two of the region's most prominent families.[24]

What did these children get in return for their training in "husbandry" and rural "housewifery"? Beyond basic support, they received little that would enable them to escape economic marginality. On the eve of independence, the supply of quality, unimproved land in New England was vanishing.[25] Likely in recognition of that fact, Boston's Overseers of the Poor required masters to compensate the boys for the lack of lucrative training with high freedom dues intended to help them stay off the poor rolls.[26] However, the dues were insufficient for a boy to purchase enough land to support a family.[27] The boys bound to husbandry entered adulthood as poor agricultural wage laborers, a status they would likely keep for the rest of their adult lives if they remained in New England.[28]

The overseers' tendency to place Boston's poor children in these western communities did not continue after 1794; thereafter most children found themselves sent elsewhere. In fact, the total number of children bound by the Overseers of the Poor declined as well, from 105 children bound between 1790 and 1794, to 69 bound in the next five years, down to 60 in the first five years of the nineteenth century. This decline did not reflect any significant reduction in the number of the poor in Boston.[29] Nor did it reflect any decline in demand for labor in Worcester County and the Connecticut River Valley; the intensification of agricultural production only accelerated at this point.[30] At the same time, some merchants were beginning to capitalize upon household manufacturing, providing families with the raw materials with which to spin and to weave—these were the beginnings of rural outwork in western Massachusetts.[31] The women and children working at these enterprises were part of the new labor force that New England entrepreneurs would utilize, in part, to sustain the development of textile manufacturing.[32]

The development of manufacturing was even more intense in Essex County. By 1789 in Lynn, for example, families were processing leather provided on credit, producing at least 175,000 shoes each year, doubling in the following decade.[33] Only one boy found himself apprenticed in that city in the postwar period.[34] Meanwhile, by the 1790s merchants had already begun to experiment with mechanized mills, beginning with the Beverly Cotton Manufactory, which began operation late in 1787, followed by a sailcloth manufactory in Boston, a cotton mill in Worcester, and a duck cloth manufactory in Haverhill in 1789.[35] These communities likewise took few apprentices during this period who might have worked in these enterprises.[36]

One might suspect that these enterprises were drawing on another source for poor apprentices. The city of Salem, for example, bound out seventy-three children in the 1790s and sixty children in the following decade.[37] Even there, city officials indentured only a handful of the poor children to these industries.[38] How, then, can the apparent contradiction between the demand for labor and the lack of placements be explained?

We can find the answer by considering *all* poor children, not just those bound as apprentices. Demand for poor children's labor persisted, albeit in a different form. In western Massachusetts, the decline in placements coincided precisely with what Winifred Rothenberg has identified as the development of a rural farm labor market.[39] While the sons of poorer western farmers comprised a large portion of this new group of wageworkers, Bostonians also sent their own teenaged sons to work on the growing number of large farms. These poor boys probably helped comprise the fifth of contract laborers whom Jack Larkin identified as working on the Ward family farm in Shrewsbury between 1787 and about 1830 who had come from more than fifteen miles away.[40]

The region's new manufacturing enterprises also drew heavily on poor children's labor. Investors in the Beverly Cotton Manufactory, for example, based the manufactory's business model on the use of child labor.[41] The Boston Sailcloth Manufactory also advertised that it employed "a great number of the poor" shortly after commencing operations; George Washington, who visited that same year, described "twenty-eight looms at work, and fourteen girls, spinning with both hands, the flax being fastened to the waist. Children (girls) turn the wheels for them; and with this assistance, each spinner can turn out fourteen pounds of thread per day."[42]

Employers, in other words, continued to employ the city's poor boys and girls, but given competition from wageworkers, they no longer committed to long-term contracts for children who might take years to reach a high level of productivity. Outwork and the new forms of manufacture also made it less necessary to train boys in the "art and mystery" of a craft; less skilled workers would suffice. Apprentices found themselves at the bottom of the labor queue; now that potential masters had access to what they perceived as more desirable, cheaper laborers, they no longer hired apprentices. Not surprisingly, the single largest destination for boys bound to craft apprenticeships after 1784 was Maine, where many households lacked other labor options.[43] Meanwhile, the proliferation of these other opportunities left poor families with other employment options for their offspring; overseers likely found fewer children who required placement overall.

Poor apprentices' employment in western Massachusetts in the years following the Revolution was an indicator of change. Wealthy farmers who had a hard time finding sufficient supplies of labor amid intensified production discovered that the "underutilized" young, urban poor could fit their needs quite nicely. We might speculate, for example, that the sons of the Northampton merchant Levi Shephard, who saw Elizabeth Bennet come of age while working in their father's home from 1793 until 1805, learned this lesson well. Just four years after the completion of her indenture, they established the Northampton Cotton and Woolen Manufacturing Company. In large part it owned its success to its labor source: the young poor. Shortly after commencing operations, for example, the operation advertised for boys between six and sixteen to work as carders, spinners, and weavers.[44] This also helps to explain why, when employers advertising in the *Hampshire Gazette* in the following decades advertised for boys to work as farm laborers or for "eight young ladies as apprentices" to straw hat-making, they indicated that "those from a distance will be preferred."[45] The children bound by Boston Overseers of the Poor helped foreshadow this kind of demand.

The consequences of change for poor children were ambiguous. After all, masters technically guaranteed poor apprentices basic literacy; no law protected boys and girls working in less formal relationships. While well intended, reforms enacted in 1789 required that children admitted to free public schools already be able to read; parents who lacked the ability to transmit this skill had no choice but to send their offspring to private schools for basic literacy training.[46] This was obviously beyond the means of Boston's poor residents; their only alternative was a handful of charity schools established by churches after the turn of the century. Those charity schools had very little success; poor parents could not afford the loss of their children's income while at school.[47] Consequently, by 1817 the Boston School Committee reported that more than 7 percent of the city's school-age population did not attend any school.[48] Nearly a generation of Boston's impoverished boys and girls had grown "up to manhood, unable to read or write."[49] Ironically, the city that established the first, most comprehensive public system of free schools to train children offered almost nothing to its poorest residents, marking them socially as a distinct class.

In Charleston, the city embarked on an entirely new plan for training the children of impoverished residents after the Revolution. Just three years after Charleston's incorporation, the new city commissioners for the poor began to investigate creating a residential orphanage. In the autumn of 1790, city elites signified their desire to school the city's poor whites when they established the Charleston Orphan House, declaring that they had designed it "for the purpose of supporting and educating poor and orphan children and those of poor and disabled parents who are unable to support and maintain them."[50] Within the first ten years, 265 children were admitted, more than 70 percent of whom were brought by their parents.[51] In fact, it seems parents were so eager to have their children admitted that the commissioners began inquiring seriously into their families' economic circumstances; several were turned away as "they were not in such low circumstances as to be objects [of] charity."[52] During that decade, it seems that over 3 percent of the city's white boys and girls were schooled in the Orphan House at any given point, comparable to the 2 percent of underage boys and girls serving as pauper apprentices in Boston at the same time.[53] Overall, John E. Murray estimates that the Orphan House served most of its intended constituency.[54]

By contrast with contemporary northern poorhouses, the Orphan House did much more than simply warehouse the children of the city's poor whites; the commissioners prioritized education and required that wards take part in a full-time regimen of schooling. The house was on the forefront of what many historians have described as the movement to create "well-ordered" asylums after the Revolution.[55] Children were divided into "classes," each under the care and supervision of an appointed nurse who ensured that they appear neat and clean, reporting to the house matron, herself "accountable for the morals and conduct of all the children."[56] Children spent a full day in school "kept every day in the year," except for Sundays and Saturday afternoons. All were required to attend for four hours in the morning and three hours after lunch, doubtless to learn the catechism, to read, and to spell. As John E. Murray has found, teachers were very effective.[57] The commissioners also provided the boys with more advanced schooling; they ordered boys eight and over to be sent to a private school run by Philip Besselieu, most likely alongside children whose parents paid tuition. Girls did not have this opportunity, but the commissioners did not neglect them entirely; regulations stipulated that "when the girls are of ability they shall attend the steward, one hour and a half in the morning and the same in the afternoon, for the purpose of being instructed in writing and arithmetic."[58]

The commissioners did not intend to maintain children indefinitely in the Orphan House. They expected from the outset that the boys and girls would eventually be transferred to masters "as shall teach them such profession, trade or occupation as may be suited to their genius and inclination."[59] Within the first three years of operation, however, they deemed only nine children ready to leave the institution as apprentices; those boys and girls were an average age of fourteen when they left with their new masters. This represented an increase in the length of poor children's maintenance above the colonial period.[60] After that point, the commissioners indentured the boys and girls at a relatively consistent age of thirteen.[61]

The schooling provided by the Orphan House appears to have significantly affected the boys' apprenticeship opportunities. Within the first decade, the commissioners bound just under one-third to lower-status work, either with mariners, or in apprenticeships with bakers, blacksmiths, tailors, or shoemakers—occupations where they would be likely to work alongside the city's skilled slaves and later face competition from them for wages.[62] Masters took the majority of these boys between 1797 and 1799, years in which their demand for unskilled labor may have increased given a 1796 law requiring employers to hire one white laborer or apprentice per four enslaved artisans.[63] At the same time, the commissioners were able to place over 30 percent of the boys in elite crafts or in apprenticeships with city merchants and professionals.[64] Opportunities only improved over the next decade, when about half of the boys secured apprenticeships in high-status crafts or with city grocers and merchants.

Why did Charleston's commissioners treat poor children so differently from their northern counterparts? We can find the answer prior to the Revolution, by considering the colonial precedents for the Orphan House. The Orphan House was not the first effort to school Charleston's poor children; since the 1740s the city's parish churchwardens (then vested with the responsibility for poor relief) regularly sent poor children to school. In fact, by 1757 their written policy required that all children under six who received poor relief attend to school; as a result, by the 1760s the poor children were withdrawn from the labor market until their early teens.[65] We can best understand this policy by considering the part of the city's poor population for whom the churchwardens did not offer any relief: blacks, both free and enslaved. Blacks' increased visibility in the city alarmed the elite, who regularly complained of their disorderly assembly and rioting after 1720, when the number of blacks in the city began to grow dramatically, comprising more than half the total population.[66] Especially frightening was the fraternization of blacks and the city's poor whites.[67] The churchwardens seem to have hoped that schooling the white poor would provide part of the solution. Not coincidentally, the schooling of poor white children took off after the Stono Rebellion and the fire in Charleston in 1740, which was suspected to be the work of black arsonists. In the previous chapter, Gabriele Gottlieb suggested that the early 1750s were years of special concern for elites about social order and racial unrest, marked by a peak in executions.[68] By schooling poor white children in a residential setting apart from the workhouse, churchwardens were simultaneously making an investment in the future. They hoped to train these children to be orderly citizens, while reducing their physical contact at a young and impressionable age with disorderly blacks in the poorhouse and in the community.[69]

Schooling could also answer the concerns of the city's laboring whites, who were fearful of economic competition from blacks.[70] Affording the children of the city's poor the chance for some formal education could help give them a chance at obtaining better apprenticeships that demanded literacy skills. This in turn would lead to a more lucrative occupation.

The local political climate also likely influenced elite Charlestonians' creation of a residential asylum for poor white children. In the war's aftermath, an alarming "spirit of mobing" plagued the city, as artisans and laborers targeted British merchants and returning Loyalists with whom they believed the legislature had been too lenient.[71] The incorporation of the city itself seems to have been motivated by the desire to quell protests, and city elites quickly acted to control the lesser sort, regulating the movements of blacks and sailors.[72] Protests continued, however, and criticism began to force elites to acknowledge mechanics' concerns as the decade concluded. Elites' creation of the Orphan House, therefore, seems to reflect both their fears and their recognition of the potential power of the city's white laboring population. Providing white laborers' children with access to the tools of social mobility and rational citizenship could have been an effort either to relieve some of the political pressure or to train these children to exercise that political power wisely in the future.

There was, however, a very important exception to the growing emphasis placed upon advancement among these white children: the Orphan House's female charges were very limited in their occupational opportunities. Beyond curricular differences, and unlike the requirements for boys, house regulations stipulated that the nurses would train the girls to work around the Orphan House when they were "of ability to do so," helping to care for the younger children.[73] The commissioners also determined that the girls were officially eligible for indenture two years earlier than the boys.[74] There is some evidence that in the first years of operation, they sought to place these girls in the few crafts available to women; over one-third of the girls who were indentured would learn mantua-making and millinery in the first decade. The remaining majority were consigned to domestic work.[75] But by the early nineteenth century, just as boys' opportunities expanded, these limited craft opportunities almost disappeared.[76] That difference stemmed in part from a persistent demand for poor white girls' service in the city's middling income families, who confined slave purchases to adult males.[77] Moreover, some families preferred white girls, like one prospective master who advertised specifically for "a white servant girl, who knows how to cook, wash and iron clothes."[78] Girls' placement also demonstrated a belief that it was more important to make social distinctions based on work between black and white boys. Charleston's elites learned that as freemen poor white boys might someday be a political force to be reckoned with; it made sense to deflate the potential that they would identify with the "profanis vulgus." By contrast, within Charleston's social hierarchy, white women would remain dependents, who acquired status through marriage to white freemen.[79] The elite effort to construct race by educating poor whites was a highly gendered strategy.

What kind of education did poor children receive in Philadelphia after the Revolution, in the same state in which the *Keppele* decision was rendered? Here, as in Boston, the primary method for training the children of the poor was the publicly administered apprenticeship system. By 1790, the volume of children bound by the city's new Guardians of the Poor had recovered from a wartime slump. At the same time, these children experienced a dramatic decline in vocational opportunities. In the flush prewar years, the Guardians of the Poor apprenticed poor boys to learn a wide range of crafts; nearly half placed in the city during the 1760s found themselves in apprenticeships with artisans in middling-status crafts.[80] During the first half of the 1790s, by contrast, more than 60 percent of the boys were bound to the lowest status trades— as tailors, coopers, cordwainers, mariners—or simply to work as servants.

Why the change? Artisans who could offer the poor boys a vocational education with some chance for social mobility had increasing access to alternate, preferred sources of labor. As Sharon Salinger has shown, these merchants and artisans were the beneficiaries of the rising number of adult workers, skilled and unskilled, who were willing to work for cheap wages. Overall, artisans' demand for even adult indentured servants had declined.[81] To no surprise, their demand for poor children was slight, at best. As the free adult labor force grew, apprenticeship opportunities for children at the bottom of the socioeconomic ladder in middling crafts dwindled.

So where was the demand for poor children's labor? Over time, the poor boys had an increasing likelihood of placement with shoemakers and mariners. Shoemaking in particular underwent significant reorganization in the Revolutionary period, as masters concentrated more on the commercial than the manufacturing aspects of their craft, widening the social gap between themselves and their employees.[82] Master cordwainers in particular were the beneficiaries of economic recovery in the 1790s, as international demand for North American shoes expanded.[83] Seeking to remain competitive, merchants attempted to lower their costs by reducing labor expenditures. The result, in part, appears to have been a greater reliance on the cheap labor of poor children, much to the chagrin of the city's journeymen, who would begin to organize to fight the changes by 1794.[84]

Perhaps the most striking change in the postwar period was the appearance of a new group of poor children who were not bound to learn any trade, but rather to work simply as servants. Girls, of course, had been bound to apprentice in "housewifery" from the outset, essentially code for work as domestic servants. These girls were now joined by boys such as nine-year-old George McHutchin, bound to Michael Eblin, who agreed to ensure that McHutchin learn only to read and write and no more, or Jonathan Watkins, bound at thirteen to William Massey, who committed to send him to school for only two years. In total, boys such as these would account for 8 percent of *all* young males bound as apprentices by both their parents and the Guardians of the Poor prior to 1806, a dramatic increase since the prewar period, when no boys were bound as "apprentices" to learn the trade of a "waiter" or a domestic servant.[85]

As William Massey's "apprentice," Jonathan Watkins served his eight years in the same household as three other boys. However, the Guardians of the Poor did not bind these children; they were part of a new category of poor bound laborers: emancipated African American children who, via the act of gradual emancipation of 1780 were required to serve as indentured servants until the age of twenty-eight.[86] For two generations, these black servants, most of whom were children eighteen and under, served as a new source of unskilled bound labor for Philadelphians. The majority of these children were indented under the oversight of the Pennsylvania Abolition Society, which recorded contracts for more than one thousand boys and girls between 1792 and 1800, dwarfing the number of white children bound by the Guardians of the Poor, and the number of indentured immigrants under fifteen who were bound annually in the 1790s and 1800s.[87] These black children were a new and very important source of poor labor upon whom wealthy Philadelphians could draw to serve as domestic laborers. The vast majority of these children were, like all of the white children bound prior to 1795 and the white girls bound thereafter, indentured to serve wealthy merchants, professionals, and gentlemen within the city itself.[88] They were one of the important "classes" of children referred to in *Keppele* whose servitude, born of "necessity," was permissible. Their status no doubt inspired Justice Bradford's comment about young servants holding an ambiguous, degraded position between slaves and freemen; the association of recently emancipated blacks with servitude had racialized youthful work in the absence of education.

However, the group of boys bound as "domestic servants" or "waiters" was not racially exclusive. African American boys were joined by whites such as Frederick Shirtz, whose mother bound him to serve the merchant John

Dubary for a year, or David Walker, whose mother bound him to serve an innkeeper as a domestic servant for three years; each master was responsible for sending them for just one semester of evening school in return.[89] These placements seem to have been a strategy poor parents used when confronted with a lack of alternate resources for their offspring. At the same time, wealthy merchants' demand for domestic servants appears to have risen substantially in the postwar period.[90] Demand for girls in particular was high; as Farley Grubb has shown, merchants and other wealthy elites accounted for more than 30 percent of the purchasers of all German redemptioner girls under fifteen entering the state *as a whole* between 1787 and 1804—no other occupational group took more. Native-born poor children also helped fulfill the rising demand for such service laborers.

In the second half of the decade, just as African American children began to flood the market for young laborers, there does seem to have been some slight improvement in the opportunities available to some of the poor white boys. After 1795, the Guardians of the Poor apprenticed 14.5 percent of the boys to trades that would require academic training beyond basic arithmetic—triple the number placed in comparable trades during the 1760s.[91] This pattern reversal correlates with what historians have identified as some growing interest among city elites in providing free schooling for these impoverished children. During the 1790s, numerous private groups endeavored to establish their own free schools for the poor, some of which could provide an extensive education. The efforts of the Philadelphia Society for the Establishment and Support of Charity Schools are indicative.[92] The initial group of fifty-one boys the society admitted to its charity school was truly drawn from among the city's poorest families.[93] These boys remained, on average, until they were about twelve, and one-fifth remained in the school until fourteen years of age or older. They acquired substantially more than basic literacy and numeracy instruction: at least 37 percent were exposed to advanced subjects, such as the son of a laborer who attended for seven years and took instruction in bookkeeping and Latin grammar.

By far the most popular and successful efforts to instruct poor children in the city, however, were the numerous Sunday schools established after 1790. Elite proponents drew on the example of Sunday schools for the poor in England where children were instructed after religious services in "reading, and in the first principles of the Christian religion"; they advocated a similar plan as early as 1785.[94] In 1790, benefactors organized as the Society for the Institution and Support of First Day or Sunday Schools in Philadelphia, and they opened their first school the following year. Within just the first three weeks, the society proudly proclaimed that it had admitted more than 120 students, "who would otherwise be debarred from the plainest education."[95] Five years later, the society reported that it had educated nearly one thousand children; by the end of the decade, well over two thousand boys and girls had taken advantage of the Sunday Schools.[96] These schools were quickly joined by a number of part-time schools for the city's growing population of free African American children.[97]

Historians have generally explained this proliferation of plans to school poor children in Philadelphia in one of two ways. Many, such as Lawrence Cremin, have emphasized the overall importance of republican rhetoric, combined with the evangelical fervor unleashed by independence from Britain, which encouraged the establishment of schools "teaching a truth properly grounded in evangelical doctrine, as . . . a bulwark of the Republic."[98] Others have emphasized aspects of these plans designed to control the poor, and the limitations on the amount of schooling provided, in particular the Sunday schools' stated objective of providing instruction only in reading and writing, "those useful and necessary branches of education, to which," they proclaimed, "we mean to confine them."[99]

These explanations are not mutually exclusive; both certainly help to explain support for these plans. However, neither takes account of the economic context, which helps explain the ambiguous commitment to instructing the young impoverished. Following the war, good apprenticeship opportunities for poor children that might afford a chance to rise out of poverty dwindled as free adult wage laborers multiplied. At the same time, the demand for workers with advanced literacy and mathematical skills was on the increase. It was not only possible to remove a handful of poor white children from the labor force until their mid-teens; it also made sense to train them to fit the new labor demands. Yet these efforts were very limited, a reflection of persistent demand for young labor in the most menial jobs. The most successful plans to school the poor, both white and black, were designed not to interfere with that labor. The Sunday schools, after all, were constitutionally constrained from offering the kind of instruction that might qualify students for occupational mobility; they were also conducted only when instruction would not interfere with work time. Schooling opportunities for poor children did little to reverse a trend toward a segmented market for young labor; they might have even encouraged it.

Despite the rhetoric employed in the decision, it appears that *Respublica v. Keppele* did not reflect any marked change in attitude toward the training of children at the bottom of the social hierarchy in the wake of the Revolution.

In Charleston opportunities for the advanced instruction of young whites, boys in particular, did expand. Here, elites had a stake in creating a social boundary between the offspring of the white poor and blacks, who could more than fill demand for unskilled laborers locally. That interest did not extend to girls, however, likely because of a persistent demand for their domestic labor. Administrators' desire to construct racial distinctions led them to extend educational resources to poor boys that would enable them to transcend their status, but not to their sisters. However, in Boston and Philadelphia support for any extensive free schooling for the poor, white or black, was lacking, particularly as demand for their cheap labor in expanding sectors of the economy increased. In Massachusetts in particular, the utilization of the labor of Boston's poor children in the decades following independence seems to have set important precedents for early nineteenth-century manufacturing. Exclusion from advanced instruction in both cities appears to have effectively blocked the poor from the vocational education that would have offered release from poverty later in life.

The comparison of efforts to educate the poor is an important reminder that elites did act deliberately to construct a system of social stratification during the early national period, using the very mechanism that many advocated to train the individuals to act as political citizens. At the same time, the diverse agendas and outcomes of these plans are important reminders that no single framework for understanding social stratification works for the period. Elites' concern for educational opportunities for the poor, and thus the salience of class boundaries, was linked in a fundamental sense to their desire to construct racial status distinctions. Nonetheless, Philadelphia's servant children remind us that even those racial prerogatives were secondary considerations, given demand for cheap labor.

Afterword:
Constellations of Class in Early North America and the Atlantic World

Christopher Tomlins

Fashion has a flair for the topical, no matter where it stirs in the thickets of long ago; it is a tiger's leap into the past. This jump, however, takes place in an arena where the ruling class gives the commands. The same leap in the open air of history is the dialectical one, which is how Marx understood the revolution.

—Walter Benjamin, "Theses on the Philosophy of History," no. 14

Does class matter? Legions of professional peers tell us that class—like God—is dead.[1] So why insist that concepts of class and class struggle retain explanatory salience? Is it to advertise a commitment to writing the history "from below" of ordinary people, their quotidian adversities and occasional triumphs? That of itself requires no embrace of class concepts. The possibility that class is a generalizable social phenomenon may be a conclusion to be drawn from such history, but class is no essence immanent within it.[2] Does it convey, then, a sharpened, more compassionate commitment, to retrieve those people (in Thompson's romantic words) from "the enormous condescension of posterity" by underscoring the moral validity and historical significance of their collective agency at moments of "acute social disturbance"?[3] Such an objective is emotionally satisfying, to be sure, but these days at least falsely premised. For posterity no longer condescends. Mostly it does not bother to recall at all; particularly in the United States, its face turns always to the future. But when posterity does glance pastward, it is less with condescension than with a tourist's enthusiastic naïveté. Posterity consumes the mnemonic commodities sold in historical areas, cheers their skirmishing reenactors, sheds a tear over the bathetic scripts that chart our heritage. "History comes alive at Charles Towne Landing, where Native Americans, English, Africans and Barbadians came together to create the first successful English colony in Carolina in 1670. Interacting with each other and the land, these groups each made important contributions and shaped the history of the region."[4]

Perhaps the objective is not sentiment but science. By categorizing behavior, organization, and action might we not uncover a shared impulse to stratify that convinces us our subjects, no matter how diverse, are in some human essential all alike? Our empiricism, however, reconstitutes history as sociology. So to sociologize our history lends it a positivism of our own invention, which discounts that which is not social.[5]

In their introduction to this collection, Simon Middleton and Billy G. Smith traverse the half-century thicket of historiographical and epistemological debates that have rendered the class concept both attractive and problematic. They also identify a tendency on display in a number of the chapters in this book[6]—conceiving class in terms of its effects—which, they argue, may provide a fruitful point of conjunction for hitherto conflicting interpretive positions. What is the promise of this discourse of effects? Theoretical innovation. Class, one may propose, is a "place" (a position, a locale) correspondent with a mode of production; as such it is a structural condition of social relations.[7] But it is unobservable as such, hence unknowable except in theory. Empirically, we encounter class only as effects—fragmented, particularized, fluid, evanescent—manifest on the occasions when class butts into our plural worlds of experience (economic, political, cultural, linguistic).[8] We discover that in the heads of flesh-and-blood people, class is not an experience in common; it may not even be a common experience.[9]

The chapters presented here, in their different ways, do much to demonstrate how and why a theory of class as effects might be found useful and productive by other scholars who also think class matters. So judged, the project has served an important purpose. We can be pleased with what we have achieved. But before we pack up and turn for home let us pause a moment to consider again what we have achieved, this time from a distinct standpoint. Let us examine what we have produced in relation to its mode of production—professional history. Tourism is a mode of production that creates one set of historical products. Professional history is another. Each imposes certain epistemological conditions on its subjects.

The dominant métier of professional history is the placement of subjects in relation to each other within a continuum we call historical time.[10] When historians say that a subject has been "historicized," they mean it has been located in its "appropriate" historical-temporal context. Although attempts are always being made to limit the universe of subjects according, say, to the application of professional canons of "significance," the general tendency is for the universe of subjects to expand constantly. Indeed, current historical practice tends to celebrate expansion, for expansion enriches the continuum of historical time by producing an ever deepening "complexity" in relations among historically located subjects that "fills in" the continuum's "empty" spaces.[11] The production of complexity satisfies the purposes of professional history as a mode of production, both by continuously producing "new" history (and new historians), and by occasioning necessarily endless argument among practitioners over the contingencies of placement—the proper locations for history's subjects, their proper contexts, the proper criteria to be considered.[12] But, however diverse their practices and methodologies of placement may be, historians' commitment to "historicizing" suggests a form of common engagement, a philosophy for historical practice.

Historians of class and class struggles must consider the relationship of their historical practice to this mode of production. Are they participants in it, engaged in locating class and class struggles as subjects in historical time, or critics of it? The importance of the question is heightened when one considers that engagement with matters of class and class struggle leads willy-nilly to an encounter with an entirely distinct philosophy of history, historical materialism,[13] which accords a very specific agency to class and class struggle and, in its most resolute incarnations, entirely washes its hands of professional history's mode of production.[14] What, in *this* light, is our discourse of "effects"? A sophisticated reconceptualization of the materialist claim? An expression of ambivalence about that claim? A disorderly retreat from it? Are historians of class and class struggles willing to locate themselves amid the production of "complexity?"[15]

I confess, myself, to a certain reluctance. "We need history," Nietzsche wrote, "for reasons different from those for which the idler in the garden of knowledge needs it." We need it "for the sake of life and action." We should serve history "only to the extent that history serves life."[16] Genealogically, if in no other way, the authors of these chapters are legatees of an original and transformative resituation of expressions of class and class struggle initiated by Marx to create a philosophy of history dedicated precisely to the service of life and action. Rather than debate how what has been written here will create some more complexity, "fill in" some more historical time, let us instead contemplate how one might pursue *that* legacy.[17]

Why, then, study class and class struggle? First, because these convulsive phenomena offer much more than a stage for the production of historical complexity: rather, they structure the universe of time under discussion. Second, because as such, class and class struggle remain a route to an absolutely distinct understanding of history. Third, because only through that distinct understanding can one begin to grasp what, as historians, we owe the past.[18]

The Tradition of the Oppressed: Memory and Time

> *We were cut off from the comprehension of our surroundings; we glided past like phantoms. . . . We could not understand because we were too far and could not remember because we were traveling in the night of first ages, of those ages that are gone, leaving hardly a sign—and no memories.*
>
> —*Joseph Conrad,* Heart of Darkness

If, as I propose, we retain a pronounced measure of respect for the claims made by historical materialism on behalf of class and class struggle, how do we elide the dogmas—that old insistence on the foundational salience of the economic, on the determinative force of productive relations, the insignificance of individual intentionality, the iron march of inevitability—that encased those claims and eventually provoked the postmaterialist (postmodernist) move? How do we re-create historical materialism's most extraordinary achievement—the gaping ontological rent it tore in historicism's continuum? To do so one must realize that the "cartoon" or orthodox historical materialism with which we are most familiar was largely the product of the rigidities of the Third International and of the terrible decades of the mid-twentieth century. Historical materialism comes in other varieties.

As the greatest single example of historical materialism's imaginative promise, consider the work of Walter Benjamin. Here I will confine myself almost entirely to his *Theses on the Philosophy of History*, written, as Alex Callinicos (invoking Victor Serge) hauntingly notes, at "midnight in the century."[19] The *Theses* confront orthodox historical materialism with three utterly fundamental challenges. "Three moments must be made to penetrate the foundations of the materialist view of history: the discontinuity of historical time; the destructive power of the working class; the tradition of the oppressed."[20] Each induces a fundamental upheaval in received conceptions of memory and historical time. The first, "discontinuity," assails orthodox historical materialism's bow to the Enlightenment ideal of historical progress. For the continuum of "forwards" it substitutes a radical uncertainty about the course of historical time, a critique of the very idea of historical time itself, and a conception of Revolution as the complete interruption of time, a "Messianic cessation of happening." The second, "destructive power," identifies the working class as the agent of interruption, stressing the working class's dawning awareness that it has the capacity to "make the continuum of history explode." The third, "the tradition of the oppressed," unites the first and second in founding the consciousness of that capacity on memory—but memory of a particular kind: not reconstruction but recognition, a galvanic conjunction between now and then, a sudden seizure upon the past "as an image which flashes up at the instant when it can be recognized."[21] Memory, constantly threatened with obliteration,[22] is the key to formation of historical knowledge "not [in] man or men but the struggling, oppressed class itself." Historical knowledge is how the oppressed come to know themselves as "the last enslaved class" and as "the avenger that completes the task of liberation in the name of generations of the downtrodden."[23] Together, these three fundamental interventions in historical materialism swerve it off the path of progress and into the eschatology of redemption.[24]

Benjamin's *Theses* emphatically do *not* present historical materialism as one of a plurality of modes of analysis available to professional historians, but rather as the generator of a completely distinct genus of historical knowledge. One sees this most clearly in Benjamin's critique of historicism—the idea, to which I have adverted, of history itself as a practice that fixes (though always contingently) objects in place in historical time the better to establish, or disavow, causal or relational connections between them. Stretching before humanity, in the historicist imagination, lies homogenous empty time through which humanity progresses. Stretching behind lies the same time now strewn with objects, like so much flotsam left in the wake of a ship, which may or may not be stable as such (currents shift, weather changes, bloated corpses bob to the surface, others, waterlogged, sink) but which has "reality"—the historicist's past has "an eternal image" that cannot be altered, for it is what has been—open for endless exploration, recovery, and debate.[25] Past, present, and future time exist in a single continuum, "a current," the flow of a stream, "a chain of events." To know a past moment, one must place it in context, purge oneself of what came after so as to know the past *on its own terms*.[26] Contrast this with Benjamin's radically disjunctive conception of history as "time filled by the presence of the now [*Jetztzeit*]," in which the past has life *only* in the present, where (as we have seen) it "flits by" unexpectedly as an image or a memory to be seized and made historical knowledge "at the instant when it can be recognized," like a mayfly in heat, or lost;[27] and in which the present is always, potentially, a moment not of transition to the next moment in the continuum, and so on ad infinitum, but of time brought screeching to a stop—"a Messianic cessation of happening, or put differently, a revolutionary chance in the fight for the oppressed past."[28] One who takes this position recognizes that only the present can establish causes; and so he "stops telling the sequence of events like the beads of a rosary. Instead he grasps the constellation which his own era has formed with a definite earlier one." He understands the present as "the time of the now" in which, as for Jews awaiting the Messiah, "every second of time [is] the strait gate through which the Messiah might enter."[29]

Twenty years after Benjamin's death, the critique of orthodox historical materialism that we associate with the beginnings of the new (post-1950s) left showed few traces of his philosophy of history. True, the Anglo-American canon took up the agency of "the oppressed," manifested most influentially in its Thompsonian incarnation as a repudiation of orthodoxy's base/super-structure metaphor in favor of the exploration of experience and conscious-ness. Yet even then, and mostly since, that commitment was oddly shorn of the anti-historicist philosophy that gave "the tradition of the oppressed" its reason for being. For even as they were recovered and celebrated, even senti-mentalized, the oppressed were "historicized," explored in and for their own sequestered moments. Their consciousness became a matter of feeling, an in-clination, inexplicable outside a particular historical context.[30] The Thomp-sonian conceptualization of class, as the editors have reminded us, was resistant to generalization beyond the particular circumstances of its signi-fier, the subjective, time-bound, experience itself.[31] That empirically rich (complex) history was spawned is not in dispute, but the absence of Ben-jamin's disjunctive conception of historical time acted as a caesura between past and present, surrendering historical practice to the placement of objects in context, the filling of historical time, to history as a processual continuum in which the past cannot enter the present.[32]

Marx's foundational intellectual purpose as a philosopher of history was precisely to escape German historicism and place historical practice in the service of a revolutionary project—the struggle to achieve a class*less* so-ciety. Yet in the twentieth century historical materialism has always lived on the precipice of assimilation to historicism, a vulnerability only increased by the encasement of historical practice in a professionalized discourse that may certainly engender a rich plurality of means to know of class—as evidenced in these pages—but eschews, even inhibits, any hint of purpose for that knowledge. Unfortunately, without such purpose we become merely prospectors in a dusty landscape. We recover the matter of class by straining familiar modalities of social stratification and their reproduction—work and labor systems, status structures, educational systems—through a conceptual sieve to recover residual evidentiary traces. We discover new matter for class by filtering in like manner many other phenomena (individual and collective, plebeian and non-plebeian) that one might term markers of identity—social, cultural, ethnic, gendered, racial, and religious—and of self-presentation— deportment, language, dramaturgy, speech and pronunciation, emotional bearing, professed belief. Class then becomes an account, an inventory of all these fragments, "a shifting totality of social relations"[33] that the historian compiles for a succession of subjects to refine their locations in historical time.[34]

Efforts to sustain class as "a useful category of historical analysis" are important as such.[35] It is no bad thing to struggle to keep class analysis fashionable in professional academic discourse. Working toward concordance upon what kind of relational structure class is and what its analytic uses might be as a historiographical project, however, do not instruct us in "the tradition of the oppressed." Concretely, then, do we find in all or any of these chapters the potential for historical knowledge that "blasts a specific era out of the homogenous course of history?" Can we use them to grasp "the constellation which [our] own era has formed with [that] definite earlier one," to take "a tiger's leap" into "the open air of history?"[36] How?

Constellating Eras: The Atlantic World

> *The Director of Companies was our captain and our host. We four affectionately watched his back as he stood in the bows looking to seaward. On the whole river there was nothing that looked half so nautical. He resembled a pilot, which to a seaman is trustworthiness personified. It was difficult to realize his work was not out there in the luminous estuary, but behind him, within the brooding gloom.*
>
> —*Joseph Conrad,* Heart of Darkness

Joseph Conrad's novella, *Heart of Darkness*,[37] tells of the harvesting of ivory from Africa by an entity known simply as "the Company." The tale is told in London, that "monstrous town," to an audience of eponymous listeners known only as "The Director of Companies . . . The Lawyer . . . [and] The Accountant."[38] The listeners stand for the swarming together of particular structures of production and extraction with particular forms of knowledge and expertise. What they have in common in their swarming is their will to improve; what the storyteller, Marlow, identifies as their shared "devotion to efficiency."[39]

Conrad's story describes how this conjunction of institutions and knowledge constructs Marlow's early twentieth-century Atlantic world. The secret of the Company's success lies in its deployment of particular techniques that "watch its back." Law—"an insoluble mystery from the sea"— enchains African labor, whether by straightforward criminalization or by "the legality of time contracts." Accountancy—"apple-pie" bookkeeping— assures the Company ascendancy in "the merry dance of death and trade." Constant distractions gnaw at efficiency—"the groans of th[e] sick," the heat, the babble of uncouth natives. "When one has got to make correct entries," says the Company's chief accountant, "one comes to hate those savages—hate them to the death." Kurtz, the legendary chief of the Company's "Inner Station," is the greatest distraction of all. Once the Company's pride, the "emissary of pity and science" it sent to transform the inhabitants of the inner territories with the disciplines of progress,[40] Kurtz becomes an obstacle to the Company's designs. He turns himself into a primitive sovereign, an upriver barbarian monarch who scorns the Company's "peddling" and roams "beyond the bounds of permitted aspirations." The Company is greatly relieved at his death.[41]

Heart of Darkness exposes an exploitative conjunction of institutions, locales, discourses, and oceanic/riverine connections that entangle the entire early twentieth-century world in the trails that attach dark colonized hinterlands to dark metropolitan hearts—"waterway[s] leading to the uttermost ends of the earth."[42] *This* Atlantic World originated in the Atlantic World of the seventeenth and eighteenth centuries. My goal here is to underscore the constellation of these eras. I will argue that we should locate "early North America and the Atlantic World" within that constellation by the history we write of it.

Heart of Darkness was published in London in 1902. It has since been fully assimilated to North American intellectual and popular culture by intermediaries as varied as Perry Miller, Francis Ford Coppola, and most recently Peter Jackson. Each did so, consciously or not, by blasting out specific historical eras and laying them alongside each other. Coppola made *Heart of Darkness* the textual template for a later imperialism's technologies of pity, science, and progress (*Apocalypse Now*, 1979). Jackson created an indelible allegorical link between the murmuring dispossessed of 1930s New York and the exploitation—and exemplary execution—of a rebellious Conradian monster (*King Kong*, 2005). The most interesting of all is Perry Miller, who assimilated the Africa of *Heart of Darkness* to "his" United States to serve as an undeclared time-bound thesis to a timeless North American antithesis. In the preface to *Errand into the Wilderness*, Miller famously tells how, as a young man sitting at a particular place and time on the banks of the Congo River, he conceived his foundational "narrative of the movement of European culture into the vacant wilderness of America" in a moment of urgent desire to "expound my America to the twentieth century." Miller's African epiphany was of North America's elemental difference: an instantiation very specifically *not* of Atlantic empire, but rather of transcendent theological mission. His exposition occluded every countervailing possibility—the economic, the imperial—by displacing all of them onto the "tawdry" Africa of his youth.[43] Amy Kaplan has laid bare some of the subtextual implications of Miller's vision:

In Miller's formulation, the origins of America stem from a dyadic relationship between Europe and an empty continent, [but] his presence in Africa introduces a triangular relationship that destabilizes this dyad. The presence of Africa—and the absence of its inhabitants—both reproduce the imaginary vacancy of the wilderness and threaten to disrupt this closed dyadic relationship by introducing a repressed third realm of the unnarrated stories of colonization, slavery and resistance that link the histories of both continents.[44]

As history, *Errand* was most certainly a "constellating" narrative but, as Kaplan suggests, one whose main purpose required that it occlude rather than explore its referents. By comparison, in the Atlantic World of this book's chapters, that "third realm" is no longer contained, no longer the darkness outside Miller's "rank of spotlights."[45] The Atlantic World of these chapters is not created out of dyadic Euro-American geographies, imaginary vacant interiors, or repressed histories. It is unimaginable *without* Africa, without the polyglot islands and seaboard of the North American landmass, without the interior and its peoples, colonization and slavery, classes and struggle.[46]

What these chapters describe, cumulatively, is the early Atlantic World as a commercial system. Its characteristics, as Simon Newman puts it, are "massive movement[s] of people and goods."[47] But these movements, one should immediately add, occur always within particular institutional formations—assemblages of mercantile capital called trading companies and partnerships;[48] assemblages of jurisdiction, called cities, corporations, manors, plantations, households;[49] and everywhere, necessarily, the enabling assemblages of sovereign authority, with its legislatures, councils, courts; its letters patent, charters, statutes, opinions, and decisions; and its increasingly elaborated juridical-penal complexes.[50] Without these formations, massive movement has no shape. It is doubtful, indeed, whether it could take place at all.[51]

Here, in studying class and class consciousness, we inquire into how these formations come about. In other words, we sense the importance of institutional formations to the comprehension of class. In fact, that importance is clearly displayed in the Atlantic World's founding texts, which map the conjunctions of particular structures of production and extraction with particular forms of knowledge and expertise. The objective was bluntly stated at the outset by the elder Richard Hakluyt as manning, planting, and keeping: that is, transfer of population; occupation of territory; production of commodities; and establishment of possession.[52]

To explore simply one locus of conjunction that crops up repeatedly in these chapters,[53] consider the city in the creation of the Atlantic World. It is a mistake to think of cities simply as conurbations, the piling up of people and buildings. The meaning of the city in the Atlantic World lies rather in the discourse of "eutopolis"—the perfected representation of civil association and civilization, the seat of sovereignty, the center of commerce, and the citadel of Christian evangelism.[54] The implantation of eutopolis in the transatlantic wilderness moves European "culture" into American "vacancy." From the Virginia colony to New England to Carolina to Pennsylvania to Georgia, the creation of cities and townships stood at the center of colonizers' strategies for securing territory, governing mobility, planning inhabitation, and achieving perfection. The first settlements in the Chesapeake were named James *City* and Charles *City*. In New England, famously, John Winthrop's *Arbella* sermon on "Christian Charity" denominated the Massachusetts Bay colonizing project an exemplary eutopolis, "a city upon a hill." The Restoration colonies further elaborated the model. The creation of a city was prominent in the Carolina proprietors' plans. Their Fundamental Constitutions designed a meticulously detailed spatial structure to frame an elaborately hierarchical culture of governance. William Penn followed a similar course in Pennsylvania, planning a city, contiguous concentrated settlement patterns, and an elaborated political order all well in advance of actual settlement.[55]

What was being pursued in all of these cases was not simply a formal allocation of space but the creation of a spatially embodied political or civic order to receive and organize the migrating population ("the poore and Idle persons wch nowe are ether burdensome or hurtefull to this Realme at home"[56]) and direct its productive impulses: a locale, in other words, for the exercise of jurisdiction. As with the city, so with other institutional formations (companies, corporations, manors)—these too were modalities of organization essential to the greater organization of the Atlantic World itself. Population, territory, city, and colony constituted an institutional-organizational complex outside which the intimately related processes of 'manning' and 'planting' and 'keeping' could not function.

But this complex and its components were simultaneously subjects of distinct meanings imparted to them by the oppressed. Chartered privileges, municipal responsibilities, claims of customary or prescriptive rights are all sites of struggle in the early Atlantic World.[57] As Simon Middleton argues, drawing on his study of the New York City revolt of 1689, "we have to investigate not only the antagonisms that develop within processes of production and accumulation, but also the character of contemporary social power and the sense of security and unanimity it fostered prior to the fractures and resentments that provoked the revolt."[58] Tapping the broad early-modern conception of economy that encompassed an ideology of the common good, Middleton inspects the salience to the revolt of frustrated "considerations of community safety and prosperity, and ... claims for local privileges and liberties whose distribution was rationalized as the means to an orderly moral and social end."[59]

Newman's Glasgow offers us another point of purchase on such considerations and claims. That point is not situated amid the city's throngs of goods and people, however, but in the quieter precincts of its university, where dwells an ironic absentee from these pages, Adam Smith. A series of lectures that Smith delivered at the university in 1762–63 have recently been identified as a historical moment outside the temporality of the economic liberalism that Smith involuntarily anchors, in that the central question for determination is not how individual liberty—political and economic—is to be maximized *against* rent-seeking strata of governance (whether princes or cities or merchant guilds or incorporated monopolies) but rather what rules should direct civil governments in the pursuit of their main objectives, identified as "the maintenance of justice, the provision of police [sanitation, security, plenitude], the raising of revenue and the establishment of arms."[60] On the cusp of the nineteenth century, in other words, the "safety and prosperity" described by Middleton suddenly rear up again from a hundred years before, not as some quaint atavistic spasm of a decayed premodern municipal discourse of economic justice, but as key elements of a "jurisprudence of security" embraced by the greatest of all modern economists. In Smith's lectures, the foundations of economics are built on law and government; security—economic and social, local and translocal—is one of the most important objects of his attention. Indeed by addressing security in the context of this distinctly nonliberal conjunction of governance, law, and economy, Smith, one can argue, sought a resolution in the apparent conflict between private right and collective interest. As Smith would later point out in *The Wealth of Nations*, security in market transactions is self-actuating, hence "invisible," because the work of transacting is governed by the impulse of self-interest. But the sentiment of self-interest does not stand alone from "sympathy, or feeling for one's fellow man," which Smith's earlier work suggests as "an antecedent principle and overall conditioner of the moral, legal and social environment in which the price system operates."[61] In other words, the Smithian formulation of the province of civil government renders the concept expansively, the means of producing what Smith's "rude" American contemporary William Manning would identify as the object of all governance: the "safety & happiness" not of "the few" but of all.[62] Such are the conjunctions that define the Atlantic World figured as a "constellation of eras" and defy history as continuum.

In his "Theorizing Class in Glasgow and the Atlantic World," Simon Newman argues, in effect, that class is the product of modernity's "stirring up" of the patterns of an older world amid gathering social and economic complexity, and that class consciousness is a sloughing off of old ways amid a dawning realization of opportunity, often frustrated, for collective self-improvement.[63] This, it seems to me, requires that one continue to place one's bets on the Enlightenment's ideal of history as progress. Certainly, so doing, Newman is in good company. As we have seen, E. P. Thompson was keen to discard orthodox materialism's economic determinism but never its historicism. The English working class made itself within the continuum of historical time. Hence, it had to behave, as it were, in sequence—certain of its actions could not take place before "their" time. If they did, then they were something other than they appeared to be.[64]

Such a history, ever facing forward, imagining—yearning?—that better will come, is an understandable and perhaps necessary opiate. But it can never accommodate the disjunctive constellations of eras that lend the tradition of the oppressed its explosive power: it participates too much in the creation of a necessary order of things. In such a history, William Manning cannot invoke those "considerations of community safety and prosperity" in 1798 that Simon Middleton finds in New York a century before without some sophisticated modern gently chiding his nostalgia for a world left behind by the rough acquisitiveness of the early republic.[65]

To explore the Atlantic World system of the seventeenth century in terms suggested by the Atlantic World system of the late eighteenth century, or of the early twentieth, or of now, or vice versa, is to sin against history as continuum. It is to commit anachronism, place our objects of study in the "wrong" moments of historical time.[66] The historicist would have us treat the class struggles of early North America and the Atlantic World as done with. Like spears that hang on the wall of a museum, they exhibit what *was*. We may reach for them, examine them, turn them this way and that. They may excite our curiosity, but not our fear or desire for vengeance. This history domesticates its readers. It does not seduce or unnerve, anger or threaten.[67]

Walter Benjamin's "angel of history" was always turned toward the past. "Where we perceive a chain of events, he sees one single catastrophe, which keeps piling wreckage upon wreckage and hurls it in front of his feet." The angel "would like to stay, awaken the dead, and make whole what has been smashed." But he is caught in a storm that blows from paradise. It "propels him into the future to which his back is turned, while the pile of debris before him grows skyward. This storm is what we call progress." If class and class struggles in early North America and the Atlantic World are to excite more than academic curiosity, their historians must have done with the ideology of progress and its temporal caesura. Only then can we learn that in the constellation of eras, all that already has been continues to be present to us—perhaps as that which becomes available at a spectral moment,[68] or perhaps incognito until recognized by one who will recall it,[69] or perhaps as a volcano, extinct until the moment that it erupts "like a flash of lightning in the clouds. We live in the flicker."[70]

Nunc Stans

> The tradition of the oppressed teaches us that "the state of emergency" in which we live is not the exception but the rule.
>
> —Walter Benjamin, "Theses on the Philosophy of History," no. 8

What does the tradition of the oppressed teach us about the relationship between class and struggle in that early Atlantic World in constellation with which we live now? It teaches, I think, the normality of empire and how class and struggle arise both *within* empire and against it.

The triadic Atlantic World on display in these chapters was created and sustained in processes of law-organized colonization. It remains with us as such, though now organized by international law as one component in a larger, global system. International law is generally treated as "Westphalian" in origin, a system of sovereign state interactions, dating from the mid-seventeenth century and later extended to the peripheral states of European settlement in North America and Australasia. In this *jus publicum Europaeum*, "war is regarded as being conducted among equal European sovereign states, in which combatants recognized each others as *justi hostes*, just enemies" who did not question each other's sovereign character or moral standing.[71] Suppose, however, one has voyaged outside a recognizable (on one's own terms) state system. Suppose one is not engaging another "just enemy" but has intruded upon the lands of "brutes." This is the earlier, formative era of international law developed in the late sixteenth and early seventeenth centuries, a pre-Westphalian law of nations that addresses not interstate relations but the rights of the community of the civil and the humane in their interactions with those outside that community, barbarians. In his *De Iure Belli* (1588), for example, Alberico Gentili, the Regius Professor of Civil Law at Oxford, argued that nature had established among men "kinship, love, kindliness, and a bond of fellowship" from which all who violated nature were excluded, brutes upon whom war might justly be made.[72] Alongside the interior gestures of courtesy that autonomous self-governing sovereign Westphalian states paid each other, that is, lay another realm of action far more characteristic of world historical experience that invoked the judgments of "nature" and the community of the humane as necessary and sufficient basis for making war to civilize (humanize, improve, instruct) barbarity. Here was the origin of the discourse of sovereign right that would sustain European empires for half a millennium as they expanded into the zones of exception they had created for themselves beyond the boundaries of the medieval map.[73]

Colonizing, one may argue, is the normalization of exception.[74] It occurs in the world's barbaric zones as an unending condition of emergency—the unending necessity that order and civility be visited upon the disordered. But colonizing is as potent a metaphor for the state's attempts to create "due regulation and order" in locales of exception within the physical boundaries of the homeland as much as in the world beyond, and in fact connects the two. In England, for example, significant legislative-juridical intensification of labor discipline took place during the eighteenth century. But that intensification exemplifies a pattern we can denominate the "internal colonization of the island." The two ideas exist together in the political economy of Daniel Defoe, who wrote vehemently in 1724 of the absolute necessity to quash the leisure preference of the poor and to discipline work, and who over the next two years described the disorder of Britain's extra-metropolitan extremities in his closely related *Tour Through the Whole Island of Great Britain*.[75] The "domestic" relationship between colonizing the island and mobilizing labor reproduces aspects of the relationship between mobilizing labor and empire abroad. In conjunction, they suggest that class formation and empire are apposite processes.[76]

Like those of the Hakluyts, Defoe's travel narratives and his writings on economics constantly stressed the intimate relationship between English domestic prosperity and order, labor mobilization, and transoceanic colonizing. Thus, in his *Plan of the English Commerce*: "An Encrease of Colonies encreases People, People encrease the Consumption of Manufactures, Manufactures Trade, Trade Navigation, Navigation Seamen, and altogether encrease the Wealth, Strength and Prosperity of *England*."[77] Eighty years on, one finds Patrick Colquhoun's treatises on *The Police of the Metropolis* (1796), *The Commerce and Police of the River Thames* (1800), and *Indigence* (1806) contemplating a further and systematic consolidation of the terms of all transactions involving labor power around the money wage (an intensification of work discipline, an assault on leisure-preference, and a persistent criminalization of perquisites), complemented by "a free circulation of labour" and extended, in his *Wealth, Power and Resources of the British Empire* (1814) into a full-blown imperial political economy. Newman's "massive movement[s] of people and goods" become ever more sophisticated in their conceptual and institutional organization.[78]

In the work of the Hakluyts, colonization and labor interact as strategies of "improvement." A disorderly population that threatens social order within the realm is improved (as is the realm, by subtraction) by shipping it to plantations overseas where it can become a productive labor force that "improves" the colonized wilderness. In Defoe's version, disorderly population is no longer exported. Intensified discipline at home becomes part of the repertoire of improvement, improving a realm that is simultaneously undergoing improvement by the expanded opportunities for domestic consumption and wealth accumulation that commodity-producing, manufacture-demanding colonies provide. In Colquhoun's version, the generalization of the wage form improves all the labor of the empire, binding all into one political economy by the full extension of free circulation and commensurability throughout a commercial empire. It no longer matters who is where. By Conrad's time, the empire has arrived at peak efficiency. Exporting its disciplines to the furthest extremity, to the heart of each continent, extracts the greatest measure of improvement possible. As Colquhoun had envisaged, relations of production and exchange have been systematically reproduced throughout an imperial political economy. Conrad observes the mechanics of the system at close hand:

Black shapes crouched, lay, sat between the trees leaning against the trunks. . . . The work was going on. The work! And this was the place where some of the helpers had withdrawn to die. . . . They were not enemies, they were not criminals, they were nothing earthly now—nothing but black shadows of disease and starvation, lying confusedly in the greenish gloom. Brought from all the recesses of the coast in all the legality of time contracts, lost in uncongenial surroundings, fed on unfamiliar food, they sickened, became inefficient, and were then allowed to crawl away and rest.[79]

Profanity and Justice

> *The current amazement that the things we are experiencing are "still" possible in the twentieth century is <u>not</u> philosophical. This amazement is not the beginning of knowledge—unless it is the knowledge that the view of history which gives rise to it is untenable.*
> —Walter Benjamin, "Theses on the Philosophy of History," no. 8

If empire and its unremitting zest for improvement is what called the Atlantic World into being as such, and if we may then consider class formation and class struggles, in all their plurality, an effect of empire and its zest for improvement, what can the tradition of the oppressed tell us about the objectives of class struggle?

Empire is an expression of sovereign order—of the attempt to create jurisdictional "unity of decision" throughout a territory, or territories. Modern sovereignty—the sovereignty of the last half millennium—has its origins in Europe and "was born and developed in large part through Europe's relationship with its outside . . . particularly through its colonial project."[80] That relationship, I have argued, was expressed as the claim of European sovereigns to rule over the zones of exception that lay beyond their self-endowed community of the humane. Although Michael Hardt and Antonio Negri have recently suggested that this "juridical power to rule over the exception" is a new paradigm of imperial authority, the evidence of early modern humanism's law of nations suggests otherwise.[81]

If empire is constituted by movement into and claims to rule over the extra-metropolitan zones and locales of exception outside civility that European law has repeatedly constructed as the object of improvement, class struggle expresses itself as a retort, a claim to interrupt or negate that invokes a distinct sovereignty, one that comes precisely from the "outside" that law creates to sustain its claims of civility. Class struggle is then an uprising from among those very "barbarians" of all stripes called into existence by law's self-representation as civility's war upon barbarity. It comes from among and on behalf of all those who inhabit the zones of emergency and exception that are the normality of the oppressed wherever and whenever they may be.[82]

In these chapters, the languages of popular rights abroad, as Newman says, in the Atlantic World, appear to express something of a claim to a sovereignty distinct from and opposed to that of empire. In Thomas Paine's revolutionary *Common Sense*, for example, we discover opposed to the "Royal Brute of Britain" a dispersed sovereignty residing in the people, the only legitimate foundation for a form of jurisdiction (rule of law) to which all should be subject.[83] Is this how the tradition of the oppressed manifests itself? In struggles to create an improved rule of law? Historicism would have us believe so, for law is to a very important extent the medium in which historicism expresses its message of progress.[84] But for Benjamin at least, the tradition of the oppressed found no expression, or instrument of interruption, in law, whatever its appearance. Law's authority was the authority of the profane, created and preserved (produced and reproduced) by the violence of state power over life and death. Interruption required of the oppressed a capacity for a distinct, revolutionary, violence—the "divine violence, which . . . may be called sovereign violence" that "instead of founding law . . . destroys it"[85] in the name of an ultimate, Messianic cessation, a "day of judgment" in which mankind would finally receive "the fullness of its past."[86]

Benjamin's was truly a poetic justice.[87] His day of judgment could come about only through the fanatic energy of a supreme sovereignty, for that was the only conceivable foundation for the ending of law and the possibility of a final epoch of justice.[88] "Only the Messiah himself consummates all history," he wrote in his *Theologico-Political Fragment*, "in the sense that he alone redeems, completes, creates its relation to the Messianic." Precisely for this anti-historicist reason, historical materialism "can easily be a match for anyone if it enlists the services of theology, which today, as we know, is wizened and has to keep out of sight."[89]

Was this eschatological conjunction one that might have been familiar to the oppressed of the Atlantic World? To some, at least, if we are to take seriously what E. P. Thompson has to tell us of William Blake.[90] Blake is nowhere in these chapters—another ironic absentee—but he is to be found nonetheless at the revolutionary climacteric of the stories of class and struggle that these chapters tell, in the fevered London of the early 1790s. London was fevered in large part by Painite Jacobinism and its rights talk, but Thompson keeps Blake at a remove from the Jacobins. "For Blake," he says, "had always been decisively alienated from the mechanical materialist epistemology and psychology which he saw as derived from Newton and Locke. And he did not for a moment shed his suspicion of radicalism's indebtedness to this materialism." Blake was no Enlightenment scion. Though he might agree with the Jacobins' assault upon state and church repression, "it did not follow that humanity's redemption . . . could be effected by a political reorganization of these institutions alone. *There must be some utopian leap, some human rebirth, from Mystery to renewed imaginative life*."[91]

Blake's theology was neither wizened nor out of sight but immanent in his every depiction of the oppressed. Let us take just one example, the poem "London" from the *Songs of Experience*. Thompson writes, "Every reader can, without the help of a critic, see London simultaneously as Blake's own city, as an image of the state of English society and as an image of the human condition."[92] It was not in Blake's nature to compromise, nor did he:

I wander thro' each charter'd street,
Near where the charter'd Thames does flow.
And mark in every face I meet
Marks of weakness, marks of woe.

In every cry of every Man,
In every Infants cry of fear,
In every voice; in every ban,
The mind-forg'd manacles I hear

How the Chimney-sweepers cry
Every blackning Church appalls,
And the hapless Soldiers sigh,
Runs in blood down Palace walls,

But most thro' midnight streets I hear
How the youthful Harlots curse
Blasts the new-born Infants tear
And blights with plagues the Marriage-hearse[93]

Blake's "London" was Patrick Colquhoun's London, the world's greatest commercial metropolis, the riverine heart of an imperial political economy, inhabited by a laboring population disciplined by the charters and bans of law and magistracy and church. Blake left unscathed not one fragment of Colquhoun's city. All (city, river, every street, every inhabitant) had been "charter'd" (hired, expropriated), absorbed into an unrelieved commerce in things and people, sold out by church and king. The marks and corruptions of hire were evident in every face and activity, heard in every voice. Manacles of "deceit, self-interest, absence of love, of law, repression and hypocrisy" clasped everyone, whether barrow boy or prostitute.[94]

"London" is a bitter root to chew on, hell on Earth. Still, it ends not in "weakness" and "woe" (the first verse), fear (the second), or hapless sighs (the third), but in a snarl of anger, a curse. It is the city that has been betrayed, not the city that has done the betraying. And always beside London as hell on Earth, Blake glimpses another city, Jerusalem, immanent, the spectral London that "could also be the millennial city, of that time when the moral and self-righteous law should be overthrown, and the Multitude return to Unity."[95] Blake's spectral London was humanity redeemed; its time, of course, was messianic; and the unity to which the multitude returned was that of a mankind whose past had now become "citable in all its moments."[96]

Conrad's "monstrous" London, "within the brooding gloom," was hell too. People lived out their lives on its "solid pavement" amid "neighbours ready to cheer you or to fall on you, stepping delicately between the butcher and the policeman, in the holy terror of scandal and gallows and lunatic asylums." Their labors were "monkey tricks" performed on tightropes at "half-a-crown a tumble," and heartache the rest of the price. The city's dark effluvium now stained the entire world. Yet Conrad too allows a hint of spectral possibility, of a "mysterious stillness watching," of unearthly conjunctions and a "now" shot through with chips of messianic time.[97]

The present belongs in this constellation of eras. "Multitude" is what Hardt and Negri have named the contemporary successor to the polyphonous multivalent mobile class—Benjamin's "oppressed"—whose early Atlantic origins and manifestations have been traversed in the chapters in this volume. "Multitude" is the present generation of barbarians, "the set of all the exploited and the subjugated," which confronts "Empire" just as past generations, to an important degree, confronted "imperialism." But it does so, they claim, in a fashion more immediate, less divisible by "cleavages and borderlines of race, gender, language, culture" and nation. For empire (globalization by a less anodyne name) has created multitude in its own image of incessant and accelerating circulation, of ubiquitous mobility. But precisely through its circulation, the multitude "reappropriates space and constitutes itself as an active subject" claiming entry—a circulation, self-constitution, and claim made enormously and abruptly manifest in U.S. cities in the immigration law reform protests of March, April, and May of 2006.[98]

Hardt and Negri ask how the multitude can become a political subject. Their answer—through a political discourse free of "metaphysical and

transcendent mediations" that simply expresses the multitude's own imma-
nence as a singularity. "There is not finally here any determinism or utopia; this
is, rather, a radical counterpower, ontologically grounded . . . on the actual activity of the multitude, its creation, production, and power." This is "a materialist teleology."[99] We have been dealing with these themes throughout: that
"counterpower" (struggle) cannot be formed on the basis of some promise of
a better future but only by reference to its own actuality, known only by history; but also that, to reject mediations, materialism is not enough: one must
allow a glimpse of the messianic. For we know from both Blake and Benjamin
that what the messianic is, precisely and absolutely, is the end to all mediations.

There is no theology within Hardt's and Negri's materialism, no immanent
"City of God" to which the multitude might turn. Its only place is "the earthly
city." The other "has lost all honor and legitimacy."[100] Blake could not have
agreed. Benjamin could, precisely because he knew that "from the standpoint of
history" the oppressed had only "the order of the profane" (the earthly city) in
which to struggle. "Theocracy has no political but only a religious meaning."
The City of God was "not the goal, but the end."[101] Yet precisely because the City
of God was the end and not the goal, the specter of messianic possibility could
be ever present. The possibility of reaching beyond the profane—beyond
"progress," beyond "improvement," beyond "homogenous, empty time"—to
the strait gate of messianic cessation, absolute justice, was, we have seen, the key
to Benjamin's conception of history and of revolution. The mediations of the
profane were otherwise insurmountable, surrender to a disabling, unending law
and historicism inevitable.[102] Every one of the *Theses*, consequently, addresses
the possibility of how the oppressed might end history, "blast open the continuum," in order to reach the messianic.[103] Who is to say that this is not the greatest of all ambitions for history, the ultimate act of hope—that before midnight
strikes us, at any time in any century, it might *stop*?

Conclusion: Why History Matters

> *The situation in which we who inhabit a seemingly common earth do not
> all do so with space, validity and pleasure, may properly be described as
> tragic. But not declined as an inescapable and irremediable given, an un-
> relievable historicism, or a mysterious condition.*
> —*Francis Barker,* The Culture of Violence

To our contemporary historicists—historical positivists—Walter Benjamin's
belief that the oppressed might end history is an absurdity, a waste of their

time; his disjunctive historical materialism nothing more than a pernicious grubbing under the foundations of the idea of history itself. The point of their historical practice is precisely to show that history is both endless and sequestered from life and struggle, an eternal filling up of time with objects that are always left in their own time, contained by caesurae of chronology and period and progress, so that (for example) we will read "London" without any stir to the mind that its anger might suddenly fuse with—erupt into, amplify—our current amazements.

Might we not ask in reply, for whom does *this* history really matter? Positivism, whether historical or legal, cannot explain our current amazements, which materialism desires at least to address. It can imagine them only as objects that are placed in and immediately contained by their temporal contexts. And so each thing that still happens becomes instantly one in an infinite series of past happenings, each placed in its moment, each leading to the next moment, and so ever on, but ever severed from now.

Why should we demand that history (*this* history) end? Because our home has been made "a new found Golgatha."[104] Because we are deafened by "London's" keening. Because, in the dying light of a fire, "a nigger [is] being beaten."[105] Because midnight has come to the century.[106] Our demand blasts each of these specific moments "out of the homogenous course of history" and creates them now anew, an eschatological constellation. Of that constellation we can ask another question. Is it this? "How long will we tolerate *this*?"[107]

Notes

Introduction

We thank Dan Richter, Greg Nobles, and an anonymous referee for their very useful comments on this essay.

1. On these academic and structural developments, see Greg Nobles, "Class," in *A Companion to Colonial America*, ed. Daniel Vickers (Malden, Mass.: Blackwell Publishers, 2003), 259–88; Patrick Joyce, *Democratic Subjects: The Self and the Social in Nineteenth-Century England* (Cambridge: Cambridge University Press, 1994), introduction; Patrick Joyce, ed., *Class* (Oxford: Oxford University Press, 1995), 3–16; and Chris Weedon, *Feminism, Theory, and the Politics of Difference* (Oxford: Blackwell, 1999), especially chapter 6.

2. Among recent publications that accord class a prominent role in their analysis of early America and the Atlantic World are Peter Linebaugh and Marcus Rediker, *The Many-Headed Hydra: Sailors, Slaves, Commoners, and the Hidden History of the Revolutionary Atlantic* (Boston: Beacon, 2000); Gary B. Nash, *The Unknown American Revolution: The Unruly Birth of Democracy and the Struggle to Create America* (New York: Viking, 2005); Nobles, "Class," 259–88; Billy G. Smith, ed., *Down and Out in Early America* (University Park: Pennsylvania State University Press, 2004); and Keith Wrightson, "Class," in *The British Atlantic World, 1500–1800*, ed. David Armitage and Michael J. Braddick (New York: Palgrave, 2002), 133–53. See also three special journal issues: "Class and Early America," *The William and Mary Quarterly*, 3rd ser., 63 (April 2006); "Deference in Early North America," *Early American Studies: An Interdisciplinary Journal* 3, no. 2 (fall 2005); and "Class Analysis in Early America and the Atlantic World: Foundations and Future," *Labor: Studies in Working Class History of the Americas* 1, no. 4 (winter 2004).

3. This paragraph draws on Peter Calvert, *The Concept of Class: An Historical Introduction* (London: Fontana, 1983), 11–93; Andrew Milner, *Class* (London: Sage Publications, 1999), 1–52; and Gary Day, *Class* (London: Routledge, 2001), introduction.

4. For the development of a language of "sorts" that simplified the previously more precise and elaborate notions of estate and degree, see Keith Wrightson, *English Society, 1580–1680* (1982; reprint, London: Routledge, 1993), chapter 1; Wrightson, "Estates, Degrees, and Sorts: Changing Perceptions of Society in Tudor and Stuart England," in *Language, History, and Class*, ed. Penelope Corfield (Oxford: Basil Blackwell, 1991), 32–44; Wrightson, "'Sorts of People' in Tudor and Stuart England," in *The Middling Sort of People: Culture, Society, and Politics in England, 1550–1800*, ed. Jonathon Barry and Christopher Brooks (Basingstoke: Macmillan, 1994), 28–51; and Wright, "Class," in *The British Atlantic World, 1500–1800*, ed. David Armitage and

Michael J. Braddick (Basingstoke: Palgrave, 2002), 133–54. On the colonial American side of the Atlantic, see Billy G. Smith, *The "Lower Sort": Philadelphia's Laboring People, 1750–1800* (Ithaca, N.Y.: Cornell University Press, 1990).

5. For accessible statements of these core principles, see Marx's introduction to *A Contribution to the Critique of Hegel's Philosophy of Right*, and his preface to *A Contribution to the Critique of Political Economy*, both in Rodney Livingstone and Gregor Benton, trans., *Karl Marx: Early Writings* (1975; reprint, London: Penguin Books, 1992), 243–59, 424–29.

6. Among the most important books about early America by American Progressive historians are Charles A. Beard, *An Economic Interpretation of the Constitution of the United States* (New York, 1913; reprint, New York: Free Press, 1986); Carl L. Becker, *The History of Political Parties in the Province of New York, 1765–1776* (Madison: University of Wisconsin Press, 1909); and Arthur Schlesinger, Sr., *The Colonial Merchants and the American Revolution* (1918; reprint, New York: F. Unger, 1957).

7. Raphael Samuel, "The British Marxist Historians I," *New Left Review* 120 (March-April 1980): 21–96; Eric Hobsbawm, "The Historians' Group of the Communist Party," in *Rebels and Their Causes: Essays in Honour of A. L. Morton*, ed. M. Cornforth (London: Lawrence and Wishart, 1978), 21–47; Harvey J. Kaye, *The British Marxist Historians* (Cambridge: Cambridge University Press, 1984), 1–23, 221–50; Richard Hoggart, *The Uses of Literacy: Aspects of Working-Class Life, with Special References to Publications and Entertainments* (London: Chatto and Windus, 1957); and Raymond Williams, "Culture Is Ordinary," in *Studies in Culture: An Introductory Reader*, ed. Ann Gray and Jim McGuigan (London: Arnold, 1997), 5–14.

8. E. P. Thompson, as quoted in Kaye, *British Marxist Historians*, 172. Also see Raymond Williams, *The Long Revolution* (Harmondsworth: Penguin, 1961).

9. Classic British studies include Edward P. Thompson, *The Making of the English Working Class* (New York: Pantheon Books, 1963); Eric J. Hobsbawm, *Primitive Rebels: Studies in Archaic Forms of Social Movement in the Nineteenth and Twentieth Centuries* (New York: Praeger, 1963). Among American contemporaries and later acolytes are Herbert Gutman, *Work, Culture, and Society in Industrializing America: Essays in American Working-Class and Social History* (New York: Vintage, 1966); Jesse Lemisch, "The American Revolution Seen from the Bottom Up," in *Towards a New Past: Dissenting Essays in American History*, ed. Barton J. Bernstein (New York: Pantheon Books, 1968), 3–46; Eric Foner, *Tom Paine and Revolutionary America* (New York: Oxford University Press, 1976); Gary B. Nash, *The Urban Crucible: Social Change, Political Consciousness, and the Origins of the American Revolution* (Cambridge, Mass.: Harvard University Press, 1979), 3–25; Sean Wilentz, *Chants Democratic: New York City and the Rise of the American Working Class* (New York: Oxford University Press, 1984); Marcus Rediker, *Between the Devil and the Deep Blue Sea: Merchant Seamen, Pirates, and the Anglo-American Maritime World, 1700–1750* (Cambridge: Cambridge University Press, 1987).

10. Andy Wood reviews the debate in the English context in his *The Politics of Social Conflict: The Peak Country, 1520–1770* (Cambridge: Cambridge University Press, 1999), chapter 1.

11. Ibid. Thus, Keith Wrightson's early modern English society "was not a society dominated by class affiliation; for however strong the awareness of status within

a specific local context, broader class consciousness was inhibited . . . by their lack of alternative conceptions of the social order, their envelopment in relationships of communality and deference, by the localism which gave those ties force and meaning and by a lack of institutions which might organize and express a horizontal group consciousness of a broader kind." Wrightson, *English Society*, 64–65. Gordon S. Wood offers a similar view of eighteenth-century America in his *The Radicalism of the American Revolution* (New York: Vintage Books, 1993), 23–24.

12. Nobles, "Class," 262. See also Stanley Aronowitz, *How Class Works: Power and Social Movement* (New Haven, Conn.: Yale University Press, 2003), 12–19.

13. Nobles, "Class," 262. For some of the earliest significant work of these scholars, see Jesse Lemisch, "Jack Tar in the Streets: Merchant Seamen and the Politics of Revolutionary America," *William and Mary Quarterly*, 3rd ser., 25 (1968): 373–407; Lemisch, "The American Revolution Seen from the Bottom Up," in *Towards a New Past*, 3–45; Staughton Lynd, *Class Conflict, Slavery, and the United States Constitution* (Indianapolis: Bobbs-Merrill, 1967); Gary B. Nash, ed., *Class and Society in Early America* (Englewood Cliffs, N.J.: Prentice-Hall, 1970); and Alfred F. Young, ed., *The American Revolution: Explorations in American Radicalism* (DeKalb: Northern Illinois University Press, 1976).

14. Joyce Appleby, Lynn Hunt, and Margaret Jacob, *Telling the Truth about History* (New York: W. W. Norton, 1994), 152–60. Among the pioneering efforts to understand the *mentalité* of common people were Michael Merrill, "Cash Is Good to Eat: Self-Sufficiency and Exchange in the Rural Economy of the United States," *Radical History Review* 4 (1977): 42–71; James A. Henretta, "Families and Farms: *Mentalité* in Pre-industrial America," *William and Mary Quarterly*, 3rd ser., 35 (1978): 3–32; and Christopher Clark, "The Household Economy, Market Exchange, and the Rise of Capitalism in the Connecticut Valley, 1800–1860," *Journal of Social History* 13 (1979): 169–90.

15. Of course, the perspective of most social historians was considerably more complex. Many of them examined the economic and demographic environment as a way ultimately to understand the lives of past people.

16. For England, see Julia Swindells and Lisa Jardine, *What's Left? Women in Culture and the Labor Movement* (London: Routledge, 1990), 24–46. For America, see Lois Rita Helmbold and Ann Schofield, "Women's Labor History, 1790–1945," *Reviews in American History* 17 (1989): 500–513; Joan Wallach Scott, *Gender and the Politics of History* (New York: Columbia University Press, 1988), chapters 3 and 4. For race, see Clarence E. Walker, "How Many Niggers Did Karl Marx Know? Or a Peculiarity of the Americans," in his *Deromanticizing Black History: Critical Essays and Reappraisals* (Knoxville: University of Tennessee Press, 1991), 1–33.

17. Peter Novick, *That Noble Dream: The "Objectivity Question" and the American Historical Profession* (Cambridge: Cambridge University Press, 1988); Gary B. Nash, Charlotte Crabtree, and Ross E. Dunn, *History on Trial: Culture Wars and the Teaching of the Past* (New York: Knopf, 1997). The criticisms leveled by historians of gender and race and the reactionary commentary that accompanied the rightward tilt of Anglo-American politics challenged accounts by class historians of the social and political struggles that accompanied a contested transition to capitalism. For example, in 1998 Eugene Genovese justified setting up the alternative professional

association, the Historical Society, by denouncing scholars whose research offered "more an exercise in self-expression than an effort to deal with objective reality." *The Washington Times*, April 29, 1998.

18. The classification is from Novick, *That Noble Dream*, 523. Hayden White, "The Burden of History," in his *Tropics of Discourse: Essays in Cultural Criticism* (Baltimore: Johns Hopkins University Press, 1978), 28.

19. The literature on this topic is vast, but useful starting points include Peter Schottler, "Historians and Discourse Analysis," *History Workshop Journal* (1988): 37–65; Joan Scott, "The Evidence of Experience," *Critical Inquiry* 17 (summer 1991): 773–97; John E. Toews, "Intellectual History after the Linguistic Turn: The Autonomy of Meaning and the Irreducibility of Experience," *American Historical Review* 92 (1987): 879–907.

20. Gareth Stedman Jones, *The Languages of Class: Studies in English Working-Class History, 1832–1982* (Cambridge: Cambridge University Press, 1983), 90; Anna Clark, *The Struggle for the Breeches: Gender and the Making of the British Working Class* (Berkeley: University of California Press, 1995). For France, see Michael Sonenscher, *Work and Wages: Natural Law, Politics, and the Eighteenth-Century French Trades* (Cambridge: Cambridge University Press, 1989).

21. Scott, *Gender and the Politics of History*, 42–43. Also see Denise Riley, *Am I That Name? Feminism and the Category of "Women" in History* (Basingstoke, Hampshire: Macmillan, 1988).

22. Two books indicated a new departure in thinking about race and identity: David Roediger, *The Wages of Whiteness: Race and the Making of the American Working Class* (London: Verso, 1991); and Alexander Saxton, *The Rise and Fall of the White Republic: Class, Politics, and Mass Culture in Nineteenth-Century America* (London: Verso, 1990). However, note the continuing dissimilarities in conceptual approaches to the history of slavery evident in the differences between Kathleen Brown, *Good Wives, Nasty Wenches, and Anxious Patriarchs: Gender, Race, and Power in Colonial Virginia* (Chapel Hill: University of North Carolina Press, 1996) and Ira Berlin, *Many Thousands Gone: The First Two Centuries of Slavery in North America* (Cambridge, Mass.: Harvard University Press, 1998). For Native Americans, see Daniel Richter's lament of the essentialism that undermined the fortunes of ethnohistory in "Whose Indian History," *William and Mary Quarterly*, 3rd ser., (1993): 379–94.

23. Gareth Stedman Jones, "Anglo-Marxism—Discursive Approach to History," in *Was Bliebt von Marxistischen Perpektiven in der Geschichtforschung?*, ed. Alf Ludtke (Gottingen: Wallstein Verlag, 1997), 151–209; William H. Sewell, "Toward a Post-Materialist Rhetoric for Labor History," in *Rethinking Labor History*, ed. Lenard R. Berlanstein (Chicago: University of Illinois Press, 1993), 15–39; Jacque Ranciere, "The Myth of the Artisan: Critical Reflections on a Category of Social History," in *Work in France: Representations, Meaning, Organization, and Practice*, ed. S. L. Kaplan and C. J. Koepp (Ithaca, N.Y.: Cornell University Press, 1986), 317–34; and Jacques Ranciere, *The Nights of Labor: The Worker's Dream in Nineteenth-Century France*, trans. John Drury (Philadelphia: Temple University Press, 1989), preface.

24. For the continued commitment to the Thompsonian framework, see the introduction and essays in *Labor Histories: Class, Politics, and Working-Class Experience*, ed. Julie Greene, Bruce Laurie, and Eric Arnesen (Urbana: University of Illinois Press,

1998). For a defense of this approach, see Bryan D. Palmer, *Descent into Discourse: The Reification of Language and the Writing of Social History* (Philadelphia: Temple University Press, 1990), chapters 1 and 4.

25. Two commentaries, published within a year of each other, captured the sense of impasse reached by those engaged in the study of class. For Sonya Rose "class identities are formed, and political solidarities generated, discursively . . . [and] do not spring forth in an unmediated fashion from productive relations." However, for Julie Greene, Bruce Laurie, and Eric Arnesen "class is not merely a discursively constructed phenomenon best understood in relation to language," and further "to isolate language from the material conditions in which it is produced . . . obliterates analytical distinctions between forms of knowledge and conditions of their production." Sonya Rose, "Class Formation and the Quintessential Worker," in *Reworking Class*, ed. John R. Hall (Ithaca, N.Y.: Cornell University Press, 1997), 148; Greene, Arnesen, and Laurie, eds., *Labor Histories*, 3.

26. The evaluation of political and economic processes in our world draws on interpretations ranging from the news magazine *The Economist* (especially the September 16, 2006 edition) to Robert Brenner, *The Economics of Global Turbulence* (London: Verso, 2006).

27. Rather than spend too much energy arguing about the "correct" interpretation of class, class and radical historians need, as Staughton Lynd urges, to reclaim themes and narratives that have been seized by conservative scholars. Staughton Lynd, "Revisiting Class in Early America: Personal Reflections," *Labor: Studies in Working-Class History of the Americas* 1, no. 4 (winter 2004): 27–34.

28. For example, see David Harlan's evaluation of Quentin Skinner's methodological conflation of speech acts with written texts, which, Harlan argues, is necessary to evade the poststructuralist conception of the autonomy of language and the intertextual accumulation of meaning that would otherwise prevent the recovery of authorial intentions that are essential for Skinner's hermeneutic project. David Harlan, "Intellectual History and the Return of Literature," *American Historical Review* 94, no. 3 (June 1989): 583–93; and his discussion of similar compromises worked out by scholars such as Thomas Haskell, David Hollinger, James Kloppenberg, and Joyce Appleby in David Harlan, *The Degradation of American History* (Chicago: University of Chicago Press, 1997), chapter 4. Also see Miguel A. Cabrera's assessment of Gareth Stedman Jones's proposal for the expansion of intellectual history informed by the study of political language outlined in Gareth Stedman Jones, "Anglo-Marxism— Discursive Approach to History," 151–209, in Miguel A. Cabrera, "Linguistic Approach or Return to Subjectivism? In Search of an Alternative to Social History," *Social History* 24, no. 1 (January 1999): 74–79.

29. Pierre Bourdieu, "What Makes a Social Class? On the Theoretical and Practical Existence of Social Groups," *Berkeley Journal of Sociology: A Critical Review* 32 (1987): 1–19.

30. For example, Sonya Rose draws upon Iris Marion Young's reworking of John Paul Sartre's concept of seriality and proposes the view that individuals come to inhabit related and serial subject positions when they confront determining opportunities and constraints with an origin and logic from outside of themselves. Sonya Rose, "Class Formation and the Quintessential Worker," 150–51; Marion Young,

"Gender as Seriality: Thinking about Women as a Social Collective," *Signs* 19 (spring 1994): 713–38. Christopher Tomlins, "Subordination, Authority, Law: Subjects in Labor History," *International Labor and Working-Class History* 47 (spring 1995): 78–80. Tomlins invoked terms suggested by Marxist-feminist theories of standpoint, especially Maureen Cain, "Realism, Feminism, Methodology, Law," *International Journal of the Sociology of Law* 14 (1986): 259–61. Also see Nancy C. M. Harstock, "The Feminist Standpoint: Developing the Ground for a Specifically Feminist Historical Materialism," in *Discovering Reality: Feminist Perspectives on Epistemology, Metaphysics, and Philosophy of Science*, ed. Sandra Harding and Merril B. Hintikka (Amsterdam: D. Reidel Publishing Company, 1983), 283–311; and the important essay by Seth Rockman, "The Contours of Class in the Early Republic City," *Labor: Studies in Working-Class History of the Americas* 1, no. 4 (winter 2004): 91–107.

31. Here we are borrowing Joan Scott's terminology in *Gender and the Politics of History*, 42.

32. Nobles, "Class," 264.

33. Linebaugh and Rediker, *The Many-Headed Hydra*. See also Rediker, "The Revenge of Crispus Attucks; or, The Atlantic Challenge to American Labor History," *Labor: Studies in Working-Class History of the Americas* 1, no. 4 (winter 2004), 40–42.

34. We have borrowed the metaphor of sedimentation from Steve Hindle, *The State and Social Change in Early Modern England* (Basingstoke: Palgrave, 2000), introduction. For the continuing transformation and exploitation of global empire, see Michael Hardt and Antonio Negri, *Empire* (Cambridge, Mass.: Harvard University Press, 2000).

35. Peggy K. Liss, *Atlantic Empires: The Network of Trade and Revolution, 1713–1826* (Baltimore: Johns Hopkins University Press, 1983); Stephen J. Hornsby and Michael Hermann, *British Atlantic, American Frontier: Spaces of Power in Early Modern British America* (Hanover, N.H.: University Press of New England, 2004); April Hatfield, *Atlantic Virginia: Intercolonial Relations in the Seventeenth Century* (Philadelphia: University of Pennsylvania Press, 2003); Peter A. Coclanis, ed., *The Atlantic Economy during the Seventeenth and Eighteenth Centuries: Organization, Operation, Practice, and Personnel* (Columbia: University of South Carolina Press, 2005).

36. Dror Wahrman, *The Making of the Modern Self: Identity and Culture in Eighteenth-Century England* (New Haven, Conn.: Yale University Press, 2005), chapter 5.

37. Edward P. Thompson, "The Patricians and the Plebs," in his *Customs in Common: Studies in Traditional Popular Culture* (New York: New Press, 1991), 16–97; Dror Wahrman, *Imagining the Middle Class: The Political Representation of Class in Britain, c. 1780–1840* (Cambridge: Cambridge University Press, 1995).

38. Raymond Williams, *Keywords: A Vocabulary of Culture and Society* (New York: Oxford, 1976), 60.

Chapter 1. Theorizing Class in Glasgow and the Atlantic World

1. Robert Reid, *Glasgow in the Olden Time: Local Memorabilia; Contributed by Senex*, in *Glasgow, Past and Present, Illustrated in Dean of Guild Court Reports and in*

the Reminiscences and Communications of Senex, Aliquis, J. B. Etc., 3 vols. (Glasgow: David Robertson and Co., 1884), 1:371. Reid's articles appeared in the *Glasgow Herald* between November 1848 and May 1851 under the pseudonym Senex and were then collected together with the reminiscences of other aged locals and published in book form. Details of his life are in the "Autobiography of Robert Reid," *Glasgow, Past and Present*, 3:489–96.

2. For a thorough investigation of the ways in which tobacco merchants reinvested profits into different manufactories, see T. M. Devine, *The Tobacco Lords: A Study of the Tobacco Merchants of Glasgow and Their Trading Activities, c. 1740–90* (Edinburgh: John Donald, 1975), 34–51.

3. John Sinclair, "City of Glasgow," in *The Statistical Account of Scotland 1791–1799: Edited by Sir John Sinclair*, vol. 7, *Lanarkshire and Renfrewshire* (East Ardsley, Wakefield: E. B. Publishing Limited, 1973), 294–95.

4. Account by emigrants from Scotland, Treasury Papers, T1/500, National Archives (Public Record Office), as quoted in Sharon V. Salinger, *"To Serve Well and Faithfully": Labor and Indentured Servants in Pennsylvania, 1682–1800* (Cambridge: Cambridge University Press, 1987), 84.

5. Marjory Harper has harnessed a wealth of primary source material in order to demonstrate that the death of the Highland feudal system resulted both from forced and voluntary movement from the land. See Marjory Harper, *Adventurers and Exiles: The Great Scottish Exodus* (London: Profile, 2003).

6. For more on the varying experiences of these Highlanders, see George Donaldson, *The Highland Clearances: People, Landlords, and Rural Turmoil* (Edinburgh: Birlinn, 2000); T. M. Devine, *Clanship to Crofters' War: The Social Transformation of the Scottish Highlands* (Manchester: Manchester University Press, 1994); T. M. Devine, ed., *Scottish Emigration and Scottish Society* (Edinburgh: John Donald, 1992); Harper, *Adventurers and Exiles*; David Dobson, *Scottish Emigration to Colonial America, 1607–1785* (Athens: University of Georgia Press, 1994); Irene Maver, *Glasgow* (Edinburgh: Edinburgh University Press, 2000); T. M. Devine and Gordon Jackson, eds., *Glasgow: Beginnings to 1830* (Manchester: Manchester University Press, 1995).

7. Maver, *Glasgow*, 9–10, 12–14; George Eyre-Todd, *History of Glasgow*, vol. 3, *From the Revolution to the Passing of the Reform Acts, 1832–33* (Glasgow: Jackson, Wylie and Co., 1934), 39–40.

8. T. M. Devine, "Urbanisation," in *People and Society in Scotland*, vol. 1, *1700–1830*, ed. T. M. Devine and R. Mitchinson (Edinburgh: John Donald, 1988), 29.

9. W. W. Knox, *Industrial Nation: Work, Culture, and Society in Scotland, 1800–Present* (Edinburgh: Edinburgh University Press, 1999), 37.

10. T. M. Devine, "The Golden Age of Tobacco," in *Glasgow*, vol. 1, *Beginnings to 1830*, ed. T. M. Devine and Gordon Jackson (Manchester: Manchester University Press, 1995), 140–41. In addition to Devine's work on the tobacco trade and the rise of the tobacco lords, see Jacob M. Price, "The Rise of Glasgow in the Chesapeake Tobacco Trade, 1707–1775," *The William and Mary Quarterly*, 3rd ser., 11 (1954): 179–99; and Price, *Capital and Credit in British Overseas Trade: The View from the Chesapeake, 1700–1776* (Cambridge, Mass.: Harvard University Press, 1980), 140–46.

11. Devine, *The Tobacco Lords*, v.

12. On the evolution of relationships among merchants in the Atlantic World, see also the chapters in this volume by Jennifer Goloboy and Andrew Schocket.

13. Devine, *The Tobacco Lords*, 15–24.

14. Ibid., 34–35.

15. Ibid., 35–44.

16. Sinclair, *The Statistical Account of Scotland,* 298.

17. For the best exploration of the role of seafaring communities in the production and distribution of laboring identity, see Peter Linebaugh and Marcus Rediker, *The Many-Headed Hydra: The Hidden History of the Revolutionary Atlantic* (Boston: Beacon Press, 2000). For an excellent summary of negotiation as a construct for analysis of the developing relationships between people of different classes, races, and status groups, see Alfred F. Young, "Afterword: How Radical Was the American Revolution?," in *Beyond the American Revolution: Explorations in the History of American Radicalism*, ed. Alfred F. Young (DeKalb: Northern Illinois University Press, 1993), 317–64.

18. John Buchanan, "Queen Street," in *Glasgow Past and Present, Illustrated in Dean of Guild Court Reports and in the Reminiscences and Communications of Senex, Aliquis, J. B. Etc.*, 3 vols. (Glasgow: David Robertson and Co., 1884), 2;423.

19. Robert Reid, "Odds and Ends—Gorbals Banishments," in *Glasgow Past and Present, Illustrated in Dean of Guild Court Reports and in the Reminiscences and Communications of Senex, Aliquis, J. B. Etc.*, 3 vols. (Glasgow: David Robertson and Co., 1884), 1:351.

20. John Butt, "Housing," in *The Working Class in Glasgow, 1750–1914*, ed. R. A. Cage (London: Croom Helm, 1987), 29–32.

21. Maver, *Glasgow*, 28–29.

22. R. A. Cage, "Health in Glasgow," in *The Working Class in Glasgow, 1750–1914*, ed. R. A. Cage (London: Croom Helm, 1987), 67, 61–62.

23. Robert Reid, "Mr. Cunninghame's House in Gorbals Street, Etc.—The Gorbals Island," in *Glasgow Past and Present, Illustrated in Dean of Guild Court Reports and in the Reminiscences and Communications of Senex, Aliquis, J. B. Etc.*, 3 vols. (Glasgow: David Robertson and Co., 1884), 1:283.

24. Sinclair, *The Statistical Account of Scotland 1791–1799*, Table 2, 306.

25. R. A. Cage, "The Nature and Extent of Poor Relief," in *The Working Class of Glasgow, 1750–1914*, ed. R. A. Cage (London: Croom Helm, 1987), 83–84; Eyre-Todd, *History of Glasgow*, 3:50–51.

26. Maver, *Glasgow*, 24.

27. Dr. Mathie Hamilton, "The King's Birthday in the Olden Time," in *Glasgow Past and Present, Illustrated in Dean of Guild Court Reports and in the Reminiscences and Communications of Senex, Aliquis, J. B. Etc.*, 3 vols. (Glasgow: David Robertson and Co., 1884), 1:258–59.

28. For a discussion of this historiography, see W. Hamish Fraser, *Conflict and Class: Scottish Workers, 1700–1838* (Edinburgh: John Donald, 1988), 1–10.

29. Ibid., 3, 10.

30. Ibid., 22–23.

31. Ibid., 24, 26–27.

32. Sinclair, *The Statistical Account of Scotland 1791–1799*, 296.

33. Fraser, *Conflict and Class*, 31–33.

34. Maver, *Glasgow*, 51–52.

35. Quoted in Maver, *Glasgow*, 25.

36. Knox, *Industrial Nation*, 57–58.

37. Dr. Mathie Hamilton, "Volunteers in Glasgow During the War of 1793," in *Glasgow Past and Present, Illustrated in Dean of Guild Court Reports and in the Reminiscences and Communications of Senex, Aliquis, J. B. Etc.*, 3 vols. (Glasgow: David Robertson and Co., 1884), 1:243–44.

38. Hamilton, "The King's Birthday," 258–60.

39. Reid, "Mr. Cunninghame's House," 286.

40. Robert Reid, "Olden Memorabilia," in *Glasgow Past and Present, Illustrated in Dean of Guild Court Reports and in the Reminiscences and Communications of Senex, Aliquis, J. B. Etc.*, 3 vols. (Glasgow: David Robertson and Co., 1884), 1:342–43.

41. Unpublished diary of John Mackinnon, quoted in A. J. S. Gibson and T. C. Smout, *Prices, Food, and Wages in Scotland, 1550–1780* (Cambridge: Cambridge University Press, 1995), 13.

42. Anonymous, "Supplementary Scraps," in *Glasgow Past and Present, Illustrated in Dean of Guild Court Reports and in the Reminiscences and Communications of Senex, Aliquis, J. B. Etc.*, 3 vols. (Glasgow: David Robertson and Co., 1884), 1:560.

43. Knox, *Industrial Nation*, 43.

44. Maver, *Glasgow*, 30–31.

45. For example, two separate articles in a single issue of one Glasgow newspaper reported Boston's riots against the Stamp Act in some detail. See "London Oct. 8" and "Extract of a Letter from Boston, August 26," in *Glasgow Journal*, 17 October 1765. I am grateful to Bradley A. Jones for these references.

46. See Bradley A. Jones, "The American Revolution, Glasgow, and the Making of the Second City of the Empire," in *Europe's American Revolution*, ed. Simon P. Newman (Houndmills: Palgrave Macmillan, 2006), 1–25.

47. E. P. Thompson, "Eighteenth-Century English Society: Class Struggle without Class?" *Social History* 3 (1978): 149, 150.

48. Fernand Braudel, *The Mediterranean and the Mediterranean World in the Age of Philip II*, trans. Siân Reynolds (1949; reprint, New York: Harper and Row, 1976).

49. For a detailed discussion of this process, see Keith Wrightson, "Class," in *The British Atlantic World, 1500–1800*, ed. David Armitage and Michael J. Braddick (Basingstoke: Palgrave, 2002), 133–53.

50. For others, particularly African American slaves, such possibilities were far more limited. However, as slave culture developed in the Americas, it developed a class of people as much as it developed a "race," and slaves clearly were conscious of themselves, their position, and their needs and wants in relations to those of other classes.

51. Thompson's classic exploration of the implications of this position is in his influential essay "Eighteenth-Century English Society," 133–65. In his magisterial *The Making of the English Working Class* (London: Victor Gollancz, 1963), Thompson provided a deeply researched case study, one that he continued in *Customs in Common: Studies in Traditional Popular Culture* (New York: The New Press, 1991).

52. Pierre Bourdieu, "What Makes a Social Class," *Berkeley Journal of Sociology* 22 (1998): 1–18.

53. For a classic statement of this position, see E. P. Thompson, "Patrician Society, Plebian Culture," *Journal of Social History* 7 (1974): 382–405. See also Thompson, "The Patricians and the Plebs," in his *Customs in Common*, 16–96; and Thompson "Eighteenth-Century English Society."

54. Examples of works challenging the traditional view include Daniel Vickers, *Farmers and Fishermen: Two Centuries of Work in Essex County, Massachusetts, 1630–1850* (Chapel Hill: University of North Carolina Press, 1994); Christine Leigh Heyrman, *Commerce and Culture: The Maritime Communities of Colonial Massachusetts, 1690–1750* (New York: Norton, 1984); and Stephen Innes, *Labor in a New Land: Economy and Society in Seventeenth-Century Springfield* (Princeton, N.J.: Princeton University Press, 1983).

55. Karl Marx, *Capital*, vol. 1, trans. Ben Fowkes (1867; reprint, London: Penguin, 1990), 447.

56. Thompson, "Eighteenth-Century English Society," 150.

57. Simon Middleton, "Rethinking Class in Early America: The Struggle for Rights and Privileges in Seventeenth-Century New York" (paper presented at the annual conference of the Omohundro Institute of Early American History and Culture, Glasgow, 2001), 3.

Chapter 2. Stratification and Class in Eastern Native America

1. Karen Ordahl Kupperman, *Indians and English: Facing Off in Early America* (Ithaca, N.Y.: Cornell University Press, 2000), 92–93. For a differing view of the same issues, see Nancy Shoemaker, *A Strange Likeness: Becoming Red and White in Eighteenth-Century North America* (New York: Oxford University Press, 2004), 35–60.

2. Helen C. Rountree, *The Powhatan Indians of Virginia: Their Traditional Culture* (Norman: University of Oklahoma Press, 1989), 100–113; Frederic W. Gleach, *Powhatan's World and Colonial Virginia: A Conflict of Cultures* (Lincoln: University of Nebraska Press, 1997), 28–34; Kathleen J. Bragdon, *Native People of Southern New England, 1500–1650* (Norman: University of Oklahoma Press, 1996), 142.

3. Joshua Piker, *Okfuskee: A Creek Indian Town in Colonial America* (Cambridge, Mass.: Harvard University Press, 2004), 21–28; Bruce G. Trigger, "Maintaining Economic Equality in Opposition to Complexity: An Iroquoian Case Study," in *The Evolution of Political Systems: Sociopolitics in Small-Scale Sedentary Societies*, ed. Steadman Upham (Cambridge: Cambridge University Press, 1990), 127–30.

4. Lawrence A. Clayton, Vernon James Knight, Jr., and Edward C. Moore, eds., *The De Soto Chronicles: The Expedition of Hernando De Soto to North America in 1539–1543*, 2 vols. (Tuscaloosa: University of Alabama Press, 1993), 1:83; Karen Ordahl Kupperman, *Captain John Smith: A Select Edition of His Writings* (Chapel Hill: University of North Carolina Press, 1988), 155.

5. Lafitau, *Customs of the American Indians*, 1:290–93.

6. David Peterson De Vries, "Voyages from Holland to America, A.D. 1632 to 1644," *New York Historical Society Collections*, 2nd ser., 3 (1857): 96–97.

7. Elman R. Service, *Primitive Social Organization: An Evolutionary Perspective* (New York: Random House, 1962); Morton H. Fried, *The Evolution of Political Society: An Essay in Political Anthropology* (New York: Random House, 1967).

8. The literature critiquing and elaborating evolutionary typologies is vast. For useful overviews, see Thomas E. Emerson, *Cahokia and the Archaeology of Power* (Tuscaloosa: University of Alabama Press, 1997), 12–18; and Timothy Earle, "Archaeology, Property, and Prehistory," *Annual Review of Anthropology* 29 (2000): 39–60. Service and Fried developed their typologies as heuristic devices for understanding theoretical principles about what Fried called "the evolution of political society." Despite their unfortunate use of terms such as "primitive," their main concern was not to make invidious comparisons between what they also unfortunately called "higher" and "lower" levels of political organization observed in contemporary ethnography. On this point, see, in particular, Service, "Our Contemporary Ancestors," in his *Primitive Social Organization*, 7–9. The bulk of Service's and Fried's critics, when not assaulting crypto-racist evolutionary frameworks, complain that societies in the real world fail to conform to easy four-part categorizations. However, both Timothy K. Earle, a leading modern heir to the Service-Fried tradition , and Steadman Upham, a thoughtful critic, note that such complaints utterly miss the point of heuristic devices. Timothy K. Earle, "Chiefdoms in Archaeological and Ethnohistorical Perspective," *Annual Review of Anthropology* 16 (1987): 279–81. As Upham observes, "This lack of congruence results directly from the fact that the societal types of Service and Fried are composites and do not exist in their entirety in the real world; they are categorical representations of reality that condense meaningful variability." Steadman Upham, "Analog or Digital?: Toward a Generic Framework for Explaining the Development of Emergent Political Systems," in *The Evolution of Political Systems: Sociopolitics in Small-Scale Sedentary Societies*, ed. Steadman Upham (Cambridge: Cambridge University Press, 1990), 88–91. As shown by the title of Upham's edited collection, and by his article's clever attempt to replace "digital" types with a more fluid "analog" model, anthropologists interested in processes of change in political systems almost invariably fall back on some kind of typological thinking, even in the process of criticizing it. Perhaps the epitome of this phenomenon is Gary Feinman and Jill Neitzel, "Too Many Types: An Overview of Sedentary Prestate Societies in the Americas," *Advances in Archaeological Method and Theory* 7 (1984): 39–102, a widely cited article that attacks the proliferation of typological categories based on lists of supposed characteristics by carrying out a complicated survey of trait lists for some 106 "middle-range" societies in North and South America. However competently those lists of traits may have been compiled from ethnological and ethnohistorical studies, the whole mode of reasoning they represent—abstracted from all context either for the cultures described or for the scholarship in which they are embedded—seems utterly antithetical to Feinman's and Neitzel's call for "long-term processual analyses" and "diachronic, contextual studies" of "the causal processes and sequences of change that are responsible for societal variability" (78).

9. See Robert D. Drennan, "Regional Demography in Chiefdoms," in *Chiefdoms in the Americas*, ed. Robert D. Drennan and Carlos A. Uribe (Lanham, Md.: University Press of America, 1987), 313–15; Patricia Galloway, *Choctaw Genesis, 1500–1700* (Lin-

coln: University of Nebraska Press, 1995), 38–40; and Timothy K. Earle, *How Chiefs Come to Power: The Political Economy in Prehistory* (Stanford, Calif.: Stanford University Press, 1997), 1–16.

10. Service, *Primitive Social Organization.*

11. Fried, *The Evolution of Political Society,* 52, 109–17, 133–34, 185–86, 225–26.

12. Service, *Primitive Social Organization,* 119. On the "'conditional' sedentism" of estuarine New England groups, see Bragdon, *Native People of Southern New England,* 55–59. For an argument for similar characteristics among Lenapes, see Marshall Joseph Becker, "A Summary of Lenape Socio-Political Organization and Settlement Pattern at the Time of European Contact: The Evidence for Collecting Bands," *Journal of Middle Atlantic Archaeology* 4 (1988): 79–83.

13. Helen Rountree and E. Randolph Turner III, *Before and after Jamestown: Virginia's Powhatans and Their Predecessors* (Gainesville: University Press of Florida, 2002), 36–51; Margaret Holmes Williamson, *Powhatan Lords of Life and Death: Command and Consent in Seventeenth-Century Virginia* (Lincoln: University of Nebraska Press, 2003); Martin D. Gallivan, *James River Chiefdoms: The Rise of Social Inequality in the Chesapeake* (Lincoln: University of Nebraska Press, 2003).

14. Stephen R. Potter, *Commoners, Tribute, and Chiefs: The Development of Algonquian Culture in the Potomac Valley* (Charlottesville: University of Virginia Press, 1993).

15. Bragdon, *Native People of Southern New England,* 40–43 (quotation), 55–79.

16. Daniel K. Richter, *The Ordeal of the Longhouse: The Peoples of the Iroquois League in the Era of European Colonization* (Chapel Hill: University of North Carolina Press, 1992), 30–49; Charles Hudson, *The Southeastern Indians* (Knoxville: University of Tennessee Press, 1976), 211–26.

17. For an overargued but nonetheless interesting discussion of this, see Alex W. Barker, "Powhatan's Pursestrings: On the Meaning of Surplus in a Seventeenth-Century Algonkian Chiefdom," in *Lords of the Southeast: Social Inequality and the Native Elites of Southeastern North America,* ed. Alex W. Barker and Timothy R. Pauketat, Archaeological Papers of the American Anthropological Association 3 (1992): 61–80.

18. Bragdon, *Native People of Southern New England,* 147–48. In 1636, Jean de Brébeuf observed that, among the Hurons, "several families have their own private trades, and he is considered Master of one line of trade who was the first to discover it. The children share the rights of their parents in this respect, as do those who bear the same name; no one goes into it without permission, which is given only in consideration of presents; he associates with him as many or as few as he wishes." Thwaites, *The Jesuit Relations,* 10:221–23.

19. See, for example, Mark W. Mehrer, *Cahokia's Countryside: Household Archaeology, Settlement Patterns, and Social Power* (DeKalb: Northern Illinois University Press, 1995).

20. Earle, *How Chiefs Come to Power,* 67–104. The differential control of *labor* by chiefs seldom enters into the equation, despite its obvious importance for the construction of, for instance, the earthworks at Cahokia and other Mississippian centers. The importance of captive taking in warfare throughout eastern North America and the significance of captives as a labor source that can usefully be seen as a form of en-

slavement suggests, however, that this resource may have been an important factor in the stratification of eastern chiefdoms. For suggestive comments on indigenous Native American slavery, see William A. Starna and Ralph Watkins, "Northern Iroquoian Slavery," *Ethnohistory* 38 (1991): 34–57; and Brett Rushforth, "'A Little Flesh We Offer You': The Origins of Indian Slavery in New France," *William and Mary Quarterly*, 3rd ser., 60 (2003): 777–808.

21. Susan M. Frankenstein and Michael J. Rowlands, "The Internal Structure and Regional Context of Early Iron Age Society in South-Western Germany," *Institute of Archaeology Bulletin* 15 (1978): 73–112, quotations from 76.

22. Mary W. Helms, "Political Lords and Political Ideology in Southeastern Chiefdoms: Comments and Observations," in *Lords of the Southeast: Social Inequality and the Native Elites of Southeastern North America*, ed. Alex W. Barker and Timothy R. Pauketat, Archaeological Papers of the American Anthropological Association 3 (1992): 187–88.

23. Frankenstein and Rowlands, "The Internal Structure and Regional Context of Early Iron Age Society," 81.

24. Earle, "Chiefdoms in Archaeological and Ethnohistorical Perspective," 297.

25. Mary Douglas and Baron Isherwood, *The World of Goods* (New York: Basic Books, 1979); Timothy R. Puketat, "The Reign and Ruin of the Lords of Cahokia: A Dialectic of Dominance," in *Lords of the Southeast: Social Inequality and the Native Elites of Southeastern North America*, ed. Alex W. Barker and Timothy R. Pauketat, Archaeological Papers of the American Anthropological Association 3 (1992): 31–51; Emerson, *Cahokia and the Archaeology of Power*, 33–35. See also Marcel Mauss, *The Gift: The Form and Reason for Exchange in Archaic Societies*, trans. W. D. Halls (London: Routledge, 2002); and Maurice Godelier, *The Enigma of the Gift*, trans. Nora Scott (Chicago: University of Chicago Press, 1999).

26. Emerson, *Cahokia and the Archaeology of Power*, 258.

27. Thwaites, *The Jesuit Relations*, 10:183–85.

28. Christopher L. Miller and George R. Hamell, "A New Perspective on Indian-White Contact: Cultural Symbols and Colonial Trade," *Journal of American History* 73 (1986): 311–28. It should be noted that Miller and Hamell explicitly object to "the all too common tautological device of simply defining such items as 'luxury,' 'prestige,' and 'status' goods, thus inherently valuable and desirable" (315).

29. James W. Bradley, *Evolution of the Onondaga Iroquois: Accommodating Change, 1500–1655* (Syracuse, N.Y.: Syracuse University Press, 1987), 69–78.

30. Laurier Turgeon, "The Tale of the Kettle: Odyssey of an Intercultural Object," *Ethnohistory* 44 (1997): 1–29, quotations from 10.

31. Ibid., 17.

32. Ibid., 15. Turgeon's euphonious insight remains valid, despite the theological difficulty that the last things that define *eschatology* are not involved.

33. Thwaites, *The Jesuit Relations*, 10:75.

34. Kupperman, *Indians and English*, 109 (quotation); Roy Harvey Pearce, *The Savages of America: A Study of the Indian and the Idea of Civilization* (Baltimore: Johns Hopkins University Press, 1953); Robert F. Berkhofer, Jr., *The White Man's Indian: Images of the American Indian from Columbus to the Present* (New York: Knopf, 1978); Olive Patricia Dickason, *The Myth of the Savage and the Beginnings of French Colonialism in*

the Americas (Edmonton: University of Alberta Press, 1984); Gordon M. Sayre, Les Sauvages Américains: Representations of Native Americans in French and English Colonial Literature (Chapel Hill: University of North Carolina Press, 1997).

35. Shoemaker, A Strange Likeness, greatly advances our understanding of these dynamics.

36. Kupperman, Captain John Smith, 156.

37. Neal Salisbury, Manitou and Providence: Indians, Europeans, and the Making of New England, 1500–1643 (New York: Oxford University Press, 1982), 236.

38. Marvin T. Smith, "Aboriginal Population Movements in the Early Historic Period Interior Southeast," in Powhatan's Mantle: Indians in the Colonial Southeast, ed. Peter H. Wood, Gregory A. Waselkov, and M. Thomas Hatley (Lincoln: University of Nebraska Press, 1991), 21–34; Alan Gallay, The Indian Slave Trade: The Rise of the English Empire in the American South, 1670–1717 (New Haven, Conn.: Yale University Press, 2002), 23–39; Steven C. Hahn, The Invention of the Creek Nation, 1670–1763 (Lincoln: University of Nebraska Press, 2004), 13–26.

39. Raymond Fogelson, "Who Were the Aní-Kutání? An Excursion into Cherokee Historical Thought," Ethnohistory 31 (1984): 255–63.

40. Thwaites, The Jesuit Relations, 10:229–31.

41. Bruce G. Trigger, Natives and Newcomers: Canada's 'Heroic Age' Reconsidered (Kingston, Ont.: McGill-Queen's University Press, 1985), 226–97; Richter, The Ordeal of the Longhouse, 50–74.

42. Treaty minutes, July 12, 1697, New York Colonial Manuscripts, vol. 41, folio 93, New York State Archives, Albany.

43. Lafitau, Customs of the American Indians, 1:293.

44. Earle, "Chiefdoms in Archaeological and Ethnohistorical Perspective," 281; Galloway, Choctaw Genesis, 67–74; Emerson, Cahokia and the Archaeology of Power, 17–18; Frankenstein and Rowlands, "The Internal Structure and Regional Context of Early Iron Age Society," 78–79; Fried, The Evolution of Political Society, 185–86 (quotation).

45. Patricia E. Rubertone, "The Historical Archaeology of Native Americans," Annual Review of Anthropology 29 (2000): 425–46.

46. Frankenstein and Rowlands, "The Internal Structure and Regional Context of Early Iron Age Society," 79, 83.

47. Dena F. Dincauze and Robert J. Hasenstab, "Explaining the Iroquois: Tribalization on a Prehistoric Periphery," in Centre and Periphery: Comparative Studies in Archaeology, by Timothy C. Champion (London: Unwin Hyman, 1989), 67–87. On Moundville's trading networks, see Christopher S. Peebles, "Moundville from 1000 to 1500 AD as Seen from 1840 to 1985 AD," in Chiefdoms in the Americas, ed. Robert D. Drennan and Carlos A. Uribe (Lanham, Md.: University Press of America, 1987), 21–41.

48. For an exploration of some of these transformations, see Fenton, The Great Law and the Longhouse.

49. See David Silverman, "Deposing the Sachem to Defend the Sachemship: Land Sales and Native Political Structure on Martha's Vineyard, 1680–1740, Explorations in Early American Culture 5 (2001): 9–44; and John Wood Sweet, Bodies Politic: Negotiating Race in the American North, 1730–1830 (Baltimore: Johns Hopkins University Press, 2003), 15–57.

50. See, for example, Claudio Saunt, *A New Order of Things: Property, Power, and the Transformation of the Creek Indians, 1733–1816* (New York: Cambridge University Press, 1999); Timothy Shannon, "Dressing for Success on the Mohawk Frontier: Hendrick, William Johnson, and the Indian Fashion, *William and Mary Quarterly*, 3rd ser., 53 (1996): 13–42; Daniel K. Richter, *Facing East from Indian Country: A Native History of Early America* (Cambridge, Mass.: Harvard University Press, 2001), 151–88; and Gail D. MacLeitch, "'Red' Labor: Iroquois Participation in the Atlantic Economy," *Labor: Studies in Working-Class History of the Americas* 1, no. 4 (winter 2004): 69–90.

51. David Guldenzopf, "The Colonial Transformation of Mohawk Iroquois Society" (Ph.D. diss., State University of New York, Albany, 1987), 97–130, 143–45.

52. Ibid., 134 (quotations), 148.

53. Ibid., 148–49; William H. Carter, "The 'Enormous Expence' of Indian Presents: The Gift Economy of Revolutionary Iroquoia" (paper presented at the McNeil Center for Early American Studies, Philadelphia, October 14, 2005), 17–24; Isabel Thompson Kelsay, *Joseph Brant, 1743–1807: Man of Two Worlds* (Syracuse, N.Y.: Syracuse University Press, 1984), 390–91, 521–96.

54. Carl F. Klinck and James J. Talman, eds., *The Journal of Major John Norton, 1816* (Toronto: The Champlain Society, 1970), 284–85. Brant's struggles to gain the right for his people to sell land directly to Euro-Americans are set in broader context in Alan Taylor, *The Divided Ground: Indians, Settlers, and the Northern Borderland of the American Revolution* (New York: Knopf, 2006), 331–41; and James W. Paxton, "Kinship, Communities, and Covenant Chains: Mohawks and Palatine Germans in New York and Upper Canada, 1712–1830" (Ph.D. diss., Queen's University, 2006).

55. William Apes[s], *Eulogy on King Philip, as Pronounced at the Odeon, in Federal Street, Boston* (Boston: published by the author, 1836), 55–56, 39.

Chapter 3. Subaltern Indians, Race, and Class in Early America

1. I use "Indian" and "Native" interchangeably—"Native" rather than "Native American" because the latter is awkward when used frequently, and "American" is a European name. Capitalizing "Native" as a proper noun is grammatically correct and prevents confusion as to whether I mean people of primarily aboriginal or immigrant (European or African) ancestry and social identity. Canadians now commonly use the term First Peoples; my capitalization of "Native" fulfills the same purpose.

2. Jenny Hale Pulsipher, *Subjects unto the Same King: Indians, English, and the Contest for Authority in Colonial North America* (Philadelphia: University of Pennsylvania Press, 2005), 1–20; Nancy Shoemaker, *A Strange Likeness: Becoming Red and White in Eighteenth-Century North America* (New York: Oxford University Press, 2004), 36–50; Karen O. Kupperman, *Settling with the Indians: The Meeting of English and Indian Cultures in America, 1580–1640* (Totowa, N.J.: Rowman and Littlefield, 1980), 49–58.

3. Immanuel Wallerstein, *The Capitalist World-Economy* (New York: Cambridge University Press, 1979); Thomas Hall, *Social Change in the Southwest, 1350–1880* (Lawrence: University Press of Kansas, 1989).

4. James Axtell, *Natives and Newcomers: The Cultural Origins of North America* (New York: Oxford University Press, 2001), 84–116.

5. Christopher Hill, *The World Turned Upside Down: Radical Ideas during the English Revolution* (London: Maurice Temple Smith, 1972); Axtell, *Natives and Newcomers*, 189–213.

6. Peter Linebaugh and Marcus Rediker, *The Many-Headed Hydra: Sailors, Slaves, Commoners, and the Hidden History of the Revolutionary Atlantic* (Boston: Beacon Press, 2000), 30–35.

7. Eric Wolf, *Europe and the People without History* (Berkeley: University of California Press, 1982), 158–94; Axtell, *Natives and Newcomers*, 112–40.

8. Helen Rountree, *Pocahontas's People: The Powhatan Indians of Virginia through Four Centuries* (Norman: University of Oklahoma Press, 1990), 142–52, 180, 182–83; Jean R. Soderlund, "The Delaware Indians and Poverty in Colonial New Jersey," in *Down and Out in Early America*, ed. Billy G. Smith (University Park: Pennsylvania State Press, 2004), 289–311; Daniel Mandell, *Behind the Frontier: Indians in Eighteenth-Century Eastern Massachusetts* (Lincoln: University of Nebraska Press, 1996); Wendy B. St. Jean, "Inventing Guardianship: The Mohegan Indians and Their 'Protectors,'" *New England Quarterly* 72 (1999): 362–87.

9. Mandell, *Behind the Frontier*, 137–40, 179–80; Rountree, *Pocahontas's People*, 145; Jean R. Soderlund, "Class, Ethnicity, and Native Americans in Eighteenth-Century New Jersey," presented at the Omohundro Institute of Early American History and Culture meeting, 2001, Glasgow, Scotland; John A. Strong, *The Montaukett Indians of Eastern Long Island* (Syracuse, N.Y.: Syracuse University Press, 2001), 45.

10. Rountree, *Pocohontas's People*, 145; Mandell, *Behind the Frontier*, 37, 62, 194, 196, 199–201.

11. Daniel Mandell, "'To Live More Like My Christian English Neighbors': Natick Indians in the Eighteenth Century," *William and Mary Quarterly*, 3rd ser., 48 (1991): 566–71; Kevin McBride, "Historical Archaeology of the Mashantucket Pequots, 1637–1900, a Preliminary Analysis," in *The Pequots in Southern New England: The Rise and Fall of an American Indian Nation*, ed. Laurence M. Hauptman and James D. Wherry (Norman: University of Oklahoma Press, 1990); John Wood Sweet, *Bodies Politic: Negotiating Race in the American North, 1730–1830* (Baltimore: Johns Hopkins University Press, 2003), 36–43.

12. Samson Occom, "A Short Narrative of My Life," reprinted in Colin G. Calloway, *The World Turned Upside Down: Indian Voices from Early America* (Boston: Bedford Books, 1994), 55, 60.

13. Mandell, *Behind the Frontier*, 26, 36–40; David Silverman, "The Impact of Indentured Servitude on the Society and Culture of Southern New England Indians, 1680–1810," *New England Quarterly* 74 (2001): 662.

14. Gideon Hawley to Peter Thacher, January 1, 1794, Hawley Letters, Massachusetts Historical Society (MHS); David Silverman, *Faith and Boundaries: Colonists, Christianity, and Community among the Wampanoag Indians of Martha's Vineyard, 1600–1871* (New York: Cambridge University Press, 2005); Strong, *The Montaukett Indians*, 53; Daniel Vickers, "The First Whalemen of Nantucket," *William and Mary Quarterly*, 3rd ser., 40 (1983): 560–83; Mandell, *Behind the Frontier*, 49, 111, 140, 197–98; Mark A. Nicholas, "Mashpee Wampanoags of Cape Cod, the Whalefishery, and Sea-

faring's Impact on Community Development," *American Indian Quarterly* 26 (2002): 165–97.

15. Gail MacLeitch, "'Red' Labor: Iroquois Participation in the Atlantic Economy," *Labor: Studies in the Working-Class History of the Americas* 1, no. 4 (winter 2004): 69–90.

16. John Sainsbury, "Indian Labor in Early Rhode Island," *New England Quarterly* 48 (1975): 379; Margaret Ellen Newell, "The Changing Nature of Indian Slavery in New England, 1670–1720," in *Reinterpreting New England Indians and the Colonial Experience*, ed. Colin Calloway and Neal Salisbury (Boston: Colonial Society of Massachusetts, 2003), 106–36; Ruth Wallis Herndon and Ella Wilcox Sekatau, "Colonizing the Children: Indian Youngsters in Servitude in Early Rhode Island," in *Reinterpreting New England Indians and the Colonial Experience*, ed. Colin Calloway and Neal Salisbury (Boston: Colonial Society of Massachusetts, 2003), 137–73; Silverman, "The Impact of Indentured Servitude," 625–37, 640–42; Vickers, "The First Whalemen of Nantucket," 577–78; Strong, *The Montaukett Indians*, 44–45.

17. Gideon Hawley to Andrew Oliver, December 9, 1760, Hawley Journal and Letters, Congregational Library, Boston, quoted in Silverman, "The Impact of Indentured Servitude," 347.

18. Rountree, *Pocohontas's People*, 136–39.

19. Timothy Dwight, *Travels in New England and New York*, 4 vols. (New Haven, Conn.: S. Converse, 1821–22; reprint, Cambridge, Mass.: Harvard University Press, 1969), 3:14; Barry O'Connell, ed., *On Our Own Ground: The Complete Writings of William Apess, a Pequot* (Amherst: University of Massachusetts Press, 1992), xxx–xxxii, 7–22; Jedidiah Morse, *A Report to the Secretary of War of the United States on Indian Affairs* (Washington, D.C., 1820), 71.

20. Trudie Lamb Richmond and Amy E. Den Ouden, "Recovering Gendered Political Histories: Local Struggles and Native Women's Resistance in Colonial Southern New England," in *Reinterpreting New England Indians and the Colonial Experience*, ed. Colin Calloway and Neal Salisbury (Boston: Colonial Society of Massachusetts, 2003), 174–213; Jean O'Brien, "'Divorced' from the Land: Resistance and Survival of Indian Women in Eighteenth-Century New England," in *After King Philip's War: Presence and Persistence in Indian New England*, ed. Colin Calloway (Hanover, N.H.: University Press of New England, 1997), 144–77.

21. Rountree, *Pocohontas's People*, 154; Strong, *The Montaukett Indians*, 84; Silverman, "The Impact of Indentured Servitude," 659–61.

22. Silverman, "The Impact of Indentured Servitude," 656–57.

23. Ibid., 654.

24. Alden Vaughan, "From White Man to Redskin: Changing Anglo-American Perceptions of the American Indian," *American Historical Review* 87 (1982): 917–53.

25. Thomas Hutchinson, *History of the Colony of Massachusetts*, 3 vols. (Boston: Thomas and John Fleet, 1764), 1:283; Vaughan, "From White Man to Redskin," 938.

26. Rountree, *Pocohontas's People*, 140.

27. Lorenzo Greene, *The Negro in Colonial New England, 1620–1776* (New York: Columbia University Press, 1942; reprint, Port Washington, N.Y.: Kennikat Press, 1966), 134–42; Vaughan, "From White Man to Redskin," 934–35.

28. Vaughan, "From White Man to Redskin"; Daniel Mandell, "The Saga of Sara

Muckamugg: Indian and African American Intermarriage in Colonial New England," in *Sex, Love, Race: Crossing Boundaries in North American History*, ed. Martha Hodes (New York: New York University Press, 1998), 72–90; Daniel Mandell, "Shifting Boundaries of Race and Ethnicity: Indian-Black Intermarriage in Southern New England, 1760–1880," *Journal of American History* 85 (1998): 466–501.

29. Joanne Melish, *Disowning Slavery: Gradual Emancipation and "Race" in New England, 1780–1860* (Ithaca, N.Y.: Cornell University Press, 1998); Sweet, *Bodies Politic*, 303, 341–45.

30. James H. Kettner, *The Development of American Citizenship, 1608–1870* (Chapel Hill: University of North Carolina Press, 1978), 173–333; Gordon S. Wood, *The Radicalism of the American Revolution* (New York: Knopf, 1992), 25–33.

31. Wood, *Radicalism of the American Revolution*, 229–369; Edward Countryman, "Indians, the Colonial Order, and the Social Significance of the American Revolution," *William and Mary Quarterly*, 3rd ser., 53 (1996): 355; Michael Merrill and Sean Wilentz, eds. *The Key of Liberty: The Life and Democratic Writings of William Manning, "a Laborer," 1747–1814* (Cambridge, Mass.: Harvard University Press, 1993); George B. Kirsch, "Jeremy Belknap and the Problem of Blacks and Indians in Early America," *Historical New Hampshire* 34 (fall/winter 1979): 202–22.

32. Rountree, *Pocohantas's People*, 187.

33. Samson Occum to Richard Law, December 5, 1789, Occom Papers, Connecticut Historical Society, quoted in David W. Conroy, "In 'Times' Turned 'Upside Down': Race and Gender Relations in Mohegan, 1760–1860" (paper delivered at the Old Sturbridge Village Colloquium on Early New England Society and Culture, Sturbridge, Mass., March 1995 [in author's possession]), 31, also passim; William DeLoss Love, *Samson Occom and the Christian Indians of New England* (Boston: Pilgrim Press, 1899), 302.

34. Moses Howwoswee, 1792 census, miscellaneous documents, Massachusetts Historical Society (MHS).

35. Rountree, *Pocohantas's People*, 192–95; Mandell, "Shifting Boundaries of Race and Ethnicity."

36. Sweet, *Bodies Politic*, 316–17.

37. Laura Murray, ed., *To Do Good to My Indian Brethren: The Writings of Joseph Johnson, 1751–1776* (Amherst: University of Massachusetts Press, 1998), 46–47; Connecticut Archives, Indians, 1st ser., vol. 2, 312ab, 300.

38. William J. Brown, *The Life of William J. Brown of Providence, R.I.* (1883; reprint, Freeport, N.Y.: Books for Libraries Press, 1971), 10.

39. Mashpees to Massachusetts General Court, July 1788, in documents relating to passed legislation (hereafter PL), ch. 30, Acts of 1788, Massachusetts Archives, Boston; Benjamin Allen to Massachusetts General Court, December 29, 1845, Unpassed Senate, no. 12207, Massachusetts. Archives.

40. Mashpee petition, July 1788, PL ch. 38, Acts of 1788; Dwight R. Adams, George Carmichael, Jr., and George B. Carpenter, *Report of the Committee of Investigation; A Historical Sketch and Evidence Taken, Made to the House of Representatives at Its January Session, A.D. 1880* (Providence, 1880), Appendix B, 31–32; Connecticut Archives, Indians, 1st ser., vol. 2, 312ab; D. L. Child, H. Stebbins, and D. Fellows, Jr., "Report [on the Condition of the Native Indians and Descendants of Native Indians,

in This Commonwealth]," *Mass. House Reports* 68 (Boston, 1827); John Milton Earle, "Report to the Governor and Council Concerning the Indians of the Commonwealth under the Act of April 6, 1859," *Mass. Senate Reports* 96 (Boston, 1861).

41. Earle, "Report" (1861)., 6; Child, Stebbins, and Fellows, "Report" (1827), 12.

42. Mandell, *Behind the Frontier*, 143–58.

43. William S. Simmons, *Spirit of the New England Tribes: Indian History and Folklore, 1620–1984* (Hanover, N.H.: University Press of New England, 1986), 168–71, 268–69.

44. Ebenezer Skiff, Gay Head, to Frederick Baylies, February 3, 1823, miscellaneous documents, Massachusetts Historical Society (MHS); F. W. Bird, Whiting Griswold, and Cyrus Weekes, "Report on Condition and Circumstances of Indians Remaining within This Commonwealth," *Mass. House Reports* 46 (Boston, 1849), 21.

45. Albert C. Koch, *Journey Through a Part of the United States of North America in the Years 1844–1846* (Carbondale: Southern Illinois University Press, 1972), 24–25.

46. Bird, Griswold, and Weekes, "Report" (1849), 21.

47. Ibid., 23.

48. See generally Winifred Barr Rothenberg, *From Market-Places to a Market Economy: The Transformation of Rural Massachusetts, 1750–1850* (Chicago: University of Chicago Press, 1992).

49. Immanuel Wallerstein, "The Construction of Peoplehood: Racism, Nationalism, Ethnicity," in *Race, Nation, Class: Ambiguous Identities*, eds. Etienne Balibar and Immanuel Wallerstein (1988; trans. New York: Verso, 1991), 78–79.

50. Eric Foner notes that, while northern ideology celebrated social advancement, the actual experience of freed African Americans was downward mobility; Foner, "Free Labor and Nineteenth-Century Political Ideology," in *The Market Revolution in America: Social, Political, and Religious Expressions, 1800–1880*, ed. Melvyn Stokes and Stephen Conway (Charlottesville: University of Virginia Press, 1996), 112–13.

51. Mashpee census, July 1, 1793, Hawley manuscripts, Houghton Library, Harvard University (thanks to Andrew Pierce for this census); 1800 Mashpee census, Hawley file, SPG Collection, Peabody-Essex Institute, Salem, Massachusetts; Mandell, "Shifting Boundaries of Race and Ethnicity."

52. Earle, "Report" (1861), 34.

53. Linebaugh and Rediker, *The Many-Headed Hydra*, 15, also 20–26.

54. Letter from justices of peace, selectmen, and other inhabitants of Barnstable, Sandwich, and Falmouth, December 22, 1788, PL ch. 38, Acts of 1788.

55. "William Penn," Boston *Advocate*, December 1833, quoted in William Apess, "Indian Nullification of the Unconstitutional Laws of Massachusetts," in *On Our Own Ground: The Complete Writings of William Apess, a Pequot*, ed. Barry O'Connell (Amherst: University of Massachusetts Press, 1992), 199; Rountree, *Pocahontas's People*, 142–52, 180, 182–83.

56. Mashpee to Massachusetts. legislature, July 1788, PL ch. 38, Acts of 1788.

57. Edward Kendall, *Travels through the Northern Parts of the United States in the Years 1807 and 1808*, 2 vols. (New York, 1809), 2:163–66, 194–95.

58. Earle, "Report" (1861), 6.

59. Marcus Rediker, *Between the Devil and the Deep Blue Sea: Merchant Seamen,*

Pirates, and the Anglo-American Maritime World, 1700–1750 (New York: Cambridge University Press, 1987), 293.

60. Frederick Baylies and Joseph Thaxter to Massachusetts legislature, September 22, 1818, Indian Guardian Accounts, box 3, folder 15. See also Christiantown to Massachusetts legislature, January 29, 1805, PL ch. 84, Acts of 1804.

61. Kendall, *Travels through the Northern Parts*, 2:163–66.

62. William J. Rorabaugh, *The Alcoholic Republic: An American Tradition* (New York: Oxford University Press, 1979); Peter C. Mancall, *Deadly Medicine: Indians and Alcohol in Early America* (Ithaca, N.Y.: Cornell University Press, 1995).

63. Hawley, report to legislature, September 2, 1795, Savage Papers, 2:218, Massachusetts Historical Society.

64. Zaccheus Howwoswee and others, Gay Head Indians, to Massachusetts General Court, in "Report on Act to Prohibit the Sale of Ardent Spirits to the Gay Head Indians," *Mass. House Reports*, 48 (Boston, 1838), 2.

65. Strong, *The Montaukett Indians*, 45.

66. John Avery, *History of the Town of Ledyard, 1650–1900* (Norwich, Conn.: Noyes and Davis, 1901), 260.

67. Dwight, *Travels in New England*, 3:14, 18.

68. Harriett Merrifield Forbes, *The Hundredth Town: Glimpses of Life in Westborough, 1717–1817* (Westborough, Mass., 1889), 170. Various records in the Hassanamisco guardian accounts show Sarah Philips as an adult member of the community circa 1790–1830, and a receipt from 1851 notes that she had recently died; John Milton Earle Papers, folders 1–2, 5, box 3, American Antiquarian Society, Worcester, Massachusetts.

69. Strong, *The Montaukett Indians*, 90.

70. See, for example, Henry David Thoreau, *Walden* (1854; reprint, New York: Modern Library, 1937), 17; Avery, *History of the Town of Ledyard*, 259–60; Frank G. Speck, *Eastern Algonkian Block–Stamp Decoration: A New World Original or an Acculturated Art*, Research Series No. 1, Archaeological Society of New Jersey, State Museum (Trenton, 1947); Ann McMullen and Russell G. Handsman, eds., *A Key into the Language of Woodsplint Baskets* (Washington, Conn.: American Indian Archaeological Institute, 1987); Ann McMullen, "Native Basketry, Basketry Styles, and Changing Group Identity in Southern New England," in *Algonkians of New England: Past and Present*, ed. Peter Benes (Boston: Boston University Press, 1993), 76–88; Ann McMullen, "Talking Through Baskets: Meaning, Production, and Identity in the Northern Woodlands," in *Basketmakers: Meaning and Form in Native American Baskets*, ed. Linda Mowat, Howard Murphy, and Penny Dransalt (Oxford: Pitt Museum, University of Oxford, 1992), 24; Samuel Orcutt and Ambrose Beardsley, *History of Derby, Connecticut, 1642–1880* (Springfield, Mass.: Springfield Printing Company, 1880), 50; Forbes, *The Hundredth Town*, 178.

71. On the persistence of "preindustrial" workways as a means of protest or cultural tenacity, see Herbert Gutman, *Work, Culture, and Society in Industrializing America: Essays in American Working-Class and Social History* (New York: Knopf, 1976), 1–70.

72. Douglas L. Jones, "The Strolling Poor: Transiency in Eighteenth-Century Massachusetts," *Journal of Social History* (1975): 28–39; Karen V. Hansen, *A Very Social*

Time: Crafting Community in Antebellum New England (Berkeley: University of California Press, 1994).

73. "Report of the House Commissioners on the Subject of the Pauper System," *Mass. House Reports* 6 (Boston 1833), 6. The commissioners also noted that "these unhappy fellow beings often travel with females, sometimes, but not always, their wives; while yet, in the towns in which they take up their temporary abode, they are almost always recognized, and treated, as sustaining this relation." Such "informal marriages" were also common among Indians and "lower sorts."

74. Dwight, *Travels in New England*, 2:15–16.

75. Rothenberg, *From Market-Places to a Market Economy*, 150, 156, 174. Rothenberg found that a wage market for farm laborers emerged in Massachusetts generally in 1800, but later (1822) in the central region, due to its delayed settlement until after 1713. She also found no records of women being hired as farm laborers.

76. William Apess, "A Son of the Forest," and "An Indian's Looking-Glass for the White Man" (1833), in *On Our Own Ground: The Complete Writings of William Apess, a Pequot*, ed. Barry O'Connell (Amherst: University of Massachusetts Press, 1992), 61, 155.

77. Committee on Indians of the Commonwealth, "[Report to the] House of Representatives, June 3, 1869 [on Marshpee Hearings]," *Mass. House Reports* 502 (Boston, 1869), 15, 20–21, 25, 26.

78. Daniel Vickers, "Competency and Competition: Economic Culture in Early America," *William and Mary Quarterly*, 3rd ser., 43 (1990): 19.

Chapter 4. Class Struggle in a West Indian Plantation Society

This chapter has been much improved by the comments of audiences at the Early Modern History Seminar at the University of Durham and the Caribbean Studies Seminar at the Institute of Commonwealth Studies, University of London, as well as by R. C. Nash. Special thanks go to Billy Smith, Simon Middleton, Greg Nobles, and an anonymous referee for the University of Pennsylvania Press, as well as my fellow ranch-going conferees.

1. William Smith, *A Natural History of Nevis, and the Rest of the English Leeward Charibee Islands in America* (Cambridge: J. Bentham, 1745), 23. The tendency of British elites to valorize rusticity is discussed eloquently in Martin J. Wiener, *English Culture and the Decline of the Industrial Spirit, 1850–1980* (Cambridge: Cambridge University Press, 1981).

2. See Edmund Morgan, *American Slavery, American Freedom: The Ordeal of Colonial Virginia* (New York: W. W. Norton and Company, 1975), passim; Trevor Burnard, *Mastery, Tyranny, and Desire: Thomas Thistlewood and His Slaves in the Anglo-Jamaican World* (Chapel Hill: University of North Carolina Press, 2004), 151.

3. ". . . Les François arrivèrent a bout au même moment que les Anglais faisoient décente a l'autre, sans avoir aucune connaissance de leurs arrivées, ce qui causa entre eux une dispute terrible, et un procez qui ne put être termine autrement, sinon, que l'Isle seroit partagée entre les deux nations également, que la chasse, la pêche, la

soufrière, les salines et les étangs seroient en commun. . . ." G[autier] D[u] T[ron-choy], *Journal de la campagne des isles de l'Amérique* (Troyes: Jacques LeFebvre, 1709), 35. All translations are mine, unless otherwise indicated.

4. Richard Pares, *War and Trade in the West Indies, 1739–1763* (Oxford: Clarendon Press, 1936), 232.

5. Margaret Deanne Rouse-Jones, "St. Kitts, 1713–1763: A Study of the Development of a Plantation Colony" (Ph.D. diss., Johns Hopkins University, 1977), 1.

6. "Quoique S. Christophe seroit une des plus grandes Isles du vent, ce n'est pas celle ou il y a de plus de terrein en valeur; on a vu ci-devant que le milieu est occupe par de hautes montagnes. . . . Ainsi, on n'évalue qu'a vingt-quatre mille acres, ou trente-cinq mille arpens, le terrein propre a la culture du Sucre." Jacques Bellin, *Description géographique des Isles Antilles possedees par les Anglois* (Paris, 1758), 109.

7. Noel Deerr, *The History of Sugar* (London: Chapman and Hall, 1949); Richard Dunn, *Sugar and Slaves: The Rise of the Planter Class in the English West Indies, 1624–1713* (Chapel Hill: University of North Carolina Press, 1973); Richard Sheridan, *Sugar and Slavery: An Economic History of the British West Indies* (Baltimore: Johns Hopkins University Press, 1974); and Sidney Mintz, *Sweetness and Power: The Place of Sugar in Modern History* (New York: Viking, 1985).

8. Samuel Martin, *An Essay upon Plantership*, 4th ed. (London: A. Millar, 1765), passim.

9. "An Act for the Encouraging and Promoting the Settling of This Island," April 11, 1698, *Acts of Assembly, Passed in the Charibbee Leeward Islands, from 1690, to 1730* (London: John Baskett, 1734), 30.

10. "An Act for the further promoting the Number of the Inhabitants of this Island, and more particularly encouraging the King's Soldiers, now to be disbanded, to continue therein, by enabling them to become Settlers amongst us," December 24, 1700, *Acts of Assembly*, 111–12.

11. "An Act for encouraging the Importation of White Servants to this Island," Antigua, July 11, 1716, *Acts of Assembly*, 159.

12. In an act of 1689, Leeward governor Christopher Codrington, Sr. mandated that "every Man that shall be hurt, maimed, or wounded in their Majesties Service for Defence of this Island, shall have the whole Charge of his Maintenance and Cure until he be restored to good Health, borne and paid out of the publick Stock of this Island; and also . . . to every man disabled in the said Service, the full Quantity of Three thousand pounds of Sugar by the Year. . . ." "An Act for Encouragement of poor Soldiers valiantly to behave themselves in their Majesties Service for Defence of this Island," Antigua, February 13, 1689, *Acts of Assembly*, 75.

13. Walter Hamilton to Council, March 15, 1706, in *Calendar of State Papers, Colonial: America and West Indies* (Vaduz: Kraus Reprint Ltd., 1964), 23: 83, hereafter simply *Calendar*.

14. Ibid.

15. Ibid., 85, 87.

16. Mr. Stanley, Nevis, to Mr. John Tonstall, April 16, 1706, in C[olonial] O[ffice] 184/1: Nevis: Original Correspondence, National Archives of Great Britain, Kew, London.

17. Daniel Parke to Mr. Secretary Hedges, October 4, 1706, in *Calendar* 23: 254–55.

18. On the hostilities between Parke and Codrington, see Natalie Zacek, "A Death in the Morning: The Murder of Daniel Parke, Antigua, 1710," in *Cultures and Identities in Colonial British America*, ed. Robert A. Olwell and Alan Tully (Baltimore: Johns Hopkins University Press, 2005).

19. Parke to Council of Trade and Plantations, October 31, 1706, *Calendar* 23: 284; Parke to Hedges, October 31, 1706, *Calendar* 23: 285–86.

20. Parke to Council of Trade and Plantations, October 31, 1706, *Calendar* 23: 284.

21. Ibid.

22. Rouse-Jones, "St. Kitts," 16.

23. Similar ideas for creating a yeoman class to act as a buffer between great planters and slaves and as a defensive force against external attack were proposed for Georgia and Virginia; for the latter, see T. H. Breen, "Of Time and Nature: A Study of Persistent Values in Colonial Virginia," in *Puritans and Adventurers: Change and Persistence in Early America* (New York: Oxford University Press, 1980), 187–91; and Peter Thompson, "William Bullock's 'Strange Adventure': A Plan to Transform Seventeenth-Century Virginia," *William and Mary Quarterly*, 3rd ser., 61 (2004): passim. My thanks to Lorena Walsh for this point.

24. David L. Niddrie, "An Attempt at Planned Settlement in St. Kitts in the Early Eighteenth Century," *Caribbean Studies* 5 (1966): 11.

25. In March 1706 the French commander d'Iberville and his forces had ravaged the islands. On Nevis, they burned "not only several boyling houses but the very dwelling houses themselves, not leaving at their going away above 20 standing on the whole island, the town [Charlestown] excepted," as well as having dismantled and removed the sugar mills and boiling coppers and seized more than three thousand slaves. At St. Kitts, d'Iberville's forces made off with an additional six hundred slaves, as well as all of the mills and coppers along the leeward coast from Brimstone Hill to Basseterre. See Gordon C. Merrill, *The Historical Geography of St. Kitts and Nevis, the West Indies* (Mexico City: Instituto Panamericano de Geografía e Historia, 1958), 67.

26. "The Case of the Poor distressed Planters, and other Inhabitants of the Islands of Nevis, and St. Christophers, in America," in a volume entitled "Law Cases," BL516m.17, British Library, London, 18.

27. "The Humble Petition of several Proprietors of Plantations in the Islands of Nevis and St. Christophers in America, and Merchants Trading to the same; on behalf of Themselves and other the Inhabitants and Traders to the aforesaid Islands" (London, 1707), broadside.

28. Ibid.; "The Case of the Sufferers of Nevis and St. Christophers (London, 1714), broadside.

29. Thanks to R. C. Nash for emphasizing this point and providing an idea of the modern value of the sum granted.

30. John Campbell, *Candid and Impartial Considerations on the Nature of the Sugar Trade* (London: R. Baldwin, 1763), 13.

31. "The humble Peticon of Elizabeth Renoult Widdow" and "The Humble

Petition of Alletta De La Coussaye of St. Cristophers," in C.O. 152/10: Board of Trade: Original Correspondence, Leeward Islands, 1713–1716, National Archives, Kew.

32. Campbell, *Candid and Impartial Considerations*, 43.

33. "The Case of the Sufferers."

34. Sir Alan Burns, *History of the British West Indies* (London: George Allen and Unwin Ltd., 1954), 437.

35. Campbell, *Candid and Impartial Considerations*, 43.

36. Dunn, *Sugar and Slaves*, 14.

37. Peter Linebaugh, *The London Hanged: Crime and Civil Society in the Eighteenth Century* (Cambridge: Cambridge University Press, 1992), xxiii. Elsewhere in his introduction, Linebaugh deftly questions "the relationship between the organized death of living labour (capital punishment) and the oppression of the living by dead labour (the punishment of capital) (xv). Joan Dayan's work in progress on the continuum incorporating racial slavery, imprisonment, and capital punishment has been integral to my thoughts about the relationship of poor whites and free and enslaved blacks in a slave society; see Dayan, "Legal Slaves and Civil Bodies," *Nepantla* 2 (2001): 3–39.

38. These episodes are discussed in detail in chapter 2 of my dissertation, "Dangerous Tenants: Conflict and Community in a Colonial British American World, 1670–1770" (Ph.D. diss., Johns Hopkins University, 2000). See also Hilary Beckles, "'Black Men in White Skins': The White Working Class in West Indian Slave Society," *Journal of Imperial and Commonwealth History* 15 (1986): 1.

39. See Natalie Zacek, "West Indian Taverns as Sites of Working-Class Sociability and Resistance" (paper presented to the Southern Labor Studies Conference, Miami, April 2002).

40. "An Act for establishing a Market at the Town of Basseterre, Old Road, Sandy Point, and Deep Bay, in the Island of St. Christopher; and for regulating and ascertaining the Prices of Beef, Mutton, Veal, Pork, and Turtle," *Acts of Assembly, Passed in the Island of St. Christopher; From 1711, to 1735, Inclusive* (London: John Baskett, 1739), 135.

41. It is important to recall that the "French lands," though newly acquired by the English, were not necessarily in a "frontier" state. In many instances, English islanders took over fully functioning French sugar plantations, some of which retained their complements of slaves, allowing the ceded lands almost immediately to contribute substantially to the island's productivity.

42. "An Act to enable the several Parts of this Island, formerly belonging to the French, to choose and send Representatives to serve in the Assemblies of this Island," *Acts of Assembly, St Christopher*, 121.

43. Rouse-Jones, "St. Kitts," ii.

44. Ibid., 44. Bailyn is quoted in Robert M. Weir, *Colonial South Carolina: A History* (Columbia: University of South Carolina Press, 1997), 235.

45. "An Act for obliging the Church-wardens and Vestrymen of the Parish of St. George Basseterre to keep Watch in the Town of Basseterre, and Irish Town, by Night; and for preventing Robberies, and other Disorders that are frequently committed therein," *Acts of Assembly, St. Christopher*, 158; Sir Probyn Inniss, *Historic Basseterre: The Story of a West Indian Town* (Basseterre, 1985), 14.

46. St. Kitts requested an entire regiment in 1738 and again in 1746 and called for two hundred further soldiers in 1770; see Andrew Jackson O'Shaughnessy, *An Empire Divided: The American Revolution and the British Caribbean* (Philadelphia: University of Pennsylvania Press, 2000), 47, 51.

47. Rouse-Jones, "St. Kitts," 221.

Chapter 5. Class at an African Commercial Enclave

1. The British National Archives (BNA), Kew Gardens: Public Records Office (PRO), Treasury 70 Series, African Companies (T 70), vol. 31, June 14, 1766.

2. The "Gold Coast" was the name for modern Ghana, and Cape Coast Castle is located about one hundred miles west of the nation's capital, Accra. PRO T 70/31, July 13, 1766, BNA. Cudjoe Caboceer, the Cape Coast *birempon*, was the town's de facto leader.

3. PRO T 70/31, January 31, 1767, BNA.

4. Among the best analyses of how eighteenth-century workers (bound and free) "bargained" (in a host of ways) with employers and owners is Alfred F. Young, "How Radical Was the American Revolution," in *Beyond the American Revolution*, ed. Alfred F. Young (Dekalb: Northern Illinois University Press, 1993).

5. The global assortment of commodities being imported into Cape Coast specifically, and the Gold Coast in general, were luxury goods in that they did not destroy or replace locally or regionally produced items; rather, they served as consumer goods. Their luxury status did not make them benign.

6. See, for example, Gary B. Nash and Jean R. Soderlund, *Freedom by Degrees: Emancipation in Pennsylvania and Its Aftermath* (New York: Oxford University Press, 1991); and Billy G. Smith, "Resisting Inequality: Black Women Who Stole Themselves in Eighteenth-Century America," in *Inequality in Early America*, ed. Carla Gardina Pestana and Sharon V. Salinger (Hanover, N.H: University Press of New England, 1999), 134–59.

7. PRO T 70/33, February 19, 1786, BNA.

8. See Peter Linebaugh and Marcus Rediker, *The Many-Headed Hydra: Sailors, Slaves, Commoners, and the Hidden History of the Revolutionary Atlantic* (Boston: Beacon Press, 2000).

9. Kwame Yaboa Daaku, *Trade and Politics on the Gold Coast, 1600–1720: A Study of African Reaction to European Trade* (Oxford: Clarendon Press, 1970), 33, illustrates the coastal economic dependency on the canoemen. Other works concerning the importance of canoemen to West Africa include Robert Smith, "The Canoe in West African History," *Journal of African History* 11, no. 4 (1970): 515–33; and Peter C. W. Gutkind, "The Canoemen of Southern Ghana," in *The Workers of African Trade*, ed. Catherine Coquery-Vidrovitah and Paul E. Lovejoy (London: Sage Publications, 1985). For a contemporary description of the coastal canoemen and the ritual for successfully crossing the breakers, see Paul Erdmann Isert, *Letters on West Africa and the Slave Trade: Journey to Guinea and the Caribbean Islands in Columbia*, trans. and ed. Selena Axelrod Winsnes (Copenhagen: 1758; reprint, Oxford: Oxford University Press,

1992), 27–28. For examples of Gold Coast canoemen being utilized along other coastal regions, see Robin Law, *Ouidah: The Social History of a West African Slaving Port, 1727–1892* (Athens: Ohio University Press and James Currey Publishers, 2005).

10. PRO T 70/30, June 9, 1755, BNA.

11. PRO T 70/30, July 1, 1754, BNA. Gutkind, "The Canoemen," 38, called this a "formal strike."

12. PRO T 70/29, July 11, 1751; PRO T 70/69, December 30, 1778; PRO T 70/152, May 16, 1780, BNA. In 1780, the African Committee demanded the end of giving *dashees* for all but three-hand intelligence canoes (a canoe manned by three canoemen). Strikes and wage disputes also characterized the relationship between white employers and African employees in the British colony island of Bulama (now part of Guinea Bisseau) in the 1790s. See the accounts in Philip Beaver, *African Memoranda: Relative to an attempt to establish a British Settlement on the island of Bulama, on the western Coast of Africa, in the year 1792 . . . and the Introduction of Letters and Religion to its Inhabitants but more particularly as the Means of Gradually Abolishing African Slavery* (London: printed for C. and R. Baldwin, 1805).

13. PRO T 70/152, June 16, 1780, BNA.

14. Ibid. Gutkind, "The Canoemen," 27, illustrates that this continual company fear of the canoemen and *bomboys* pilfering company goods had a long coastal tradition.

15. A "palaver" was a coastal dispute. Once a palaver started, each side retained the right to *panyar* either goods or peoples that they held until the dispute was settled through the arbitration of the local *penyins* (elders) and elites. If the company helped to settle a palaver, it was expected to provide numerous presents and *dashees*.

16. Brodie Cruikshank, *Eighteen Years on the Gold Coast of Africa* (London: Hurst and Blackett, 1853; reprint, New York: Barnes and Noble, 1966), 37.

17. The consequences of the slave trade for West Africa are studied in Daaku, *Trade and Politics*, Harvey M. Feinberg, *Africans and Europeans in West Africa: Elminas and Dutchmen on the Gold Coast during the Eighteenth Century* (Philadelphia: American Philosophical Society, 1989); Per O. Hernæs, *Slaves, Danes, and Coast Society: The Danish Slave Trade from West Africa and Afro-Danish Relations on the Eighteenth-Century Gold Coast* (Trondheim: Department of History, University of Trondheim, 1995); J. E. Inikori, ed., *Forced Migration: The Impact of the Export Slave Trade on African Societies* (New York: Africana Publishing Co., 1982); Robin Law, *The Slave Coast of West Africa 1550–1750: The Impact of the Atlantic Slave Trade on an African Society* (Oxford: Clarendon Press, 1991); and John Thornton, *Africa and Africans in the Making of the Atlantic World, 1400–1680* (Cambridge: Cambridge University Press, 1992).

18. PRO T 70/1021, May 18, 1764, BNA. *Negannepauts* were a blue and white cotton, either striped or checked; *bejutapauts* were a coarse bleached cotton, either striped or checked; *tapseils* were a cheap, striped cotton-silk blend.

19. PRO T 70/1022, March 3, 1765, BNA.

20. PRO T 70/1028, April 20, 1769, BNA.

21. PRO T 70/1009, January 3, 1755, BNA.

22. PRO T 70/30, March 14 and April 22, 1753, BNA.

23. PRO T 70/31, January 10, 1764, BNA.

24. PRO T 70/31, December 24, 1762, BNA. Daaku, *Trade and Politics*, 37, defines

the value of one *ackie* to be five shillings; sixteen *ackies* were worth one ounce of gold (or the inflated coastal value of four pounds).

25. PRO T 70/31, July 13, 1766 and January 31, 1767, BNA.
26. PRO T 70/30, March 10, 1753, BNA.
27. PRO T 70/1469, BNA.
28. PRO T 70/32, July 29, 1774, BNA.
29. PRO T 70/69, December 5, 1774, BNA.
30. PRO T 70/1325, and T 70/1335, BNA.
31. PRO T 70/152, February 1, 1772, BNA.
32. Suzanne Miers and Igor Kopytoff, "Slavery as an Institute of Marginality," in *Slavery in Africa: Historical and Anthropological Perspectives*, ed. Suzanne Miers and Igor Kopytoff (Madison: University of Wisconsin Press, 1977). Also see Akosua Adoma Perbi, *A History of Indigenous Slavery in Ghana: From the 15th to the 19th Century* (Accra: Sub-Saharan Publishers, 2004).
33. PRO T 70/31, May 10, 1764, BNA.
34. Cape Coast consisted of several town quarters, each divided into wards associated with the *asafo* companies. Company records usually referred to Cape Coast as having two parts, Upper and Lower Towns, although occasional mention was made of four parts divided into wards. PRO T 70/32, January 20, 1780; PRO T 70/152, August 16, 1772, BNA. A. W. Lawrence, *Trade Castles and Forts of West Africa* (Stanford, Calif.: Stanford University Press, 1964), 69, claimed that the company slaves were full citizens of Lower Town. See also Arthur Ffoulkes, "The Company System at Cape Coast Castle," *Journal of the African Society* 7 (1908): 262.
35. Ty M. Reese, "Liberty, Insolence, and Rum: Cape Coast and the American Revolution," *Itinerario: International Journal on the History of European Expansion and Global Interaction* 28, no. 3 (fall 2004): 18–37, explores instances in which the local peoples blockaded the castle during a palaver with the company.
36. PRO T 70/31, July 20, 1765, and October 25, 1765, BNA.
37. PRO T 70/31, March 31, 1768, BNA. They did not go to war.
38. PRO T 70/30, September 8, 1753, BNA.
39. PRO T 70/31, January 10, 1764, BNA.
40. PRO T 70/466, BNA.
41. PRO T 70/486, BNA.
42. PRO T 70/155, BNA.
43. PRO T 70/145, January 25, 1781, BNA.

Chapter 6. A Class Struggle in New York?

1. Francis Nicholson and Council to the Board of Trade, May 15, 1689, in *Documents Relative to the Colonial History of the State of New York*, ed., E. B. O'Callaghan and Berthold Fernow, 15 vols. (Albany, N.Y., 1856–67), 3:575 (hereafter *DRCNY*); New York Historical Society, *Collections* (1868): 260–61 (hereafter NYHS); Declaration of the Freeholders of Suffolk County, Long Island, *DRCNY*, 3:577, 591. Also see Nicholas Bayard's account of these events, *DRCNY*, 3:632.

2. Stephen van Cortlandt to Edmund Andros, July 9, 1689, *DRCNY*, 3:594. Three days later, five of the six militia captains issued a declaration signed by four hundred men, explaining that "notwithstanding our severall pressures and griviences thes many years under a wicked arbitrarie Power exercise by our Late popish governr Coll Dongan & . . . his wicked Creatures and Pensionaries," they had resolved to wait for relief from England, but the latest series of outrages led them to think "delay Dangerous so we have unanimously Resolved to Live no Longer in such a Danger but to secure the ffort . . . and we declare to be Entirely and Openly Opposed to papists and their Religion." See "Declaration of the Inhabitants Soudjers Belonging Under the Severall Companies of Train Band of New Yorke," in *Documentary History of the State of New York*, ed. E. B. O'Callaghan, 4 vols. (Albany, N.Y., 1849–51), 2:10–11 (hereafter *DHSNY*). This chapter draws upon material discussed in more detail in Simon Middleton, *From Privileges to Rights: Work and Politics in Colonial New York City* (Philadelphia: University of Pennsylvania Press, 2006).

3. Charles M. Andrews, *The Colonial Period in American History* (New Haven, Conn.: Yale University Press, 1934–38), 3:135, and Charles M. Andrews, *Narratives of the Insurrections, 1675–1690* (New York, 1915), 4–5. Also see Mariana Griswold Van Rensselaer, *History of the City of New York in the Seventeenth Century*, 2 vols. (New York: Macmillan Company, 1909), 2:564–67; Charles W. Spencer, "The Rise of the Assembly, 1691–1760," in *History of the State of New York*, ed. A. C. Flick (New York: New York State Historical Association, 1933–37). Economic and class discontents are discussed in Bernard Mason, "Aspects of the New York Revolt of 1689," *New York History* 30 (January 1949): 165–80.

4. Jerome K. Reich, *Leisler's Rebellion: A Study of Democracy in New York, 1664–1720* (Chicago: University of Chicago Press, 1953), preface and 172–73. Reich considered the rebellion as an urban variant of rural "early colonial democratic movements," arguing that Leisler's Rebellion kept "alive the rather puny 'democratic' tradition in New York" and lay "the foundation for a political party when this 'democratic' tendency assumed larger proportions" in the Jacksonian era.

5. Gary B. Nash, *The Urban Crucible: Social Change, Political Consciousness, and the Origins of the American Revolution* (Cambridge, Mass.: Harvard University Press, 1979), 44–47; and Edwin G. Burrows and Mike Wallace, *Gotham: A History of New York City to 1898* (New York: Oxford University Press, 1999), 100.

6. For a statement of the rebels' aims, see "Representation of Committee of Safety, 9 Nov. 1689," *DRCNY*, 3:630–34. Although the rebellion brought middling city residents into positions of unusual public prominence, the Leislerians also included wealthy merchants who had served in the provincial administration, some of whom rejoined the governing elite following the return of royal rule. See David Voorhees, "The 'Fervent Zeale' of Jacob Leisler," *William and Mary Quarterly* 3rd ser., 51 (July 1994): 447–72.

7. Michael G. Hall, Lawrence H. Leder, and Michael Kammen, eds., *The Glorious Revolution in America: Documents on the Colonial Crisis of 1689* (Chapel Hill: University of North Carolina Press, 1964), 84–85; Thomas J. Archdeacon, "The Age of Leisler—New York City, 1689–1710: A Social and Demographic Interpretation," in *Aspects of Early New York Society and Politics*, ed. Jacob Judd and Irwin Polishook (Tarrytown, N.Y.: Sleepy Hollow Restorations, 1974), 73, 79; John Murrin, "English Rights

as Ethnic Aggression," in *Authority and Resistance in Early New York*, ed. William Pencak and Conrad E. Wright (New York: New York Historical Society, 1988), 56–94; Donna Merwick, "Being Dutch: An Interpretation of Why Jacob Leisler Died," *New York History* (October 1989): 373–404; David William Voorhees, "In Behalf of the One True Religion: Leisler's Rebellion in Colonial New York" (Ph.D. diss., New York University, 1988).

8. Joyce D. Goodfriend, *Before the Melting Pot: Society and Culture in New York City, 1664–1730* (Princeton, N.J.: Princeton University Press, 1992); and Adrian Howe, "Accommodation and Retreat: Politics in Anglo-Dutch New York City, 1700–1760" (Ph.D. diss., University of Melbourne, 1984).

9. Craig Muldrew, *The Economy of Obligation: The Culture of Credit and Social Relations in Early Modern England* (Basingstoke: MacMillan, 1998); Albert O. Hirschman, *The Passions and the Interests: Arguments for Capitalism before Its Triumph* (Princeton, N.J.: Princeton University Press, 1977); and James Tully, "After the Macpherson Thesis," in his *An Approach to Political Philosophy: Locke in Contexts* (London: Cambridge University Press, 1993), 71–95. For early North America, see Naomi Lamoreaux, "Rethinking the Transition to Capitalism in the Early American Northeast," *Journal of American History* 90 (September 2003): 437-62; Christine Leigh Heyrman, *Commerce and Culture: The Maritime Communities of Colonial Massachusetts, 1690–1750* (New York: W. W. Norton and Company, 1984); Daniel Vickers, *Farmers and Fishermen: Two Centuries of Work in Essex County, Massachusetts, 1630–1850* (Chapel Hill: University of North Carolina Press, 1994); and Margaret Ellen Newell, *From Dependency to Independence: Economic Revolution in Colonial New England* (Ithaca, N.Y.: Cornell University Press, 1998).

10. Richard Dagger, "Rights," in *Political Innovation and Conceptual Change*, ed. Terence Ball et al. (Cambridge: Cambridge University Press, 1989), 292–303. Also see Richard Tuck, *Natural Rights Theories* (Cambridge: Cambridge University Press, 1979), 143–56; and Knud Haakonssen, *Natural Law and Moral Philosophy: From Grotius to the Scottish Enlightenment* (New York: Cambridge University Press, 1996), 15–31, 310–21. The beginnings of this municipal culture and implication of civic privileges in the later history of the city are explored further in Middleton, *From Privileges to Rights*.

11. For an overview of this early modern European political culture, see the essays in Martin van Gelderen and Quentin Skinner, eds., *Republicanism, a Shared European Heritage: Republicanism and Constitutionalism in Early Modern Europe* and *Republicanism, a Shared European Heritage: The Values of Republicanism in Early Modern Europe* (Cambridge: Cambridge University Press, 2002), passim. The concept of liberty referred to here is discussed by Skinner in four of his essays: "Machiavelli on the Maintenance of Liberty," *Politics* 18 (1983): 3–15; "The Idea of Negative Liberty: Philosophical and Historical Perspectives," in *Philosophy in History*, ed. R. Rorty, J. B. Schneewind, and Q. Skinner (Cambridge: Cambridge University Press, 1984), 199–221; "The Republican Idea of Liberty," in *Machiavelli and Republicanism*, ed. G. Bock, Q. Skinner, and M. Viroli (Cambridge: Cambridge University Press, 1990), 293–309; and *Liberty before Liberalism* (Cambridge: Cambridge University Press, 1998), 16–36.

12. My argument regarding the role of anti-popery in New York's revolt is adapted from Peter Lake, "Anti-Popery: The Structure of a Prejudice," in *Conflict in*

Early Stuart England: Studies in Religion and Politics, 1603–1642, ed. Richard Cust and Ann Hughes (Harlow: Longman, 1989), 72–107. For the playing out of these themes in seventeenth-century English politics, see Derek Hirst, *Authority and Conflict: England 1603–1658* (London: Edward Arnold, 1985), 84–87; and Paul D. Halliday, *Dismembering the Body Politic: Partisan Politics in England's Towns, 1650–1730* (Cambridge: Cambridge University Press, 1998).

   13. For overviews of the recent flourishing of studies on Dutch New York, see Eric Nooter and Patricia U. Bonomi, eds., *Colonial Dutch Studies: An Interdisciplinary Approach* (New York: New York University Press, 1988); Nancy Anne McClure Zeller, ed., *A Beautiful and Fruitful Place: Selected Rennsselaerswijck Seminar Papers* (Albany, N.Y: New Netherland Publishing, 1991); Wayne Bodle, "Themes and Directions in Middle Colonies Historiography, 1980–1994," *William and Mary Quarterly,* 3rd ser., 51 (July 1994): 357–58; and Joyce D. Goodfriend, "Writing/Righting Dutch Colonial History," *New York History* 80 (January 1998): 5–28.

   14. The New Amsterdam merchants' campaign against the West India Company figured prominently in nineteenth-century histories of early New York; see Edmund B. O'Callaghan, *History of New Netherland,* 2 vols. (New York: D. Appleton and Co., 1855), 1:392; and John Romeyn Brodhead, *History of the State of New York,* 2 vols. (New York: Harper and Brothers, 1853–71), 2:246. These were criticized by later scholars for their Whiggish view of the struggle as part of an emerging North American democratic tradition; see Philip L. White, "Municipal Government Comes to Manhattan," *New York Historical Society Quarterly* 37 (1953): 146–57. Recent studies have reconsidered the role of New Amsterdam's merchants and the struggle for rights, privileges, and representative government in the town; see Morton Wagman, "Civil Law and Colonial Liberty in New Netherland," *De Halve Mean* 55 (spring 1980): 1–5; Morton Wagman, "The Origins of New York City's Government: From Proprietary Control to Representative Government," *De Halve Maen* 57, no. 1 (February 1983): 6–11; and Oliver Rink, *Holland on the Hudson: An Economic and Social History of Dutch New York* (Ithaca, N.Y.: Cornell University Press, 1986). The fullest treatment is Dennis J. Maika, "Commerce and Community: Manhattan Merchants in the Seventeenth Century" (Ph.D. diss., New York University, 1995), part 1.

   15. *DRCNY,* 1:260, 268; *DHSNY,* 1:598–602. For the growth of municipal government functions after 1653, see notes on the establishment of a ferry service in David Valentine, ed., *Manual of the Corporation and City of New York* (New York: New York City Corporation, 1848), 385–86; Kenneth Scott, "New Amsterdam's Taverns and Tavern Keepers," *De Halve Maen* part 1, 39, no. 1 (April 1964): 9, 10, 15; John E. O'Connor, "The Rattle Watch of New Amsterdam," parts 1 and 2, *De Halve Maen* 43, no. 1 (April 1968): 11–12, and 43, no. 2 (July 1968): 9–12; Elva Kathy Lyon, "The New Amsterdam Weighhouse," *De Halve Maen* 69 (spring 1996): 1–10; and Adriana van Zweiten, "The Orphan Chamber of New Amsterdam," *William and Mary Quarterly,* 3rd ser., 53 (April 1996), 319–40.

   16. "Petition of the Commonalty of New Netherland &c to Director Stuyvesant, 1653," in *DRCNY,* 1:550–55.

   17. NYHS, *Collections* (1885), 19.

   18. Aside from the exclusion of free blacks and an unsuccessful attempt to exclude Jewish registrants, these privileges were shared by tradesmen regardless of their

Old World backgrounds. For example, the city's bakers included native New Amster-
damers such as Teunis and Jacob de Key, Anthony De Milt from Haarlem, and Joost
Teunissen from Naarden in the northwest Netherlands, Johan Verpronck from Bonn,
Germany, and Lawrens van der Spiegel from Vlissingen, Zeeland in the southwest
Netherlands. See lists of early immigrants to New Netherland, *DHSNY*, 3:52–63; van
der Spiegel in *New York Genealogical and Biographical Record* (January 1932): 11.

19. Historians have previously ascribed the ease of the transition in New York
City, compared to the occasional flaring of conflict in outlying towns, to dissatisfac-
tion with the West India Company's administration and a predisposition among the
Dutch settlers to accept authoritarian rule. See Michael Kammen, *Colonial New York:
A History* (New York: Oxford University Press, 1974), 73–100; and Robert C. Ritchie,
The Duke's Province: A Study of New York Politics and Society, 1664–1691 (Chapel Hill:
University of North Carolina Press, 1977), 22.

20. For the growing inequality, see Ritchie, *The Duke's Province*, 134–37; and
Goodfriend, *Before the Melting Pot*, 71. The growing disparities in the fortunes of the
town's residents were especially apparent among the town's middling sort: the levy of
1665 assessed the tanners Arian and Stoffel Van Laer, the hatter Warner Wessels, the
glazier Evert Duykinge, and the bakers Reynier Willemsen and Laurens van der
Spiegel at two florins per week. Twelve years later an assessment estimated the Van
Laers's personal wealth at the fifty-pound minimum, Wessels and Duykinge at two
hundred pounds each, and the bakers' at five and eight hundred pounds respectively.

21. On the predominance of Dutch and later Anglo-Dutch oligarchy as measured by tenure of office-holding and connection with governors and ruling council,
see Mason, "Aspects of New York's Revolt"; Thomas Archdeacon, *New York City, 1664-
1710. Conquest and Change* (Ithaca: Cornell University Press, 1976), 58–77; Voorhees,
"In Behalf of the One True Religion," 57–58; and Maika, "Commerce and Community," 322–84. Dutch merchant leaders and future anti-Leislerians included Cornelius
Steenwyck, Frederick Philipse, Nicholas Bayard, Stephen van Cortlandt, and Gabriel
Minvielle; English merchants included John Robinson, George Heathcote, William
Pinhorne, James Graham, John West, and John Winder.

22. See the warrant from James to increase duty on rum on account of drunken-
ness in order to improve the health of his subjects, *DRCNY*, 3:268; for the prohibition
on distilling grain unless it is unfit for bolting and export, see Herbert Osgood, ed.,
Minutes of the Common Council of the City of New York, 1675–1776 (New York: Dodd
and Mead, 1905), 1:25. For a discussion of the bread and meat export monopoly, see
Ritchie, *The Duke's Province*, 114; and Cathy Matson, *Merchants and Empire: Trading in
Colonial New York* (Baltimore: Johns Hopkins University Press, 1998), part 1.

23. Peter R. Christoph and Florence A. Christoph, eds., *The Andros Papers*, 3 vols.
(Syracuse, N.Y.: Syracuse University Press, 1989–91), 3:303.

24. Robert Ritchie found that the number of taxpayers assessed at 500 pounds
fell from seventy-six in 1676 to six by 1695, Ritchie, *The Duke's Province*, 194. The price
of wheat, which ordinary New Yorkers used to pay their debts, stagnated or fell, from
4s 6d a bushel in 1680 to 3s in 1682, and from 4s in 1684 to 3s and 6d in 1691. In the
same period, the price of real property in the city increased threefold. See Matson,
Merchants and Empire, 106, and Voorhees, "In Behalf of the One True Religion," 58.

25. Bartlett Burleigh James and J. Franklin Jameson, eds., *Journal of Jasper*

Danckaerts, 1679–1680 (New York, 1941), 239–44. Although Danckaerts met with local notables, he spent most of his time in the company of small-time traders and artisans, men such as Arnoldus de la Grange, who "had a small shop, as almost all the people here have, who gain their living by trade, namely in tobacco, liquours, thread and pins, and other knick knacks," and the carpenters Gerrit Evertsen van Dun and Jacob Swarts, who had worked in the city for more than thirty years.

26. Ibid., 244.

27. These suspicions might have been enhanced by the knowledge that Frederick Philipse, who was well known as one of Andros's closest confidants, began shipping large numbers of raw hides to England in the late 1670s and 1680s Philipse. See Patricia Bonomi, *A Factious People: Politics and Society in Colonial New York* (New York: Columbia University Press, 1971), 61.

28. The surviving text of the examination of the coopers who had all signed a document agreeing pricing for standard work further highlights the evasive tactics adopted by the powerless when called to account. The coopers were summoned to appear before Andros and the council, where they "acknowledge[d] their subscription, but pretend[ed] no ill intent." Richard Elliot (the official culler) "first pretends great Ignorance saith nothing to the purpose," Evert Wessels testifies "that it [the agreement] was writt at Peter Stevensen['s house]," William Waldron says "that Crookes bro: (a seaman) writte it." Christoph and Christoph, *The Andros Papers*, 2:185.

29. "Humble Petition of the company of carters belonging to the city of New York," in *New York Colonial Manuscripts*, 80 vols. (Albany, N.Y. State Archives), 39:109. For a similarly brusque treatment of a group of disobedient city porters who were dismissed in September 1685, see MCC, 1:169. See also Graham Hodges, *New York City Cartmen* (New York: New York University Press, 1987).

30. "Thomas Dongan's Report to the Committee of Trade on the Province of New York, 22 February 1687," in *DHSNY*, 1:150, 161. For civil disturbances, introduction of military patrols, new Sabbath laws, and closer regulation of strangers and movement into and out of the city, see MCC, 1:27, 28, 90, 147, 266, and 390. In 1684, following the reorganization of the city into five wards, the common councilmen instructed each of the constables to hire eight additional watchmen at twelve pence per night, making New York more closely policed than English towns with four times the population. See Carl Bridenbaugh, *Cities in the Wilderness: The First Century of Urban Life* (New York: Oxford University Press, 1938), 76–77, 80.

31. Gary S. DeKrey, "Radicals, Reformers, and Republicans: Academic Language and Political Discourse in Restoration London," in *A Nation Transformed: England after the Restoration*, ed. Alan Houston and Steve Pincus (New York: Cambridge University Press, 2001), 71–100; and Jacob Price, *Holland and the Dutch Republic in the Seventeenth Century* (Oxford: Clarendon Press, 1994), part 1.

Chapter 7. Middle-Class Formation in Eighteenth-Century North America

I thank Constance Furey, Sarah Knott, Seth Rockman, Alexandra Shepard, and especially the editors, Simon Middleton and Billy Smith, for their helpful suggestions.

1. "Man and Woman of the Year: The Middle Americans," *Time Magazine*, January 5, 1970, 10–17; now "Middle Class" on the *Time Magazine* website: http://www.time.com/time/personoftheyear/archive/stories/index.html (as of March 6, 2007). *Time Magazine* was not the first to notice the rising discontent of the middle class. See also Richard N. Goodwin, "Sources of the Public Unhappiness," *New Yorker*, January 4, 1969, 38–58; Peter Schrag, "The Forgotten American," *Harper's Magazine*, August 1969, 27–34; and "The Troubled American: A Special Report on the White Majority," *Newsweek*, October 6, 1969, 29–73.

2. See, for example, Harold D. Lasswell, "The Psychology of Hitlerism as a Response of the Lower Middle Classes to Continuing Insecurity," *Political Quarterly* 4 (1933): 373–84; David J. Saposs, "The Role of the Middle Class in Social Development: Fascism, Populism, Communism, Socialism," in *Economic Essays in Honor of Wesley Clair Mitchell* (New York: Columbia University Press, 1935), 393–424; and Svend Ranulf, *Moral Indignation and Middle Class Psychology: A Sociological Study* (Copenhagen: Levin and Munksgaard, 1938).

3. For negative and positive assessments of mid-twentieth-century American culture centered on the middle class, see Reinhold Niebuhr, *The Irony of American History* (New York: Charles Scribner's Sons, 1952); and Louis Hartz, *The Liberal Tradition in America: An Interpretation of American Political Thought Since the Revolution* (New York: Harcourt, Brace and World, 1955).

4. The middle class would serve as the proverbial canary in the coal mine for scholars surveying the damage inflicted upon the American economy by "Reaganomics" in the 1980s. See, for example, Katherine S. Newman, *Falling from Grace: The Experience of Downward Mobility in the American Middle Class* (New York: Free Press, 1988); Barbara Ehrenreich, *Fear of Falling: The Inner Life of the Middle Class* (New York: Pantheon Books, 1989); and Frederick R. Strobel, *Upward Dreams, Downward Mobility: The Economic Decline of the American Middle Class* (Lanham, Md.: Rowman and Littlefield, 1993).

5. For recent theoretical reassessments of the concept of class, see Wai Chee Dimock and Michael T. Gilmore, eds., *Rethinking Class: Literary Studies and Social Formations* (New York: Columbia University Press, 1994); Michael Denning, *The Cultural Front: The Laboring of American Culture in the Twentieth Century* (London: Verso, 1996); John R. Hall, ed., *Reworking Class* (Ithaca, N.Y.: Cornell University Press, 1997); J. K. Gibson-Graham, Stephen Resnick, and Richard D. Wolff, eds., *Re/Presenting Class: Essays in Postmodern Marxism* (Durham, N.C.: Duke University Press, 2001); Stanley Aronowitz, *How Class Works: Power and Social Movement* (New Haven, Conn.: Yale University Press, 2003); and Sherry B. Ortner, *New Jersey Dreaming: Capital, Culture, and the Class of '58* (Durham, N.C.: Duke University Press, 2003).

6. This is the standard "liberal" critique of class; the standard "conservative" critique of class instead stresses the supposed fluidity of social mobility in the United States.

7. Rockman's monograph will be the fruition of a series of seminal articles. See Seth Rockman, "The Contours of Class in the Early Republic City," *Labor: Studies in Working-Class History of the Americas* 1, no. 4 (2004): 91–107; Seth Rockman, "Class and the History of Working People in the Early Republic," *Journal of the Early Republic* 25 (2005): 527–35; and Seth Rockman, "The Unfree Origins of American Capitalism,"

in *The Economy of Early America: Historical Perspectives and New Directions*, ed. Cathy Matson (University Park: Pennsylvania State University Press, 2005), 335–61.

8. Rockman's strategy tends toward a synchronic analysis of the working class, but I know it to be attentive to historical change as well. In turn, my strategy tends toward a diachronic analysis of the middle class, but it is also attentive to material structures.

9. See John S. Gilkeson, Jr., *Middle-Class Providence, 1820–1940* (Princeton, N.J.: Princeton University Press, 1986); Stuart M. Blumin, *The Emergence of the Middle Class: Social Experience in the American City, 1760–1900* (Cambridge, Mass.: Harvard University Press, 1989); Theodore Koditschek, *Class Formation and Urban-Industrial Society: Bradford, 1750–1850* (Cambridge: Cambridge University Press, 1990); R. J. Morris, *Class, Sect, and Party: The Making of the British Middle Class, Leeds, 1820–1850* (Manchester: Manchester University Press, 1990); Dror Wahrman, *Imagining the Middle Class: The Political Representation of Class in Britain, c. 1780–1840* (Cambridge: Cambridge University Press, 1995); David Garrioch, *The Formation of the Parisian Bourgeoisie, 1690–1830* (Cambridge, Mass.: Harvard University Press, 1996); D. S. Parker, *The Idea of the Middle Class: White-Collar Workers and Peruvian Society, 1900–1950* (University Park: Pennsylvania State University Press, 1998); Carol E. Harrison, *The Bourgeois Citizen in Nineteenth-Century France: Gender, Sociability, and the Uses of Emulation* (Oxford: Oxford University Press, 1999); and Robert D. Johnston, *The Radical Middle Class: Populist Democracy and the Question of Capitalism in Progressive Era Portland, Oregon* (Princeton, N.J.: Princeton University Press, 2003).

10. See Mary P. Ryan, *The Cradle of the Middle Class: The Family in Oneida County, New York, 1790–1865* (Cambridge: Cambridge University Press, 1981); Bonnie G. Smith, *Ladies of the Leisure Class: The Bourgeoisies of Northern France in the Nineteenth Century* (Princeton, N.J.: Princeton University Press, 1981); Karen Halttunen, *Confidence Men and Painted Women: A Study of Middle-Class Culture in America, 1830–1930* (New Haven, Conn.: Yale University Press, 1982); Nancy Armstrong, *Desire and Domestic Fiction: A Political History of the Novel* (New York: Oxford University Press, 1987); Leonore Davidoff and Catherine Hall, *Family Fortunes: Men and Women of the English Middle Class, 1780–1850* (Chicago: University of Chicago Press, 1987); Peter Earle, *The Making of the English Middle Class: Business, Society, and Family Life in London, 1660–1730* (Berkeley: University of California Press, 1989); Paul Langford, *A Polite and Commercial People: England, 1727–1783* (Oxford: Clarendon Press, 1989); John Seed, "From 'Middling Sort' to Middle Class in Late Eighteenth- and Early Nineteenth-Century England," in *Social Orders and Social Classes in Europe since 1500: Studies in Social Stratification*, ed. M. L. Bush (London: Longman, 1992), 114–35; Jonathan Barry, "Introduction," in *The Middling Sort of People: Culture, Society, and Politics in England, 1550–1800*, ed. Jonathan Barry and Christopher Brooks (New York: St. Martin's Press, 1994), 1–27; John Smail, *The Origins of Middle-Class Culture: Halifax, Yorkshire, 1660–1780* (Ithaca, N.Y.: Cornell University Press, 1994); Margaret Hunt, *The Middling Sort: Commerce, Gender, and the Family in England, 1660–1750* (Berkeley: University of California Press, 1996); Alan Kidd and David Nicholls, "Introduction: The Making of the British Middle Class?," in *The Making of the British Middle Class?: Studies of Regional and Cultural Diversity since the Eighteenth Century*, ed. Alan Kidd and David Nicholls (Phoenix Mill, Gloucestershire: Sutton Publishing,

1998), xv–xl; Catherine E. Kelly, *In the New England Fashion: Reshaping Women's Lives in the Nineteenth Century* (Ithaca, N.Y.: Cornell University Press, 1999); Christine Adams, *A Taste for Comfort and Status: A Bourgeois Family in Eighteenth-Century France* (University Park: Pennsylvania State University Press, 2000); Burton J. Bledstein and Robert D. Johnston, eds., *The Middling Sorts: Explorations in the History of the American Middle Class* (London: Routledge, 2001); Brian P. Owensby, *Intimate Ironies: Modernity and the Making of Middle-Class Lives in Brazil* (Stanford, Calif.: Stanford University Press, 1999); Margaret C. Jacob and Matthew Kadane, "Missing, Now Found in the Eighteenth Century: Weber's Protestant Capitalist," *American Historical Review* 108 (2003): 20–49; and Amy Schrager Lang, *The Syntax of Class: Writing Inequality in Nineteenth-Century America* (Princeton, N.J.: Princeton University Press, 2003).

11. This chapter interrogates the intended audience and stated content of these books, without considering their authors (mostly anonymous or obscure) or their readers. Original American books in these genres were not authored before the 1780s.

12. On the social terminology of "class" in eighteenth-century England, see Mary Poovey, "The Social Constitution of 'Class': Towards a History of Classificatory Thinking," in *Rethinking Class: Literary Studies and Social Formations*, ed. Wai Chee Dimock and Michael T. Gilmore (New York: Columbia University Press, 1994), 15–56; Keith Wrightson, "'Sorts of People' in Tudor and Stuart England," in *The Middling Sort of People: Culture, Society, and Politics in England, 1550–1800*, ed. Jonathan Barry and Christopher Brooks (New York: St. Martin's Press, 1994), 28–51; John Seed, "From 'Middling Sort' to Middle Class in Late Eighteenth- and Early Nineteenth-Century England," in *Social Orders and Social Classes in Europe since 1500*, ed. M. L. Bush (London: Longman, 1992), 114–35; Penelope J. Corfield, "Class by Name and Number in Eighteenth-Century Britain," in *Language, History, and Class*, ed. Penelope J. Corfield (Oxford: Basil Blackwell, 1991), 101–30; Keith Wrightson, "Estates, Degrees, and Sorts: Changing Perceptions of Society in Tudor and Stuart England," in *Language, History, and Class*, ed. Penelope J. Corfield (London: Basil Blackwell, 1991), 30–52; Keith Wrightson, "The Social Order of Early Modern England: Three Approaches," in *The World We Have Gained: Histories of Population and Social Structure*, ed. Lloyd Bonfield, Richard M. Smith, and Keith Wrightson (Oxford: Basil Blackwell, 1986), 177–202; Steven Wallech, "'Class Versus Rank': The Transformation of Eighteenth-Century English Social Terms and Theories of Production," *Journal of the History of Ideas* 57 (1986): 409–31; David Cressy, "Describing the Social Order of Elizabethan and Stuart England," *Literature and History* 3 (1976): 29–44; and Asa Briggs, "The Language of 'Class' in Early Nineteenth-Century England," in *Essays in Social History*, ed. M. W. Flinn and T. C. Smout (Oxford: Clarendon Press, 1960), 154–77.

13. For recent work conceptualizing agency, see Walter Johnson, "On Agency," *Journal of Social History* 37 (2003): 113–24; Sherry B. Ortner, "Specifying Agency: The Comaroffs and Their Critics," *Interventions* 3 (2001): 76–84; Laura M. Ahearn, *Invitations to Love: Literacy, Love Letters, and Social Change in Nepal* (Ann Arbor: University of Michigan Press, 2001); Special Issue, *History and Theory* 40, no. 4 (December 2001); Lois McNay, *Gender and Agency: Reconfiguring the Subject in Feminist and Social Theory* (Cambridge: Polity Press, 2000); Mustafa Emirbayer and Ann Mische, "What Is Agency?," *American Journal of Sociology* 103 (1998): 962–1023; and Ellen

Messer-Davidow, "Acting Otherwise," in *Provoking Agents: Gender and Agency in Theory and Practice*, ed. Judith Kegan Gardiner (Urbana: University of Illinois Press, 1995), 23–51. For a recent, exceptionalist account of "agency culture" and "agency civilization" in American history, see James E. Block, *A Nation of Agents: The American Path to a Modern Self and Society* (Cambridge, Mass.: Harvard University Press, 2002).

14. The following analysis is based on my examination of hundreds of English and colonial American imprints spanning the sixteenth through eighteenth centuries, as held in the Newberry Library (Chicago), the Huntington Library (Pasadena), Digital Evans, Eighteenth-Century Collections Online, and Early English Books Online.

15. J. P., *The Merchant's Dayly Companion* (London: H. Clark, 1684), 388.

16. Thomas Watts, *An Essay on the Proper Method for Forming the Man of Business* (London, 1716), 16–19.

17. N. H., *The Compleat Tradesman, or, the Exact Dealers Daily Companion* (London, 1684), 2.

18. First English imprint, 1681; first colonial imprint, 1710.

19. First English imprint, 1687; first colonial imprint, 1703.

20. First English imprint, 1727; first colonial imprint, 1748.

21. Quotes from the title page and preface of Thomas Hill, *The Young Secretary's Guide: or, A Speedy Help to Learning*, 3rd ed. (Boston: B. Green and J. Allen, 1703).

22. See a complete list of occupations in William Mather, *The Young Man's Companion: or, Arithmetick Made Easie*, 5th ed. (London: J. Mayos, 1699), 5–6.

23. See Thomas Hill, *The Young Secretary's Guide: or, A Speedy Help to Learning*, 4th ed. (Boston: T. Fleet, 1713), 33.

24. See George Fisher, *The American Instructor: Or, Young Man's Best Companion*, 9th ed. (Philadelphia: B. Franklin and D. Hall, 1748), 54.

25. On the truncated social hierarchy in the North American colonies relative to England, see Gordon S. Wood, *The Radicalism of the American Revolution* (New York: Alfred A. Knopf, 1992), chapter 7.

26. See the unpaginated preface to [John Hill], *The Young Secretary's Guide: or, A Speedy Help to Learning* (Boston: B. Green, for Nicholas Buttolph, 1707).

27. See Hill, *The Young Secretary's Guide*, 4th ed., 35.

28. My book manuscript, *In My Power: Letter Writing in Early America*, includes a fuller range of identity categories. The category of gender, for instance, would move from cultural background to foreground in the mid-eighteenth century with respect to epistolary culture.

29. The best synthetic account of the commercializing colonial economy is John J. McCusker and Russell R. Menard, *The Economy of British America, 1607–1789*, 2nd ed. (Chapel Hill: University of North Carolina Press, 1991).

30. On commercialization and the "Great Awakening" in early America, see Richard L. Bushman, *From Puritan to Yankee: Character and the Social Order in Connecticut, 1690–1765* (Cambridge, Mass.: Harvard University Press, 1967), parts 3–4; and John L. Brooke, *The Heart of the Commonwealth: Society and Political Culture in Worcester County, Massachusetts, 1713–1861* (Cambridge: Cambridge University Press, 1989), chapters 2–3. On commercialization and the "consumer revolution" in early America, see Richard L. Bushman, *The Refinement of America: Persons, Houses, Cities* (New York: Alfred A. Knopf, 1992), chapters 1–6; and Cary Carson, Ronald Hoffman,

and Peter J. Albert, eds., *Of Consuming Interests: The Style of Life in the Eighteenth Century* (Charlottesville: University Press of Virginia, 1994).

31. See, for example, Fisher, *The American Instructor.*

32. A compelling account of intense boundary work, with respect to race and gender in the latter eighteenth-century America, is Mechal Sobel, *Teach Me Dreams: The Search for Self in the Revolutionary Era* (Princeton, N.J.: Princeton University Press, 2000).

33. See Hill, *The Young Secretary's Guide*, 4th ed., 35–36.

34. See the title page to N. H., *The Compleat Tradesman, or, the Exact Dealers Daily Companion*, 2nd ed. (London, 1684).

35. See, for example, the unpaginated preface to Hill, *The Young Secretary's Guide*, 4th ed.

36. On the material culture of letter writing, see Konstantin Dierks, "Letter Writing, Stationery Supplies, and Consumer Modernity in the Eighteenth-Century Atlantic World," *Early American Literature* 41 (2006): 474–94.

37. The maritime dimension of this communications infrastructure is discussed in Ian K. Steele, *The English Atlantic 1675–1740: An Exploration in Communication and Community* (New York: Oxford University Press, 1986); and Kenneth J. Banks, *Chasing Empire Across the Sea: Communications and the State in the French Atlantic, 1713–1763* (Montreal: McGill-Queen's University Press, 2002).

38. The canonical book on the variable and shifting salience of identity categories in early America, especially gender and race, is Kathleen M. Brown, *Good Wives, Nasty Wenches, and Anxious Patriarchs: Gender, Race, and Power in Colonial Virginia* (Chapel Hill: University of North Carolina Press, 1996).

Chapter 8. Business Friendships and Individualism in a Mercantile Class of Citizens in Charleston

I thank the organizers and other attendees of the Class and Class Struggle conference for the comments on this chapter. I also appreciate the assistance of my family—particularly my son, Matthew Sigmond, who was the smallest conference participant.

1. Charles Machin Memoir, William L. Clements Library, University of Michigan. I silently modernized the punctuation in this quote.

2. By "merchant," I mean an individual engaged in international trade, either on his own account or on commission. Since these men were often extremely mobile, I include letters dating from before and after their sojourns in Charleston. In the memoir previously cited, for example, Machin was based in Savannah during the incident in question, and only later did he move to work in Charleston, where he was nearly immediately imprisoned for debt. This chapter relies primarily on letters written by and to merchants based in Charleston from 1763 to 1833. For a complete bibliography, see Jennifer Lee Goloboy, "'Success to Trade': Charleston's Merchants in the Revolutionary Era" (Ph.D. diss., Harvard University, 2003), 191–97. This chapter draws from arguments, evidence, and language in my dissertation.

3. On merchants identifying themselves as a "class of citizens," see, for example, the *Pennsylvania Gazette* (Philadelphia), December 31, 1783 and December 1, 1784. Also see George C. Rogers, Jr., et al., eds., *The Papers of Henry Laurens*, vol. 4, *Sept. 1, 1763–Aug. 31, 1765* (Columbia: University of South Carolina Press, 1974), 254; and Thomas Smith, So. Car., to John Ferguson Esq. [dear Ferguson], Messrs. Ogden, Ferguson and Co., New York, January 13, 1827, Ferguson Papers, New York Genealogical and Biographical Society.

4. In addition to Susan Branson's chapter in this book, which analyzes early nineteenth-century middle-class culture, see Burton J. Bledstein and Robert D. Johnston, eds., *The Middling Sorts: Explorations in the History of the American Middle Class* (New York: Routledge, 2001); Stuart M. Blumin, *The Emergence of the Middle Class: Social Experience in the American City, 1770–1900* (New York: Cambridge University Press, 1989); Leonore Davidoff and Catherine Hall, *Family Fortunes: Men and Women of the English Middle Class, 1780–1850* (Chicago: University of Chicago Press, 1987); Elizabeth Fox-Genovese, *Within the Plantation Household: Black and White Women of the Old South* (Chapel Hill: University of North Carolina Press, 1988); Margaret R. Hunt, *The Middling Sort: Commerce, Gender, and the Family in England, 1680–1780* (Berkeley: University of California Press, 1996); Alan Karras, "The World of Alexander Johnston: The Creolization of Ambition, 1762–1787," *Historical Journal* 30 (1987): 53–76; Mary P. Ryan, *Cradle of the Middle Class: The Family in Oneida County, New York, 1790–1865* (New York: Cambridge University Press, 1981); and Jonathan Sperber, "Burger, Burgertum, Burgerlichkeit, Burgerliche Gesellschaft: Studies of the German (Upper) Middle Class and Its Socialcultural World," *Journal of Modern History* 69 (1997): 271–97.

5. I thank Joe Torre for his insight into the eighteenth-century economic mind.

6. Hunt, *The Middling Sort*, 1–5.

7. Jonathan Barry makes a similar argument for the British middle class, contrasting its situation with that of the poor and the gentry, whose fortunes seemed more predetermined and less dependent on individual effort. Barry, "Introduction," in *The Middling Sort of People: Culture, Society, and Politics in England, 1550–1800*, ed. Jonathan Barry and Christopher Brooks (New York: St. Martin's Press, 1994), 15–16.

8. Reinhard Bendix, *Max Weber: An Intellectual Portrait* (Berkeley: University of California Press, 1977), esp. 257–68; Sam Whimster, *The Essential Weber, a Reader* (New York: Routledge, 2004), chapters 13–14. One reason for the difference in Schocket's and my formulations might be that Philadelphia's commercial elite succeeded in maintaining its economic status and becoming socially dominant after the Revolution. In Charleston, in contrast, merchants lost both their financial and social authority to a planter elite.

9. I thank Marina Moskowitz and Dallett Hemphill for their insights about these issues.

10. Blumin, *Emergence*; Richard Bushman, *The Refinement of America: Persons, Houses, Cities* (New York: Alfred A. Knopf, 1992), esp. ch. 8; Ryan, *Cradle*.

11. I thank Lisa Norling, whose work on the increasingly impersonal nineteenth-century economy and its social effects inspired this research; Norling, *Captain Ahab Had a Wife: New England Women and the Whalefishery, 1720–1870* (Chapel Hill: University of North Carolina Press, 2000), 137–38, and Norling, "Commerce, Credit, and Coverture: Kezia Coffin and the Limits to Married Women's Enterprise in Revolution-

ary New England" (paper presented at the Seventh Annual Omohundro Conference, Glasgow, Scotland, July 14, 2001). See also Gordon Wood's remarks on patronage in *The Radicalism of the American Revolution* (New York: Vintage, 1993), 340.

12. Peter Coclanis, *The Shadow of a Dream: Economic Life and Death in the South Carolina Low Country, 1670–1920* (New York: Oxford University Press, 1989), 144.

13. Russell R. Menard, "Slavery, Economic Growth, and Revolutionary Ideology in the South Carolina Lowcountry," in *The Economy of Early America: The Revolutionary Period, 1763–1790*, ed. Ronald Hoffman, John J. McCusker, Russell R. Menard, and Peter J. Albert (Charlottesville: University Press of Virginia, 1988), 257. Menard estimated the average annual import value to be £436,400.

14. R. C. Nash, "The Organization of Trade and Finance in the Atlantic Economy: Britain and South Carolina, 1670–1775," in *Money, Trade, and Power: The Evolution of Colonial South Carolina's Plantation Society*, ed. Jack P. Greene, Rosemary Brana-Shute, and Randy J. Sparks (Columbia: University of South Carolina Press, 2001), 85.

15. [Francis Clayton], Charlestown, to Mr. Sheilds, Cowes, March 30, 1763, Hogg and Clayton Letter Book and Accounts, located in the Rare Book, Manuscript, and Special Collections Library, Duke University (hereafter cited as Duke).

16. [Unknown] to Mr. Dreghorn, July 29, 1763, Hogg and Clayton Letter Book and Accounts, Duke.

17. [Josiah Smith] to Mr. William Manning, London, December 5, 1772, Josiah Smith Letter Book, *Records of Ante-bellum Southern Plantations: From the Revolution through the Civil War*, ed. Kenneth M. Stampp and Randolph Boehm (Frederick, Md.: University Publications of America, 1985–96), series J, part 3. The original letter book is collection #3018 in the Southern Historical Collection, Wilson Library, University of North Carolina, Chapel Hill (hereafter cited as UNC).

18. Jonathan Purdy, New York, to Mr. Paul Rapelye, Charleston, December 19, 1820, Records of Napier, Rapelye, and Bennet, South Caroliniana Library, University of South Carolina (hereafter cited as USC).

19. David Lamb, Glasgow, to Robert Henderson Esq., Philadelphia, August 11, 1800, Robert Henderson Papers, (PHi) 1692, Historical Society of Philadelphia (hereafter cited as HSP).

20. David Lamb, Glasgow, to Mr. Robt. Henderson, Philadelphia, February 19, 1800, Robert Henderson Papers, 1692, HSP.

21. Zeph[aniah] Kingsley, Liverpool, to James Hamilton, Esq., February 28, 1805, James Hamilton Papers, Duke.

22. Isabella Hamilton, Clapton, to "My Dear Mr. Hamilton," February 2, 1805, James Hamilton Papers, Duke.

23. This description complements the world of women described by Carroll Smith-Rosenberg, "The Female World of Love and Ritual: Relations between Women in Nineteenth-Century America," *Signs: Journal of Women in Culture and Society* 1 (1975): 1–30.

24. George Nelson to Mr. William Fiddy, Charleston, June 6, 1797, George Nelson Letter Copy Book #3720, UNC.

25. Geo. Nelson, London, to Brother and Sister [not Brother Fras.], Houlton near Wragley, October 9, 1794, George Nelson Letter Copy Book #3720, UNC.

26. G. Nelson, London, to Mr. S. Bellamy, 41 Queen St. N. York, October 6, 1794, George Nelson Letter Copy Book #3720, UNC.

27. George Nelson Letter Copy Book #3720, UNC.

28. Daniel W. Stowell, ed. *Balancing Evils Judiciously: The Proslavery Writings of Zephaniah Kingsley* (Gainesville: University Press of Florida, 2000), 2–5.

29. Hunt, *The Middling Sort*, 33–34.

30. The mercantile involvement in the politics concerning trade between Britain and South Carolina is considered in Rebecca Starr, *A School for Politics: Commercial Lobbying and Political Culture in Early South Carolina* (Baltimore: Johns Hopkins University Press, 1998).

31. Stuart Bruchey, *Enterprise: The Dynamic Economy of a Free People* (Cambridge, Mass.: Harvard University Press, 1990), 231.

32. Menard, "Slavery," 257.

33. "South Carolina Produce exported, from the port of Charles-Town only, from the 1st day of November, 1763, to the 1st of November, 1764," *The South-Carolina Gazette*, Monday, October 29 to Monday, November 5, 1764. See also *South-Carolina Gazette*, Monday, October 8 to Monday, October 15, 1764; *South-Carolina Gazette*, Saturday, April 27 to Saturday, May 4, 1765.

34. George C. Rogers, Jr., et al., eds., *The Papers of Henry Laurens*, vol. 5, *Sept. 1, 1765- July 31, 1768* (Columbia: University of South Carolina Press, 1976), 661, 499.

35. R. C. Nash, "South Carolina and the Atlantic Economy in the Late Seventeenth and Eighteenth Centuries," *Economic History Review* 45 (1992): 682.

36. *Miller's Planters' and Merchants' Almanac, for the Year of our Lord 1829* (Charleston: A. E. Miller, [1828?]).

37. L. Trapmann, Charleston S/C, to Messrs. Ogden, Ferguson and Co., New York, February 18, 1830, Ogden, Ferguson, Day Co. Records, New York Historical Society (hereafter NYHS).

38. Ralph W. Hidy, *The House of Baring in American Trade and Finance: English Merchant Bankers at Work, 1763–1861* (Cambridge, Mass.: Harvard University Press, 1949), 75.

39. See, for example, Robt. Wilson, Liverpool, to Mr. James Hamilton of St. Simons, care of Richd. Carnochan, Esq., Charleston, July 24, 1811 (which is written on a preprinted letter) for an analysis of the volume of imports and price current from Duff Findlay, and Co., Liverpool, July 20, 1811, James Hamilton Papers, Duke.

40. Trapmann, Schmidt and Co., Charleston, to Messrs. McConnel and Kennedy, Manchester, January 1, 1824; October 9, 1824; February 21, 1825; June 4, 1825, all in the McConnel and Kennedy Papers, USC. L. Trapmann, Charleston, to Mr. Thomas Lamb, Boston, June 12, 1826, Lamb Family Papers, Massachusetts Historical Society, Boston; Peterson, Jahncke and Co., Charleston, to Messrs. Ogden, Day and Co., New York, September 15, 1823, Ogden, Ferguson, Day Co. Records, NYHS.

41. Jno. Fraser and Co., Charleston, to Messrs. Ogden, Ferguson and Co., New York, September 3, 1828; W. C. Molyneux, Charleston, to Messrs. Ogden, Ferguson and Co., New York, December 2, 1828; both in Ogden, Ferguson, Day Co. Records, NYHS.

42. "Gazette Weekly Letter Sheet, 1831," Monday, March 28, 1831, by Simms and

Duryea, included in Joseph Battersby, Charleston, to Messrs. Ogden, Ferguson and Co., New York, March 30, 1831, Ogden, Ferguson, Day Co. Records, NYHS.

43. The practice of reprinting trade statistics from other cities in the local newspaper might have encouraged quantification. See *City Gazette and Daily Advertiser*, April 5, 1821, which printed exports from Savannah.

44. Patricia Cline Cohen, *A Calculating People: The Spread of Numeracy in Early America* (New York: Routledge, 1999), 152, 40.

45. John Longsdon, Charleston, to Messrs. McConnel and Kennedy, Manchester, April 10, 1819, McConnel and Kennedy, USC.

46. Fred[rick] Smith, Warm Springs, Va., to Messrs. Ogden, Ferguson and Co., New York, August 22, 1832, Ogden, Ferguson, Day Co. Records, NYHS.

47. Charles Rosenberg, *The Cholera Years: The United States in 1832, 1849, and1866* (Chicago: University of Chicago Press, 1987), 40.

48. Gourdin and Smith, Charleston, to Messrs. Ogden, Ferguson and Co., New York, April 2, 1832, Ogden, Ferguson, Day Co. Records, NYHS.

49. John Hill, *The Young Secretary's Guide: or, A Speedy Help to Learning*, 24th ed. (Boston: Heart and Crown, for Thomas Fleet, 1750), 28.

50. Anonymous, *The Complete American Letter-Writer, and Best Companion for the Young Man of Business* (New York: M'Farlane and Long for Scott, 1807), 19–20.

51. Ibid., esp. 22–36. See also Toby L. Ditz, "Shipwrecked; or, Masculinity Imperiled: Mercantile Representations of Failure and the Gendered Self in Eighteenth-Century Philadelphia," *Journal of American History* 81 (1994): 51–80.

52. Anonymous, *The Complete American Letter-Writer*, 35. Emphasis in original.

53. George C. Rogers, Jr., *Evolution of a Federalist: William Loughton Smith of Charleston (1758–1812)* (Columbia: University of South Carolina Press, 1962), 230–33.

54. Naomi R. Lamoreaux, *Insider Lending: Banks, Personal Connections, and Economic Development in Industrial New England* (New York: Cambridge University Press, 1994), esp. 27–30.

55. See Jesus Cruz's discussion of the "bourgeois revolution" paradigm in Jesus Cruz, *Gentlemen, Rourgeois, and Revolutionaries: Political Change and Cultural Persistence among the Spanish Dominant Groups, 1750–1850* (New York: Cambridge University Press, 1996), esp. 262–63; Blumin, *The Emergence of the Middle Class*, 9–10; Debby Applegate, "Henry Ward Beecher and the 'Great Middle Class': Mass-Marketed Intimacy and Middle-Class Identity," in *The Middling Sorts: Explorations in the History of the American Middle Class*, ed. Burton J. Bledstein and Robert D. Johnston (New York: Routledge, 2001), 109. On the assumed link between the German middle class and political liberalism, see Sperber, "Burger," 273–74.

56. Davidoff and Hall, *Family Fortunes*, 13.

Chapter 9. Corporations and the Coalescence of an Elite Class in Philadelphia

1. For the most sweeping historiographical treatment of the issue of the extent to which the American Revolution was truly revolutionary, see Alfred Young, "American Historians Confront 'The Transforming Hand of Revolution,'" in *The Transforming*

Hand of Revolution: Reconsidering the American Revolution as a Social Movement, ed. Ronald Hoffman and Peter Albert (Charlottesville: University Press of Virginia, 1995), 346–494.

2. Gary J. Kornblith and John M. Murrin, "The Dilemmas of Ruling Elites in Revolutionary America," in *Ruling America: A History of Wealth and Power in a Democracy*, ed. Steve Fraser and Gary Gerstle (Cambridge, Mass.: Harvard University Press, 2005), 27–63. For a treatment of this phenomenon in Pennsylvania in particular, see Robert L. Brunhouse, *The Counter-revolution in Pennsylvania, 1776–1790* (1942; reprint, New York: Octagon Books, 1971).

3. One of the few to address this issue is Doron Ben Atar, *Trade Secrets: Intellectual Piracy and the Origins of American Industrial Power* (New Haven, Conn.: Yale University Press, 2004).

4. The establishment of the Sierra Leone Company by Parliament in 1791 represented an exception to the rule.

5. Pauline Maier, "The Revolutionary Origins of the American Corporation," *William and Mary Quarterly*, 3rd ser., 50 (1993): 51, 83.

6. James W. Hurst, *The Legitimacy of the Business Corporation in the Law of the United States, 1780–1970* (Charlottesville: University Press of Virginia, 1970), 1, 7.

7. Although the historiography on early North American corporations is not vast, it does span the twentieth century, including such works as John P. Davis, *Corporations: A Study of the Origin and Development of Great Business Combinations and of Their Relation to the Authority of the State* (1905; reprint, New York: Capricorn Books, 1961); Guy S. Callender, "The Early Transportation and Banking Enterprises of the States in Relation to the Growth of Corporations," *Quarterly Journal of Economics* 17 (November 1902): 111–62; Joseph S. Davis, *Essays in the Earlier History of American Corporations*, 2 vols. (Cambridge, Mass.: Harvard University Press, 1917); Joseph Blandi, *Maryland Business Corporations, 1783–1852* (Baltimore: Johns Hopkins University Press, 1934); Shaw Livermore, *Early American Land Companies: Their Influence on Corporate Development* (New York: Commonwealth Fund, 1939); William Miller, "A Note on the Business Corporations in Pennsylvania, 1800–1860," *Quarterly Journal of Economics* 55 (November 1940): 150–60; Oscar Handlin and Mary F. Handlin, "Origins of the American Business Corporation," *Journal of Economic History* 5 (May 1945): 1–23; Oscar Handlin, *Commonwealth: A Study of the Role of Government in the American Economy* (Cambridge, Mass.: Harvard University Press, 1947); Louis Hartz, *Economic Policy and Democratic Thought: Pennsylvania, 1776–1860* (Cambridge, 1948); John W. Cadman, *The Corporation in New Jersey, 1791–1875* (Cambridge, Mass.: Harvard University Press, 1949); Edwin M. Dodd, *American Business Corporations until 1860: With Special Reference to Massachusetts* (Cambridge, Mass.: Harvard University Press, 1954); Hurst, *Legitimacy*; Ronald E. Seavoy, *The Origins of the American Business Corporation, 1784–1855: Broadening the Concept of Public Service During Industrialization* (Westport, Conn.: Greenwood Press, 1982); and Maier, "Revolutionary Origins."

8. For the most recent and persuasive arguments concerning British corporate business activity in the eighteenth century, see Ron Harris, *Industrializing English Law: Entrepreneurship and Business Organization, 1720–1844* (New York: Cambridge University Press, 2000).

9. Benjamin Franklin to Jean-Baptiste Leory, November 13, 1789, as quoted in

Bartlett and Kaplan, eds., *Familiar Quotations*, 16th ed. (Boston: Little, Brown and Company, 1992), 310.

10. See David Hancock, *Citizens of the World: London Merchants and the Integration of the British Atlantic Community, 1735–1785* (New York: Cambridge University Press, 1995).

11. Charles G. Paleske, *Observations on the Application for a Law to Incorporate "The Union Canal Company" Respectfully Submitted to the Members of Both Houses of the Legislature of Pennsylvania* (Philadelphia: Duane, 1808), 7.

12. Theodore Thayer, "The Land Bank System in the American Colonies," *Journal of Economic History* 13, no. 2 (spring 1953): 145–59; Mary M. Schweitzer, *Custom and Contract: Household, Government, and the Economy in Colonial Pennsylvania* (New York: Columbia University Press, 1987), 115–68; Edwin J. Perkins, *American Public Finance and Financial Services, 1700–1815* (Columbus: Ohio State University Press, 1994), 29–84.

13. Robert Gough, "Towards a Theory of Class and Social Conflict: A Social History of Wealthy Philadelphia, 1775–1800" (Ph.D. diss., University of Pennsylvania, 1978), 671–701.

14. Thomas M. Doerflinger, *A Vigorous Spirit of Enterprise: Merchants and Economic Development in Revolutionary Philadelphia* (Chapel Hill: University of North Carolina Press, 1986), 245.

15. Ibid., 244.

16. For example, Alexander Brown, the founder of the nineteenth-century Brown family transatlantic empire, emigrated from Ireland to Baltimore in the 1790s. Edwin J. Perkins, *Financing Anglo-American Trade: The House of Brown, 1800–1880* (Cambridge, Mass.: Harvard University Press, 1975), 19.

17. Kenneth Morgan, "Business Networks in the British Export Trade to North America, 1750–1800," in *The Early Modern Atlantic Economy*, ed. John J. McCusker and Kenneth Morgan (New York: Cambridge University Press, 2000), 41–42.

18. Ralph Hidy, *The House of Baring in American Trade and Finance: English Merchant Bankers at Work, 1763–1861* (Cambridge, Mass.: Harvard University Press, 1949), 29.

19. Thomas Mortimer, *Every Man His Own Broker: or, A Guide to Exchange-Alley, in Which the Nature of the Several Funds, Vulgarly Called the Stocks, Is Clearly Explained*, 6th ed. (London: S. Hooper, 1790).

20. Joseph Hume Francis, *History of the Bank of England* (Chicago: Euclid Publishing Company, 1888), 206.

21. See John Brewer, *The Sinews of Power: War, Money, and the English State, 1688–1783* (New York: Knopf, 1989), 88–134.

22. See Henry Hamilton, *An Economic History of Scotland in the Eighteenth Century* (Oxford: Clarendon Press, 1963); and Richard Saville, *Bank of Scotland: A History, 1695–1995* (Edinburgh: Edinburgh University Press, 1996), 249–78.

23. See Saville, *Bank of Scotland*, 1–278; and Charles W. Munn, *The Scottish Provincial Banking Companies, 1747–1864* (Edinburgh: John Donald Publishers, 1981).

24. Although the Bank of North America had a Pennsylvania charter, it clearly was originally intended as an institution of national scope.

25. John Phillips, *A General History of Inland Navigation, Foreign and Domestic:*

Containing a Complete Account of the Canals Already Executed in England, with Considerations on Those Projected (London: I. and J. Taylor, 1792), 84.

26. Compiled through analysis of Joseph Priestley, *Historical Account of the Navigable Rivers, Canals, and Railways throughout Great Britain* (London, 1831).

27. For a brief discussion of the role of business decision-making rules and routines in the adaptation of new techniques and technologies, see Richard R. Nelson, *Understanding Technical Change as an Evolutionary Process*, Professor Dr. F. de Vries Lectures in Economics 8 (New York: Elsevier Science Publishing Company, Inc., 1987).

28. Francis, *History of the Bank of England*, 58–63; William Robert Scott, *The Constitution and Finance of English, Scottish, and Irish Joint-Stock Companies to 1720*, vol. 3, *Water Supply, Postal, Street-Lighting, Manufacturing, Banking, Finance, and Insurance Companies; Also Statements Relating to the Crown Finances* (New York: Peter Smith, 1951), 253–56; *Charters, Laws, and By-Laws, of the Bank of Pennsylvania* (Philadelphia: Clark and Raser, 1830), 2–21.

29. *Charters, Laws, and By-Laws, of the Bank of Pennsylvania*, 2–21.

30. For example, in June 1814 Henry Drinker, the cashier for the Bank of North America, called a meeting of the cashiers of Philadelphia banks to discuss their policy regarding the notes of the forty-one banks that the state legislature had just chartered. June 17, 1814, Excerpt of Minutes of Board of Directors, Historical Records, Box 1, 1807–20, Farmers and Mechanics Bank, Accession 1658, Hagley Museum and Library, Wilmington, Delaware.

31. Bishop Carleton Hunt, *The Development of the Business Corporation in England, 1800–1867* (New York: Russell and Russell, 1969), 10; from 1791 to 1793, state governments chartered seven canal companies, more than in any other three-year period in the United States until the explosion of the early 1820s that was inspired by the Erie Canal.

32. Phillips, *A General History of Inland Navigation*, 348–56.

33. William Smith, *An Historical Account of the Rise, Progress, and Present State of the Canal Navigation in Pennsylvania. With an Appendix, Containing, Abstracts of the Acts of the Legislature Since the Year 1790, and the Grants of Money for Improving Roads and Navigable Waters throughout the State; to Which Is Annexed, "An Explanatory Map"* (Philadelphia: Zachariah Poulson, Jr., 1795); and Charles Vallancey, *A Treatise on Inland Navigation, or, the Art of Making Rivers Navigable, of Making Canals in All Sorts of Soils, and of Constructing Locks and Sluices* (Dublin: George and Alexander Ewing, 1763), 4. Passages from Smith's book had appeared as part of the entry for James Brindley in Andrew Kippis, *Biographia Britannica: or, The Lives of the Most Eminent Persons Who Have Flourished in Great Britain and Ireland*, vol. 2, 2nd ed. (London: W. and A. Strahan, 1780), 591–604. This work, in turn, contains long quotes from *The History of Inland Navigations, Particularly Those of the Duke of Bridgewater, in Lancashire and Cheshire; and the Intended One Promoted by Earl Gower and the Other Persons of Distinction in Staffordshire, Cheshire, and Derbyshire*, 2nd ed. (London: T. Lowndes, 1769), with which Smith also was most likely familiar. Also see Phillips, *A General History of Inland Navigation*; and Richard Whitworth, *The Advantages of Inland Navigation; or, Some Observations Offered to the Public, to Shew That an Inland Navigation May Be Easily Effected Between the Three Great Ports of Bristol, Liverpool,*

and Hull; Together With a Plan for Executing the Same (London: R. Baldwin, 1766), both of which contain information that appeared in Smith's *An Historical Account* and other North American works.

34. See Whitworth, *The Advantages of Inland Navigation*, 17–24; and George Heberton Evans, Jr., *British Corporation Finance, 1775–1850: A Study of Preference Shares* (Baltimore: Johns Hopkins University Press, 1936), 11–25.

35. See, for example, the charters of both the Schuylkill and Susquehanna Canal Company and the Delaware and Schuylkill Canal Company. Smith, *An Historical Account*, 23–44. For a brief discussion of some of the structural similarities between British and North American corporations, see Maier, "Revolutionary Origins."

36. William Barton, *Observations on the Nature and Use of Paper-Credit . . . Including Proposals for a National Bank* (Philadelphia: R. Aitken, 1781), 40.

37. Thomas Willing to William Phelps, et al., January 16, 1784, as quoted in Doerflinger, *A Vigorous Spirit of Enterprise*, 284.

38. "Remarks on Money, and the Bank Paper of the United States: Together with a Review of Governor Snyder's Objections to the Bank Bill Passed by Two of the Legislative Branches of the State of Pennsylvania, at Their Session of 1812–1813" (Philadelphia, 1814), 14, 15.

39. Robert C. Alberts, *The Golden Voyage: The Life and Times of William Bingham, 1752–1804* (Boston: Houghton-Mifflin, 1969), 106.

40. "List of Stockholders Who Have Completed Shares in the Delaware and Schuylkill Canal Navigation," 1807, Society Miscellaneous Collection, Box 4-B, Historical Society of Pennsylvania.

41. John Wilson to Joseph Pemberton, January 12, 1782, Pemberton Papers, Historical Society of Pennsylvania.

42. Mark Prager and Co. to James St. Ferrall, Philadelphia, February 9, 1797, Prager Letter Book, Historical Society of Pennsylvania, as quoted in Robert E. Wright, "Bank Ownership and Lending Patterns in New York and Pennsylvania, 1781–1831," *Business History Review* 73 (spring 1999): 42.

43. Edwin J. Perkins, *American Public Finance and Financial Services, 1700–1815* (Columbus: Ohio State University Press, 1994), 260.

44. See Evans, *British Corporation Finance*.

45. Tom W. Smith estimated the average personal wealth per decedent in Philadelphia in 1791 to be between $604 and $660. Tom W. Smith, "The Dawn of the Urban-Industrial Age: The Social Structure of Philadelphia, 1790–1830" (Ph.D. diss., University of Chicago, 1980), 69. In "Bank Ownership and Lending Patterns," Wright asserted that bank stockholding reached "a broad segment of the population," noting that stockholding extended beyond merchants and that some women held stock as well. However, given the cost of stocks, the number of shares available, the median holding of shares, the size of the total population, and median wealth figures, that definition of "wide segment" encompasses no more than 10 percent of the general population.

46. Matthew Carey, ed., *Debates and Proceedings of the General Assembly of Pennsylvania, on the Memorials Praying a Repeal or Suspension of the Law Annulling the Charter of the Bank* (Philadelphia: Carey and Co., 1786), 10.

47. Bank lending policy has been a matter of some historiographic dispute.

Nonetheless, historians agree that the Philadelphia banks (especially the first three, the Bank of North America, the Bank of Pennsylvania, and the Bank of Philadelphia) lent most of their money (in terms of both dollars and number of loans) to the upper quarter of the population in terms of wealth.

48. See Brunhouse, *The Counter-Revolution in Pennsylvania*; and Douglas M. Arnold, *A Republican Revolution: Ideology and Politics in Pennsylvania, 1776–1790* (New York: Garland, 1989) for analyses of Pennsylvania politics during the 1780s.

49. See Terry Bouton, "A Road Closed: Rural Insurgency in Post-Independence Pennsylvania," *Journal of American History* 87 (December 2000): 855–87.

50. For the most recent consideration of colonial Pennsylvania politics, see Richard R. Beeman, *The Varieties of Political Experience in Eighteenth-Century America* (Philadelphia: University of Pennsylvania Press, 2004), 204–42.

51. Randall S. Kroszner, "Free Banking: The Scottish Experience as a Model for Emerging Economies," in *Reforming Financial Systems: Historical Implications for Policy*, ed. Gerard Caprio, Jr. and Dimitri Vittras (New York: Cambridge University Press, 1997), 41–64.

52. Robert Ralston to Samuel Richards, July 24, 1811, Historical Records, Box 1, 1807–1820, Farmers and Mechanics Bank, Accession 1858, Hagley Museum and Library, Wilmington, Delaware.

53. David Armitage, "Three Concepts of Atlantic History," in *The British Atlantic World, 1500–1800*, ed. David Armitage and Michael J. Braddick (New York: Palgrave Macmillan, 2002), 11–30.

54. John, Lord Sheffield, *Observations on the Commerce of the American States* (Dublin: Luke White, 1784), 134.

55. *Report of the Senate, Appointed to Enquire into the Extent and Causes of the Present General Distress* (Lancaster: Commonwealth of Pennsylvania, 1820), 3.

Chapter 10. Class, Discourse, and Industrialization in the New American Republic

1. To avoid burdensome language, this chapter uses the terms "America," "American," and "Americans" to describe the region or the people who lived in the United States (or the colonies that became that nation). Martin J. Burke, *The Conundrum of Class: Public Discourse on the Social Order in America* (Chicago: University of Chicago Press, 1995), 1–21.

2. Weber's emphasis on culture is most obvious in *The Protestant Ethic and the Spirit of Capitalism* (New York: Charles Scribner's Sons, 1952) but it is also evident in his other essays. For example, in "Class, Status, Party," Weber notes that while class is primarily linked to economic status, the degree to which communal action results from class situation "is linked to general cultural conditions, especially to those of an intellectual sort." See Weber, "Class, Status, Party," in *From Max Weber: Essays in Sociology*, ed. H. H. Gerth and C. Wright Mills (New York: Oxford University Press, 1944), 184.

3. Rolla M. Tryon, *Household Manufactures in the United States* (Chicago: Uni-

versity of Chicago Press, 1917), 123–63. For a general overview, see Lawrence A. Peskin, *Manufacturing Revolution: The Intellectual Origins of Early American Industry* (Baltimore: Johns Hopkins University Press, 2003), 61–64.

4. *Pennsylvania Gazette*, March 7, 1765, 2; February 16, 1769, 3; *Boston Gazette*, January 4, 1768, 3; Peskin, *Manufacturing Revolution*, 30–44.

5. *Pennsylvania Gazette*, May 1, 1766, 3; *Boston Gazette*, August 8, 1774, 3; *New York Journal*, July 14, 1768, 3.

6. *New York Journal*, September 8, 1768, 2; September 15, 1763, 3; *Pennsylvania Gazette*, January 25, 1779, 3; May 24, 1770, 2.

7. Richard Alan Ryerson, *The Revolution Has Now Begun* (Philadelphia: University of Pennsylvania Press, 1978), 56; *New York Journal*, November 24, 1774, 1; Staughton Lynd, "The Mechanics in New York Politics, 1774–1788," *Labor History* 5 (fall 1964): 227.

8. Peskin, *Manufacturing Revolution*, 71–75.

9. *New York Independent Gazette*, January 24, 1784, 2; *Philadelphia Independent Gazetteer*, July 19, 1783, 3.

10. *Boston Gazette*, September 19, 1785, 3. The former Sons of Liberty were the shipwright Gibbons Sharp and the hat maker Sarson Belcher.

11. *New York Journal*, October 20, 1785, 2; *Boston Gazette*, October 10, 1785, 3.

12. *Boston Gazette*, April 18, May 9, and October 10, 1785; *Pennsylvania Gazette*, May 18 and June 8, 1785.

13. *Laws of Pennsylvania*, August 1785, 669; Victor S. Clark, *History of Manufactures in the United States* (New York: McGraw Hill, 1929) 1:62; William Frank Zornow, "Massachusetts Tariff Policies, 1775–1789," *Essex Institute Historical Collections* 90 (1954): 212; Zornow, "New York Tariff Policies, 1775–1789," *New York History* 37 (1956) 44-45.

14. Billy Smith, *The "Lower Sort": Philadelphia's Laboring People, 1750–1800* (Ithaca, N.Y.: Cornell University Press, 1990), 126–49; John Bézis-Selfa, *Forging America: Ironworkers, Adventurers, and the Industrious Revolution* (Ithaca, N.Y.: Cornell University Press, 2004); Simon Middleton, *From Privileges to Rights: Work and Politics in Colonial New York City* (Philadelphia: University of Pennsylvania Press, 2006). The author thanks Simon Middleton for sharing his work in manuscript form.

15. Anonymous, "Observations on the Federal Procession on the Fourth of July, 1788," *American Museum* 4 (July 1788): 77; *Maryland Journal*, May 6, 1788, 2–3; *New York Daily Advertiser*, August 2, 1788, 1; *Boston Gazette*, February 11, 1788, 3. Emphasis added.

16. Minutes of the General Society of Mechanics and Tradesmen of the City of New York (hereafter GSMT), November 18, 1788 (located at their headquarters, New York City); *New York Daily Advertiser*, February 6, 1789, 2.

17. Thomas C. Cochran, ed., *The New American State Papers: Manufactures* (Wilmington: Scholarly Resources, 1972), 1:33–37.

18. For the constitutions of the Philadelphia, New York, Baltimore, and Boston societies, see *American Museum* 2 (August 1787): 167–69; *New York Daily Advertiser*, March 21, 1789, 2; *Maryland Journal*, May 15, 1789, 2; *Massachusetts Centinel*, September 13, 1788, 3.

19. Lawrence A. Peskin, "From Protection to Encouragement: Manufacturing

and Mercantilism in New York City's Public Sphere, 1783–1795," *Journal of the Early Republic* 18 (1998): 606–13; Peskin, *Manufacturing Revolution*, 98–104.

20. *Pennsylvania Gazette*, July 9, 1788; *Massachusetts Centinel*, September 13, 1788, 3; Samuel Miles, "Address of the Board of Managers of the Pennsylvania Society for the Protection of Manufactures and the Useful Arts," *American Museum* 2 (October 1787): 361–62.

21. *New York Daily Advertiser*, February 6, 1790, 2.

22. Joseph Stancliffe Davis, *Essays in the Earlier History of American Corporations* (Cambridge, Mass.: Harvard University Press, 1917), 1:422; George Logan, "At a Meeting of the Germantown Society for Promoting Domestic Manufactures," *American Museum* 12, appendix (1792), 222–23.

23. *Pennsylvania Gazette*, October 10, 1792, 1.

24. Gary John Kornblith, "From Artisans to Businessmen: Master Mechanics in New England, 1789–1850" (Ph.D. diss., Princeton University, 1983), 96–97; Joseph T. Buckingham, *Annals of the Massachusetts Charitable Mechanics Association* (Boston: Crocker and Brewster, 1853), 6, 17–49.

25. *Boston Gazette*, January 13, 1800, 3–4.

26. Buckingham, *Annals*, 118.

27. John E. Crowley, *This Sheba Self: The Conceptualization of Economic Life in Eighteenth-Century America* (Baltimore: Johns Hopkins University Press, 1974).

28. Baltimore: Mechanics Bank (1806). Philadelphia: Farmers' and Mechanics' Bank (1807), Mechanics Bank (1814). New York City: Mechanics Bank (1810). Boston: Manufacturers and Mechanics Bank (1814).

29. *Baltimore American*, June 30, 1806, 3, and May 22, 1806, 2. Farmers' and Mechanics' Bank Records, Hagley Museum and Library, Wilmington, Delaware.

30. Buckingham, *Annals*, 130.

31. For details, see Peskin, *Manufacturing Revolution*, 145–52.

32. Steffen, *The Mechanics of Baltimore* (Urbana: University of Illinois Press, 1984), 196; *Baltimore American*, June 30, 1806, 3. For candidate lists, see *Baltimore American*, June 26, 1806, 3; June 27, 1806, 3; June 28, 1806, 3; June 30, 1806, 3.

33. Minutes of the GSMT, February 21, 1810, July 4, 1810, and passim.

34. *Aurora*, October 22, 1808.

35. *Aurora*, May 27, 1809, 2. On "mechanicians," see Anthony F. C. Wallace, *Rockdale: The Growth of an American Village in the Early Industrial Era* (New York: Alfred Knopf, 1980), 211–37; and David Freeman Hawke, *Nuts and Bolts of the Past* (New York: Harper and Row, 1988), 27–44.

36. Cynthia Shelton, *The Mills of Manayunk* (Baltimore: Johns Hopkins University Press, 1986), 7–25.

37. F. W. Taussing, *The Tariff History of the United States* (1932; reprint, New York: Augustus M. Kelley, 1967), 68–108; Edward Stanwood, *American Tariff Controversies in the Nineteenth Century* (New York: Houghton Mifflin, 1903), 160–289; R. W. Thompson, *The History of the Protective Tariff Laws* (1888; reprint, New York: Garland, 1974), 110–209; Clark, *History of Manufactures*, 1:274–79; Charles Sellers, *Market Revolution* (New York: Oxford University Press, 1991), 285–96.

38. *American State Papers*, Finance, 4:390, 3:452.

39. On Gray, McLean, and Wilkinson, see William R. Bagnall, *The Textile Indus-*

tries of the United States (1893; reprint, New York: A. M. Kelly, 1971), 318, 496; and the *Dictionary of American Biography* entry for Wilkinson . Other prominent manufacturer delegates included Elijah Paine (Vermont), James Rhodes (Rhode Island), and J. E. Sprague (Massachusetts). For the list of delegates to Harrisburg, see *Proceedings of the General Convention at Harrisburg*, 10; reprinted in *Niles' Register*, August 11, 1827.

40. Mathew Carey, *Autobiographical Sketches in a Series of Letters Addressed to a Friend* (Philadelphia: John Clarke, 1829), 1:123, 150–52.

41. John Niven, *Martin Van Buren* (New York: Oxford University Press, 1983), 188.

42. John R. Commons, ed., *History of Labour in the United States* (1918; reprint, New York: Augustus M. Kelley, 1966), 1:193, 237.

43. Daniel Feller, *The Jacksonian Promise: America, 1815–1840* (Baltimore: Johns Hopkins University Press, 1995), 131; Commons, *History of Labour*, 194, 304.

44. Thomas Skidmore, *The Rights of Man to Property!* (New York: Alexander Ming, 1829), 273; Commons, *History of Labour*, 295–96.

45. Ronald Schultz, *The Republic of Labor: Philadelphia Artisans and the Politics of Class, 1720–1830* (New York: Oxford University Press, 1993), 228–30.

Chapter 11. Sex and Other Middle-Class Pastimes in the Life of Ann Carson

1. Ann Carson, *The History of the Celebrated Mrs. Ann Carson, Widow of the Late Unfortunate Lieutenant Richard Smith* . . . (Philadelphia, 1822).

2. Both the Baker family's and the Carson family's income and housing ranked them slightly above the average for Philadelphia households. Susan E. Klepp and Susan Branson, "A Working Woman: The Autobiography of Ann Baker Carson," in *Life in Early Philadelphia: A Documentary History*, ed. Billy G. Smith (University Park: Pennsylvania State University Press, 1995), 156, note 1.

3. Carson wrote her memoir with the help of Mary Clarke Carr. There is a distinct possibility that Carr actually wrote most of the *History*. Sixteen years later, Carr told her side of the story in her continuation of Carson's life (published under the name Mary Clarke), *The Memoirs of the Celebrated and Beautiful Mrs. Ann Carson, Daughter of an Officer of the U.S. Navy and Wife of Another, Whose Life Terminated in the Philadelphia Prison*, 2nd ed., 2 vols. (Philadelphia and New York, 1838). All quotations from the *History* are taken from what is essentially the second edition of that work, the *Memoirs*. Clarke, *Memoirs*, 1:191.

4. John Binns to Simon Snyder, Philadelphia, 9 p.m. Wednesday, July 10, 1816; Correspondence of Simon Snyder, case 76, vol. 1, Historical Society of Pennsylvania. Had Carson's plan not succeeded, she was prepared to kidnap Snyder's son, or John Binns (the editor of the *Democratic Press*), or Binns's young son. Prisoners for Trial Docket (January 1816–January 1818), Philadelphia City Archives.

5. Clarke, *Memoirs*, 1:21. This may have been John Montgomery. He is listed as "councillor at law," in *Matchett's Baltimore Director for 1827* (Baltimore, 1827), 189. Montgomery was the Maryland State Attorney General in 1811, and in 1820 he became mayor of Baltimore. See Index of Office Holders in Edward C. Papenfuse, et al.,

Archives of Maryland, Historical List, New Series, vol. 1 (Annapolis: Maryland State Archives, 1990).

6. Clarke, *Memoirs,* 2:10 (Carson's emphasis). For details of the kidnapping and trial, see Susan Branson, "'He Swore His Life Was in Danger From Me': The Attempted Kidnapping of Governor Simon Snyder," *Pennsylvania History* 67, no. 3 (summer 2000): 349–60.

7. This is my paraphrasing of John Seed's definition of the middle class in his essay, "From 'Middling Sort' to Middle Class in Late Eighteenth- and Early Nineteenth-Century England," in *Social Orders and Social Classes in Europe since 1500: Studies in Social Stratification,* ed. M. L. Bush (London: Longman, 1992), 115.

8. See the chapter by Konstantin Dierks in this book. Burton J. Bledstein confirms these different paths to class identity: "One could enter the middle class piecemeal, through discriminating practices: in family activities, child-rearing procedures, gender relations, techniques of worship, work habits, labor relations, education and health methods, recreation routines, and personal as well as domestic consumption patterns." Burton J. Bledstein and Robert D. Johnson, eds., *The Middling Sorts: Explorations in the History of the American Middle Class* (New York: Routledge, 2001), 9.

9. Seed, "From 'Middling Sort' to Middle Class in Late Eighteenth- and Early Nineteenth-Century England," 125.

10. The term "middling interest" was in use (and in print) both as a political identification and as a social one by the 1820s. Lydia Maria Child believed the audience for her books was the "middling class"; see the preface to her *The Mother's Book* (1831). Historians disagree about the timing of middle-class formation as well the definition of this class. I am not concerned so much with its origins as with identifying it in a time and place in which people began consciously to use the term middling sorts or middling interests, and to identify themselves as such. Konstantin Dierks's chapter in this book addresses the eighteenth-century development of this self-identification.

10. Clarke, *Memoirs,* 1:19.

12. Ibid., 1:89–90. Sean Wilentz, *Chants Democratic: New York City and the Rise of the American Working Class, 1788–1850* (New York: Oxford University Press, 1984); Gary J. Kornblith, "From Artisans to Businessmen: Master Mechanics in New England, 1789–1850" (Ph.D. diss., Princeton University, 1983); Lisa Lubow, "Artisans in Transition: Early Capitalist Development and the Carpenters of Boston, 1787–1837" (Ph.D. diss., University of California, Los Angeles, 1987).

13. Susan Branson, "Women and the Family Economy in the Early Republic: The Case of Elizabeth Meredith," *Journal of the Early Republic* 16 (spring 1996): 47–71.

14. Carson recognized the value of women's contributions to this transition in family fortunes and regretted that it did not happen in her own family. Carson's mother, unlike Elizabeth Meredith, did not help with family business or conduct a business of her own. Mrs. Baker's husband considered her "incapable of conducting any business. . . ." Said Carson, "Had he permitted my mother to keep a *shoe, grocery,* or *grog shop,* now at this time our family might have been opulent, and some of its members probably lawyers, doctors, and even clergymen. The parents of numbers of our various professional characters were then of that class of society." Clarke, *Memoirs,* 1:25.

15. Gertrude Meredith to William Meredith, September 2, 1800, Meredith Family Papers, Historical Society of Pennsylvania. Gertrude Meredith was the daughter of Samuel Ogden and the niece of Gouverneur Morris. Concern with child rearing and an emphasis on emotion and attachment to children was not confined to mothers. See Shawn Johansen, *Family Men: Middle-Class Fatherhood in Early Industrializing America* (New York: Routledge, 2001).

16. Gertrude Meredith to William Meredith, February 7, 1805; May 3, 1804. Gertrude seemed overly concerned with the appearance of refinement. She disparaged her uncle Morris's library because the books appeared "more like the purchases of a great economist than a man of fortune. The editions are few of them elegant and the greater proportion of them very common indeed, and some in boards." Gertrude Meredith to William Meredith, September 6, 1802.

17. Consumption is a topic most recently considered in terms of gender roles. Elaine S. Abelson, *When Ladies Go A-Thieving: Middle-Cass Shoplifters in the Victorian Department Store* (New York: Oxford University Press, 1990); Lori Merish, *Sentimental Materialism: Gender, Commodity Culture, and Nineteenth-Century American Literature* (Durham, N.C.: Duke University Press, 2000). C. Dallett Hemphill discusses the ways in which the middle class sought to define itself through manners, speech, and behavior—all precisely explained in, and encouraged by, conduct books. See C. Dallett Hemphill, *Bowing to Necessity: A History of Manners in America, 1620–1860* (Oxford: Oxford University Press, 1999), esp. chapter 7. The literature on the subject of the formation of middle-class identity and respectability includes the following: Mary Beth Norton, "The Evolution of White Women's Experience in Early America," *American Historical Review* 89 (1984): 593–619; Stuart M. Blumin, *The Emergence of the Middle Class: Social Experience in the American City, 1760–1900* (New York: Cambridge University Press, 1989): 66–137; Jane H. Pease and William H. Pease, *Ladies, Women, and Wenches: Choice and Constraint in Antebellum Charleston and Boston* (Chapel Hill: University of North Carolina Press, 1990); Patricia Cline Cohen, "Unregulated Youth: Masculinity and Murder in the 1830s City," *Radical History Review* 52 (1992): 33–52; Patricia Cline Cohen, "The Helen Jewett Murder: Violence, Gender, and Sexual Licentiousness in Antebellum America," *NWSA Journal* 2 (1990): 374–89; Steven Ruggles, "Fallen Women: The Inmates of the Magdalen Society Asylum of Philadelphia, 1836–1908," *Journal of Social History* 16 (1982–83): 65–82; Christine Stansell, *City of Women: Sex and Class in New York, 1789–1860* (Urbana: University of Illinois Press, 1987); and Carroll Smith-Rosenberg, *Disorderly Conduct: Visions of Gender in Victorian America* (New York: Oxford University Press, 1985).

18. The *Sun*'s and the *Herald*'s coverage of the Helen Jewett and Mary Rogers murder cases exemplified this type of journalism. Andie Tucher, *Froth and Scum: Truth, Beauty, Goodness, and the Ax Murder in America's First Mass Medium* (Chapel Hill: University of North Carolina Press, 1994); Patricia Cline Cohen, *The Murder of Helen Jewett: The Life and Death of a Prostitute in Nineteenth-Century New York* (New York: Alfred A. Knopf, 1998); and Amy Gilman Srebnick, *The Mysterious Death of Mary Rogers: Sex and Culture in Nineteenth-Century New York* (Oxford: Oxford University Press, 1995). For earlier criminal accounts, see Daniel E. Williams, "Rogues, Rascals, and Scoundrels: The Underworld Literature of Early America," *American Studies* 24, no. 2 (fall 1983): 5–19.

19. One of the earliest of these North American confessions is *The Vain Prodigal Life, and Tragical Penitent Death of Thomas Hellier* (London, 1680). Hellier, a Virginia indentured servant, murdered his master and mistress.

20. Daniel A. Cohen, *Pillars of Salt, Monuments of Grace: New England Crime Literature and the Origins of American Popular Culture, 1674–1860* (New York: Oxford University Press, 1993), 158–59. Burroughs's autobiography was also printed in Boston (1804) and Philadelphia (1812).

21. Daniel Cohen has noted that early North American sentimental fiction is much like modern "docudrama." Cohen, *Pillars of Salt, Monuments of Grace*, 168. For a discussion of early North American sentimental fiction, readership, and class, see Cathy N. Davidson, *Revolution and the Word: The Rise of the Novel in America* (New York: Oxford University Press, 1986).

22. Clarke, *Memoirs*, 1:77. Carson's sentiments are suspiciously similar to those expressed by Constantia Dudley in Charles Brockden Brown's *Ormond* (1799), whom Brown says was "mistress of the product of her own labor." Dudley, like Carson, articulates ideals of independence, intelligence, and self-reliance for women. Ernest Earnest, *The American Eve in Fact and Fiction, 1775–1914* (Urbana: University of Illinois Press, 1974), 32–33; and Steven Watts, *The Romance of Real Life: Charles Brockden Brown and the Origins of American Culture* (Baltimore: Johns Hopkins University Press, 1994), 89–100.

23. Clarke, *Memoirs*, 1:131. Carson confessed to her readers that on at least one occasion she was embarrassed to be a storekeeper, since she sought to conceal from a potential beau her "humble employment." Ibid., 1:85.

24. Ibid., 1:76. Carson opened her shop just prior to the crisis with Britain, which culminated in the War of 1812. Few North American merchants had new stock of chinaware, and Carson's supply was in high demand.

25. Ibid., 1:95.

26. Ann Carson to Stephen Girard, September 2 and 4, 1811, Girard Papers, series 2, reel 49, no. 392, American Philosophical Society, Philadelphia. Her imprisonment for debt was revealed during Richard Smith's murder trial in 1816. *The Trials of Richard Smith . . . as principal, and Ann Carson, alias Ann Smith, as accessary, for the murder of Captain John Carson, on the 20th day of January, 1816, at a Court of oyer and terminer held at Philadelphia, May, 1816, by the judges of the Court of common pleas, Judge Rush . . . president; together with the arguments of counsel, the charges and sentence of the president. Taken in short hand by J. C., a member of the Philadelphia bar* (Philadelphia: Thomas Desilver, 1816).

27. Clarke, *Memoirs*, 2:33.

28. Ibid., 1:87. This notion harkens back to the eighteenth-century idea of "competency"—the goal being to secure financial security rather than merely acquire wealth. See Branson, "Women and the Family Economy in the Early Republic."

29. Ibid., 1:185, 2:34.

30. Ibid., 2:60.

31. Ibid., 1:180. Her dislike of these working-class men, of course, was intimately bound up with her trials. She not only found mechanics and tradesmen to be "ignorant, mean, and selfish," but also dangerous: "when invested with power, [they are] arbitrary, cruel, and vindictive." Ibid., 1:30.

32. *Weekly Magazine of Original Essays* (Philadelphia, May 1798).

33. Clarke, *Memoirs*, 1:215, 2:33.

34. Ibid., 2:11. The class origin of Carson's compatriots is not as unlikely as it might seem. They would have needed a certain level of education as well as skill to carry out counterfeiting and other illegal activities. Daniel A. Cohen has noted that members of flash gangs in Massachusetts also came from comfortable backgrounds. Daniel A. Cohen, "A Fellowship of Thieves: Property Criminals in Eighteenth-Century Massachusetts," *Journal of Social History* 22 (1988): 70.

35. Karen Halttunen writes, "In the cities of early industrial America, the personal appearance of a stranger did not offer reliable clues to his identity." This was due in part to the Industrial Revolution, which Halttunen says enabled "rising classes to imitate the dress and conduct of the older elites." Karen Halttunen, *Confidence Men and Painted Women: A Study of Middle-Class Culture in America* (New Haven, Conn.: Yale University Press, 1982), 37. See also Claudia B. Kidwell and Margaret C. Christman, *Suiting Everyone: The Democratization of Clothing in America* (Washington, D.C.: Smithsonian Institution, 1974). See also Richard L. Bushman, *The Refinement of America: Persons, Houses, Cities* (New York: Knopf, 1993) for a discussion of the sharp line the middle class drew to separate themselves from the lower classes. The diffusion of gentility confused the issue of class because more people could afford the outward semblance of it.

36. Hemphill, *Bowing to Necessity*, 130–31. This behavior accompanied dress and consumption (both material and cultural). Concern with social and class distinctions burgeoned in the 1820s. Hemphill notes the growth in the number of conduct books offered for sale in the United States. Nine of every ten of these new works were directed at (and written by) middle-class North Americans. Carson compared Madison rather unfavorably to herself: "I discovered that fame had, as usual, been very far from the truth, as Mrs. Madison is not so tall, much thicker, and inclining to *em bon point*." Clarke, *Memoirs*, 2:26.

37. Clarke, *Memoirs*, 2:65, 66.

38. Black women, according to Carson, made up "a large majority in our female republic." Ibid., 2:68.

39. Ibid., 1:177.

40. Ibid., 2:67. Carson also received a knife and fork.

41. Ibid., 2:68. She mentions this again a few pages later: "The cell was then filled with negroes, whose odour, added to the effluvia from the common sewer, formed a complication of stenches sufficient to create infectious and malignant distempers." Ibid., 2:71.

42. Ibid., 1:229.

43. Ibid., 1:194. To my personal chagrin, Carson also dismissed an entire section of South Jersey: "That part of Jersey [around Burlington] was strongly prejudiced against me, being generally ignorant, consequently inquisitive, weak, credulous people. . . ." Ibid., 1:184.

44. Ibid., 1:205.

45. It is unclear if she succeeded in either of these ambitions. Mary Clarke Carr recounted that "fifty copies were disposed of in a day for several days in succession" after it went on sale. She also claimed that "it was written for by the President, vice

President, Gov. of Pennsylvania, and a great number of members of Congress, of both houses." Ibid., 2:103. However, under the terms of their contract with the printer, De-silver, Carson and Carr had to wait until his portion of the books was sold before they could make any profit. Ibid., 2:104. Carson chose to trade her share of the books for counterfeit notes on Stephen Girard's bank. This adventure got her arrested again. While serving a seven-year sentence on the counterfeiting charge, Carson died in the Philadelphia penitentiary of typhoid fever in April 1824. She was thirty-eight years old.

46. *Democratic Press,* Saturday, January 25, 1823.

47. Think of the classic 1960s sitcom *The Beverly Hillbillies*—a comedy all about pretenders/aspirers to a class above themselves.

Chapter 12. Leases and the Laboring Classes in Revolutionary America

1. William Lowry's lease, April 14, 1767, roll 8, Livingston-Redmond Family Pa-pers, 1630–1900, thirteen rolls of microfilm, Franklin Delano Roosevelt Library, Hyde Park, New York (hereafter LP). See also the leases for Hendrick Stiever, April 19, 1748; John Peter Lowree, March 19, 1760; and Nicholas Luych, May 1, 1763, all in rolls 6, 7, and 8, LP. I have converted all currency to 1775 £NY. For £NY in 1775, roughly £165 NY equaled £100 sterling, or approximately £5 to £3. See John McCusker, *How Much Is That in Real Money? A Historical Price Index for Use as a Deflator of Money Values in the Economy of the United States* (Worcester, Mass.: American Antiquarian Society, 1992), appendix A, and table A-2; and Edward Countryman, *A People in Revolution: The American Revolution and Political Society in New York, 1760–1790* (New York: W.W. Norton and Company, 1988), 344, note 7. Assessment Rolls, 1779, microfilm, A-FM, N66, #71, New York State Library, Manuscripts and Special Collections (hereafter NYSL).

2. To avoid burdensome language, this chapter uses the terms "America," "Amer-ican," and "Americans" to describe the region or the people who lived in the United States (or the colonies that became that nation).

3. "Record Book of Leases for Bethlehem Rensselaerswyck, 1771–1800," Albany Institute of History and Art, Albany, N.Y.; lists of leases in boxes 36, 84, and 86, Van Rensselaer Manor Papers (hereafter VRMP), NYSL; Abraham Ten Broeck's Lease Ledger, box 84, VRMP, NYSL; Alan Taylor, *William Cooper's Town: Power and Persua-sion on the Frontier of the Early Republic* (New York: A. A. Knopf, 1995), 77–78, 98–99; and Reeve Huston, *Land and Freedom: Rural Society, Popular Protest, and Party Poli-tics in Antebellum New York* (Oxford: Oxford University Press, 2000), 14–15.

4. Daniel Vickers, "Working the Fields in a Developing Economy: Essex County, Massachusetts, 1630–1675," in *Work and Labor in Early America,* ed. Stephen Innes (Chapel Hill: Published for the Institute of Early American History and Culture by the University of North Carolina Press, 1988), 63–66; Steven Sarson, "Landlessness and Tenancy in Early National Prince George's County, Maryland," *William and Mary Quarterly,* 3rd ser., 56 (2000): 569–98 (hereafter *WMQ*); Gregory Stiverson, *Poverty in a Land of Plenty: Tenancy in Eighteenth-Century Maryland* (Baltimore: Johns Hopkins University Press, 1977); James T. Lemon, *The Best Poor Man's Country: A Geographi-*

cal Study of Early Southeastern Pennsylvania (Baltimore: Johns Hopkins University Press, 1972); and Lucy Simler, "Tenancy in Colonial Pennsylvania: The Case of Chester County," *WMQ*, 3rd ser., 43 (1986): 542–69.

5. Gordon S. Wood, *The Radicalism of the American Revolution* (New York: A. A. Knopf, 1993), 170. Edmund Morgan reasserts this point in his review of September 22, 2005 in the *New York Review of Books* of Gary Nash's *The Unknown American Revolution: The Unruly Birth of Democracy and the Struggle to Create America* (New York: Viking, 2005). Samuel P. Huntington, *Political Order in Changing Societies* (New Haven, Conn.: Yale University Press, 1968), 298–99; see also Ronald Schultz, "A Class Society? The Nature of Inequality in Early America," in *Inequality in Early America*, ed. Carla Gardina Pestana and Sharon V. Salinger (Hanover, N.H.: University Press of New England, 1999), 204–21. Karl Marx, *The Eighteenth Brumaire of Louis Bonaparte*, in *The Marx-Engels Reader*, ed. Robert Tucker (New York: International Publishers, 1978), 595. For the fuller development of what could be called the declension narrative of the American economy that depicts the colonial and Revolutionary society as precapitalist and more egalitarian, and the industrial society as unequal, see Carl Bridenbaugh, *Cities in the Wilderness: The First Century of Urban Life* (New York: Ronald Press Co., 1938); Carl Bridenbaugh, *The Colonial Craftsman* (Chicago: University of Chicago Press, 1961), 5–72; Jack P. Greene, *Pursuits of Happiness: The Social Development of Early Modern British Colonies and the Formation of American Culture* (Chapel Hill: University of North Carolina Press, 1988), 170–203; and Stephen Innes, *Creating the Commonwealth: The Economic Culture of Puritan New England* (New York: W. W. Norton, 1995), 64–107. In 1966, Gordon S. Wood famously argued that colonial and Revolutionary Virginia was largely devoid of class strife, but he did so only by ignoring slaves and tenants. He repeats the argument on a broader scale some thirty years later. Gordon S. Wood, "Rhetoric and Reality in the American Revolution," *WMQ*, 3rd ser., 23 (1966): 3–32.

6. John Locke, *Two Treatises of Government*, ed. Peter Laslett (1960; reprint, Cambridge: Cambridge University Press, 1994), 299, chapter 5, §45; and G. E. Aylmer, "The Meaning and Definition of 'Property' in Seventeenth-Century England," *Past and Present* 86 (1980): 87–97.

7. Karl Marx, Preface to *A Contribution to the Critique of Political Economy in Early Writings* in *Marx after Marxism: The Philosophy of Karl Marx*, ed. Tom Rockmore (Oxford: Blackwell Publishers, 2002), 114-23; E. P. Thompson, *The Making of the English Working Class* (London: Pantheon Books, 1963); E. P. Thompson, "Eighteenth-Century English Society: Class Struggle without Class," *Social History* 3 (1978): 133–65; Alfred F. Young, Afterword to *Beyond the American Revolution: Explorations in the History of American Radicalism*, ed. Alfred F. Young (DeKalb: Northern Illinois University Press, 1993), 317–64; John R. Hall, "The Reworking of Class Analysis," in *Reworking Class*, ed. John R. Hall (Ithaca, N.Y.: Cornell University Press, 1997), 1–40; Pierre Bourdieu, "What Makes a Social Class," *Berkeley Journal of Sociology* 22 (1998): 1–18; Erik Olin Wright, "Rethinking, Once Again, the Concept of Class Structure," in *Reworking Class*, ed. John R. Hall (Ithaca, N.Y.: Cornell University Press, 1997), 45, 60–62; Ronald Schultz, "A Class Society?," 203–21; Keith Wrightson, "Class," in *The British Atlantic World, 1500–1800*, ed. David Armitage and Michael J. Braddick (New York: Palgrave Macmillan, 2002), 133–53; and Stanley Aronowitz, *How Class Works:*

Power and Social Movement (New Haven, Conn.: Yale University Press, 2003), 1–11, 15, 39, 50.

8. Paul A. Gilje and Howard B. Rock, Introduction to *Keepers of the Revolution: New Yorkers at Work in the Early Republic*, ed. Paul A. Gilje and Howard B. Rock (Ithaca, N.Y.: Cornell University Press, 1992), 1–23, quotes on 4, 6, and 8; and Stephen Innes, *Creating the Commonwealth: The Economic Culture of Puritan New England* (New York: W. W. Norton and Company, 1995), 64–107.

9. Rowland Berthoff and John M. Murrin, "Feudalism, Communalism, and the Yeoman Freeholder: The American Revolution Considered as a Social Accident," in *Essays on the American Revolution*, ed. Stephen G. Kurtz and James H. Hutson (Chapel Hill: Published for the Institute of Early American History and Culture by the University of North Carolina Press, 1973), 261. See also Gary B. Nash, *The Urban Crucible: Social Change, Political Consciousness, and the Origins of the American Revolution* (Cambridge, Mass.: Harvard University Press, 1979); Billy G. Smith, "The Material Lives of Laboring Philadelphians, 1750–1800," *WMQ*, 3rd ser., 38 (1981): 163–202; Billy G. Smith, *The "Lower Sort": Philadelphia's Laboring People, 1750–1800* (Ithaca, N.Y.: Cornell University Press, 1990); the essays by Susan Klepp, Simon P. Newman, Gary B. Nash, and Ruth Herndon, among others, in *Down and Out in Early America*, ed. Billy G. Smith (University Park: Pennsylvania State University Press, 2003); and Simon P. Newman, *Embodied History: The Lives of the Poor in Early Philadelphia* (Philadelphia: University of Pennsylvania Press, 2003).

10. Brendan McConville, *Those Daring Disturbers of the Public Peace: The Struggle for Property and Power in New Jersey, 1701–1786* (Ithaca, N.Y.: Cornell University Press, 1999); Alan Taylor, "Agrarian Independence: Northern Land Rioters after the Revolution," in *Beyond the American Revolution: Explorations in the History of American Radicalism*, ed. Alfred. F. Young (DeKalb: Northern Illinois University Press, 1993), 237; Allan Kulikoff, *From British Peasants to Colonial American Farmers* (Chapel Hill: University of North Carolina Press, 2000); and Allan Kulikoff, *The Agrarian Origins of American Capitalism* (Charlottesville: University Press of Virginia, 1992). For the link between republicanism and yeoman farmers, see Robert E. Shalhope, "Toward a Republican Synthesis: The Emergence of an Understanding of Republicanism in American Historiography," *WMQ*, 3rd ser., 29 (1972): 49–80. Joyce Appleby warns against making the link, but then makes it, in "Commercial Farming and the 'Agrarian Myth' in the Republic," *Journal of American History* 68 (1982): 833–49.

11. Thomas Jefferson, *Notes on the State of Virginia*, ed. William Peden (Chapel Hill,: University of North Carolina Press, 1982), 164–65.

12. See, for example, Robert Weibe, *The Opening of American Society: From the Adoption of the Constitution to the Eve of Disunion* (New York: Knopf, 1984); Wood, *The Radicalism of the American Revolution*; and Joyce Appleby, *Inheriting the Revolution: The First Generation of Americans* (Cambridge, Mass.: Belknap Press of Harvard University Press, 2000).

13. Elizabeth Fox-Genovese and Eugene Genovese, *Fruits of Merchant Capital: Slavery and Bourgeois Property in the Rise and Expansion of Capitalism* (New York: Oxford University Press, 1983), chapter 1; Allan Kulikoff, "The Transition to Capitalism in Rural America," *WMQ*, 3rd ser., 44 (1989): 120–44; Kulikoff, *The Agrarian Origins of American Capitalism*; and Edward Countryman, "The Uses of Capital in

Revolutionary America: The Case of New York Loyalist Merchants," *WMQ*, 3rd ser., 49 (1992): 3–28.

14. This line of thinking dominates the literature on urban laborers in the nineteenth century. Much of it is built around the themes laid out in Thompson's magisterial *The Making of the English Working Class*. See Herbert Gutman, *Work, Culture, and Society in Industrializing America: Essays in American Working-Class and Social History* (New York: Knopf, 1976); Howard B. Rock, *Artisans of the New Republic: The Tradesmen of New York City and the Rise of the American Working Class, 1788–1850* (New York: New York University Press, 1979); Sean Wilentz, *Chants Democratic: New York City and the Rise of the American Working Class, 1788–1850* (New York: Oxford University Press, 1984); and Bruce Laurie, *Artisans into Workers: Labor in Nineteenth-Century America* (New York: Hill and Wang, 1989).

15. I illustrate these points for other Hudson Valley manors in *Land and Liberty: Hudson Valley Riots in the Age of Revolution* (DeKalb: Northern Illinois University Press, 2004). For Livingston Manor, see "The Livingston Manor Patent," June 22, 1686, in *The Documentary History of the State of New York*, ed. E. B. O'Callaghan, 4 vols. (Albany: Weed, Parsons and Company, Public Printers, 1856–83), 3:625; leases in rolls 6, 7, and 8, LP; leases in rolls 1 and 52 in the Robert R. Livingston Papers, fifty-seven rolls of microfilm, New York Historical Society, New York, New York (hereafter NYHS); the Livingston Manor Rent Ledger, 1767–84, NYHS; and the Assessment Rolls, 1779, microfilm roll A-FM, N66 #71, NYSL. For Van Rensselaer Manor, including the Claverack,, see "A List of Indentures 1699–1744," and "Leases Granted by Stephen Van Rensselaer Esquire and his ancestors for lands," September 1, 1790, both in the VRMP, NYSL; see also Kilian Van Rensselaer's will, June 18, 1718, Townsend Collection, box 1, NYSL. For a list of tenants, see "Abstract of Deeds given by Stephen Van Rensselaer Esq dec'd. with the Quit Rent due in upon each Lott Respectively," no date, VRMP, Family, Mrs. Benjamin Wadworth Arnold Collections, Albany Institute of History and Art, Albany, New York (hereafter AIHA); VRMP, boxes 36, 84, and 86, NYSL; "The List of Tenants," Van Rensselaer Family Papers, Vlie House, box 3, AIHA; and the "Record Book of Leases for Bethlehem Rensselaerswyck, 1771–1800," AIHA.

16. My general statements on leases issued in the Hudson Valley in the colonial eighteenth century comes from my reading of the extent leases for Philipsburgh, Cortlandt Manor, Beekman's Precinct, Livingston Manor (including Clermont), and Rensselaerswyck (including Claverack). See the leases in the Philipse Papers, PT 249, 8904 #26, Sleepy Hollow Restoration Library, Tarrytown, New York (hereafter SHRL); Van Cortlandt Papers, folders v. 2204, v. 2206, v. 2194, and v. 1697, SHRL; the leases in rolls 6, 7, and 8, LP; leases in rolls 1 and 52 in the Robert R. Livingston Papers, NYHS; "Leases Granted by Stephen Van Rensselaer, Esquire and his ancestors for lands," September 1, 1790, VRMP, NYSL; and the lists of leases in boxes 36, 84, and 86 of the VRMP, NYSL.

17. For Livingston Manor and Clermont, see Rent Rolls and Leases, rolls 6 and 7, LP; and the Rent Rolls in Robert R. Livingston Papers, roll 52. For Rensselaerswyck, including Claverack, see the leases in boxes 36, 84, and 86, VRMP, NYSL; and Abraham Ten Broeck, Lease Ledger, box 84, VRMP, NYSL.

18. For Livingston Manor, see the payments of Ephraim Reese and Frans Brusie in the Livingston Manor Rent Ledger, 1767–84, NYHS. The ledger contains the rent

information for 370 tenants, and I have calculated average rent payments from it and from existing leases and rent records for the manor found in rolls 6, 7, and 8, LP. For the Van Rensselaers, see, for examples, the rent payments for Jacob I. and Levinias Lansing, William Hogan, Wouter Becker, Mattys Bovie, Daniel Boss, Jacob Outhoudt, and Jacob Loock in the Rensselaerswyck Ledger A of Rents, 1768–89, Rensselaerswyck Manor Papers, NYSL.

19. Van Rensselaer's Book of Tithes, 1758–[70], Rensselaerswyck Papers, NYSL; and Ledger B of Rents for Rensselaerswyck, 1769–89, VRMP, box 75, NYSL.

20. See the Rent Rolls for Clermont for 1756 and 1759 in the Robert R. Livingston Papers, roll 52; and for his statement, see Robert R. Livingston to Robert Livingston, Jr., New York City, March 17, 1762, Robert R. Livingston Papers, roll 1.

21. I have calculated these figures from the Livingston Manor Rent Ledger, 1767–89, NYHS, which includes the yearly rent paid by between 266 and 330 tenants, out of 370 total, over the given period. The number of tenants fluctuated because tenants moved on and off the manor, and others did not pay rent every year. The figure, however, is lower than the number of tenants who appear on tax lists for the manor in 1779. I did not use information from damaged or partial entries.

22. Memorandum between Robert Livingston, Jr., and Jacobus Proper, May 1, 1763; "Articles of Agreement" signed by Robert Livingston, Jr., and Johan Barnhart Koens, October 7, 1763, roll 7, LP. See also the sales of William Krankhyte's improvements to Philip Fells for £100, of which Livingston kept £69 to cover Krankhyte's one-quarter sales fee and outstanding debt, roll 7, LP. For a discussion of tenants paying off their debt when they sold their improvements, see Philip Harmanse to Robert R. Livingston, February 25, 1775, Robert R. Livingston Papers, roll 18. For the sales of improvements elsewhere in the valley, see Solomon Horton's Loyalist Claim, PR AO 12, vol. 18, October 1786; see the records in Abraham Ten Broeck's Debit and Credit Accounts of the Manor, 1763–87, VRMP, box 41, NYSL; letters from John Duncan to Ten Broeck, Hermitage, September 22, 1769, Ten Broeck Family Papers, Box 1, AIHA; and the Rensselaerswyck Rent Ledger B, 1769–89, VRMP, box 75, NYSL. Philip Schuyler later followed the paths of his neighbors; see the letters to Schuyler from Hannah Brewer (1784) and from James Perry (1786), both in Local Land Papers, roll 13, Schuyler Papers, NYPL; and see the Schuyler Account Book, 1769–95, Schuyler Papers, roll 15.

23. See Ledger B of Rents for Rensselaerswyck, 1769–89, VRMP, box 75, NYSL; Abraham Ten Broeck recounted some of these figures in an unaddressed letter, February 16, 1764, Letters of Abraham Ten Broeck Papers, 1753–83, VRMP, box 53, NYSL. Ten Broeck administered the estate from the middle of the 1760s until the last patroon reached maturity in 1785. Robert Van Deusen's lease is in the Van Rensselaer Papers, September 10, 1718, and is discussed in Sung Bok Kim, *Landlord and Tenant in Colonial New York: Manorial Society, 1664–1775* (Chapel Hill: Published for the Institute of Early American History and Culture by the University of North Carolina Press, 1978), 168.

24. Robert Livingston, Jr., cited in Cynthia Kierner, *Traders and Gentlefolk: The Livingstons of New York, 1675–1790* (Ithaca, N.Y.: Cornell University Press, 1992), 87, and see 41–43 and 92–93; and the Livingston Manor Rent Ledger, 1767–89, NYHS.

25. "A General Accot. of Goods rec'd per the Manor Sloop," 1767; "Sales of 342 tons of Pig Iron," March 30, 1767, both in Robert R. Livingston Papers, roll 16. See also

Walter Livingston's Waste Book, 1765–67, Robert R. Livingston Papers, roll 16; and John Abeel to Robert Livingston, Jr., New York City, November 13, 1766, roll 8, LP.

26. Quotes from Solomon Schutt's lease, 1749, roll 6, LP. See also Ephraim Goes's lease, 1734, and William Lowry's lease, 1769, both in rolls 6 and 8, LP. For Rensselaerswyck, see Abraham Ten Broeck's Lease Ledger, box 84, VRMP, NYSL. For Schuyler's Saratoga lands, see his leases to William Steward, 1770, William Foster, 1785, and David Bennington, 1795, in Land Papers, Saratoga Patent, Schuyler Papers, reel 14, NYSL.

27. I base my figures for realty holdings in the Hudson Valley on assessments made according to "An Act for raising monies by tax to be applied towards the public exigencies of this State," passed by the New York State legislature in 1779. Assessors rated realty at one shilling per pound for all improved land, "including wood lands, kept for the purpose of fuel and timber and deemed parts and parcel of an improved farm." Realty also included, according to the act, houses, barns, mills, stores, and other buildings, but land made up the bulk of the assessment. Assessors rated personalty at six pence per pound of personal estate held within the state, but the legislature had resolved that the personalty of each citizen should be assessed only if it exceeded the "debts due from each respective person, or value thereof, at the time of the assessing." The assembly also provided that a "tax of one shilling per pound shall . . . be raised on the amount of all unimproved lands . . . not subject to a right of commonage of any kind whatsoever." In other words, landlords paid less for unimproved and uninhabited land. See "An Act for raising monies by tax," passed March 2, 1779, Chapter 16, Laws of New York, 2nd sess., quotes on 103 and 108; and the reaffirmation of the act on October 23, 1779, ibid. Assessors in 1779 based their assessments on the value of New York currency in 1775, equaling roughly £5 NY to £3 sterling. The list is the most complete list for New York in the second half of the eighteenth century and thus allows for regional comparisons. See the Assessment Rolls, 1779, microfilm, roll A-FM, N66 #71, NYSL.

28. Thomas S. Wermuth, *Rip Van Winkle's Neighbors: The Transformation of Rural Society in the Hudson River Valley, 1720–1850* (Albany: State University of New York Press, 2001), chapters 1 and 2; and Kim, *Landlord and Tenant*, 183–202.

29. Countryman, *A People in Revolution*, 243; and, Huston, *Land and Freedom*, chapter 1.

30. David M. Ellis, *Landlords and Farmers in the Hudson-Mohawk Region, 1790–1850* (Ithaca, N.Y.: Cornell University Press, 1946), 42–43; Alfred F. Young, *Democratic Republicans of New York: The Origins, 1763–1797* (Chapel Hill: Published for the Institute of Early American History and Culture by the University of North Carolina Press, 1967), 534–35; Taylor, *William Cooper's Town*, 57–114; and Huston, *Land and Freedom*, 14–18.

31. Rent Ledger for the manor, roll 8, LP; and the Livingston Manor Rent Ledger, 1767–84, NYHS; Ellis, *Landlords and Farmers*, 42–43; and Young, *Democratic Republicans*, 534–35.

32. Livingston Manor Rent Book, 1767–87, NYHS; Kim, *Landlord and Tenant*, 238; Huston, *Land and Freedom*, chapter 1. I base these figures on leases signed by tenants between 1779 and 1797, in the "Lists of Tenants on Rensselaerswyck on the east side of Hudson's River," box 86, VRMP, NYSL; List of Leases in boxes 36 and 84, and

Abraham Ten Broeck's Lease Ledger, box 84, all in VRMP, NYSL; John Devoe to Abraham Ten Broeck, Heldebergh Patent, August 13, 1785; and Ephraim Woodworth to Ten Broeck, Stillwater, August 24, 1785, Ten Broeck Family Papers, box 1, AIHA; and Huston, *Land and Freedom*, 25–27.

33. Huston, *Land and Freedom*, 27–28; and the leases for Rensselaerswyck at NYSL.

34. James C. Scott, *Domination and the Arts of Resistance: Hidden Transcripts* (New Haven, Conn.: Yale University Press, 1990).

35. Peter DeWitt's Ledger A, 1750–59, DeWitt Papers, box 47, NYSL; DeWitt's Account Journal, DeWitt Papers, 1764–89, box 47, NYSL; and Kierner, *Traders and Gentlefolk*, 96–97.

36. Rent Ledger A, VRMP, NYSL; Stephen Van Rensselaer to Abraham Ten Broeck, February 1, 1786, Abraham Ten Broeck Papers, NYSL; "Notice to Tenants," January 14, 1795, Watervliet, and "Proclamation to Tenants," no date, Watervliet, both in box 1; and the "Names of Tenants who have called at the Office & Settled their accounts, 1797," box 38, all in VRMP, NYSL.

37. "Abstract of the Rental of the Manor Rensselaerswyck, October 22nd 1797," box 60, VRMP, NYSL.

38. A manuscript of the broadside resides in the Philip Schuyler Papers, NYPL, dated December 14, 1790; "Address of General Philip Schuyler to the Tenants of Lands at Hillsdale, derived Through His Wife from her Father, John Van Rensselaer," November 12, 1790, cited in Ellis, *Landlords and Farmers*, 34, note 65; and Young, *Democratic Republicans*, 204.

39. Alexander Coventry's diary, October 25, 1791, NYSL; the minutes for *The People of the State of New York agt. Thomas Southward, Jonathon Arnold, John West, Abel Hacket, Ebenezer Hatch, Robert Boze, John Rodman, Joseph Fickner, and Jacob Virgil*, December 2, 1791, and *The People v. Peter Showerman*, 8 February 8, 1792, both in the Court of Oyer and Terminer Minutes, 1788–1831, Clerk of Common Courts in Hudson, New York (hereafter CCCH); Ellis, *Landlords and Farmers*, 34–36.

40. "A Letter," *Albany Gazette*, October 31, 1791, in Young, *Democratic Republicans*, 204–5; Franklin Ellis, *The History of Columbia County, New York* (Philadelphia: Everts and Ensign, 1878), 62, 236; *The People of the State of New York agt. Thomas Southward*, December 2, 1791, CCCH.

Chapter 13. Class and Capital Punishment in Early Urban North America

I thank Marcus Rediker, John Donoghue, Billy G. Smith, Simon Middleton, and the Atlantic History Research Seminar at the University of Pittsburgh for their helpful comments and suggestions.

1. The accounts of Dolly and Liverpoole appear, respectively, in the *South Carolina Gazette*, August 1, 1769 (extraordinary issue), and the *Georgia Gazette*, August 16, 1769; Ames is in Samuel Mather, *Christ Sent to Heal the Broken Hearted* (Boston, 1773), 36. For the execution of the wheelbarrow men, see *Freeman's Journal*, October 14, 1789.

2. A classic analysis of the use of violence as a means of social control is Leonard L. Richards, *"Gentlemen of Property and Standing": Anti-Abolition Mobs in Jacksonian America* (London: Oxford University Press, 1970). Steven Mintz likewise considers issues of social control in *Moralists and Modernizers: America's Pre-Civil War Reformers* (Baltimore: Johns Hopkins University Press, 1995), chapter 1.

3. I compiled three sets of data for each of the port cities of Boston, Philadelphia, and Charleston in the second half of the eighteenth century. The first set consists of executions in each city, including information about the alleged crime, the condemned's social, economic, and ethnic background, and the execution itself. The second set includes executions in Massachusetts, Pennsylvania, and South Carolina. Court records of capital crimes supplied most of the information in the third set of data. I supplemented these sources with newspaper reports, legislative accounts, and financial registers. Sources for Charleston provided the least reliable information, since records for neither slave courts nor the Court of General Sessions (with the exception of the years 1769–76) still exist.

4. *Pennsylvania Gazette*, May 14, 1800; and *The Execution of LaCroix, Berouse, and Baker for Piracy: The Last Words and Dying Confession of the Three Pirates, Who Were Executed This Day* (Philadelphia: Folwell's Press, 1800), 8.

5. On execution rituals, see Louis P. Masur, *Rites of Execution: Capital Punishment and the Transformation of American Culture, 1776–1865* (New York: Oxford University Press, 1989); Ronald A. Bosco, "Lectures at the Pillory: The Early American Execution Sermon," *American Quarterly* 30 (summer 1978): 156–76; Peter Linebaugh, *The London Hanged: Crime and Civil Society in the Eighteenth Century* (New York: Cambridge University Press, 1992); V. A. C. Gatrell, *The Hanging Tree: Execution and the English People, 1770–1868* (New York: Oxford University Press, 1994).

6. *Pennsylvania Gazette*, May 17, 1764.

7. Douglas Hay, "Property, Authority, and the Criminal Law," in *Albion's Fatal Tree: Crime and Society in Eighteenth-Century England*, ed. Douglas Hay et al. (New York: Pantheon Books, 1975), 26–27, 40–49.

8. The account of Webster and Smart appeared in the *Pennsylvania Gazette*, May 7, 1752, and July 9, 1772; Rogers's words were recorded in the *Charleston City Gazette*, June 17, 1788.

9. *South Carolina Gazette*, August 29, 1754.

10. *Pennsylvania Gazette*, January 30, 1753.

11. *City Gazette*, October 20, 1795.

12. *Pennsylvania Gazette*, October 20, 1784; and Henry K. Brooke, *Book of Murders, Containing an Authentic Account of the Most Awful Tragedies That Have Been Committed in This Country* (Philadelphia, 1858), 27.

13. For examples, see *A Brief Account of the Execution of Elisha Thomas* (Dover, 1788); *The Grafton-Minerva*, July 28, 1796; *The Herald*, August 19, 1797.

14. *A Solemn Farewell to Levi Ames: Being a Poem Written a Few Days before His Execution, for Burglary, Oct. 21, 1773* (Boston, 1773).

15. *Morning Post*, November 21, 1786.

16. *Columbian Herald*, June 28, 1787.

17. *Boston Weekly News-Letter*, May 20, 1756.

18. *Pennsylvania Gazette*, April 21, 1773.

19. *American Bloody Register*, appendix 1.

20. *Pennsylvania Packet*, October 29, 1778.

21. E. P. Thompson, "Eighteenth-Century English Society: Class Struggle without Class?," *Social History* 3 (May 1978): 133–65, quote 145.

22. *Pennsylvania Gazette*, September 12, 1765.

23. Anne Rowe Cunningham, ed., *Letters and Diary of John Rowe* (New York: New York Times and Arno Press, 1969), 88. See also William Pencak, "Play as Prelude to Revolution: Boston, 1765–1776," in *Riot and Revelry in Early America*, ed. William Pencak, Matthew Dennis, and Simon P. Newman (University Park: Pennsylvania State University Press, 2000), 132.

24. Cunningham, *Letters and Diary of John Rowe*, 261.

25. Quoted in Thomas J. Humphrey, "Crowd and Court: Rough Music and Popular Justice in Colonial New York," in *Riot and Revelry in Early America*, ed. William Pencak, Matthew Dennis, and Simon P. Newman (University Park: Pennsylvania State University Press, 2000), 113–14.

26. *Columbia Gazette*, March 28, 1794.

27. While Philadelphia and Charleston executed about two people annually in the second half of the eighteenth century, Boston put one person to death every two years. In per capita terms, Bostonians witnessed one execution for every 696 inhabitants, while Philadelphians and Charlestonians experienced one per 347 inhabitants and one for every 128 inhabitants, respectively. These numbers are based on the average population of the cities in the second half of the eighteenth century. The city's populations are from Allan Kulikoff, "The Progress of Inequality in Revolutionary Boston," *William and Mary Quarterly*, 3rd ser., 28 (July 1971): 393; Billy G. Smith, *The "Lower Sort:" Philadelphia's Laboring People, 1750–1800* (Ithaca, N.Y.: Cornell University Press, 1990), 206; and Walter Fraser, *Charleston! Charleston! The History of a Southern City* (Columbia: University of South Carolina Press, 1989), 178.

28. The moratorium resulted in part from jury nullification, as jurors refused to convict the accused of capital crimes. Instead, they either acquitted or found the accused guilty of a lesser crime. See Gabriele Gottlieb, "'Rattling the Chains:' Penal Reform, Capital Punishment, and Social Order in Late Eighteenth-Century Philadelphia" (unpublished paper).

29. Officials executed twelve people between 1784 and 1789 and five others in the 1790s. On class differences in the cities, see Gary B. Nash, *The Urban Crucible: Social Changes, Political Consciousness, and the Origins of the American Revolution* (Cambridge, Mass.: Harvard University Press), 1979.

30. For the sixteen cases with known ages, the mean was 25.5 years, with nine people younger than 25 (the youngest being 17). The race of slightly more than half of the executed are identified in the records. An unusual amount is known about the condemned of Boston because many of them were the subject of broadsides and pamphlets. While the information of those publications cannot always be trusted, in some cases it can be confirmed with court records. For a discussion of the credibility of crime narratives, see Peter Linebaugh, "The Ordinary of Newgate and His Account," in *Crime in England, 1500–1800*, ed. J. S. Cockburn (Princeton, N.J.: Princeton University Press, 1977), 246–69, especially 263–64.

31. *Life, Last Words, and Dying Confession of John Bailey: A Black Man, Who Was*

Executed at Boston This Day, Being Thursday, October 14, 1790, for Burglary (Boston, 1790).

32. *Dying Confession . . . Pirates, viz. Collins, Furtado, and Palacha, Who Were . . . at Boston, This Day, Being the Thirteenth of July, 1794, for the Murder of Mr. Enoch Wood* (Boston, 1794).

33. The Superior Court of the Judicature is the court in which capital cases were tried.

34. Nine executions occurred in 1778 and 1783, with slightly lower numbers in the intervening years. Nine people were hanged in the two years following the war, and ten more suffered that fate during 1788–89, the period when the U.S. Constitution was being created and debated. Only ten days after the Constitution was adopted, Abraham and Levi Doan, notorious highway robbers, Tories, and outlaws, were hanged without the benefits of a trial. On crime in Pennsylvania, see Jack D. Marietta and G. S. Rowe, *Troubled Experiment: Crime and Justice in Pennsylvania, 1682–1800* (Philadelphia: University of Pennsylvania Press, 2006).

35. Based on twelve known cases, the average age of the executed was 26.2. The race of the condemned is hard to verify. Court records generally do identify the defendant's race, although I was able to determine race in other sources, such as newspapers and letters.

36. *An Account of the Robberies Committed by John Morrison and His Accomplices, in and Near Philadelphia, 1750* (Philadelphia, 1750–51), 11.

37. For economic conditions and poverty in Philadelphia and early North America, see Smith, *The "Lower Sort,"* especially chapter 3; Gary B. Nash, "Poverty and Poor Relief in Pre-Revolutionary Philadelphia," *William and Mary Quarterly,* 3rd ser., 33 (January 1976): 3–30; and Billy G. Smith, ed., *Down and out in Early America* (University Park: Pennsylvania State University Press, 2003).

38. In 67 percent of "true bills" (404 cases)—those indictments that went to trial—the accused was charged with a property crime. In 75 percent of the cases, the trial ended in the conviction of the defendant: 68 percent were guilty verdicts according to the indictments, and another 6 percent were partial verdicts with convictions of a lesser crime. Seventy trials (23 percent) ended in a death sentence and thirty-eight defendants were executed, meaning that 54 percent of those capitally convicted were hanged. The execution rate was higher for personal crimes, although the overall conviction rate for such crimes was lower (65 percent) compared to that for property crimes (75 percent). There were fifty-five convictions for personal crimes in eighty-three cases. Sixteen of those (all of them indictments for murder) resulted in death sentences; twelve of those defendants were executed. Positive indictments and subsequent trials for political crimes (seventy-four cases) were almost as frequent as those for personal crimes (eighty-three cases) during the second half of the eighteenth century. While jurors found forty-five defendants guilty, only three death sentences were pronounced and two men were hanged, speaking to the unpopularity among Philadelphians for charges such as treason. "Reproductive crimes" appeared least frequently in the Superior Court. Five of the nine cases ended in conviction, including three sentences of death. Two people, "Mulatto" Elizabeth for infanticide and Francis Courtney for rape, suffered hanging. For the majority of years, transcripts of at least one of the court sessions are available, although a few years are missing completely.

39. At least ninety-seven people, the majority of them slaves, were put to death in Charleston between 1750 and 1800. Only seven executions can be documented with certainty during the Revolutionary War, although the records are incomplete.

40. On the paranoia about the actuality of slave revolts during the Revolution, see Sylvia R. Frey, *Water from the Rock: Black Resistance in a Revolutionary Age* (Princeton, N.J.: Princeton University Press, 1991).

41. Forty-five people were executed in Charleston during the Revolutionary War. There were fourteen executions in 1788; twelve people (including six members of a highway robbery gang and six pirates) were hanged within days of each other. Eighteen of the twenty-four slaves who were condemned between 1783 and 1800 died during the 1790s. The account of the three slaves executed in 1797 appears in the *Boston Gazette*, December 18, 1797. For the fear of slave revolts, see Herbert Aptheker, *Negro Slave Revolts in the United States, 1526–1860* (New York: International Publishers, 1939), 96.

42. Forty-nine of the condemned were slaves. Unfortunately, the limitations of Charleston's records mean it is difficult to establish a complete social profile of the executed.

43. J. Hector St. John de Crèvecoeur, *Letters from an American Farmer* (New York: E. P. Dutton, 1957), 167–68.

Chapter 14. Class Stratification and Children's Work in Post-Revolutionary Urban America

1. *Respublica v. Keppele*, 2 Dallas 197 and 1 Yeates 233 (Pennsylvania, 1793).

2. For the best discussion of the case and its implications, see Holly Brewer, *By Birth or Consent: Children, Law, and the Anglo-American Revolution in Authority* (Chapel Hill: University of North Carolina Press, 2005), 230–87.

3. For example, see Lawrence Cremin, *American Education: The National Experience, 1783–1876* (New York: Harper and Row, 1980); Brewer, *By Birth or Consent*, 124–28; Stanley Schultz, *The Culture Factory: Boston Public Schools, 1789–1860* (New York: Oxford University Press, 1973); and Carl Kaestle, *Pillars of the Republic: Common Schools and American Society, 1780–1860* (New York: Hill and Wang, 1983).

4. *Respublica v. Keppele*, 2 Dallas 197 (Pennsylvania, 1793).

5. Ibid.

6. *Respublica v. Catherine Keppele*, 1 Yeates 233 (Pennsylvania, 1793).

7. Max Weber, "Class, Status, and Party," in *From Max Weber: Essays in Sociology*, ed. H. H. Gerth and C. Wright Mills (New York: Oxford University Press, 1946), 180–82.

8. See Ian Quimby, *Apprenticeship in Colonial Philadelphia* (New York: Garland, 1985), 99–117; Christine Daniels, "Alternative Workers in a Slave Economy: Kent County, Maryland, 1675–1810" (Ph.D. diss., Johns Hopkins University, 1990); John E. Murray and Ruth Herndon, "Markets for Children in Early America: A Political Economy of Pauper Apprenticeship," *Journal of Economic History* 62 (June 2002): 356–82; and Karin Zipf, *Labor of Innocents: Forced Apprenticeship in North Carolina*

1715–1919 (Baton Rouge: Louisiana State University Press, 2005); also see the conference papers written for "Proper and Instructive Education: Children Bound to Labor in Early America" (McNeil Center for Early American Studies, Philadelphia, November 1–2, 2002).

9. Ruth Herndon, "A Better Bargain Than Poor Relief: Servant Apprenticeship in Southern New England, 1720–1820" (paper presented at the "Proper and Instructive Education" conference, McNeil Center for Early American Studies, Philadelphia, November 1–2, 2002), 30.

10. See Sharon Braslaw Sundue, "Industrious in Their Stations: Young People at Work in Boston, Philadelphia, and Charleston 1735–1785" (Ph.D. diss., Harvard University, 2001), 124–84.

11. I am beholden to Seth Rockman, who has redefined "class" as a system of economic production whereby economic power and powerlessness are reproduced. A key mechanism for the reproduction of class would be the system of pauper apprenticeship and education, which, this chapter argues, had a very different impact on the reproduction of class, given local labor needs and racial hierarchies. Seth Rockman, "The Contours of Class in the Early Republic City," *Labor: Studies in Working-Class History of the Americas* 1, no. 4 (winter 2004): 91–107.

12. From 1775 through 1783, 36 of the total 105 children bound as apprentices were sent to these western counties, 25 in Worcester County alone. "List of Apprentices Bound by the Boston Overseers of the Poor, 2 April 1758 to 20 January 1790," Boston Overseers of the Poor Records, Massachusetts Historical Society, Boston. By sending these children to the hinterland to relieve city dwellers of the burden of their care and meet farmers' demands for labor, the overseers set a precedent for nineteenth-century programs that placed poor, urban "orphans" with families in need of extra hands in western states, albeit without a legal contract stipulating respective responsibilities. Marilyn Irvin Holt, *The Orphan Trains: Placing Out in America* (Lincoln: University of Nebraska Press, 1992).

13. See, for example, Robert Gross, *The Minutemen and Their World* (New York: Hill and Wang, 1976), 142; and Ross Beales, "The Reverend Ebenezer Parkman's Farm Workers, Westborough, Massachusetts, 1728–82," *Proceedings of the American Antiquarian Society* 99 (1989): 139–40.

14. From 1775 through 1782, forty-one of the forty-six boys bound were placed in husbandry, representing an all-time high; by contrast, from 1770 through 1774 only twenty-seven of the seventy-eight boys bound were placed in husbandry apprenticeships. "List of Apprentices," Boston Overseers of the Poor Records.

15. Marcus Jernegan, *Laboring and Dependent Classes in Colonial America 1607–1783* (Chicago: University of Chicago Press, 1931), 105–7. See also Herndon, "A Better Bargain Than Poor Relief," 21–22.

16. James Draper, *History of Spencer, Massachusetts from Its Earliest Settlement to the Year 1860*, 2nd ed. (Worcester, Mass.: H. J. Howland, 1841), 78. Mary McDougall Gordon likewise confirms that many of Massachusetts's towns provided public education that was of questionable quality following the Revolution. Mary McDougall Gordon, "Union with the Virtuous Past: The Development of School Reform in Massachusetts, 1789–1837" (Ph.D. diss., University of Pittsburgh, 1974), 130–80.

17. Not only did the proportion of boys apprenticed to husbandry increase, but

the absolute number of boys did as well. From 1783 through 1789, twenty-six of the fifty boys were placed with farmers, versus twenty-five of the fifty-eight total from 1790 through 1794; twenty-five of the forty from 1795 through 1799, and thirty-nine of the forty-seven from 1800 through 1805. Lawrence Towner, "The Indentures of Boston's Poor Apprentices: 1735–1805," *Proceedings of the Colonial Society of Massachusetts* 43 (March 1962): appendix.

18. Barry Levy has also described the tendency for Boston's poor children to form part of an inter-town supplemental labor market. He described elites like Mandell as exceptional; over the entire period 1734–1806 most urban children serving apprenticeships in rural areas found themselves in young, harder-pressed households. After the war, however, that pattern shifted. Barry Levy, "Girls and Boys: Poor Children and the Labor Market in Colonial Massachusetts," *Pennsylvania History* 64 (1997): 298–303.

19. Lucius R. Paige, *History of Hardwick, Massachusetts* (Boston: Houghton Mifflin, 1883), 416.

20. In Westfield, of eight men who took thirteen apprentices after 1774, at least six were wealthy and prominent community members. See ibid. In Hardwick, four of the five men who took seven apprentices were from the town elite. Ibid., 124–28, 337.

21. Winifred Rothenberg, "The Market and Massachusetts Farmers, 1750–1855," *Journal of Economic History* 81 (1981): 283–314; Rothenberg, "The Emergence of a Capital Market in Rural Massachusetts, 1730–1838," *Journal of Economic History* 45 (1985): 781–808; Rothenberg, *From Market-Places to a Market Economy: The Transformation of Rural Massachusetts, 1750–1850* (Chicago: University of Chicago Press, 1992); Christopher Clark, *The Roots of Rural Capitalism: Western Massachusetts, 1780–1860* (Ithaca, N.Y.: Cornell University Press, 1990), 59–64, 71–83.

22. Clark, *The Roots of Rural Capitalism*, 71–74, 93–117; Daniel Vickers, *Farmers and Fishermen: Two Centuries of Work in Essex County, Massachusetts, 1630–1850* (Chapel Hill: University of North Carolina Press, 1994), 247–57, 309–23.

23. Laurel Ulrich, "Wheels, Looms, and the Gender Division of Labor in Eighteenth-Century New England," *William and Mary Quarterly*, 3rd ser., 55 (January 1998): 3–38; Joan Jensen, *Loosening the Bonds: Mid-Atlantic Farm Women, 1750–1850* (New Haven, Conn.: Yale University Press, 1986). For the relationship between this kind of production and early-nineteenth century proto-industrial outwork, see Thomas Dublin, *Transforming Women's Work: New England Lives in the Industrial Revolution* (Ithaca, N.Y.: Cornell University Press, 1994), 1–77.

24. Elizabeth McCulloch was bound to Israel Williams, Jr. on June 22, 1773; Elizabeth Bennet was bound to Levi Shepherd on October 4, 1793. Towner, "Boston's Poor Apprentices," 455, 462. For the Williams's family prominence and Levi Shepherd's mercantile activities, see Clark, *The Roots of Rural Capitalism*, 29, 41–2.

25. Gloria L. Main and Jackson T. Main, "The Red Queen in New England?" *William and Mary Quarterly*, 3rd ser., 56 (January 1999): 140–41.

26. Murray and Herndon, "Markets for Children in Early America," 365–69.

27. Dues could buy about ten acres of unimproved land during the 1760s; if this had been extremely productive land, it could have supported one adult. For an evaluation of land required for subsistence, see Bettye Hobbs Pruitt, "Self-Sufficiency and

the Agricultural Economy of Eighteenth-Century Massachusetts," *William and Mary Quarterly*, 3rd ser., 41 (July 1984): 341–42. Lawrence Towner comes to the same conclusion about the boys' inability to subsist as farmers. Towner, "Boston's Poor Apprentices," 432.

28. See Jack Larkin's analysis of poor farm wage laborer's perpetual landlessness in early nineteenth-century Worcester County in Jack Larkin, "'Labor Is the Great Thing in Farming': The Farm Laborers of the Ward Family of Shrewsbury, Massachusetts, 1787–1860," *Proceedings of the American Antiquarian Society* 99 (1989): 216–18.

29. Almshouse admissions remained consistent throughout the period. Register of Admissions to Almshouse, December 12, 1768–September 30, 1788; October 1, 1788–July 30, 1795, Boston Overseers of the Poor Records, box 9, Massachusetts Historical Society.

30. August 3, 1792, Minutes of the Trustees, 1792–1805, Massachusetts Society for Promoting Agriculture, box 33, Massachusetts Historical Society. The first premiums offered included rewards for the "largest quantity of beef raised upon the fewest acres," the "greatest stock upon the least quantity of land," and "the largest quantity and best quality of wool from the fewest number of sheep."

31. Clark, *The Roots of Rural Capitalism*, 176–77.

32. Dublin, *Transforming Women's Work*, 29–75.

33. Vickers, *Farmers and Fisherman*, 311–19.

34. Jeremiah Gray was bound to Mr. Joseph Fuller of Lynn on November 3, 1799. Towner, "Boston's Poor Apprentices," 465.

35. William Bagnall, *The Textile Industries of the United States* (Cambridge, Mass.: Riverside Press, 1893), 89–131.

36. Ebenezer Silvester was bound to Capt. Francis Carr on March 22, 1793. Towner, "Boston's Poor Apprentices," 463. Likewise, the overseers sent only two boys to Worcester after 1789: James Keth, who was bound to Benjamin Butman, a tailor, on May 2, 1793, and Peter Hunnewell, who was bound to Mr. Arden Webb on May 2, 1792 to learn the barber's trade.

37. Book of Indentures, 1695–1847, Salem City Clerk's Office, Salem, Massachusetts.

38. Although fifteen out of the seventy-three children bound in the 1790s were indentured to learn the craft of a cordwainer, only five were bound to serve in Lynn (all with members of the Newhall family, who pioneered methods of mass shoe manufacture during the period). None of the children bound to serve from Salem were apprenticed to learn weaving, or to Beverley manufacturers. Ibid.

39. Winifred Rothenberg, "The Emergence of Farm Labor Markets and the Transformation of the Rural Economy: Massachusetts, 1750–1855," *Journal of Economic History* 48 (September 1988): 537–66.

40. Larkin, "'Labor Is the Great Thing in Farming,'" tables 2 and 6A, pp. 206, 224. Larkin found that 20.6 percent of contract laborers between 1787 and 1829, and 21.5 percent of day laborers between 1787 and 1839, were born more than fifteen miles away from Shrewsbury; it seems likely that a large number were drawn from Boston, where the poor population experienced a high degree of turnover after the Revolution. On that point, see Allan Kulikoff, "The Progress of Inequality in Revolutionary Boston," *William and Mary Quarterly*, 3rd ser., 28 (July 1971): 402, which described

only 42 percent of the bottom rung of the tax list in 1780 as remaining in Boston ten years later.

41. Bagnall, *The Textile Industries of the United States*, 91.

42. Ibid., 114–15.

43. After 1783, 14 percent of the boys bound to occupations other than husbandry went to Maine. Of all poor apprentices, 21.7 percent of the children bound after the war were sent there.

44. Clark, *The Roots of Rural Capitalism*, 112.

45. Advertisements in the *Hampshire Gazette*, April 10, 1822, May 4, 1831, and October 12, 1831, cited in ibid., 111, note 122.

46. Joseph M. Wightman, *Annals of the Boston Primary School Committee* (Boston: Rand and Avery, 1860), 18–19; Stanley K. Schultz, *The Culture Factory: Boston Public Schools, 1780–1860* (New York: Oxford University Press, 1973), 22–25.

47. Schultz, *The Culture Factory*, 25–26.

48. According to a survey of school attendance conducted in 1817 by the Boston School Committee, 4,132 children attended private school, 2,365 children attended public school, and 526 children between four and fourteen attended no school at all. Wightman, *Annals of the Boston Primary School Committee*, 22–28. For an analysis of the likelihood that this seriously underestimates the true population of unschooled Bostonians, see Schultz, *The Culture Factory*, 32–34.

49. Wightman, *Annals of the Boston Primary School Committee*, 31.

50. City Ordinance of October 18, 1790, Minutes of the Commissioners of the Charleston Orphan House, South Carolina Archive, microfilm. From the original in the Charleston City Archive.

51. For an insightful analysis of these children's backgrounds, see John E. Murray, "Bound by Charity: The Abandoned Children in Eighteenth-Century Charleston," in *Down and Out in Early America*, ed. Billy G. Smith (University Park: Pennsylvania State University Press, 2004), 218. For a list of these children, see *The History and Records of the Charleston Orphan House 1790–1860*, abstracted and transcribed by Susan L. King (Easley, S.C.: Southern Historical Press, 1984).

52. Minutes of the Charleston Orphan House, March 10, 1791, Records of the Charleston Orphan House, Charleston City Archive; see also ibid., April 7, 1791 for another inquiry into the circumstances of several children whose parents were ultimately deemed incapable of supporting them.

53. From 1790 to 1799, the Orphan House commissioners admitted 269 boys and girls to the Orphan House, or an average of 27 admitted per year for an average term of five years. Interpolation of census data indicates that there were about 4,213 white boys and girls under sixteen in the city in 1790, and 3,758 in 1800, or an average of 3,985 white boys and girls under sixteen during the period. This suggests that about 3.3 percent of eligible white boys and girls were educated in the Orphan House at any one time. By contrast, Boston's Overseers of the Poor apprenticed 175 boys and girls from 1790 to 1799, or an average of 17.5 per year for an average term of 10.2 years. Interpolation of age groups for the 1790 and 1800 censuses yields an average of 18,296 boys between ten and twenty-one and girls between seven and eighteen in Boston; on average just over 2 percent of that city's eligible minors were receiving education as pauper apprentices at any one time.

54. Murray, "Bound by Charity," 217.

55. David Rothman, *The Discovery of the Asylum: Social Order and Disorder in the New Republic* (Boston: Little, Brown, 1971), 213–14.

56. "Rules and Regulations for the Government of the Orphan House, in the City of Charleston" July 27, 1791, Minutes of the Charleston Orphan House, 1:39–42.

57. Murray, "Bound by Charity," 223.

58. "Rules and Regulations," Minutes of the Charleston Orphan House, 1:40.

59. Ibid., 38.

60. All analysis of the disposition of Orphan House inmates was calculated from the abstracted list given by King, *The History and Records*.

61. Murray, "Bound by Charity," 221–22.

62. For patterns of slaveholding among masters in these trades and the concentration of skilled slaves in these industries, see Sundue, "Industrious in Their Stations," 98, fig. 2.8. In total, twenty-three boys were placed in low-status trades: three with bakers, one with a blacksmith, six with tailors, three with shoemakers, nine with mariners, and one was bound to work on a plantation.

63. Richard Walsh, *Charleston's Sons of Liberty* (Columbia: University of South Carolina Press, 1959), 126.

64. These trades included carpentry, coachmaking, goldsmithing, gunsmithing, and printing. Twenty-three boys were given these opportunities, including one who was placed with an attorney, one with a merchant, and another each with an insurance broker, a wharfinger, and a grocer.

65. St. Phillip's Parish Rough Vestry Minutes, book 1, June 23, 1752, June 20, 1757, November 8, 1759. South Carolina Department of Archives and History.

66. Peter Wood, *Black Majority: Negroes in Colonial South Carolina from 1670 through the Stono Rebellion* (New York: Knopf, 1974), 220–24; Philip Morgan, "Black Life in Eighteenth-Century Charleston," *Perspectives in American History* 1 (1984): 188–89.

67. Walter Fraser, "Poor Children of Pre-Revolutionary Charleston," *South Carolina Historical Magazine* 84 (1983): 171–72.

68. Wood, *Black Majority*, 294–97; see also Gabriele Gottleib's chapter in this book.

69. Walter Fraser describes fears that apprentices and youths were being entertained and debauched in the city's "disorderly houses." Fraser, "Poor Children of Pre-Revolutionary Charleston," 172, 175.

70. Carl Bridenbaugh, *Cities in the Wilderness: The First Century of Urban Life in America* (New York: Knopf, 1955), 359. See also Richard B. Morris, *Government and Labor in Early America* (New York: Columbia University Press, 1946), 184–85; and *Journal of the South Carolina Common House, 1742–43*, 345–46.

71. Nathaniel Greene, cited by Jerome Nadlehaft, *The Disorders of War: The Revolution in South Carolina* (Orono: University of Maine Press, 1981), 98.

72. Ibid., 99–103.

73. "Rules and Regulations," July 27, 1791, Minutes of the Charleston Orphan House, 1:39.

74. King, *The History and Records*, 19.

75. From 1790 through 1800, ten girls were placed as domestic servants, nine as seamstresses, eight with mantua makers, and two with milliners. Ibid., 18-35.

76. From 1800 through 1809, twenty girls were placed as domestic servants and two were bound as seamstresses. Ibid., 18–53.

77. See Sundue, "Industrious in Their Stations," 98, fig. 2.8.

78. *South Carolina Gazette*, June 5, 1755, 4.

79. On the role of marriage in determining women's social status in the eighteenth-century south, see Kathleen M. Brown, *Good Wives, Nasty Wenches, and Anxious Patriarchs* (Chapel Hill: University of North Carolina Press, 1996), 101–2, 295–98.

80. From 1760 to 1769, out of 128 boys placed in Philadelphia, 59 were assigned to learn crafts that offered the opportunity for middling social and economic status. By contrast, 33 boys were placed in low-status apprenticeships, and more than three-quarters of that group were placed after 1765. "Memorandum of Indentures of the Poor," 1751–99, and Indenture Papers and Bonds, 1795–99, Philadelphia Guardians of the Poor Collection, Philadelphia City Archive.

81. Sharon Salinger, "Artisans, Journeymen, and the Transformation of Labor in Eighteenth-Century Philadelphia," *William and Mary Quarterly*, 3rd ser., 40 (1983): 65, table 1.

82. John Commons, "American Shoemakers, 1648–1895: A Sketch of Industrial Evolution," *Quarterly Journal of Economics* 24 (November 1909): 45–49.

83. Billy G. Smith, *The Lower Sort: Philadelphia's Laboring People, 1750–1800* (Ithaca, N.Y.: Cornell University Press, 1990), 123.

84. Charles Steffen likewise demonstrated the increasing reliance of Baltimore's shoemakers on the labor of youthful apprentices in his "Changes in the Organization of Artisan Production in Baltimore, 1790 to 1820," *William and Mary Quarterly*, 3rd ser., 36 (January 1979): 101–17, arguing that journeymen protests were in part a response to this changing composition of the workforce.

85. Sixty-one boys were also bound to these trades between 1800 and 1806. Apprenticeship Indentures 1800–1806, Office of the Mayor's Collection, Philadelphia City Archive.

86. Indentures of John Wee, June 17, 1794; Peter, June 9, 1796; and Valentine, July 7, 1796, Pennsylvania Abolition Society Indenture Books, reel 22, Papers of the Pennsylvania Abolition Society, Historical Society of Pennsylvania. See also Gary B. Nash and Jean R. Soderlund, *Freedom by Degrees: Emancipation in Pennsylvania and Its Aftermath* (New York: Oxford University Press, 1991), 99–166, 173–82.

87. Between 1790 and 1799, the Pennsylvania Abolition Society (PAS) recorded indentures for an average of more than 110 African American minors per year; in 1795, the number bound by the PAS peaked at an astonishing 374. Indenture Books I and II, microfilm reels 22 and 23, Papers of the Pennsylvania Abolition Society, Pennsylvania Historical Society. For the number of redemptioners under fifteen bound between 1787 and 1804, see Farley Grubb, "Immigrant Servant Labor: Their Occupational and Geographic Distribution in the Late Eighteenth-Century Mid-Atlantic Economy," *Social Science History* 9 (1985): 268–69, table 10.

88. Out of 163 black children eighteen and under indented by the PAS in 1796, the masters of 104 were traceable. Of this group, nearly 90 percent remained within Philadelphia, and more than 60 percent were bound to individuals identified as merchants, professionals, or gentlemen. Of the 60 children bound in 1801, at least 32 remained in Philadelphia, of whom just fewer than 60 percent were bound to

merchants, professionals, and gentlemen. Data from 1796, 1797, 1798, 1800, and 1802 Philadelphia Directories.

89. Apprenticeship Indentures, 1800–1806.

90. Salinger, "Artisans," 66–68, esp. table 2. A similar pattern was observed by Farley Grubb through analysis of the occupations of servant purchasers listed in the 1787–1804 register; Grubb, "Immigrant Servant Labor," 271.

91. From 1795 to 1799, 150 boys were placed in Philadelphia; 28 were placed in trades requiring advanced instruction, versus only 10 during the 1760s. Information on educational requirements comes from R. Campbell, *The London Tradesman* (London: T. Gardner, 1747).

92. "List of Students, 1801–1830," Ludwick Institute Records, Historical Society of Pennsylvania.

93. Of the initial fifty-one, information about parents was given for forty-two. Seventeen had widowed mothers, another four had mothers working in as seamstresses, and one had a mother who was a housekeeper. Four had fathers who were laborers, four had fathers who were woodsawyers, two had fathers who were shoemakers, two had fathers who were tailors, and one had a father who was a mariner. In total about 78 percent were likely to have been drawn from among the city's poorest occupational groups.

94. John Alexander, *Render Them Submissive: Responses to Poverty in Philadelphia, 1760–1800* (Amherst: University of Massachusetts Press, 1981), 145.

95. *Pennsylvania Gazette*, March 30, 1791.

96. Alexander, *Render Them Submissive*, 146.

97. Efforts to establish free schools for African Americans and the difficulties endured are explained in ibid., 146–48.

98. Cremin, *American Education*, 66–67.

99. See "The Society for the Institution and Support of First Day or Sunday Schools, Constitution, 1790," Library Company of Philadelphia, photostat (original in the American Antiquarian Society). *Pennsylvania Gazette*, March 30, 1791.

Chapter 15. Afterword

1. For the death of class, see the introduction to this volume. For conjectures on the death of God, see Friedrich Nietzsche, *The Gay Science*, trans. Walter Kaufman (New York: Vintage, 1974), 125.

2. This does not mean that one cannot theorize class structurally, or (as many historians of class now unfortunately claim) that such theorizations are of no use. For classic statements, see Louis Althusser and Étienne Balibar, *Reading Capital*, trans. Ben Brewster (London: Verso 1979); Nicos Poulantzas, *Political Power and Social Classes* (London: New Left Books, 1973); and Poulantzas, *Classes in Contemporary Capitalism* (London: New Left Books, 1975).

3. E. P. Thompson, *The Making of the English Working Class* (New York: Vintage, 1966), 12.

4. http://www.discoversouthcarolina.com/stateparks/parkdetail.asp?PID=1575

(accessed October 2004). See also Rebecca Ann Bach, *Colonial Transformations: The Cultural Production of the New Atlantic World, 1580–1640* (New York: Palgrave, 2000), 221–32.

5. For a critique of stratification theory, see R. W. Connell and T. H. Irving, *Class Structure in Australian History: Documents, Narrative, and Argument* (Melbourne: Longman Cheshire, 1980), 4–5. On the pervasiveness of sociology (reduction to the social) in framing contemporary inquiry into human subjects, see Marianne Constable, *Just Silences: The Limits and Possibilities of Modern Law* (Princeton, N.J.: Princeton University Press, 2005), 54–55, 175–76.

6. See, for example, the chapters by Ty Reese, Simon Middleton, Konstantin Dierks, Jennifer Goloboy, Susan Branson, and Sharon Braslaw Sundue.

7. Nicos Poulantzas, *State, Power, Socialism*, trans. Patrick Camiller (London: Verso, 1980), 25-27.

8. I propose this approach in my "Subordination, Authority, Law: Subjects in Labor History," *International Labor and Working Class History* 47 (spring 1995): 56–90. For a summary, see below, note 34.

9. See the introduction to this book. But always remember Marilyn Strathern's observation that "what is imagined as fragmentation may be no more derived from a world of fragments than what is imagined as integration comes from a world already a totality." Marilyn Strathern, *Partial Connections* (Savage, Md.: Rowman and Littlefield, 1991), 22.

10. See generally Kunal Parker, "Context in History and Law: A Study of the Late Nineteenth-Century American Jurisprudence of Custom," *Law and History Review* 24, no. 3 (fall 2006); and Constantin Fasolt, *The Limits of History* (Chicago: University of Chicago Press, 2004), xiii–xxi, 1–45.

11. Parker, "Context in History and Law." For various strategies of limitation, see Peter Novick, *That Noble Dream: The Objectivity Question and the American Historical Profession* (Cambridge: Cambridge University Press, 1988).

12. Strathern points out that the production of complexity encourages its own extension because its very pursuit multiplies our awareness of unexplained "remainders" or gaps. Strathern, *Partial Connections*, 119.

13. For a classic statement of the materialist conception of history, see Friedrich Engels, "Socialism, Utopian and Scientific," in *Selected Works*, by Karl Marx and Frederick Engels (London: Lawrence and Wishart, 1970), 375–428. See ibid., 382–83, in which the term designated "that view of the course of history, which seeks the ultimate causes and the great moving power of all important historic events in the economic development of society, in the changes in the modes of production and exchange, in the consequent division of society into distinct classes, and in the struggles of these classes against one another." Engels left no doubt that the materialist conception was a revolution in the conceptualization of history. See Frederick Engels, "Karl Marx," in *Selected Works*, 370–71.

14. On this matter, see the section entitled "The Tradition of the Oppressed: Memory and Time" later in this chapter.

15. These are not empty questions. In "The Revenge of Crispus Attucks; or, The Atlantic Challenge to American Labor History," *Labor: Studies in Working-Class History of the Americas* 1, no. 4 (2004): 35–45, Marcus Rediker extols the historicization of class

begun by E. P. Thompson for "subject[ing] the concept to empirical controls and remov[ing] it from the abstract, philosophical Continental system of thought in which it had long been trapped and ossified" (40). It is frankly unclear what "empirical *controls*" means. Positivism? Perhaps the phrase is better understood as empirical *investigation*. But the larger point is that Rediker apparently takes for granted a historicist philosophy of history, so that the way to render class conceptually intelligible is by locating it in the "right" historical-temporal position vis-à-vis other located subjects. Thus, much of his essay debates conventionally historicist problematics—how to expand/limit the universe of placeable subjects, how to organize historical time and space (what chronology, what periodization), and so forth. In a debate among professional historians all this may well be quite appropriate, so I shall not criticize Rediker's essay beyond its failure to address critically the rules of the historical practice it endorses. But that failure is problematic. If we make class just another subject for historicist categorization we should not be surprised that professional fashion determines its fate, and we leave ourselves no answer to decrees that it is "dead" other than the assertion that it is "not."

16. Friedrich Nietzsche, "On the Uses and Disadvantages of History for Life" (Leipzig, 1874), in *Untimely Meditations*, trans. R. J. Hollingdale (New York: Cambridge University Press, 1983), 59.

17. Frederick Engels, "Speech at the Graveside of Karl Marx," in *Selected Works*, 429–30. Here then I am noting, but rejecting (politely), the terms of debate defined in the conceptual interventions undertaken by Konstantin Dierks (in this book) and his protagonist Seth Rockman (see, for example, Rockman, "The Contours of Class in the Early Republic City," *Labor: Studies in Working-Class History of the Americas* 1, no. 4 [2004]: 91–107, mostly at 92–93).

18. On which (in addition to what follows), see Staughton Lynd, "Revisiting Class in Early America: Personal Reflections," *Labor: Studies in Working-Class History of the Americas* 1, no. 4 (2004): 27–34, at 34.

19. Alex Callinicos, *Making History: Agency, Structure, and Change in Social Theory* (Leiden and Boston: Brill, 2004), 207. Walter Benjamin, "Theses on the Philosophy of History," in *Walter Benjamin, Illuminations: Essays and Reflections*, ed. Hannah Arendt (New York: Schocken, 1968), 253–64. Benjamin was a German Jewish Marxist literary, cultural, and linguistic theorist, whose work flowered in the 1920s and 1930s. He died in September 1940 in Portbou on the Franco-Spanish border, attempting to escape Nazism. The "Theses" comprise eighteen densely interwoven propositions (hereafter referenced as "Thesis" or "Theses" followed by the appropriate arabic numeral) written in the last months of Benjamin's life. They are the crescendo, but not in any sense a summary, of his life's work. "Midnight in the century" is the English translation of *S'il est Minuit dans le Siècle*, the title of a novel published in 1939 in Paris by the Russian anarchist and revolutionary Victor Serge [Victor Lvovich Kibalchich]. The title stands for the final extinguishment of Serge's hopes as a revolutionary, confronted by Stalinism and Fascism.

20. Callinicos, *Making History*, 208–9.

21. Benjamin, Thesis no. 5, 255; Thesis no. 15, 261, and see also Walter Benjamin, "The Destructive Character," in *Walter Benjamin, Reflections: Essays, Aphorisms, Autobiographical Writing*, ed. Peter Demetz (New York: Schocken, 1978), 301–3; Thesis no. 17, 263.

22. Benjamin, Thesis no. 6.

23. Benjamin, Thesis no. 12, 260. Note that it is the "oppressed class itself" not "man or men" that is the beneficiary of materialist historical knowledge. Compare Louis Althusser's critique of humanism, notably in *For Marx* (London: Allen Lane, 1969), 221–47. See also 9–13.

24. Benjamin, Theses no. 11–12, 258–61. Benjamin's critique here is aimed principally at the reformist social democracy of the Second International, on which see also Georges Sorel, *Reflections on Violence*, trans. T. E. Hulme and J. Roth (Glencoe, Ill.: The Free Press, 1950); Benjamin shared certain important perspectives with Sorel. Many Marxists will part company with Benjamin here, refusing to surrender capitalism's "progressive aspects" hence its propulsive "force for change." Even among the most sophisticated, a residual attraction to an organizing linearity remains, which renders Benjamin's disjunctive assault on history's continuum incomprehensible. See, for example, Callinicos, *Making History*, 256–57.

25. Benjamin, Thesis no. 16, 262, and see, generally, Theses no. 13–18A, including, 260–64.

26. Benjamin, Theses no. 9, 257; no. 11, 258; and no. 7, 256.

27. Benjamin, Theses no. 14, 261; and no. 5, 255. Benjamin's awareness of the fragility of the moment of conjunction that is "historical knowledge" is overwhelming. The historicists' contention that "the truth will not run away from us" earns the ontological retort that "every image of the past that is not recognized by the present as one of its own concerns threatens to disappear irretrievably." Benjamin, Thesis no. 5, 255.

28. Benjamin, Thesis no. 17, 263. See also no. 18, 263.

29. Benjamin, Theses no. 18A and 18B, 263–64.

30. William M. Reddy, *Money and Liberty in Modern Europe: A Critique of Historical Understanding* (Cambridge: Cambridge University Press, 1987), 26, 28–89. For a distinct, though not incompatible, account of the same historiographical moment, see the chapter by Lawrence A. Peskin in this book.

31. See the introduction to this book.

32. Indeed, when confronted by the insurgence of the past he had recovered against his own present, Thompson felt obliged to disown it. See E. P. Thompson, *Whigs and Hunters: The Origin of the Black Act* (Harmondsworth: Penguin Books, 1977), 258–69; and Tomlins, "Subordination, Authority, Law," 81, note. Thompson's historicism, his rejection of disjunctive conceptions of time, is on display in E. P. Thompson, *The Poverty of Theory and Other Essays* (New York: Monthly Review Press, 1978), for example, 88–93. Compare Althusser and Balibar, *Reading Capital*, 99–100. I discuss these matters further in Christopher Tomlins, "How Autonomous Is Law?" *Annual Review of Law and Social Science* 3 (2007): 5.1–5.24.

33. John Seed, "From 'Middling Sort' to Middle Class in Late Eighteenth- and Early Nineteenth-Century England," in *Social Orders and Social Classes in Europe since 1500: Studies in Social Stratification*, ed. M. L. Bush (London: Longman, 1992), 125, as quoted by Susan Branson in her chapter in this book.

34. My own inclination as alluded to earlier (see note 8) has been to think of class quite differently, in terms suggested by Marxist-feminist theories of standpoint; that is to theorize class as an intransitive relational structure that sets conditions for the existence of knowledge—including knowledge of class itself. By this I mean that

relations of class, like those of gender and race, exist independently of our observation of them and set conditions of what (and how) we can know. (One might posit, for example, that class, like gender and race, sets conditions for the existence of knowledge in a manner analogous to certain astrophysical phenomena that "bend" light by the gravitational pull of their presence. First, one cannot observe the totality of the phenomenon, but its presence is theorizable by observation of the effect. Second, what one can observe must be recognized as a produced effect. From the observation one constitutes knowledge, but the effects observed cannot comprise the totality of the phenomenon. Class, that is, is not constituted by its signifiers, any more than is gender or race.)

35. Significantly, this book represents the third purposive engagement with contemporary historiography inspired by the conference at which the chapters in this book were first presented. I have already made occasional reference to the others: a group of articles that appeared in *Labor: Studies in Working-Class History of the Americas* 1, no. 4 (2004); and a second group that appeared in the *William and Mary Quarterly*, 3rd ser., 63, no. 2 (April 2006).

36. Benjamin, Thesis no. 14, 261.

37. Joseph Conrad, *Heart of Darkness* (1902), available at http://etext.virginia.edu/toc/modeng/public/ConDark.html (from the Signet Classics reprint: New American Library) (last visited June 2007).

38. Ibid., 65–66.

39. Ibid., 69.

40. "Each station should be like a beacon on the road towards better things, a centre for trade of course, but also for humanizing, improving, instructing." Ibid., 101.

41. Ibid., 79, 80, 82, 83, 84–85, 92, 122, 123, 138.

42. Ibid., 158.

43. Perry Miller, *Errand into the Wilderness* (Cambridge, Mass.: Harvard University Press, 1956), vii–x.

44. Amy Kaplan, " 'Left Alone with America': The Absence of Empire in the Study of American Culture," in *Cultures of United States Imperialism*, ed. Amy Kaplan and Donald E. Pease (Durham, N.C.: Duke University Press, 1993), 6 and generally 3–11.

45. Miller, *Errand*, vii.

46. For this we can thank, in particular, the chapters by Daniel Richter, Daniel Mandell, Natalie Zacek, and Ty Reese in this book.

47. See Simon Newman's chapter in this book.

48. See, for example, the chapters by Jennifer Goloboy and Andrew Schocket in this book.

49. See the chapters by Simon Middleton and Thomas Humphrey in this book.

50. See, for example, the chapters by Sharon Braslaw Sundue and Gabriele Gottlieb in this book.

51. See Christopher Tomlins, "Law, Population, Labor," in *The Cambridge History of Law in America*, ed. Michael Grossberg and Christopher Tomlins, 3 vols. (Cambridge: Cambridge University Press, 2008).

52. Richard Hakluyt (Lawyer), "Pamphlet for the Virginia Enterprise" (1585), in *The Original Writings and Correspondence of the Two Richard Hakluyts*, ed. E. G. R. Taylor (London: The Hakluyt Society, 1935), 327–38.

53. See, notably, Simon Newman's chapter on Glasgow in this book.

54. See Engin Isin, *Being Political: Genealogies of Citizenship* (Minneapolis: University of Minnesota Press, 2002), 153–89.

55. I develop this argument in Christopher Tomlins, "Framing the Fragments; Police: Genealogies, Discourses, Locales, Principles," in *The New Police Science: The Police Power in Domestic and International Governance*, ed. Markus Dubber and Mariana Valverde (Stanford, Calif.: Stanford University Press, 2006), 248–94.

56. Hakluyt, "Pamphlet for the Virginia Enterprise," 330.

57. See Christopher L. Tomlins, *Law, Labor, and Ideology in the Early American Republic* (Cambridge: Cambridge University Press, 1993), 107–27; Robert A. Leeson, *Traveling Brothers: The Six Centuries' Road from Craft Fellowship to Trade Unionism* (London: Allen and Unwin, 1979); and David Rollison, "The Specter of the Commonality: Class Struggle and the Commonwealth in England before the Atlantic World," *William and Mary Quarterly*, 3rd ser., 63, no. 2 (April 2006): 221–52.

58. See Simon Middleton's chapter in this book.

59. Ibid.

60. Lindsay Farmer, "The Jurisprudence of Security: The Police Power and the Criminal Law," in *The New Police Science: The Police Power in Domestic and International Governance*, ed. Markus Dubber and Mariana Valverde (Stanford, Calif.: Stanford University Press, 2006), 145–67. The definitive edition of Smith's famous lecture series is *Lectures on Jurisprudence*, ed. R. L. Meek, D. D. Raphael, and P. G. Stein (Oxford: Clarendon Press, 1978).

61. Paul J. McNulty, *The Origins and Development of Labor Economics: A Chapter in the History of Social Thought* (Cambridge, Mass.: MIT Press, 1980), 38.

62. William Manning, *The Key of Liberty: The Life and Democratic Writings of William Manning, "A Laborer," 1747–1814*, ed. Michael Merrill and Sean Wilentz (Cambridge, Mass.: Harvard University Press, 1993), 130; and Tomlins, *Law, Labor, and Ideology*, 1–8.

63. See Newman's chapter in this book. Lawrence Peskin embraces something of the same approach in his chapter in this book.

64. Rediker, "The Revenge of Crispus Attucks," 41.

65. Historians commonly chide their subjects for their temporal obstinacies ("before her time"; or "time had passed her by"), or alternatively indulge the most obstinate by designating them forerunners ("as early as") or remnants ("as late as") of when they *should* be. It is necessary, of course, for historians to grant time itself such breathtaking (virtually anthropomorphic) agency if they are to produce their stock-in-trade of difference and change over time.

66. Fasolt, *The Limits of History*, 6. For recent illustration, see Gordon S. Wood, *New York Review of Books* 53, no. 8 (May 2006): 48, in reply to Calvin H. Johnson.

67. Rediker captures something of the urgency of thinking differently in his conclusion to "The Revenge of Crispus Attucks," 44–45.

68. Jacques Derrida, *Specters of Marx: The State of the Debt, the Work of Mourning, and the New International*, trans. Peggy Kamuf (New York: Routledge, 1994), xx (speaking of "A spectral moment, a moment that no longer belongs to time . . . that is not docile to time, at least to what we call time").

69. Constable, *Just Silences*, 12 (speaking of the opportunity not to predict what will be but to recall what "already will have been").

70. Conrad, *Heart of Darkness*, 68. See also Benjamin, Thesis no. 6, 255 (speaking of "that image of the past which unexpectedly appears to man singled out by history at a moment of danger").

71. Mitchell Dean, "Military Intervention as 'Police' Action" (describing the theories of Carl Schmitt), in *The New Police Science: The Police Power in Domestic and International Governance*, ed. Markus Dubber and Mariana Valverde (Stanford, Calif.: Stanford University Press, 2006), 197.

72. Alberico Gentili, *De Iure Belli Libri Tres*, ed. C. Phillipson, trans. J. C. Rolfe (Oxford: Oxford University Press, 1933), 67, 123–24.

73. For example, "Kings and those who are invested with a Power equal to that of Kings, have a Right to exact Punishments, not only for Injuries committed against themselves, or their Subjects, but likewise, for those which do not peculiarly concern them, but which are, in any Persons whatsoever, grievous violations of the Law of Nature or Nations." Hugo Grotius, *The Rights of War and Peace*, 3 vols. (London: Printed for W. Innys, 1738), vol. 2, chap. 20, para. 40. See generally Richard Tuck, *The Rights of War and Peace: Political Thought and the International Order from Grotius to Kant* (Oxford: Oxford University Press, 1999), 16–139. In addition, see Christopher Tomlins, "Law's Wilderness: The Discourse of English Colonizing, the Violence of Intrusion, and the Failures of American History," in *New World Orders: Violence, Sanction, and Authority in the Colonial Americas*, ed. John Smolenski and Thomas J. Humphrey (Philadelphia: University of Pennsylvania Press, 2005), 21–46.

74. On "exception," see Giorgio Agamben, *Homo Sacer: Sovereign Power and Bare Life*, trans. Daniel Heller-Roazen (Stanford, Calif.: Stanford University Press, 1998), 18: "The particular 'force' of law consists in th[e] capacity of law to maintain itself in relation to an exteriority. We shall give the name relation of exception to the extreme form of relation by which something is included solely through its exclusion."

75. Michael Brogden, "An Act to Colonise the Internal Lands of the Island: Empire and the Origins of the Professional Police," *International Journal of the Sociology of Law* 15, no. 2 (May 1987): 179–208; Daniel Defoe, *The Great Law of Subordination Consider'd; or, The Insolence and Unsufferable Behaviour of Servants in England Duly Enquir'd Into* (London: S. Harding et al., 1724); and Daniel Defoe, *A Tour Through the Whole Island of Great Britain* (London: Penguin Books, 1971), at, for example, 460–68.

76. For recent (and distinct) explorations of which, see Douglas Hay and Paul Craven, eds., *Masters, Servants, and Magistrates in Britain and the Empire, 1562–1995* (Chapel Hill: University of North Carolina Press, 1994); and Peter Linebaugh and Marcus Rediker, *The Many-Headed Hydra: Sailors, Slaves, Commoners, and the Hidden History of the Revolutionary Atlantic* (Boston: Beacon Press, 2000).

77. Daniel Defoe, *A Plan of the English Commerce* (London: Printed for Charles Rivington, 1728), 367.

78. Patrick Colquhoun, *A Treatise on the Police of the Metropolis* (London: H. Fry, for C. Dilly, 1796); Patrick Colquhoun, *A Treatise on the Commerce and Police of the River Thames* (London: J. Mawman, 1800); Patrick Colquhoun, *A Treatise on Indigence* (London: Printed for J. Hatchard, 1806); and Patrick Colquhoun, *A Treatise on*

the Wealth, Power, and Resources of the British Empire (London: J. Mawman, 1814). See also Mark Neocleous, "Theoretical Foundations of the 'New Police Science,'" in *The New Police Science: The Police Power in Domestic and International Governance*, ed. Markus Dubber and Mariana Valverde (Stanford, Calif.: Stanford University Press, 2006), 17–41, at 29–34.

79. Conrad, *Heart of Darkness*, 82.

80. Michael Hardt and Antonio Negri, *Empire* (Cambridge, Mass.: Harvard University Press, 2000), 70.

81. Ibid., 17.

82. "What does the poverty of experience oblige the barbarian to do? To begin anew, to begin from the new." Walter Benjamin, "Erfahrung und Armut" [Experience and Poverty]" (1933), in *Gesammelte Schriften*, ed. Rolf Tiedemann and Hermann Schweppenhäussen (Frankfurt: Suhrkamp, 1972), 2:215. Hardt and Negri, *Empire*, 215.

83. Thomas Paine, *Common Sense* (Philadelphia: W and T Bradford, 1776), available at http://www.bartleby.com/133/ part III, par. 49 (visited May 2007).

84. See, for an example, Thompson's conclusion to *Whigs and Hunters*.

85. Walter Benjamin, "Critique of Violence" (1921), in *Walter Benjamin, Reflections: Essays, Aphorisms, Autobiographical Writing*, ed. Peter Demetz (New York: Schocken, 1978), 297, 300; JacquesDevvida, "Force of Law: The Mystical Foundation of Authority," in *Acts of Religion/Jacques Devvida*, ed. Gil Anidjar (New York: Routledge, 2002), 287.

86. Benjamin, Thesis no. 3, 254. And see Christopher Tomlins, "The Threepenny Constitution (and the Question of Justice)," *Alabama Law Review*, 58 (2007): 979.

87. Somewhat like Sorel, Benjamin's conception of revolutionary violence was not instrumental but expiatory. It was "without bloodshed," symbolic of apocalyptic change "for the sake of the living." Benjamin, "Critique of Violence," 297–300. Compare Sorel, *Reflections on Violence*, 202–40.

88. Benjamin, "Critique of Violence," 300.

89. Walter Benjamin, "Theologico-Political Fragment" (1919), in *Walter Benjamin, Reflections: Essays, Aphorisms, Autobiographical Writing*, ed. Peter Demetz (New York: Schocken, 1978), 312–13; Benjamin, Thesis 1, 253.

90. E. P. Thompson, *Witness against the Beast: William Blake and the Moral Law* (New York: The New Press, 1993). See also Linebaugh and Rediker, *The Many-Headed Hydra*, 290–326, on the eschatology of Jubilee.

91. Thompson, *Witness against the Beast*, 193 (emphasis added).

92. Ibid., 174.

93. Ibid., 174–75.

94. Ibid., 179–80, 184, 187–89, 191.

95. Ibid., 190–91, 194.

96. Benjamin, Thesis no. 3, 254.

97. Marlow muses at the outset, before he begins his tale, "I was thinking of very old times, when the Romans first came here, nineteen hundred years ago—the other day. Light came out of this river . . . like a running blaze on a plain, like a flash of lightning in the clouds. We live in the flicker." Conrad, *Heart of Darkness*, 68. See also 65, 103, 105, 122, and 158.

98. Hardt and Negri, *Empire*, 393, 397, 399, and generally 394–98.

99. Ibid., 66, 394–96.

100. Ibid., 396.

101. Benjamin, "Theologico-Political Fragment," 312.

102. Benjamin, "Critique of Violence."

103. Benjamin, Theses no. 16, 17, and 18.

104. Thomas Morton, *New English Canaan: or, New Canaan* (1637; reprint, New York: Arno Press, 1972), 23.

105. Conrad, *Heart of Darkness*, 90. In addition, see Richard Price, "Dialogic Encounters in a Space of Death," in *New World Orders: Violence, Sanction, and Authority in the Colonial Americas*, ed. John Smolenski and Thomas J. Humphrey (Philadelphia: University of Pennsylvania Press, 2005), 47–65.

106. See above, note 19.

107. Francis Barker, *The Culture of Violence: Essays on Tragedy and History* (Chicago: University of Chicago Press, 1993), 234.

Contributors

Susan Branson is an associate professor of American studies at Syracuse University. She wrote *These Fiery Frenchified Dames: Politics and Culture in Early National Philadelphia*. Her recent work is a shift from political culture to criminal culture. A research project on the notorious Harry Flashman's involvement in a plot to kidnap the governor of Pennsylvania led her to investigate the activities (and crimes) of Ann Baker Carson. These exploits are detailed in Branson's latest book, *Dangerous to Know: Women, Crime, and Notoriety in the Early Nineteenth Century*.

Konstantin Dierks, an assistant professor in the History Department at Indiana University, Bloomington, is currently completing a book manuscript entitled *In My Power: Letter Writing in Early America*. He recently published "Letter Writing, Stationery Supplies, and Consumer Modernity in the Eighteenth-Century Atlantic World," which was included in a special issue of *Early American Literature* devoted to "economics and early American studies" (November 2006).

Jennifer L. Goloboy received her Ph.D. from Harvard University. Her dissertation focused on merchants and middle-class culture in Charleston, South Carolina, during the Revolutionary era. She has published an essay on the early American middle class in the *Journal of the Early Republic*. Currently, she is revising her dissertation and writing and editing a book on the social history of the Industrial Revolution for ABC-Clio.

Gabriele Gottlieb, an assistant professor of history at Grand Valley State University, Michigan, is currently revising her dissertation into a book manuscript. "Theater of Death: Capital Punishment in Early America, 1750–1800" is a comparative study of the application of the death penalty in Boston, Philadelphia, and Charleston.

Thomas J. Humphrey is an associate professor of history at Cleveland State University. The author of several articles and essays on land riots in the

Revolutionary period, he has also written *Land and Liberty: Hudson Valley Riots in the Age of Revolution*. He is the co-editor, with John Smolenski, of *New World Orders: Violence, Sanction, and Authority in the Early Americas*. In addition to his continuing research on Edward J. Flashman's fervent support of Alexander Hamilton's fiscal policies, he is currently pursuing a book-length study of tenants in North America in the Revolutionary era.

Daniel R. Mandell is an associate professor of history at Truman State University, Missouri, where he has taught early American and Native American history since 1999. He is the author of *Tribe, Race, History: Native Americans in Southern New England, 1780–1880* (forthcoming); *Behind the Frontier: Indians in Eighteenth-Century Eastern Massachusetts* (1996); the *New England South* and *New England North* volumes in the series *Early American Indian Documents: Treaties and Laws* (2003); and various articles on Indians and race in early America.

Simon Middleton is a lecturer in early American history at the University of Sheffield. He is the author of *From Privileges to Rights: Work and Politics in Colonial New York City* and articles in *New York History* and *The William and Mary Quarterly* on the history of New York City. Currently, he is looking into the life of John Underhill, an English Puritan whose travels took him to the Dutch Republic, New England, and New Netherland in the first half of the seventeenth century.

Simon P. Newman has degrees in American studies and history from the University of Nottingham, the University of Wisconsin, and Princeton University. He is the Sir Denis Brogan Professor of American Studies at the University of Glasgow and author of *Parades and the Politics of the Street: Festive Culture in the Early American Republic* (1997) and *Embodied History: The Lives of the Poor in Early Philadelphia* (2003).

Lawrence A. Peskin, an associate professor of history at Morgan State University in Baltimore, has written *Manufacturing Revolution: The Intellectual Origins of Early American Industry* (2003) and several articles. He is currently completing a manuscript on the impact of Barbary captivity on the early national United States.

Ty M. Reese is an associate professor of history at the University of North Dakota. His work on the Fetu, Fante, and Cape Coast seeks to redefine the place of West Africa in the Atlantic World and to increase our understanding of the consequences of the slave trade in West Africa through a focused, rather than regional, study.

Daniel K. Richter is the Richard S. Dunn Director of the McNeil Center for Early American Studies and a professor of history at the University of Pennsylvania. He is the author of *Facing East from Indian Country: A Native History of Early America* (2001) and *The Ordeal of the Longhouse: The Peoples of the Iroquois League in the Era of European Colonization* (1992). He is the coeditor, with James H. Merrell, of *Beyond the Covenant Chain: The Iroquois and Their Neighbors in Indian North America, 1600–1800* (1987; rev. ed. 2003), and, with William A. Pencak, of *Friends and Enemies in Penn's Woods: Indians, Colonists, and the Racial Construction of Pennsylvania* (2004). His scholarly articles have appeared in *American Indian Quarterly, Ethnohistory, The Journal of American History, The Journal of the Early Republic, Pennsylvania History, Reviews in American History, The William and Mary Quarterly,* and several collaborative volumes, including *The Oxford History of the British Empire* (1998).

Andrew M. Schocket is an associate professor of history at Bowling Green State University. His publications include *Founding Corporate Power in Early National Philadelphia* (2007) and "Thinking about Elites in the Early Republic," in the *Journal of the Early Republic* (2005). He is now working on a biography of Boston King in the context of the American Revolution, the British Empire, and the Atlantic World.

Billy G. Smith, a professor of history at Montana State University, has focused primarily on the history of marginalized humans in early America, in books such as *Down and Out in Early America* (2004) and (with Susan E. Klepp) *The Infortunate: The Voyage and Adventures of William Moraley, an Indentured Servant* (1992; rev. ed. 2005). At present, he is collaborating with several contributors to this volume on a biography of the enigmatic E. J. Flashman, as well as writing *Ship of Death: The Voyage That Changed the Atlantic World* for National Geographic Books.

Sharon Braslaw Sundue is an assistant professor of history at Drew University in Madison, New Jersey. She is the author of *Industrious in Their Stations: Young People at Work in Urban America, 1720–1810*, which is forthcoming from the University of Virginia Press.

Christopher Tomlins is a member of the Research Faculty of the American Bar Foundation in Chicago, where he studies the history of Anglophone law, 1500–2000. His current interests include the relationship among migration, law, and the colonization of mainland North America; the history of law's relationship to social science disciplines; the conceptual history of "police" and police powers in Anglophone law and politics; and the materialist jurisprudence of Walter Benjamin. He is probably best known for *Law, Labor, and Ideology in the Early American Republic* (1993; rev. ed. 2002). For recent publications and a tolerable likeness, go to http://www.abfn.org/restomlins.html.

Natalie Zacek is a lecturer in history and American studies at the University of Manchester. She is completing a monograph on white society in the English West Indies from the late seventeenth century through the late eighteenth. In addition, she has published articles in *Slavery and Abolition*, *Wadabagei: A Journal of the Caribbean and Its Diaspora*, and several edited collections. Her next project focuses on the cultural meaning of the thoroughbred horse in colonial and antebellum Virginia.

Index

Acknowledgments

"All history," proclaimed Friedrich Engels, "has been a history of class struggles between dominated classes at various stages of social development." Engels, of course, was wrong; human history is much too complex and varied. Yet, his insight is powerful, and it has shaped the thinking of people for generations. None of the authors in this volume fully embraces Engels's analysis, but all recognize its importance to studying the past and understanding the present. For that, and with our tongues tucked only slightly in our cheeks and our hearts in the right place, we thank Engels, Karl Marx, E. P. Thompson, and scores of other philosophers, historians, scholars, and activists who take class inequality seriously and work hard to alleviate its causes and consequences.

Five years ago, discouraged by the supposed death of class analysis, we devised a plan to try to breathe new life into its use among historians of early America and the wider Atlantic World. Since then, we have organized several conferences and edited three journal issues dealing with these topics. With this anthology, we complete our project with considerable optimism. The work of numerous researchers, whether linked with this undertaking or not, clearly has resuscitated the patient. During this venture, we have been quite fortunate to labor with and learn from excellent scholars and compassionate human beings. Simon Newman, always generous, provided a nourishing venue for the genesis of our scheme. Well over a hundred people—many more than we originally expected—brought our project to life by their ardent participation in conferences in Montana and Philadelphia. We thank all of them as well as the individuals who carried out the truly hard work of organizing the meetings, including Diane Cattrell, Jennifer Chrisman, Deidre Manry, Trinette Ross, John Gallagher, John Lewis, Pete Faggen, Bridgette Case, Charissa Fuhrmann, Jim Bruggeman, Amy Baxter-Bellamy, Zelini Hubbard, and Dan Richter. We likewise value Adrienne Mayor for guiding academic fisherpeople, Brett Walker for not injuring anybody on his bike tours, and David Large for his skills as a "people person." We gratefully acknowledge the financial support for the conferences and the excellent judgment displayed by the offices of the Vice President for Research (Tom

McCoy), the Provost (David Dooley), and the President (Geoffrey Gamble) at Montana State University; the University of East Anglia; and the McNeil Center for Early American Studies at the University of Pennsylvania.

Although this is the last item published from our project, this collection is far from the least in terms substance. We thank, sincerely, the contributors to the volume for caring enough about the topic to write and revise their excellent chapters and for having sufficient endurance to wait for this book to be finished. "If the lower orders don't set us a good example," Oscar Wilde asked sarcastically a century ago, "what on earth is the use of them?" Fortunately, the authors of these essays as well as the people who helped with this book—even those who do not hail from the "lower orders"—set a superior example in cooperative scholarship. Greg Nobles read the manuscript several times and offered advice that was right on the mark; an anonymous referee likewise provided positive suggestions. Daniel Richter's critique of the volume was particularly helpful, and we much appreciate his decision to include it in his series. Meghan Scott was, as usual, incredibly efficient as a research assistant, and she improved the book in innumerable ways. Christine Sweeney performed very conscientiously as a copyeditor, Erica Ginsburg was a patient and helpful managing editor, and Bob Lockhart was both tolerant and supportive as the editor.

Friends and colleagues in the History and Philosophy Department at Montana State University have made it an enjoyable, stimulating place to work. Mary Murphy, Michelle Maskiell, and Tom Wessel are among the few who understand class analysis. However, and to the good fortune of one of the book's editors, Michael Reidy, Brett Walker, Kristen Intemann, Dale Martin, Edward Flashman, Susan Cohen, and Tim LeCain vastly overestimate their understanding of poker.

Our families encouraged us throughout this endeavor. Jack Smith, Carol Smith, Betty Smith, Barbara Gibson, Sage Smith, and Michelle Maskiell have been, as always, very loving and supportive. Simon thanks Billy for five years of great collaboration, Carolyn for putting up with his mental absences and diva-like mood swings, and Betsy and Rosie for being adorable.

Simon Middleton, Sheffield
Billy G. Smith, Bozeman